James Brown, John Merry Ross

Scottish History and Literature to the Period of the Reformation

James Brown, John Merry Ross

Scottish History and Literature to the Period of the Reformation

ISBN/EAN: 9783337205621

Printed in Europe, USA, Canada, Australia, Japan

Cover: Foto ©Thomas Meinert / pixelio.de

More available books at **www.hansebooks.com**

SCOTTISH HISTORY AND LITERATURE

TO THE PERIOD OF THE REFORMATION

BY

JOHN M. ROSS, LL.D.

EDITED, WITH BIOGRAPHICAL SKETCH

By JAMES BROWN, D.D.

GLASGOW
JAMES MACLEHOSE & SONS
Publishers to the University
1884

All rights reserved

NOTE.

A FEW days before he died, Dr. Ross committed this book, which was nearly ready for the press, to the care of the Editor. Its preparation, for which the favourite studies of his life qualified him, had been the occupation of such leisure as the Author could command during many years.

The Editor has had the help of competent friends in completing what was awanting, in verifying quotations and references and in revising proofs. His special thanks are due to Mr. Robert MacLehose, M.A., whose aid in consulting books not easily accessible, and in preparing the Index, has greatly lightened the Editor's labour of love. The Editor is deeply sensible of the loss which readers sustain through the lack of final revision from the Author's own hand; but, in spite of this, he sends the book forth with confidence that it is no unworthy contribution to the history of our national literature.

CONTENTS.

BIOGRAPHICAL SKETCH, - - - - - - - xiii-xxviii

CHAPTER I.
THE SCOTTISH NATIONALITY.

Its Original Elements.—Victory of the Anglic.—Sentiment with regard to the Celtic.—National Life and Polity begun in 9th Century.—Welding Influence of Assaults.—Extension of Territory.—Influence of Malcolm and the Princess Margaret.—Influences during the Reign of David.—Increase of National Spirit.—Attitude of the Clergy.—Influence of Later Events.—Disappearance of the Sense of Distinction of Race.—The Valour of the Gael recognised as typical.—All the Original Elements of Nationality remain in North Britain,
1-15

CHAPTER II.
THE LIVES OF THE EARLY SAINTS.

Ninian.—Early Notices of him by Bede.—Fuller but less trustworthy Account by Ailred.—Kentigern or Munghu.—Silence of Bede and Adamnan concerning him.—Jocelin's Biography.—Kentigern's Settlement at Glasgow.—Banishment to Wales and Return.—Missionary Expeditions.—Columba.—His Work the foundation of Scottish Nationality.—His connection with Ireland.—Migration to Iona.—Adamnan's Life.—Its Legendary Character.—Greatness of Columba's Work.—His Poetry.—His Work essentially Missionary.—His Death.—Aidan.—Cuthberht, - - - - - - - 16-34

CHAPTER III.
THE WAR OF INDEPENDENCE AND ITS MINSTRELS.

Scotland before and after Malcolm Ceannmor.—Dearth of Literature till the latter half of Fourteenth Century.—Contrast with England in this particular.—The War of Independence.—First Effort of Scottish Muse in Anglic Vernacular to celebrate that War.—Barbour's Brus and Blind Harry's Wallace considered together.—Barbour's Life.—Estimate of his Work.—How far Historical.—Notices of Blind Harry.—What we really know of Wallace.—Blind Harry's Work gives literary Expression to Wallace Cult.—Its Extravagancies.—Wallace's true position, - - - - - 35-91

CHAPTER IV.

HISTORY AND LITERATURE OF FOURTEENTH AND FIFTEENTH CENTURIES.

Rising and Discomfiture of Disinherited Barons.—David.—French Alliance.—Accession of Stewarts.—English Invasions and their Effects.—Literature of the Period.—Barbour, Fordoun, Bower, and Wyntoun, Apologists for Scotland.—Traces of Song and Romance.—Barbour, Arthurian Pieces, Huchowne, &c.—Fifteenth Century contrasted with Fourteenth.—Freedom from Foreign Aggression.—Miserable Domestic Policy.—Feuds of the Barons.—Reigns of Robert III. and of James I., II., and III.—Brighter Aspects of the Time.—Position of Commons.—Influence of Clergy.—Foundation of Universities.—Literature of the two Centuries contrasted.—Obscure Poets.—Worth of Blind Harry's Work, - - - - - - - - 92-131

CHAPTER V.

KING JAMES, HENRYSON, AND DUNBAR.

Period of James's Captivity.—The Dukes of Albany.—The King's Return.—Arrest of the Regent and his Followers, and of the Highland Chiefs.—Conspiracies against the King.—His Murder.—Character of his Administration.—His Poems "The Kingis Quhair," &c.—Robert Henryson.—His Life.—His shorter Poems.—Robene and Makyne.—Fables.—Testament of Cresseid.—William Dunbar.—Characteristics of his Time.—New Era of Scottish History.—Features of the Reign of James IV.—Decline of Feudalism.—Commerce.—Increase of Wealth.—Compulsory Education.—Lollards of Kyle.—Corruptions of the Church.—Dunbar an Image of his Time.—His Poems, Allegorical, Satirical, and Moral.—His Place in Scottish Poetry.—His Verse characterized by Distinctive Features of the National Character, - 132-218

CHAPTER VI.

THE EARLIER HALF OF THE SIXTEENTH CENTURY.

Comparative Interest of the Sixteenth Century for England and Scotland.—Need for Reformation greater in Northern Kingdom.—Severance from the Past more complete.—Approach of the Crisis.—Literary Culture and Scholarship in Earlier Half of the Century.—Group of Academic Authors.—Hector Boece.—Lives of Bishops of Aberdeen.—Scotorum Historiæ a Prima Gentis Origine.—Joannes Major.—His Residence abroad and Earlier Works.—Professorship in Glasgow and Publication of his Historia.—Characteristics of the Work.—Removal of Major to St. Andrews.—Relations to Knox.—John Bellenden.—His Translations of Boece and of Livy the Earliest Examples of Prose in Scottish Literature.—His Poetry.—James Inglis, &c.—The Complaynt of Scotland.—Conjectures as to Authorship.—Analysis, - - - - - 219-292

CHAPTER VII.
GAVIN DOUGLAS.

His Descent and Earlier History.—Becomes Provost of St. Giles' and a prominent Ecclesiastic.—Period of his Literary Activity.—The Years after Flodden.—Marriage of Queen Margaret to the Poet's Nephew.—Her Letters to the Pope in behalf of Douglas.—Plots against the Queen.—Albany recalled and made Regent.—Douglas becomes Bishop of Dunkeld.—Absence of the Regent.—Broils between Douglasses and Hamiltons.—Margaret's Quarrel with her Husband.—She joins the Regent on his Return.—Douglas becomes the Envoy of Angus and his Party to the English Court.—His unpatriotic Conduct.—Deprived of his Bishopric.—His Death.—Criticism and Analysis of his Works.—The Palice of Honour.—King Hart.—Translation of the Æneid. - - - - - - - 293-374

CHAPTER VIII.
SIR DAVID LYNDSAY.

His Birthplace.—Position of the Country during his Earlier Years.—He enters St. Salvator's College, St. Andrews.—Passes into the Royal Household.—Flodden.—Lyndsay's Attendance on the Young King, James V.—His Marriage.—James assumes the Government at the Age of Twelve.—Comes under the Power of Angus.—Overthrow of Angus.—Lyndsay begins his Literary Career.—The Dreme.—Analysis and Criticism.—The Complaynt to the Kyng.—Lyndsay appointed Lyon King of Arms.—The Testament and Complaynt of the Kyngis Papyngo.—The Boldness of Lyndsay's Utterance.—His Minor Pieces.—His Masterpiece, Ane Pleasant Satyre of the Thrie Estaitis.—Its Nature.—Outline of the Play.—Critical Estimate.—Lyndsay's Duties as Lyon-Herald.—The King's Marriages.—His Death.—Consequent Changes.—Tragedie of the Cardinall.—Lyndsay's Connection with Knox.—Reasons of his Safety.—Squire Meldrum.—The Monarchie.—The Poet's Death.—Estimate of his Work,
375-414

INDEX, - - - - - - - - - - - 415-420

SCOTTISH HISTORY AND LITERATURE.

BIOGRAPHICAL SKETCH.

John Merry Ross, the author of the following pages, was born at Kilmarnock on the 21st of April, 1833. He was the only child left to his parents, and was of such promise that, at some sacrifice, they gave him the best education that the Academy of his native town could furnish. He found for himself other educative influences in the surroundings amid which he spent his boyhood. His often solitary rambles up the Dean, by the picturesque banks of Kilmarnock Water and on through the Crawfurdland Woods; or his further stretches to the moors around Fenwick, or in the direction of Galston and Loudon Hill, served to nourish at once his love of "the green-leaved earth," and his intense sympathy with the heroic epochs of Scottish history. The town itself helped to mould him. It is one of those towns which have become manufacturing without ceasing to be agricultural—where the new ideas which follow in the wake of machinery have blended with the old ideas which are represented by farmers in home-spun buying and selling at the Cross, and by their wives and daughters, with comely though weather-worn faces, sitting with their butter and eggs spread out before them in the market. It stands in the very heart of Lowland Scotland, and on its streets one hears the deep rich Doric as it can be heard in few places besides. Ross was wont to speak proudly of his Celtic blood, and to claim kindred with the Rosses of the far-northern shire; but whatever of Celtic fervour might occasionally reveal itself in him, he was by upbringing and sympathy a true Lowland Scot, with all the staying power peculiar to the race. He was nurtured amid the memories of Burns. Kilmarnock knew the poet at his best, before the volume which it had the honour of publishing had brought him the fame which proved so perilous. His memory is cherished there with a peculiar kindliness; and sober elders of the Kirk will resent any imputation cast on his good name as hotly as they would a slander spoken against John Brown of Priesthill, Peden the Prophet, or any other Ayrshire Covenanter.

While yet a boy, Ross had some of his closest companions among elderly men, whose memories could go back to the poet's time, and who had thus drunk in at its very source that tender sympathy with nature and with lowliest forms of life which Burns brought into our literature. To one of these he confessedly owed much; and when in the college days his student-friends visited him, they were always taken to the humble room behind the little book shop, which was the home of Archibald Mackay, the venerable historian of the burgh. Ross did not sit at the old man's feet, but would, when occasion called, stoutly argue with him some disputed point in literary criticism; but he delighted in his homely wisdom, in his quaint and humorous descriptions of men and things, and yet more in his poetic flights, when, in the very dialect of Burns, he would tell, as Burns might have told, of sunset hours he had spent among the hedgerows, of the sounds that filled his ear, of the living creatures whose motions he had watched, and of the fragrance that floated on the evening breeze. I can remember that once when I was with Ross very early in our student-course, he left me to attend the funeral of Archibald Mackay's brother, John. When he returned it was evident that he had been deeply moved. He spoke to me of the ennobling influences of death, and of how he found it difficult to realize that in the scene of perfect life there should be no funerals!

In 1851, when he was eighteen years of age, Ross entered the University of Glasgow, where, in the Humanity class-room in an out-of-the-way corner of the inmost quadrangle of the old College, his pale face and finely cut features began to attract attention and to draw fellow-students around him. Neither then nor afterwards did he attain, or seek, distinction in class work. He did faithfully the exercises prescribed, but his attention was not concentrated upon them. He was occupied with a broader course of study, and devoted more time to English literature than to the Greek and Roman classics. He also, at this period, acquired a considerable knowledge of French and German literature. The only prize he won—and he won it easily—was for the poem in the class of Logic and Rhetoric. The subject prescribed was congenial—an address to Ailsa Craig—the sea-girt rock which can be seen so well from the Ayrshire heights on which he had wandered in his boyhood.

He had a quite peculiar power of turning to good account the companionships of college life, which often count for more in a student's education than the direct instruction furnished in class-rooms. Not a few of his chosen companions have risen to distinction. As many as three of them now occupy chairs in their *alma mater;* while another—Dr. John Service, who has just been taken from us—exercised, by virtue of the power of genius, an influence as a religious teacher the extent and the value of which are hardly even yet fully recognised. Nor did Ross associate only with those to whom he was drawn by their ability and culture. He gratified at once his taste for studying the quaint and curious in character and his homely brotherliness of spirit, by making friends of some whom an entrance examination would probably have excluded. He helped them over many a stile, and found his reward in their devoted attachment and in the grotesque scenes into which his friendship for them sometimes led him. One of these in particular was fired with a literary ambition, and published occasional lectures and essays, which Ross found saleable among his friends for the sake of the wild extravagance of the rhetoric. The product of the sales he effected was materially helpful to the struggling author.

The Professor to whom Ross, like many others of his time, was most deeply indebted, was one whose class he never attended, or, at most, attended fitfully and for a few weeks. He early came under the charm of Professor John Pringle Nichol, whose occasional lectures on astronomy, delivered beyond the college walls, were in these years probably the most stimulating of the means of intellectual improvement available in Glasgow. As one of the friends of the Professor's now distinguished son, Ross was welcomed to the Observatory, the genial hospitalities of which contributed not a little to the culture of those students who had the privilege of sharing them, and who gratefully appreciated the kind and fatherly interest taken in their work by a man distinguished for wide and varied learning and possessed of so much that learning cannot give.

Of influences in Glasgow beyond the academic circle which helped to make Ross what he became, the most noteworthy was his friendship for the son of the famous preacher and lecturer, Dr. William Anderson of John Street Church. This son, who bore his father's name, had by that time completed his curriculum in arts and theology, but shrank, through nervous sensitiveness, from taking license as a preacher. He had used his abundant leisure in making himself familiar with all our literature, and Ross found in one of so acute and richly cultured mind a congenial companion, whose early and sudden death powerfully impressed him. Through this companionship he was brought into contact with the venerable preacher, and felt the influence of his intense and eager intellect. It was while still an undergraduate at Glasgow that Ross made his first appearance in literature. He wrote for the *Hogg's Instructor* of these days an essay on Philip James Baillie's *Festus*, which attracted considerable attention, and revealed such power of literary criticism and such felicity of style as gave good promise for the future. The value of the performance was, as may be well believed, not underrated by the generous enthusiasm of his friends at the University.

Being destined for the ministry of the United Presbyterian Church, Ross passed from Glasgow to the classes in which the students of that Church then got their theological training, and which met in the autumn months at 5 Queen Street, Edinburgh. It was my privilege to occupy the same rooms with him during the first three sessions of our course. Faithfully we wrought together at our Hebrew and our New Testament Greek, at our Church History and our Dogmatics, facing as wisely as we could the questions which, though not raised in our class-rooms, were then beginning to perplex students of theology. Among our teachers, the one whose influence Ross felt most powerfully was Dr. Eadie, whose great learning, worn so lightly, won his respect, and whose easy friendliness of manner among the students won his heart.

At the Hall, as at school and college, he found other teachers than those who conducted him through the prescribed curriculum. The picturesqueness of Edinburgh, with its historic and literary memories, laid hold of him; and our Saturday rambles among the rich Lothian harvest fields, to Roslin and Hawthornden, or across the Braid Hills to the slopes of the Pentlands, were a continual joy. On these rambles we were generally accompanied by Alexander Smith, the gentle and richly dowered author of the *Life Drama*, who had by this time left his pattern-designing in Glasgow to become Secretary to the University of Edinburgh. We had made his acquaintance in the West, and now the acquaintance ripened into friendship. Fellowship with such a nature—in which there was the generous richness and indescribable flavour of some bountiful vintage from a sunny hillside—was in itself an education. To the last Ross was wont to speak of these Saturday excursions, with their quiet symposiums at some distant village inn, and their walks homeward amid the fragrance of harvest sunsets.

At the close of our third session Ross resolved to turn aside from his career as a theological student, and to remain in Edinburgh that he might obtain literary and educational work as a means of support. Difficulties in the way of subscribing the Westminster Confession of Faith seemed then insurmountable, and the attraction of the freer life of a *litterateur* or a teacher was powerfully felt. He never lost sympathy with the church in its high spiritual aims, and his withdrawal to another sphere of labour did not in the least interfere with his friendship for those of his associates who went forward to the ministry. Indeed his sympathies with the profession for which he was originally destined were so strong, and his difficulties were so far overcome, that after a few years' interval he returned to the study of theology, and completed his curriculum with the view of taking license as a preacher; but before the time for license arrived, circumstances had arisen which led him to devote himself to scholastic and literary work, and so the ministry was finally abandoned.

The acccomplished lady to whom he had been married was the head of an educational institution in which he had taught as English master. He continued to aid her in her work, but the greater part of his time was devoted to literary labour. He was appointed by the Messrs. Chambers sub-editor of their *Encyclopædia* under Dr. Findlater. Never surely was work of the kind that now fell to him done more conscientiously or laboriously. Ross could not brook the methods which are so common in connection with publications of this class. Scissors and paste had no place in his editorial sanctum. He was not satisfied unless even the least important articles were prepared from original sources, and unless the minutest facts and dates were carefully verified. His knowledge of French and German proved of peculiar advantage to him in this part of his work. Much as we admired his faithfulness, however, those of us who knew him grudged that he should toil on from year to year at a compilation in which he could hardly find scope for his powers. It was, therefore, matter of congratulation to all his friends when, in 1866, the Town Council of Edinburgh, under the leadership of the Lord Provost—the late William Chambers—chose him by a large majority from among a list of candidates of acknowledged eminence, and of experience greater than his in the teaching profession, to the position of senior English master in the High School.

It is not too much to say that his entrance on this office marks an epoch in the history of secondary education in Scotland. Up to that time English had, in this metropolitan grammar school, been regarded as a mere adjunct to the classics, and as such was taught by masters who were selected for the sake of their attainments in Latin and Greek without reference to their knowledge of the history and literature of their mother tongue. But the Town Council, who were then the managers of the school, had, with a wisdom which would probably be inexplicable but for the fact that the remarkable man we have already named occupied the civic chair, resolved that English should be made a separate department. They desired that boys who, destined for commercial or other than professional life, chose the modern side, should enjoy as great educational advantages and receive as exact mental training as those who took the classical course, and that those who were taught the classics might learn under the English master that the language and literature of their own land are as apt and powerful educative instruments as the languages and literature of the older civilizations. The same wisdom which dictated the resolution of the Council appeared in the choice of the first master. The success of the experiment depended on the man selected to carry it out. Had one whose chief qualification was experience in teaching English been appointed, the end in view would probably not have been gained. But when a man could be found of wide literary culture, and with well-approved literary gifts, who had made English his special study, the comparative lack of experience in the traditional methods of teaching it was rather an advantage than a drawback.

Be this as it may, the result justified the choice of the Council. From the first year of his appointment Mr. Ross contributed his part to the enhancement of the already high reputation of the historic school. Though the Rector was a man of European fame in his chosen field, he was the first to acknowledge that the English department was second to none in its efficiency and in its educational value. When the Act of 1872 brought the High School under the School Board, and statutory examiners were annually appointed to estimate the work of each year, the eulogium pronounced on the English classes became an expected feature of every report. Such men as Professors Spencer Baynes, Masson, and Minto have vied with each other in the warmth with which they have spoken of the methods employed and the results attained. These results were not reached without painstaking labour; but they were such as mere laboriousness could never have produced. Ross won the warm affection of his boys, and got them to do their best by his entire devotion to them and his interest in all that concerned them. His own burning enthusiasm spread in his classes; and even the dullest, whom the routine of class discipline would have left unmoved, were stirred to some measure of intellectual life. There are many already occupying influential positions who delight to acknowledge their indebtedness to him; and the influence of his example will long be felt in the teaching profession.

In 1871 Mr. Ross sought a wider field in which to do his chosen work as a teacher of English. He then published, in connection with the Messrs. Nelson's School Series, an edition of Milton, embracing the first four books of Paradise Lost, the third and fourth of Paradise Regained, with the chief of the minor poems, all carefully and copiously annotated. In this book teachers of English find an edition of an English classic, worthy to be set beside the scholarly annotations which lie in so great numbers to the hand of the teacher of the Greek and Roman classics. The work was most cordially received by the press, its critics only expressing their regret that the edition did not embrace all the works of our great epic poet. In 1874 the University of Glasgow recognised the professional eminence of its former alumnus, and conferred on Mr. Ross the degree of LL.D.

When *Chambers' Encyclopædia* was completed, the thorough and honest work of the sub-editor brought him a proposal from another publisher that he should undertake the editorship of a similar book, and the result was the preparation of the *Globe Encyclopædia*, to which Dr. Ross devoted the same unwearied labour and conscientious carefulness. But the new undertaking unfortunately involved the sacrifice of sleep. His work in school occupied six hours daily, and the evening was taken up with the correcting of exercises, and other duties connected with his classes. It was when he should have been retiring to rest that he had to set himself to the correcting of proof-sheets, and often to the rewriting of articles which had been sent up by careless or incompetent contributors, whom yet he could not bring himself to deprive of their means of living.

Amid these oppressive labours, he never ceased to take supervision of the girls first, and the boys afterwards, who were under the care of Mrs. Ross as boarders. Tutors were provided for those departments which Mrs. Ross herself, who is an accomplished linguist, could not undertake; but the religious instruction of the young people in his house he made his own peculiar care. His Bible lessons were most diligently prepared, and were greatly appreciated. We have the testimony of several who enjoyed the privilege of being under him, that these lessons were at once intellectually stimulating and spiritually profitable. It was one of the most noteworthy features of Dr. Ross's relations to his pupils—not in the house only, but in the school—that he sought to do his own work, and to teach them to do theirs "as ever in the Great Taskmaster's eye." When after Dr. Donaldson's appointment to the Chair of Humanity in Aberdeen, it fell to Dr. Ross to do, temporarily, the Rector's duties, he was as minutely conscientious in the preparation of the brief morning prayer with which he had to open the school, as he had always been of his class-work. It was touching to find among his papers a large collection of the prayers written at that time. They all breathe the same spirit of earnest faith and humble self-consecration; they recognise daily duties as God's work, and ask for grace that that work may be done well. Sometimes there is recognition of public calamity, or of more private sorrow, by which the boys would be taught the godly habit of owning the divine hand in all events, and of finding comfort and hope in the divine presence. It may interest the reader to see two specimens of these simple utterances of a loyal heart. Here is one written for a day when there is no outstanding event to occupy the mind:—

"Our Father who art in Heaven, we draw near to Thee this morning to ask Thy blessing on the work Thou hast given us to do. Touch our spirits as with a live coal from off Thine altar, that we may be purified from all selfishness and sin, and may offer unto Thee a holy sacrifice. Give us that wisdom that cometh from above, that we may be enabled to walk in the way of the Lord, and to keep His testimonies. Thou hast delivered us from the power of darkness and hast translated us into the Kingdom of Thy dear Son. Help us to gratefully acknowledge Thy liberating love, to rejoice in the assurance that if we put our trust in Thee, we shall never be ashamed. The eternal God is our refuge and underneath are the everlasting arms. With this faith may we go cheerfully and seriously to our allotted work from day to day, and find our highest happiness in doing what Thou wouldst have us do. Pardon all our unworthiness and graciously receive the worship which we render to Thee through Jesus Christ our Lord. Amen."

Here is another written under the shadow of some sorrow of the nature of which we have no record :—

"O God, we desire to draw near to Thee this morning and to offer Thee our humble and heartfelt thanks for all thy goodness to us during the past night. While grief and suffering have torn many hearts, Thou hast mercifully preserved us from all evil and hast caused us to go forth in health and security to our appointed callings. Give us, we beseech Thee, a spirit of true and loving sympathy with those that mourn under the sterner dispensations of Thy providence. Help us to devoutly believe that they who are stricken and we who are spared, are alike embraced in those everlasting arms that are stretched in love and pity round the whole family of man. Impress us deeply with the conviction that however dark and mysterious Thy ways may seem to outward sense, the end will show them to be wise and good and true. Grant us therefore, we beseech Thee, the patience and courage that are born of faith. May we realize that only in the path of duty we are safe, that earthly perils cannot harm us when we walk with Thee; yea, though we walk through the valley of the shadow of death, we will fear no evil, for Thou art with us: Thy rod and Thy staff comfort us. In this high assurance may we enter on all our duties in life, both when we are young and when we are old. Be with us in this day to guide and direct our steps, to guard us from all that is evil, to incite us to all that is good, and pardon the errors and shortcomings of our service for the sake of Thy Son our Lord and our Redeemer. Amen."

These simple words are in beautiful harmony with the devout and childlike spirit which ever characterized

Dr. Ross, and which became more conspicuous in his closing years. He was led to connect himself with the congregation of St. Stephen's. The deep spirituality and earnestness of the late Dr. Maxwell Nicholson laid powerful hold of Dr. Ross's mind and heart, and the death of this devoted minister in the zenith of his usefulness greatly touched him. He took an interest in the appointment of his successor, and when the choice of the congregation fell on his old fellow-student, Norman Macleod, he transferred to him the loyal affection which had been drawn forth by the gifts and graces of his predecessor. He was chosen to the eldership, and though the wide sympathies of his student-days were in no sense narrowed, and he had grown in tolerance and comprehensiveness of spirit, the difficulties he once felt about subscription had cleared away, and he gladly obeyed the call to bear office in the Christian church. We have the testimony of his minister that he failed not in the duties of his office, but "was hearty and affectionate in all that concerned the welfare of the congregation."

His home life was singularly happy. His wife wrought most ably and unweariedly with him, and was ever ready to share his anxieties. In busiest times they had a welcome for their chosen friends, and the warmth of that welcome can never be forgotten by those who were admitted to the little back parlour at 30 Great King Street to listen to Coleridgean discourse, or take part in high debate on politics or theology. Once and again the shadow of bereavement fell upon the home. Out of seven children, only four remain. Dr. Ross, though by no means reticent, never spoke much of his deepest sorrows, but all his friends could see the effects of the discipline of grief. The annual autumn holiday which comes to jaded teachers was shortened for him by his literary engagements; but the brief time of relaxation was therefore the more thoroughly enjoyed. It was almost always spent at Troon—a wind-swept, treeless promontory on the Ayrshire coast—which had its chief attraction for him in the fact that it is only separated by the green heights of Dundonald from his native Kilmarnock. He had been taken to it annually in his boyhood, and he seemed to become a boy again as year by year he escaped from his class-room and his proof sheets, to wander on the fair expanse of the sandy shore, and look across the moving water to the hills of Arran. Troon became still more attractive to him when several years ago a golf club was founded, and he had the opportunity of enjoying his favourite game within a few hundred yards of his lodging.

In connection with the election of Dr. Donaldson's successor he experienced the sorest disappointment of his life. He was the senior master left in the school; he had often acted for the Rector in his absence: he had the full confidence of his colleagues and the enthusiastic love of the boys; and so he felt that he might without presumption aspire to the rectorship. But he had to face the prejudice created by long usage against appointing any one but a classical master to the Rector's chair. It was that he might overcome this prejudice rather than he might obtain personal preferment that he was so earnest in the matter. He felt that English would never have its rightful place in our secondary schools unless the English masters were equally eligible with the classical for the highest office. The prejudice proved too strong, and though Dr. Ross's fitness for the position in all other respects, and the claim founded on long and effective service, were fully admitted, a majority of the Board were resolute that none but a classical master should be chosen. Dr. Ross, as might have been expected, bore the disappointment bravely. In a letter I had from him a few days after the election, he wrote cheerfully of his defeat and kindly of the new Rector, whom he was the first to congratulate on his appointment.

But the strain to which he was subjected during the time of uncertainty, and the final disappointment of a not unreasonable hope, wrought unfavourably on a constitution weakened by years of over-work. In the following January he was laid down with a painful internal malady, and those who loved him best feared from the first that he was smitten with a fatal stroke. The forebodings were sadly fulfilled. On the 3rd of February, at the gray dawning of the day, he passed into the eternal rest. He said in dying, "I have the most perfect conviction my anchor has been cast on sure ground, and that to me death is life." We laid him in Warriston Cemetery, amid a great company of mourners, in which not only the School Board, his colleagues, and his boys, but the University, the Municipality, the congregation of St. Stephen's, his fellow-students and friends from the west, and the general body of the citizens were largely represented.

JAS. BROWN.

St. James' Manse,
Paisley, 30th April, 1884.

SCOTTISH HISTORY AND LITERATURE.

CHAPTER I.

THE SCOTTISH NATIONALITY.

Its Original Elements.—Victory of the Anglic.—Sentiment with regard to the Celtic.—National Life and Polity begun in 9th Century.—Welding Influence of Assaults.—Extension of Territory.—Influence of Malcolm and the Princess Margaret.—Influences during the Reign of David.—Increase of National Spirit.—Attitude of the Clergy.—Influence of Later Events.—Disappearance of the Sense of Distinction of Race.—The Valour of the Gael recognised as typical.—All the Original Elements of Nationality remain in North Britain.

PERHAPS no nation in the world is more composite in its original elements than the Scotch, and yet none is more passionately patriotic. The Picts, Britons, Scots, and Angles, who divided among themselves the land north of the Tweed and the Solway down to the twelfth century, were not thoroughly fused into one political community till the War of Independence (1297-1314); and even to the present day the names "Highlander" and "Lowlander" represent profound distinctions in race, character, and language. The Caledonian Pict and the Irish Scot, through the missionary zeal of Columba and his successors, were indeed gradually blended into one indistinguishable mass of Gaels, while the Britons of Cumbria, after their transference to the rule of the Scottish kings in the tenth century, slowly yielded to the Anglic pressure from the east, and abandoning—we know not precisely when—their Welsh dialect and their Celtic habits, became at length thoroughly Teutonized in speech and sentiment. Some ethnologists, indeed, believe they can trace, alike in the early covenanting zeal and the later commercial enterprise of Lanark and Ayr, a certain Celtic fervour and enthusiasm which seem to prove that nothing is more indestructible than the lineaments of race. But in the obscure conflict of ethnological forces in North Britain, victory remained with the Anglic. From the twelfth century this became the dominant, and, in spite of rude and perilous interruptions extending over four centuries, the cohesive element in Scottish polity; that to which Scottish nationality—the most genuine, the most intense, and the most illogical thing in the world—owes its existence.

On the other hand, there has grown up, especially within the last two hundred years, what may be called romantic and poetical sentiment among the people of Scotland regarding their country and themselves. Though their civilization, and the language of their chief literature are of Anglic origin, the conviction has found expression in a thousand ways that the Celtic element in Scotland, long vanquished in political strife, and all but silenced in the courts of the muses, is yet a great and powerful factor in the national life. This conviction has to some extent remoulded the Scot. It has in various ways softened, beautified, and brightened the sombre features of Lowland character, and it has, practically at least, effaced from the popular imagination the distinction of race and the facts of history.

One might cull from the Scottish poets of the eighteenth and nineteenth centuries almost unlimited evidence of this. It is Allan Ramsay, the most thoroughly Lowland of poets in the temper of his genius, who writes the fine lines,

> "For Lochaber no more, Lochaber no more,
> We'll maybe return to Lochaber no more;"

and who (anticipating Burns in this as in so many other respects) extols with genuine enthusiasm the irresistible charms of the "Highland Laddie" and the "Highland Lassie." It is Walter Scott who, in his glorious apostrophe to his native land in the *Lay of the Last Minstrel*, not only invokes it under its oldest Celtic name of "Caledonia," but shows by his description,

> "Land of brown heath and shaggy wood,
> Land of the mountain and the flood,"

that he is thinking of Perth and Inverness, rather than of his own familiar Tweedside and Teviotdale.

Politically, of course, this feeling of nationality is far older than the eighteenth century. It is older even than the fusion of the different races. Enthusiasts can discover it with ease in the very dawn of our history. The stubborn resistance of the Caledonian tribes to the advance of the Roman arms, from the age of Agricola to the irruptions of Alaric, is held to be a proof of its venerable origin; and the elaborate illusions entertained with regard to the Culdees are sometimes employed to support the sentiment. But setting aside the fantasies and crotchets of an extravagant patriotism, we may believe, without provoking ridicule, that the germs of a distinct nationality are traceable as far back as the middle of the ninth century. The union of the Scottish and Pictish crowns in the person of Kenneth MacAlpin in 844, preceded as it was by more than two hundred years of obscure but sanguinary conflicts between kindred peoples, and by the still more obscure but salutary operations of the Columban clergy, may be fairly considered as an epoch when something like a national life and polity began. Henceforth there was a large and compact territory to defend, an effective power of resistance to foreign aggression, a rapid interfusion of races,[1] and a vigorous extension of the Scottish Church (a phrase which occurs for the first time in the reign of King Giric, 878-889). The descents of the piratical Danes and Norwegians on the eastern and western coasts, though not without a local effect on the Scottish character and speech, could only weld together more closely the two races that were assailed with equal fury, and whose territories were harried with the same savage inhumanity.

The monarchs of Alban experienced the vicissitudes that are incident to all dynasties; but the nation was never again in danger of disruption. The Picts of Orkney vanished before the colonies of Norsemen, whom the tyranny of Harfagr compelled to seek new homes; Caithness and Sutherland were held for a time by foreign Jarls; all Southern Alban, as far as the Tay, was more than once over-run and plundered by the ruthless rovers; the Hebrides were utterly sub-

[1] These Scots and Picts, belonging to the same Gaelic race and speaking kindred dialects, would amalgamate readily enough, and they would probably be found at this time established alongside of each other in homesteads, some of which would be Scottish and others Pictish. We find examples of this state of matters in Northern Russia, where the earlier Finnish population and the intruding Slavs occupy respective villages, and in parts of Greece, where the distribution of the Albanian and the Greek population presents the same features.

dued, and became a bone of contention between Scandinavian rivals; but the stability of the new state was never seriously shaken.

When the violence of these northern invaders had spent its original force in the reign of Constantine the Second (900-942) and a century of tranquillity ensued, it was seen that Alban had only waxed stronger amidst the storms of strife. She began to extend her dominion to the south. Foreign acquisitions were not likely to diminish the natural pride of the Scots. When Strathclyde and Cumbria were gifted to Malcolm by Edward of England, though the tenure of possession was one of fealty to the English King, it could hardly be overlooked that this was a region in which the people, in spite of a precarious English lordship and a temporary English episcopate, were still as thoroughly Celtic as the men of Alban; nor could it be forgotten that in the adjacent district of Galloway, the Scots of Dalriada had once found a refuge from Pictish tyranny, and thence had emerged under Kenneth MacAlpin to secure an irreversible triumph. The Cymry of the Clyde peacefully accepted the sovereignty of the Scottish Kings, though they continued for a time to be ruled by their native princes. We do not know the century in which their Welsh speech gave place to the English of Lothian, but its decay was certainly rapid, and it is improbable that it survived the close of the twelfth century. Politically they became "Scots" almost from the moment of their annexation. Nowhere did the instinct of Scottish nationality at a later period burst forth into fiercer flame. To them belongs the imperishable glory of beginning the heroic struggle for Scottish independence, and amidst the numerous conjectures to which the name of Wallace has given rise, none is more worthy of belief than that which finds in it an evidence of his Cymric descent.

Eastward of Strathclyde the Scots were also successful in extending their power. The Anglic kingdom of Northumbria, founded where Picts and Britons had once been the sole inhabitants, was invariably regarded with hostile eyes by the Celtic kings of Alban. Even before Northumbria had sunk from an independent state into a subordinate earldom of the English crown, it was repeatedly assailed by its northern neighbours, and at length, in 1018, the great victory of Carham wrested it from an incapable governor, and placed it under the permanent authority of the Scots. This was perhaps the most important event that had occurred since the days of Columba, the one that exercised the greatest influence on the course of the national history. Now, for the first time, a Scottish king had English-speaking subjects, and an element was introduced that was destined to overthrow the formal supremacy of the Celtic race, and to force the posterity of the Picts and Scots and Britons to hide their origin under Teutonic disguises, even though the *perfervidum ingenium Scotorum* still attests the real ascendancy of the Celtic character, the indestructible presence of Celtic blood.

But Lothian, even more strikingly than Strathclyde, illustrates the vigour of Scottish nationality. Peopled by a purely English race, held as an English earldom for which homage was due to the English king, there is yet no trace of a spirit of disaffection towards its Celtic rulers, or a longing to be re-united to the English crown. It loyally adhered to its new connection, as if already conscious of its future pre-eminence, as if it had foreseen from the first that its language and laws were fated to prevail in the state.

We have thus seen that before the reign of Malcolm Ceannmor, Scottish nationality was a political fact. It was mainly, however, a Celtic nationality, though it was beginning to be coloured by a Teutonic infusion. The long exile of Malcolm in Northumbria and his subsequent marriage with the Princess Margaret, sister of Eadgar Ætheling, broadened the sympathies and interests of the Celtic monarch. He had ruled in Lothian and Strathclyde before he had recovered "Scotia" from the strong hand of Macbeth; the speech of the Angles was as familiar to him as the Gaelic of his boyhood; and though the death of the usurper restored him to the land of his fathers, and placed him at the head of a Celtic state, he could never forget his southern discipline and ties, he could never resume the position of a purely Celtic chief. The piety and patriotism of his English wife stimulated his own enlightened preferences.[1] Englishmen found in his dominions a secure asylum from Norman oppression. His persistent attempts to extend his authority to the Tyne and the Tees, though entirely unsuccessful, at least prove that he was ambitious of ruling over more than a Celtic state. Yet there is not a shadow of evidence for the supposition that he wished to transform his Scottish subjects into Englishmen, or cherished a policy inimical to the supremacy of the Celt.

In the reign of his son David, however, new influences began to work. The Norman adventurers who flocked to his court, and on whom he so lavishly

---

[1] It is certain that her ecclesiastical innovations on the Culdee practices were indirectly intended to strengthen the English influence.

bestowed lands and offices, remained for generations aliens in language and feeling to the people among whom they lived. By their help the king effected a revolution in the tenure of land. "Under his auspices," says Mr. Skene, "feudalism rapidly acquired predominance in the country, and its social state and institutions became formally assimilated to Norman forms and ideas, while the old Celtic element in her constitutional history gradually retired into the background."[1] But the very favour which was shown to these unscrupulous foreigners, who were utterly indifferent to the political dignity of the nation in which they had found wealth and power, and who would have sold the independence of a Celtic community without an emotion of shame, could only intensify the feeling of nationality throughout the kingdom, and create a stronger antipathy to the violent dominion of a foreign power.

Long before the age of Wallace we have the clearest evidence that the inhabitants of Northern Britain had come to regard themselves as a distinct and separate people from the English; and that the transference of political and ecclesiastical rule from Celtic mormaers and Culdees to an Anglo-Norman baronage and hierarchy, could no more destroy this feeling than the victory of Senlac destroyed the nationality of England. Amidst all the momentous changes that Scotland witnessed during the two centuries which intervened between the deaths of Malcolm Ceannmor and Alexander the Third, nothing is more certain than this, that as she increased in political power, subduing internal revolts of disaffected chiefs, now in Galloway, now in Moray and Ross, and wresting from the obstinate hold of Norse-

---

[1] *Celtic Scotland*, vol. I., p. 460.

men the earldom of Caithness and the lordship of the Isles, her national spirit and pride also increased. The charters of David may be addressed to "all the good men of the whole land, Norman, English, and Scotch," but that is merely the precautionary exactness of a feudal lawyer. When Ailred describes the composition of the army that David commanded at the battle of the Standard, we see that the distinctions of race were still remarked. Galwegian Picts, Cumbrians of Strathclyde, Lothian English, Islesmen, Scots, and Normans are there, but the host is the Scottish host, and fights under the banner of a Scottish king. Zealous as the offspring of Margaret were for the glory of the Church, they were no less zealous for the honour of their kingdom. Alexander the Fierce, with all his love for ecclesiastics and their literature, indignantly broke off his conference with Eadmer when the English monk, who had been elected Bishop of St. Andrews, maintained the supremacy of Canterbury over every diocese in Britain; and though the penitent prelate afterwards confessed that he had changed his opinions, and was now unwilling "to derogate in any way from the liberty and dignity of Scotland," the wary monarch retained his suspicions, and refused to restore him to the see, which he had forsaken or resigned. In this controversy we are told that Alexander was supported by the whole of the Scottish clergy.

The attitude of the latter at the Council of Northampton furnishes additional evidence of the national temper. The eloquent defence of the independence of the Scottish Church, "subject to none but the Bishop of Rome," which Fordun puts into the mouth of Canon Murray, derives its force, not from its literal truth, but from the incontestable fact that the Scots were a separate people, who would never brook absorption into an English community. Even the violent and contumacious action of William the Lion in his singular quarrel (1178) with the Pope, Alexander III., seems to have worked in favour of the liberties of the Scottish Church, for only ten years later a bull of Clement III. repelled the claims of Canterbury and York, and declared the Church of Scotland "a daughter of Rome by special grace, and immediately subject to her."

It would be easy to overstate the significance of these facts. We must not suppose that the clergy of Scotland were fighting the battle of Scottish nationality with any purpose of vindicating the rights of race. Their motives were purely political, not ethnological. Before their resistless energy all traces of the native Celtic Church nearly disappeared. The old Columban monasteries, which had long ago passed into the hands of laymen, and retained nothing of their ecclesiastical character except the name, and the later communities of the Culdees which feebly strove to keep burning the flame of religion in the land, gave place to a new and more brilliant form of ecclesiastical life. Great cathedrals and abbeys were founded in all parts of the kingdom, from Dornoch in the earldom of Caithness, to Melrose on the Lothian border; and parishes began to be formed in every diocese. But the men who were active in this august transformation cared nothing for the traditions of Alban, and were cold to the fame of Iona. The lists of bishops and abbots are almost destitute of Celtic names; even the chapters of cathedrals and the monastic fraternities are mainly composed of English or Anglicized Normans, and there is no reason to doubt that, for some generations at least after the reign of David, the parochial clergy were chiefly recruited from the same foreign field. But still the result produced was the same as if the new Scottish Church had served itself heir to Ninian, Columba, and Kentigern.

In a sense it probably did this. As it brought no new religion into the land, as it did not even profess to have effected a reformation, as it merely made ample provision for the spiritual needs of the nation, it might consider itself entitled to claim the privileges of that Celtic Church which it had superseded and extinguished. This position would at once strengthen its argument for independence of Canterbury, and its hold on a people from whom it was partially separated by language and race. It would also serve to explain a phenomenon that is otherwise difficult of explanation—the rapid spread of an English dialect among a Celtic people, and a rising fervour of nationality among those who were losing the instrument by which nationality is best preserved. We cannot for a moment doubt that just as the labours of the Scottish missionaries among the Picts, and their exclusive control of the religious education of their converts for upwards of two hundred years, sufficiently accounts for the total disappearance of the Pictish tongue; so among the causes that led to the abandonment of Welsh by the Britons of Strathclyde, and of Gaelic in the Lowlands north of the Forth, must be reckoned the presence and influence of an Anglic clergy, no less than of an Anglic or Anglo-Norman nobility. But this point will be more appropriately discussed in a later chapter; here it is enough to note the effect of the policy of the Scottish clergy in confirming the popular belief that, in some real and indestructible sense, the distinct and dissimilar races of the country formed, through the force of political ties, a single and separate nation of immemorial antiquity and high renown.

When the Anglo-Norman baronage of Scotland hastened to acknowledge the sovereignty of Edward I., the people stubbornly refused to follow their natural leaders, and found a representative of their unalterable convictions in the person of William Wallace. The great struggle for independence, which began with the night assault on the English garrison at Lanark, and ended with the crowning victory of Bannockburn, planted in the heart of every genuine Scot an undying love of his country, and an invincible determination to defend its liberties, even at the expense of its prosperity. The literature of the next two centuries, during which Scotland was almost incessantly in arms to guard the treasure she had won, is largely a vindication or a record of the strife. In the sixteenth century the sense of nationality received a fresh and powerful impulse from the Reformation of religion, which bound the community together in new bonds of faith and doctrine. Still later, the grand insurrection of the kingdom in defence of its Presbyterian Church, menaced by a despotic ruler, had also an enduring influence on the character and culture of the people.

But still it cannot be denied that this political and ecclesiastical feeling of nationality was mainly a defensive foreign policy on the part of Scotland. She knew perfectly well that her people were not as homogeneous in their origin as those of England; that while they might fight under one banner, and call themselves

Scots, for the honour and independence of the kingdom, they were internally separated by the most startling differences and discords. In great international conflicts, like Bannockburn or Flodden, the Scottish Celt and the Scottish Teuton might combine to resist or assail a formidable opponent; but within the realm of Scotland itself the antagonism of race and the difference in their modes of life engendered the fiercest animosities, and made peace and security impossible along the line of the Grampians. The way in which the "Highland Host" went to work among the Covenanters of the western shires, is a conspicuous instance of the utter absence of any feeling of kinship or inward national sympathy between the savage marauders of the northern glens and the industrious farmers and traders of the southern plains.

Not till well on in the eighteenth century—till Jacobitism was no longer a source of alarm to the mass of the people, and only a poetic grief to its adherents—did the sense of distinction of race become dim, and Scotchmen generally begin to imagine that even the uncouth native of a remote Hebridean isle, to whom English was an unknown tongue, was somehow more akin to the weaver of Glasgow or the farmer of the Merse, than was the miner of Durham or the cattle-feeder of Northumberland. It was inevitable that this feeling should grow up. The course of Scottish history necessitated it, and the gradual disappearance of the Celtic dialects before the civilizing encroachments of their Anglic rival, has been one of the strongest and most persistent agents in its development. But it was also right that it should grow up. Community of laws, religion, and culture, breeds a community of sympathy that in the long run practically obliterates the sense of ethnological difference, though the consequences of such difference may indefinitely survive, and materially modify the course of national history. Such has been the case markedly in Scotland. The brilliant valour of the Gael, which has done so much to enlarge the empire and increase the renown of Britain, is now one of the proudest boasts of the entire Scottish people; and the blood of a Lowlander now flames as quickly as that of his Highland brother at the very mention of the tartaned heroes. The Spanish Peninsula, Waterloo, India, the Crimea, and many another soil,[1] call up visions of noble figures to which the Gael has more than a common claim, and memories of brave deeds in which he has more than a common share. In war the Highlander has, in fact, become the symbol of the nation. When Scott describes the landing of the British troops in Portugal, how is it that he paints his countrymen?

> "And O! loved warriors of the minstrel's land!
>   Yonder your bonnets nod, your tartans wave!
> The rugged form may mark the mountain band,
>   And harsher features, and a mien more grave;
> But ne'er in battlefield throbbed heart so brave
>   As that which beats beneath the Scottish plaid;
> And when the pibroch bids the battle rave,
>   And level for the charge your arms are laid
> Where lives the desperate foe that for such onset staid?"

It is the clans that Byron (himself half a Highlander by blood) thinks of in his memorable verses on Waterloo. In the "Soldier's Dream" it is a Highlander that lies sleeping on the battlefield under the "sentinel stars":—

[1] This was written before the victory of Tel-el-Kebir.—ED.

> "I flew to the pleasant fields traversed so oft
>   In life's morning march, when my bosom was young,
> I heard my own mountain-goats bleating aloft,
>   And knew the sweet strain that the corn-reapers sung."

Just as Highland scenery has come to be reckoned peculiarly Scottish scenery, not only by Englishmen and foreigners, but even by the inhabitants of the Lowlands themselves, to whom its lakes and glens, its stony precipices and wind-swept isles are as familiar and dear as they were once dreaded and disliked; so in some important aspects, of which war is perhaps the chief, the Highlander has become the typical Scot, and the Lowlander, who mainly shaped the fortunes of the nation and gave it its place in history, has acquiesced in the representation and is proud of the disguise. No harm can follow from this if we only keep steadily in view the true ethnological condition of Scotland, and realize the fact that while in Southern Britain the Saxons and Angles almost wholly superseded the original Cymric population, there is no evidence that a similar act ever took place in North Britain; there is no record of a Teutonic settlement except in the southeast, and there is no probability that the Picts between Drumalban and the eastern sea, or even the Cymry of Strathclyde, though they lost their language and their independence, were ever expelled from their original seats, or transformed in character by any extraordinary infusion of a Teutonic element.

CHAPTER II.

THE LIVES OF THE EARLY SAINTS.

Ninian.—Early Notices of him by Bede.—Fuller but less trustworthy Account by Ailred.—Kentigern or Munghu.—Silence of Bede and Adamnan concerning him.—Jocelin's Biography.—Kentigern's Settlement at Glasgow.—Banishment to Wales and Return.—Missionary Expeditions.—Columba.—His Work the foundation of Scottish Nationality.—His connection with Ireland —Migration to Iona.—Adamnan's Life.—Its Legendary Character.—Greatness of Columba's Work.—His Poetry.—His Work essentially Missionary.—His Death.—Aidan.—Cuthberht.

DURING the long period of eight centuries that elapses from the departure of the Romans to the war of Independence, some shining figures light up the deep obscurity in which Scottish history is involved. Of contemporary literature there was, unfortunately, little or nothing, and the lives of men like Ninian, and Kentigern, and Columba have come down to us with halos of imaginative superstition, that make biographical criticism well-nigh impossible.

The brief sketch of Bede is the earliest notice we possess of the British missionary, the record of whose labours among the Picts of Galloway is the first historic account of the Christian religion north of the Solway; but the Northumbrian monk has given us no outline, however faint, of Ninian's personality, and it is not till we reach the distant age of Ailred, seven hundred years after the Saint had passed away, that we are furnished with a narrative, which is meant for a biography, but is merely a succession of fantastic miracles recorded with all the enthusiasm of medieval credulity. The grace of Ailred's Latin cannot hide the emptiness of his rhetoric, and though we may readily believe that some dim likeness of the early saint struggles to find expression through the monkish marvels, little is added by the Abbot of Rievaux to the modest record of Bede. Perhaps we may venture to accept as historic tradition, the sweetness and gentleness of spirit which shine through Ailred's pious legends. In later ages at least the memory of Ninian was deeply revered. Chapels were dedicated to him in every part of Scotland, and pilgrimages were habitually made to the church where his dust reposed. In his mission to the Picts he was perhaps moved by motives of humanity as well as religion, and may have wished to put an end to their incessant assaults on the provincial Britons. According to Bede, he carried the gospel as far as the range of the Grampians, though it cannot be denied that we find few traces of his beneficent work in the character of those savage tribes who peopled the region to which he penetrated. No more sacred spot exists in Scotland than that where Ninian built his church of white stone. Out of devout associations which even the rigour of the Reformation has not robbed of their charm, Catholic and Protestant may here feel that they stand on the common ground of primeval Christianity, and can unite in a common veneration of the Cumbrian apostle, whose virtues are the boast of both, and into whose labours both have entered.

Kentigern is a more distinct figure than Ninian. Living two centuries after the latter, at a time when Christianity had established itself in Ireland, and had passed with the Dalriadic Scots to the western coasts of Alban; when the Britons and Cumbrians were still in arms against the Teutonic host, and the fame of Arthur the *Guledig*[1] was still fresh in the minds of his countrymen; when Columba was engaged in the conversion of the Picts, and St. David was restoring the orthodoxy of Wales, Kentigern naturally comes into contact with other historic personages, and the incidents of his vigorous apostolate could not altogether fade away into the mists of monastic fiction. But there is a singular absence of allusion to the saint in the oldest ecclesiastical literature of the island. Bede is silent regarding his work. His name is not mentioned by Adamnan, either in his life of St. Columba, or of St. David. Were it not for the notice of his death in 612, in the *Annales Cambriae*, we might almost believe that the fame of Kentigern had scarcely crossed the limits of Strathclyde, till the reign of David I., when the revival of old, and the formation of new, bishoprics gave wider circulation to the local traditions of native saints.

We are indebted to Jocelin, a monk of Furness, who flourished in the twelfth century, for all that we know of Kentigern. From his prologue we learn that earlier lives of the Cumbrian saint were "in use" in the Bishopric of Glasgow. He particularly mourns over two that he had found. One, because of its bad Latin and its bad doctrine; the other "written in the Scotic dialect," because "it is full of solecisms from end to end." The former probably still survives in the fragment executed by a foreign ecclesiastic at the request of Bishop Herbert; but the latter has certainly perished, though Jocelin leads us to suppose that its contents were transferred to his own biography, and that his chief labour

---

[1] Leader in battle. Comp. Nennius' *dux bellorum*.

had been of a literary nature, "seasoning what had been composed in a barbarous way with Roman salt." In reality Jocelin's work is cast in the same legendary mould as the life of Ninian; it is even in some parts more wildly wonderful in its thaumaturgy, but gleams of genuine history strike here and there through the dense mass of fabulous incidents which forms its substance, and by a proper application of criticism we can picture to ourselves the work and character of the saint.

Born in the first half of the sixth century, probably of royal descent, of a gracious and benignant disposition, which procured for him the name of Munghu[1] by which the people of Scotland best remembered him, we may dismiss the records of his youth into the limbo of uncertainties, and consider that he first becomes a historic figure in connection with his residence on the banks of the Molendinar burn. His mission field was mainly British, but the dedications of churches in Alban seem to show that his labours extended as far as the Dee in Aberdeen. If it also included the territories of the Picts of Galloway (as his biographer asserts) it corresponded in the main with the area of Ninian's efforts. But everything in Jocelin assumes that there had been a relapse into idolatry among the Britons of Strathclyde and their Pictish neighbours, and that the work of his predecessor was almost undone.

The causes of this are not difficult to comprehend. When Ninian lived, the authority of Rome was still felt in Britain, and the Christian religion still possessed the sanction and support of imperial power; but during the two centuries which intervened between his age and

[1] From Welsh *mwyn*, "amiable," and *cu*, "dear."

that of Kentigern events of enormous importance had occurred in Britain. The Roman government had vanished, and the greater part of the island had passed into the hands of heathen invaders from the Lowlands of Germany. The Welsh chroniclers cry aloud in their despair. Christianity was threatened with extinction. Even the brilliant series of victories over the Angles of Bernicia, won by Arthur on the borders of Strathclyde, did not avail to restore the Church of the Britons. The champion of the Christian faith perished by treachery in a pagan insurrection; the new ruler in Alcluith was a supporter of the reactionary movement, and only three years after the fall of Arthur, Kentigern was driven from his bishopric, and forced to seek a refuge in Wales. There are traces of him south of the Solway, and though confirmation of his friendship with St. David and St. Asaph is not to be found, we can hardly suppose that during an exile of several years he remained in ignorance of those illustrious contemporaries. That he founded a great monastic brotherhood on the banks of the Elgu in Denbigh is not in itself improbable. In the Red Book of St. Asaph's mention is several times made of grants to Kentigern by Maelgwyn Gwyned, the King of North Wales.

Meanwhile a Christian revival was taking place at home. A remnant had always been left among the Britons of Strathclyde, and the appearance on the scene of Rhydderch *Hael* (the 'Liberal'), who had learned Christianity in Ireland from the disciples of St. Patrick, was the sign of a coming change. Rhydderch was originally but one of several Cumbrian princes who united their forces to resist the aggressions of the Angles. Nennius, who records the struggle, is silent as to its results, but the pagans of Bernicia were probably successful, and pushed their conquests farther west into Strathclyde Dissensions now broke out among the Britons themselves. A Christian and a pagan party emerged, the former clinging to its Roman traditions, the latter influenced by Anglic associations and the memory of ancient idolatries. Rhydderch became the head of the first, and in the great battle fought at Ardderyd in Eskdale, in 573, he inflicted so disastrous a defeat on his opponents that their cause was lost for ever in Strathclyde.

That region now became a kingdom, and one of the first acts of the new monarch was to recall from exile the venerable saint of Glasgow. The meeting between Kentigern and Rhydderch at Holdelm (now Hoddam), in Dumfries-shire, may or may not be a historical fact, but Jocelin's description is at least pervaded by a historical spirit. The exhortation addressed by the apostle to the king and his people, recognises the peculiar character of the paganism that still existed in the land. The denunciation of Woden, whose soul, 'buried in hell, endureth the eternal fire,' shows the fear with which a Christian missionary regarded the presence of the Angles; his more humane refutation of their Celtic superstitions, when he urged that " the elements in which they believed as deities were creatures and formations adapted by the disposition of their Maker to the use, help, and assistance of men," illustrates the tact and the sympathy with which he sought to win or recover his countrymen to the religion of Christ.

After dwelling for a time in Holdelm, building churches and ordaining priests, Jocelin sends Kentigern on those wider missionary expeditions to which we have alluded, and only restores him to his church in Glasgow when his conquests were complete, when he had " cleansed from the foulness of idolatry and the contagion of heresy the home of the Picts," when he had reclaimed Alban " from the worship of idols and from profane rites that were almost equal to idolatry," and had sent his disciples to the Orkneys, Norway, and Ireland " to announce to the dwellers therein the name of the Lord." Much of this triumphal progress is purely imaginary. There is no evidence of Kentigern's presence in Galloway ; the northern isles were converted by Irish missionaries; and even in Alban he could only have been a fellow-worker with Scotic rivals from Iona. Jocelin records a visit of Columba to Kentigern. If such a meeting ever took place, it would surely have been known to Adamnan, but the silence of the Abbot of Iona throws suspicion on the statement, and the details in Jocelin are utterly incredible. They are meant to exalt the fame of the Cumbrian apostle, and were probably invented to enhance the dignity of the bishopric founded by David I.

Though Jocelin has drawn a picture of the saint's career that dazzles us with the splendour of his miraculous achievements, and exhausts his fancy in their description; though he makes King Rhydderch strip himself of his royal robes, and bending humbly before Kentigern, pay homage to the saint and accept his dominions as a gift from his hands, nothing is more certain than that the Church of Strathclyde, in spite of the genius and labour of its founder, was never conspicuous for its energy or zeal. History has no record of its triumphs abroad, and darkness falls on it at home when Kentigern is dead. A doubtful tradition in the continuator of Nennius ascribes to a Cumbrian prince the conversion of the northern Angles. The authority of Bede is decisive, who tells us that Paulinus, a successor of Augustine, accomplished the sacred feat; and when the victory of Penda had once more restored the worship of Woden, the revival of the Christian faith was due to the monks of Iona, and not to the disciples of Kentigern.

Indeed, the political fortunes of Strathclyde in the seventh and eighth centuries were anything but bright. The country was conquered by the Angles in the reign of that Ecgfrith who perished in battle with the Picts in 685; and though on his death some of the Britons regained their independence, Ayrshire became an Anglic possession in 750, and only six years later Alcluith surrendered, and the Celtic population abandoned the struggle. Its subsequent history is mainly a tale of devastations till it came into the hands of the Scottish kings. During all this time religion seems to have languished, for we hardly again hear of the church of Kentigern till five centuries have passed away. Glasgow owes more to the liberality of David I. than to the earlier work of St. Munghu. Without his princely beneficence, the new bishopric could never have become the site of a famous city; but it is a true and generous instinct that has led men to recall from the depths of ages the memory of the first Christian who settled on the solitary banks of the Clyde, and to associate with his name the prosperity and splendour of an imperial mart.

But by far the grandest figure in the early dawn of Scottish history is that of Columba. His work laid the first foundation of Scottish nationality. The conversion of the northern Picts, and their gradual adoption of the Scotic tongue, made the Kingdom of Alban a possibility. Kenneth Macalpin would never have reigned at Scone if Columba had never settled in Iona; and it should always be remembered that the great Celtic state beyond the Forth was for centuries the only power in Northern Britain which seemed capable of resisting conquest and fostering a national spirit. The life of the Scotic saint is familiar to his countrymen, who have instinctively felt that his mission was immeasurably more significant for them than the obscure work of Ninian, or the semi-fabulous career of Kentigern; and have even perversely sought to discover in the peculiar features of his monastic system a likeness to the modern church of the Reformation.

When Columba landed at Iona in 563, he was over forty years of age. There is no reason why Ireland should not divide the honour of his fame with her Scottish sister. He was a native of Donegal, and trained in the monastic schools of Ireland, which owed their origin to the churches of Galloway and Wales. He had played an important part in Irish history before he resolved to devote himself to a foreign mission. He had founded numerous monastic churches and had exercised a powerful influence in the tribal politics of Ulster. A scion of the royal race of northern Hy-Neill, he was moved by secular passions as well as by religious zeal, and long after he had found a new home in the Western Isles, the choleric saint is seen eagerly intermeddling in the civil broils of his native land. The Irish clans of the sixth century were as hopelessly given over to faction fights as their modern descendants, and took the part of the saint who belonged to their tribe with the proverbial fervour of the Celt. The tradition which records the censure of Columba by a vote of the clergy, and ascribes to St. Molaisi of Inishmurry the sentence of perpetual exile pronounced against him, is obviously the creation of a later age, and even as it stands, proves that he sought the help of his kinsmen to avenge an affront. It is not necessary, therefore, to accept the popular belief that he was banished to Iona to expiate ecclesiastical offences. Monks in the days of Columba were not exempt from military service. Their clan could call them to the field, and the annals of Ireland furnish sufficient proof of this curious condition of things. We read of sanguinary conflicts between rival fraternities in which hundreds were slain. That a leading member of this order, a man of the highest rank in his tribe, one moreover possessed of a temper violent and imperious, though essentially heroic, should hotly interfere in the quarrels of his brethren and make himself a host of enemies both among the clergy and the laity, was the most natural thing in the world; that in these circumstances he should seek a new sphere for his energy in a heathen land where the strife would be nobler and the triumph more glorious, was a course to which the history of the church offers many parallels, and in all probability this was the true motive of his migration to the Hebrides.

When Columba departed he severed no ties, surrendered no jurisdiction; his congregations remained in their various settlements, still subject to his authority; and he took with him no more than the prescriptive attendance of a missionary leader.[1] Nor was his

[1] Dr. Reeve's *Life of St. Columba:* Historians of Scotland, vol. VI. Introduction, p. 37.

mission even a retreat into a distant obscurity. Iona was only a day's sail from Ireland, and his countrymen were already in possession of the neighbouring coasts. Whether the band of Scots under Fergus Mor, who left Antrim at the close of the fifth century and established themselves in Kintyre and Isla, were the first of their nation to settle among the northern Picts, is a question that we need not here discuss. In the sixty years preceding the arrival of Columba, they had greatly extended their territories, but in the year 560, in the reign of the Pictish king Brude, they suffered a disastrous defeat, and the Scottish colony, again restricted to the peninsula of Kintyre, seemed in danger of expulsion from Alban. It is possible that Columba was stirred to undertake his mission to the Picts by the perilous position of his kinsmen. It may well have seemed to him that their best hope of safety and tranquillity lay in the conversion of their formidable neighbours. Nor could he forget that among the revered instructors of his youth, Finnian of Clonard, the founder of the greatest monastic school in Ireland, belonged to the race of Irish Picts. At any rate it was during this eclipse of the fortunes of the Dalriad Scots, that Columba took up his abode in Iona on the confines of the Pictish territory.

Few details of his genuine missionary labours have been recorded. Adamnan's *Life* has been happily described as a portrait and a eulogy, but not a history. The character and virtues of the saint are brightly mirrored in a hundred fables, but we would gladly surrender the whole for one chapter of genuine biography. Although written only a century after Col-

ceptible; overpowering impressions are made upon its imagination and conscience by superior intellect and sanctity; men suddenly lifted out of moral darkness by a vision of heavenly light, or out of mental torpor by a storm of heavenly enthusiasm, saw nothing in the new world around them as it really was; everything seemed of necessity miraculous, and superstition soon gave a prosaic shape and form to the exaggerations of religious fancy. A dream or a rumour hardened into a fact under the influence of a universal credulity, and had a tendency to propagate itself in a hundred different ways. The crude daemonism of heathen religions often strangely reflects itself in the Christianity by which they are overthrown; and the Scottish monks may have been insensibly led to ascribe to the victorious Columba the exercise of powers that threw into the shade the magic of Pictish wizards and sorcerers.

The work that he did was great: it was nothing less than the conversion of a nation, and it was followed by circumstances that gave it a peculiar interest. What imperial Rome accomplished in Gaul by her legions, her colonies, and her civilization, the monastic brotherhood, that traced their origin to Iona, accomplished in Pictavia by the help of religious culture alone. They effaced the native dialect of a powerful people, and compelled them to accept the language of their teachers. Men still helplessly discuss the question, "What has become of the Pictish tongue?" and in the almost total absence of *data* sometimes have proffered the absurdest answers. So complete was the triumph of the Scottish missionaries that in the course of a few centuries Irish Gaelic was in use wherever their influence extended, and has probably for more than a thousand years been the sole Celtic speech of the Highlands.[1]

We have said that Adamnan's *Life* is not a biography, and that it is impossible to ascertain from it the course of Columba's missionary and political career. From other sources we learn a few interesting and important facts. The Pictish Chronicle states that Brude was baptized by Columba in the eighth year of his reign, and in the Irish Life of the Saint we are told of a set contest in thaumaturgy between the Pictish druids and Columba, in which the former were cut off to a man. Adamnan records the coronation of Aidan as king of the Dalriad Scots, to which the Pictish Chronicle assigns the date 574; and, according to the ancient poem called the *Amra or Praise of Columcille*, he appeared in the following year, attended by an imposing retinue of his priests and bishops, at a great synod of the Irish chiefs and clergy held at Drumceat in Londonderry, to bring about among other things "a pacification between the men of Erin and Alban about Dalriada." In other words the question came up, "Are the Scots of Alban to be independent of the Scots of Erin?" A decision was given in the affirmative. The colony became an independent state, and henceforth stood on an equal footing with its Pictish neighbour.

It was on this occasion that Columba made his famous appeal on behalf of the Irish poets who were then suffering banishment on account of their extravagant demands on the resources of the tribes. It was to his eloquence they owed their recall, and the gratitude of the greatest of the minstrels finds expression in the

[1] See Skene's *Celtic Scotland*, vol. II. pp. 453-63.

Amra of Dallan Forgaill. Columba was himself a poet, and a considerable number of pieces ascribed to him still survive. The verses on his island home, bearing the title *Columcille fecit,* so fresh, simple, and picturesque, so full of boyish glad-heartedness and of wholesome religion—if they really came from his pen—present the impulsive yet fearless saint in a new and more brilliant light, and help us to realize, better than a legion of miracles would do, the everyday life and thought of those ancient servants of God who forsook the savage ways of secular existence, and in secure retreats of piety and peace spent their days in honest labours, in beneficent charities, in fraternal worship, in solitary devotion, in the cheerful enjoyment of the face of nature, and in the calm delights of sacred literature.

The work of Columba was essentially missionary. He not only set up a purer model of life in the little monastic society of Iona, but both in Pictish and Scottish territory he founded similar fraternities,[1] which remained under the jurisdiction of the mother church, and together formed one great Christian family.[2] Ireland furnished Columba and his successors with a constant supply of religious auxiliaries, who carried to their lonely retreats in the Western Isles and in the glens beyond Drumalban something of that love of learning which had made the Irish Church the admiration of Christendom. The fame of Iona attracted students from far and near. Princes and nobles sought "wisdom" in the lowly huts of the monks. Nor was their evangelistic energy limited to Celtic regions.

---

[1] See Adamnan, book 2, chap. 47.
[2] Skene, *Celtic Scotland,* book 2, chap. 4.

Columba died in the summer of 597, and in the autumn of the same year a Roman mission undertook the conversion of the English kingdoms. It has been the good fortune of Augustine and his successors to have their work recorded by the greatest historian of the dark ages, but the narrative of Bede also throws a light on the progress of the Columban Church. During the reign of Eadwine of Northumbria, the sons of Æthelfrith lived in exile among the Scots. In the pagan reaction that followed his death all traces of the Christianity introduced by Paulinus seemed to be lost; but when the victory of the "Heavenly Field" placed Oswald on the throne of his fathers, the grateful monarch turned to the isle which had given him a shelter, for help in the work of restoring the faith that had been overthrown. The venerable Aidan was sent from Iona by the elders of the Scots to exercise episcopal authority in Northumbria. He fixed his see in the isle of Lindisfarne, and preached with a noble ardour to the Angles in his Gaelic vernacular, Oswald acting as interpreter. Scottish missionaries now poured in from Dalriada. "Churches were built in several places; the people joyfully flocked together to hear the word; money and lands were given of the king's bounty to build monasteries; the Angles, great and small, were instructed by their Scottish masters in the rules and observance of regular discipline; for most of those who came to preach were monks."[1] The Easter and tonsure controversies between the rival churches of Iona and Canterbury ended in the discomfiture of the former, and thirty years after Aidan's settlement

---

[1] Bede, *Eccl. Hist.* b. 3, chap. 3.

in Lindisfarne, the Scottish monks withdrew from Northumbria, and left the care of religion to those who were more familiar with the traditions of Rome. But the work which they did was never undone. At this distance of time the controversy has dwindled into utter insignificance. We can hardly bring ourselves to believe that men could ever grow hot on such trivial questions; but the permanent restoration of the religion of Christ, where it had been trodden under foot, is a historic fact of the first importance, and a perpetual honour to the Church of Columba.

From one of the monasteries founded by Aidan, that of Melrose, came the illustrious St. Cuthberht, who renounced the world in 651. Ten years later he was chosen prior of Melrose, and signalized his office by the most chivalrous labours in the service of his Master. By virtue of a resistless eloquence, an enthusiasm that made his face when he preached like that of an angel, a deep affectionate pity for all who were poor and forlorn, he was one of the noblest evangelists of that early time. Bede, who wrote Cuthberht's life only forty years after the saint's death in Farne Isle, gives us a picture of his missionary work in the wild Cheviot hills, which even yet, after the lapse of more than a thousand years, thrills us with high emotion. We see the eager monk on his lonesome pilgrimages over desolate moors and mountains fearful to behold, swiftly passing from one cluster of rude sheilings to another, gathering the 'rustic people' into little congregations, and flashing into the dull routine of their pastoral life the glory and splendour of heavenly truths. Weeks and months would pass by before Cuthberht returned to his priory, for his energy and enthusiasm were alike inexhaustible. The

Columba died in the summer of 597, and in the autumn of the same year a Roman mission undertook the conversion of the English kingdoms. It has been the good fortune of Augustine and his successors to have their work recorded by the greatest historian of the dark ages, but the narrative of Bede also throws a light on the progress of the Columban Church. During the reign of Eadwine of Northumbria, the sons of Æthelfrith lived in exile among the Scots. In the pagan reaction that followed his death all traces of the Christianity introduced by Paulinus seemed to be lost; but when the victory of the "Heavenly Field" placed Oswald on the throne of his fathers, the grateful monarch turned to the isle which had given him a shelter, for help in the work of restoring the faith that had been overthrown. The venerable Aidan was sent from Iona by the elders of the Scots to exercise episcopal authority in Northumbria. He fixed his see in the isle of Lindisfarne, and preached with a noble ardour to the Angles in his Gaelic vernacular, Oswald acting as interpreter. Scottish missionaries now poured in from Dalriada. "Churches were built in several places; the people joyfully flocked together to hear the word; money and lands were given of the king's bounty to build monasteries; the Angles, great and small, were instructed by their Scottish masters in the rules and observance of regular discipline; for most of those who came to preach were monks."[1] The Easter and tonsure controversies between the rival churches of Iona and Canterbury ended in the discomfiture of the former, and thirty years after Aidan's settlement

---

[1] Bede, *Eccl. Hist.* b. 3, chap. 3.

in Lindisfarne, the Scottish monks withdrew from Northumbria, and left the care of religion to those who were more familiar with the traditions of Rome. But the work which they did was never undone. At this distance of time the controversy has dwindled into utter insignificance. We can hardly bring ourselves to believe that men could ever grow hot on such trivial questions; but the permanent restoration of the religion of Christ, where it had been trodden under foot, is a historic fact of the first importance, and a perpetual honour to the Church of Columba.

From one of the monasteries founded by Aidan, that of Melrose, came the illustrious St. Cuthberht, who renounced the world in 651. Ten years later he was chosen prior of Melrose, and signalized his office by the most chivalrous labours in the service of his Master. By virtue of a resistless eloquence, an enthusiasm that made his face when he preached like that of an angel, a deep affectionate pity for all who were poor and forlorn, he was one of the noblest evangelists of that early time. Bede, who wrote Cuthberht's life only forty years after the saint's death in Farne Isle, gives us a picture of his missionary work in the wild Cheviot hills, which even yet, after the lapse of more than a thousand years, thrills us with high emotion. We see the eager monk on his lonesome pilgrimages over desolate moors and mountains fearful to behold, swiftly passing from one cluster of rude sheilings to another, gathering the 'rustic people' into little congregations, and flashing into the dull routine of their pastoral life the glory and splendour of heavenly truths. Weeks and months would pass by before Cuthberht returned to his priory, for his energy and enthusiasm were alike inexhaustible. The day was spent in preaching to the poor forlorn shepherds and their families; the night in prayers and incredible austerities. Nothing in all his great career is so great as this. He was an admirable bishop, and an anchorite of the purest kind; but neither his labours to win over the Scottish monks of Northumbria to the usage of Rome and Canterbury, nor the self-denying rigours of his solitude in Farne, though they are unquestionably the cause of his ecclesiastical fame, excite the admiration of the modern world like the holy philanthropy of his missionary visits to the outcast children of poverty and desolation.

Though Cuthberht conformed to Roman usage (like Adamnan himself), he must be regarded as a product of the Church of Iona. He owes his first religious impressions to the ardour of the Celtic evangelists in Lothian. While watching the flocks of his master in the vale of the Leader he saw, in a vision, angels carrying the soul of St. Aidan to Heaven,[1] and was in consequence led to choose a monastic life, and through all his career the spirit of Columban energy is visible in his work. The fire, the eloquence, the tenderness, the austere devotion of the Scottish saints reappear in Cuthberht, and point with unmistakeable accuracy to the sources of his inspiration. After his death the spread of Christianity in Northumbria is due solely to Anglian efforts, but the building and endowment of churches is an immeasurably less heroic achievement than the first evangelization of a heathen people, or the recovery of a race that had lapsed. Cuthberht's is the greatest name in the religious history of Lothian, till the time of John Knox.

[1] *Vita Anon. S. Cuth.*

CHAPTER III.

THE WAR OF INDEPENDENCE AND ITS MINSTRELS.

Scotland before and after Malcolm Ceannmor.—Dearth of Literature till the latter half of Fourteenth Century.—Contrast with England in this particular. —The War of Independence.—First Effort of Scottish Muse in Anglic Vernacular to celebrate that War.—Barbour's Brus and Blind Harry's Wallace considered together.—Barbour's Life—Estimate of his Work—How far historical.—Notices of Blind Harry.— What we really know of Wallace. —Blind Harry's Work gives literary Expression to Wallace Cult.—Its Extravagancies.— Wallace's true Position.

THE history of Scotland from the time of Kenneth Macalpin (843) to the accession of the Stewarts is divisible into two periods, each singularly unlike the other. The first ending with the reign of Malcolm Ceannmor (1057-93) presents to us a purely Celtic state, and an almost purely Celtic community, with a corresponding social and political organization. The second exhibits the same state undergoing an almost complete transformation, in which the Celtic element was reduced to political insignificance, the decayed church of Columba giving place to the splendid reformation of David I.; feudal tenures and jurisdictions either superseding the older tribal institutions of the Picts and Scots, or breaking up the tribes into those petty clans who have in later times become so famous; the Scotic language, which the Columban missionaries had spread over the whole region north of the Forth, rapidly disappearing from the eastern seaboard before the Anglic dialect used by the foreign burgesses of the newly founded towns; a similar process going on in Strathclyde from even an earlier date; a new race of Anglic and Anglo-Norman nobles displacing to some extent [1] the older Celtic mormaers; and in fine a new conception of what is meant by the kingdom of Scotland, and the Scottish nation.

The first period has scarcely a single notable name. Some good work was of course done by the Donalds, Aeds, Girics, Indulphs, Kenneths, and other kings of Alban; but the men are shadows, and their lives are mist. One figure alone stands out conspicuous. Shakespeare has invested the obscure career of Macbeth with the splendid light of genius; and though the story of the dramatist is demonstrably false, it will certainly outlive the assaults of criticism. The real history of Macbeth shows him to have been a beneficent and successful ruler, in spite of his treacherous slaughter of his monarch. The mormaer of Moray was bound to his kinsman, the King of Alban, by no very close or ancient tie; and Duncan's unwise aggression on the Norwegian earldom of the Orkneys might seem to him a fitting opportunity for asserting his independence, or overthrowing his master. The Celtic population of "Scotia" accepted his government, and for seventeen years his authority remained unchallenged north of the Forth. His fall at Lumphanan in Aberdeenshire, in 1058, marks the close of the purely Celtic rule in Scotland; for Malcolm Ceannmor, who probably spent his youth in Northumbria, and cer-

---

[1] The greater part of the Celtic proprietary however remained, though the tenure of land was feudalized. See Robertson's *Scotland under her early Kings*, vol. II. pp. 484-501.

tainly ruled in Lothian long before he was able to wrest the Scottish throne from Macbeth, naturally was predisposed to look with favour on the English portion of his subjects.

It is hardly possible to over-estimate the influence which Malcolm's marriage with an English princess exercised on the course of Scottish history. The rare virtues of Margaret inspired her husband with a chivalrous devotion that revolutionized the policy and aims of the Celtic king. He was not content like his predecessors to carry on the traditions of Celtic supremacy, and to rule the people of Lothian as strangers and foreigners. His repeated invasions of Northumbrian territory are not to be taken as evidence of Celtic antagonism to a Teutonic race, but of an ambitious desire to extend the area of his Anglic sovereignty. The Norman Conquest sharpened the edge of Malcolm's sword, and involved him in a series of bloody wars; but the countrymen of Margaret found a secure asylum in Scotland, and her husband's devastations on the Northumbrian border filled the hamlets of Lothian with English slaves. The numerous refugees from Norman oppression civilized the manners and usages of the Scottish court. The children of the English princess were imbued with the religious sentiments of their mother, and the ecclesiastical policy which carried them far away from the traditions of the Columban church, was the fruit of their filial piety. They shared her love of pomp and ceremony; and if their introduction of feudal obligations cannot be properly described as an English innovation, it was at least suggested by their connection with the English court, and was another departure from the social system of their Celtic ancestors. The insurrections that broke out in the north were a sort of angry protest on the part of the native chiefs, who felt that the power was passing from the race to which it had once belonged, and who feared that foreign institutions were but the heralds of a new nobility. The struggles of the mormaers of Moray were unavailing. In the reign of David I. the great Celtic earldom was forfeited to the Crown, and partly divided among the Anglo-Norman knights who had come to the aid of the king from Northumberland and York. But it is an error to suppose that any serious displacement of Celtic proprietors took place in Alban generally. Whatever evidence exists goes to show that the land still remained for the most part in their hands, and generations must have passed before even the eastern and north-eastern lowlands lost their Gaelic-speaking gentry.[1] The composition of David's army at the Battle of the Standard (1138) illustrates the motley character of the Scottish population, and we may well believe that the twelfth century had closed before the Anglic tongue was recognised as the national organ of the community, and the Celtic dialects of Alban and Strathclyde had ceased to possess a political importance.

The anarchy that followed the capture of William the Lyon at Alnwick (1174) proves how superficial was the unity of the feudal kingdom of Scotland. Not only did the native lords of Galloway destroy the royal fortresses in their dominion, expel the officers of the Scottish king, and hasten to proffer their vassalage to his fortunate adversary; but many of the Scots in the north and west of Alban banded themselves together to

---

[1] See *Scotland under her early Kings*, vol. II. pp. 487 *et seq.*

crush the rising power of the English and Flemish burgesses, and to restore the supremacy of the Celt. The apparition of a Highland sennachy at the coronation of Alexander III. (1249), and his genealogical harangue delivered in Gaelic, may be considered the latest effort of the Celtic community to formally and constitutionally assert its place in Scottish history.

It is unnecessary to trace in detail the progress of feudal institutions and burghal life in Scotland, or to point out the extent to which the former was modified by "ancient custom," and to which the latter absorbed and transformed a Celtic peasantry into urban craftsmen and traders, who soon acquired Teutonic names and forgot their Gaelic speech. Before Malcolm Ceannmor's time Scotland was inhabited by a rural population, scattered over the face of the country in mean hamlets and bothies, and supporting itself mainly by flocks and herds, and by a rude and insignificant agriculture. Architecture was unknown; commerce did not exist; religion and learning were dead. Before the death of Alexander III. had left Scotland a prey to foreign ambition and rapacity, successive generations of landed proprietors, small and great, had been bound to extend the area of their cultivated land: even those who had no land were, according to Fordun, under an obligation to dig daily seven feet square of earth. Towns had sprung up, and had originated both a home and a foreign trade. Berwick, then a Scottish possession, had become the greatest port in the Isle of Britain, "the Alexandria of the North." The Church had arisen from its Culdee tomb with more than Columban vigour; by its noble structures, its educational efforts, its elaborate ritual, its parochial organization, the energy of its prelates and abbots, as well as the unbroken favour of the Scottish kings, it had recovered its spiritual authority, and was once more a power over the consciences of men. A great judiciary system had long been in operation, which required the services of the feudal baronage. In a word the kingdom was completely changed; and though numerous traces of the older state of things were still visible, in language and custom and character, Scotland had cast off for ever the uncivilized dominion of the Celt.

No one can tell exactly when the English tongue became the national language of the Scottish lowlands. It was in use in Lothian from the sixth century: it certainly spread into Strathclyde as early as the eighth, but in all likelihood did not wholly supersede the native Cymric before the growth of towns in the twelfth century. The reign of Malcolm Ceannmor saw it introduced at the Scottish court, but there is no reason to suppose that the influence of Margaret reached farther than the circle of her home and her personal friends. Outside of these, Gaelic alone would be used both by her husband and his thanes; but the disposition to acquire a knowledge of the language of the favoured province of Lothian, would grow stronger from year to year, although it might perhaps sustain a temporary check by the counter current of Norman-French which began to flow into Scotland from the time of David I. The Scoto-Norman nobles used French probably as long as their neighbours in England, *i.e.*, till after the middle of the fourteenth century. At the coronation of Alexander III. Latin forms were translated into French for the monarch's benefit; but the very necessities of their position would make it a matter of importance, to both the king and the foreign nobles, to acquire some familiarity with the vernaculars of the different parts of the kingdom. The growth of burghs and the increase of trade, through the influence of English and other Teutonic settlers, must have silently extended the area over which the English tongue was spoken. Though we have no data by which we can trace its progress from the sixth to the fourteenth century, when it first appears as a literary language, we may safely believe that during these eight hundred years it made continuous advances in the Lowland districts, and passed through the same phases of change which marked its history in the southern part of the isle. If one may hazard a conjecture where all exact knowledge is impossible, we should be inclined to say that English was never unknown to the Scottish kings from the time of Malcolm Ceannmor, though it may have fallen into disuse through the prevalence of Norman-French among the feudal nobility; and that while charters and statutes were drawn up in Latin by ecclesiastical lawyers, English had become the medium of common intercourse for the entire Lowland population of Scotland from the Moray Firth to the Solway, except in part of Galloway, as early as the reign of Alexander III.

The chief cause of our ignorance on this point is the almost total dearth of literature in Scotland till the latter half of the fourteenth century. The Church of Columba was for a time imbued with a love of learning, and to Culdee scribes we probably owe the first attempts to chronicle the national history. But nothing survives that is of earlier date than the tenth century. The *Pictish Chronicle* closes with Kenneth II., who died in 995, and as it leaves the years of his reign blank, it is supposed to have been compiled during that monarch's life. The *Duan Albanach* in the eleventh, a series of rude "chronicles" both of "Scots" and "Picts" in the next three centuries, and one or two lives of saints, are all that Scotland has to show till we reach the age of Barbour and Wyntoun and Fordun. Their historical value is great, but they are utterly destitute of grace or art, and cannot exempt the nation which produced them from the charge of literary barbarism. The brilliant revival of ecclesiastical life in the thirteenth century must have enlarged the culture of the Scottish clergy, but their intellectual activity somehow never found literary expression. The new bishoprics, monasteries, and abbeys may have been nurseries of medieval learning and administrative ability, but they cannot boast of a single famous name. From Malcolm Ceannmor to Alexander III. not a solitary poet or scholar appears to break the monotonous sterility of two hundred years. Michael Scot—an apparent exception—is half a mystery and half a myth, but he was not a product of the Scottish Church, and the works that have been ascribed to him were written in foreign lands.

Scotsmen hardly realize the immense contrast between the literary poverty of their own country in the earlier period of its history, and the literary affluence of England. But they ought both to realize and remember it, if they wish to form a right judgment on the respective civilizations of the sister kingdoms. While England was still a cluster of separate states, the venerable Bede had written his *Historia Ecclesiastica*, a work that can never be sufficiently admired ; instinct with a genuine, historic spirit, in spite of its numerous traces of monkish credulity ; the outcome of a most honourable and indefatigable labour, for every diocese and monastery at home seem to have furnished him with materials for his task, while the munificence of Benedict Biscop which enriched the Northumbrian libraries with the most valuable books that the continent possessed, allowed him to gratify still further his passion for liberal studies. Piety and criticism, learning and pictorial grace, toleration and love of truth are harmoniously blended in its pages; and one rises from reading it with an irresistible conviction that Bede, in a later and more enlightened age, would have ranked among the foremost of English historians. The authenticity of Asser's *Life of Alfred* is now perhaps more than a matter of doubt, but the so-called *Anglo-Saxon Chronicle* compiled from the humble registers of monastic houses, and more or less marking the course of events in England from the departure of the Romans to the death of Stephen, is a work of superlative value. The Homilies of Ælfric; the translations from Orosius, Boethius, and Gregory ascribed to Alfred; and the versions of the Gospels, and parts of the Old Testament, are illustrations of a desire to enlighten and broaden the minds of men by a knowledge both of God and of mankind; and however low we may rate their artistic merits, they are an everlasting honour to the England of those days.

Still nobler and more striking is the genius displayed in old English poetry. When Alban and Strathclyde and Lothian were all but voiceless in song (for the Celtic sennachies are of Irish origin, and their bardic effusions hardly deserve the name of literature), the Angles of the south had surpassed every contemporary nation in the richness and vigour of their verse.

The heroic tale of *Beowulf* is worth a thousand *Ossians*. Not one falsetto note, not one sham-antique sentiment or image, not one grotesque anachronism stains its primitive beauty and simplicity. Whether it was first composed on the heaths of Holstein or by the fiords of Slesvig, brought to Britain by the Jutish followers of Hengist and Horsa, and after the conversion of their descendants to Christianity, recast under Christian influence; whether it dates from the Danish rule of Canute; or is a purely English poem framed by some gifted priest, the companion of Willibrod on his mission to the Saxons and Danes in the seventh century, who found in the legend of the heathen prince who delivered the Danes from the ravages of a malignant fiend, some far-off shadow of the Great Redeemer, it breathes in every line the magnanimous spirit of Teutonic antiquity. The fiery ardour and boyish bravado of the warriors, the superabundant hilarity of their banquets, the fine courtesy and reverence shown to woman, the sweetness, grace, and dignity of the Lady Wealhtheow, are exquisitely pourtrayed, and remind us forcibly of that other primitive world round the eastern shores of the Mediterranean, which shines so fair in the *Iliad* and the *Odyssey*. And through all the poem, strangely mingling with its crude and yet solemn Christianity, there runs a heathen awe of the wild terrors that haunt the waste places of a half-subdued world. But the influence of the Christian religion is far more visible in other poems. The *Paraphrase*, long ascribed to Caedmon, bears witness to the deep and powerful impression made on the minds of Englishmen by the grand incidents of Scripture history. If it does not possess the graphic pictorial charm of *Beowulf*, it is inspired with a loftier and a more hallowed thought. At times from the mere majesty of his theme, the unlettered peasant of Whitby comes into no unworthy comparison with the author of *Paradise Lost*. The Exeter and Vercelli collections of old English poetry furnish additional evidence of the extent to which biblical and apocalyptic story, and church legend, had laid hold of the English mind, and was exercising over it a high and beneficent control. The *Elene* and *Christ* of Cynewulf, the *Phœnix*, *The Address of the Soul to the Body*, *Judith*, are evidences of native Christian culture to which Europe at that time could exhibit no parallel. Some of the poems we have mentioned are examples of literary art sustained through thousands of verses.

But the contrast between the two kingdoms is not confined to the period preceding the Norman Conquest. The great age of the English chroniclers has no counterpart in Scotland. Against the scanty fragments in which the story of the Picts and Scots is told over and over again with unvarying dulness, England can place the elegant, learned, and critical history of William of Malmesbury, the graphic miscellanies, historical, geographical, and political, of the vivacious Gerald de Barri, the minute and valuable annals of Ordericus Vitalis, Florence of Worcester, Eadmer, Henry of Huntingdon, William of Newbury, Roger of Hoveden, Roger of Wendover, Matthew Paris, and Nicholas Trivet. Besides this solid array of historical names, England can show a splendid list of poets, satirists, and critics, when empty silence reigns beyond the Tweed. She can point to the piquant wit and mocking humour of Walter Map, the burlesque satire of Nigel Wireker, and the classic verse of Joseph of Exeter, and the classic criticism of Geoffrey de Vinsauf, the reappearance in new forms of the vernacular literature as exemplified by the poems of Ormin, Geoffrey of Monmouth, and Robert of Gloucester, and the marvellous outburst of romantic fiction in honour of King Arthur. In short, there exists what may fairly be called an overwhelming mass of evidence to prove the superior culture and civilization of the southern kingdom.

To what extent this superiority is due to the earlier development of a national unity in England than in Scotland, might not be easy to determine; but no one can doubt that the task of welding into one political community, the separate and discordant races of the North, was immeasurably more difficult than any which the Kings of England had to face. What Scotsmen are justly proud of is the thoroughness with which the task was finally accomplished. Along with the growth of the national prosperity, through all the changes in speech and interfusion of races, in spite of a half alien nobility whose English possessions made it impossible for them to be patriots, there grew up silently among the gentry and commons of Scotland an indestructible conviction that they were members of a separate and independent nation, whose liberties could never be justly assailed by any foreign power. The Scottish policy of Edward I. brought out this conviction into the clearest light. We do not intend to discuss the merits or demerits of that policy. Those who wish to know what Englishmen have to say in its favour should consult Sir Francis Palgrave's *Documents and Records*

Illustrative of the History of Scotland, and Mr. Freeman's *History of the Norman Conquest* and his *Historical Essays*. The Scottish view of the question is argued by Mr. W. E. Robertson in an appendix to his work on *Scotland under her Early Kings* in a way that leaves nothing to be desired, and by Mr. Burns in his *Scottish War of Independence* with a dogged energy of purpose, and an honest pugnacity of spirit which are highly refreshing.

But though we do not think it necessary to discuss Edward's "Claim of Right," we have no hesitation in saying that if it had been a thousand times stronger than it was, it could by no possibility have been allowed by the Scottish people. They had got far beyond the point when a reference to a doubtful transaction in the reign of Eadward the Elder in the tenth century, could have any practical influence on their political conduct; even if that transaction had then acquired the prominence which Mr. Freeman now gives it. They knew well that over and over again when the independence of the kingdom had been challenged either in church or state, prelates and monarchs had asserted its rights with fiery pride, and no voluntary submission to an English dominion could henceforth be dreamt of. Their country might be conquered and crushed—such was indeed its fortune for a time —but Edward was never farther from the end he desired than when his soldiers garrisoned every fortress, and his governors meted out what justice they pleased to the burghers and peasants of Scotland. A fierce, even a rancorous hatred of the English rule sprang up in the hearts of the Scottish commons; and in spite of the cramp which feudal authority could exercise on the military energies of the nation, it is no exaggeration to say that the appearance of William Wallace on the scene, is the protest of an insurgent people against the violent tyranny of strangers. The War of Independence was a national war, and its real character cannot be affected by the vacillation and perfidy of the Scoto-Norman nobles, who did not share the popular passion for national freedom, and who could not always command the services of their vassals. One of its best results was the conversion of many of the nobles themselves into Scottish patriots, whose zeal for the rights and honour of the kingdom obliterated the memory of their former selfishness. Never again could England hope to conquer by divisions in the Scottish state. Faction did not instantly expire, but the malcontent barons were disinherited and driven from the land which they sought to enslave. Their return with Edward Baliol in 1332 involved Scotland again in a brief anarchy; but when the national party discovered that Scottish independence was more than jeopardized, was in fact secretly sold to England, they once more came to the rescue, and Baliol and his associates had to flee from the realm whose rights they had betrayed.

It is not without significance that the first effort of the Scottish muse in its new Anglic vernacular should be devoted to a celebration of the glorious struggle for independence. Barbour's *Brus* is a fitting tribute to the memory of the great king whose valour, patience, fortitude, and sagacity brought to a successful issue the heroic work begun by Wallace. The circumstances of its composition make it infinitely more valuable for historical biography, than the farrago of impossible fictions which Blind Harry offers as a *Life of Sir William Wallace*. With a view to point out more clearly the contrast between the two authors and their productions, though they are separated from each other by nearly a century, and though not a little important Scottish literature intervened, we shall consider them together. The historical proximity of their respective heroes may form an additional justification of this mode of treatment. These heroes, after the lapse of so many centuries, are still the dearest in Scottish history. If in reality we know less of the ill-fated warrior whose short career was closed by an ignominious and cruel death in London, than of the intrepid monarch who led his nation to victory at Bannockburn, tradition has generously stepped in to help our ignorance, and has furnished us with an ideal portrait and a romantic biography, on which we love to linger even when criticism forbids us to believe. Everywhere there are places sacred to his memory : his name, says Wordsworth, is

> " to be found, like a wild flower,
> All over his dear Country ; "

and not even the barbarous taste and ludicrous prejudice of Blind Harry can materially diminish the lofty veneration in which that name has been held in every succeeding age of Scottish history.

John Barbour, the father of the Anglic literature of Scotland, was Archdeacon of Aberdeen in the latter half of the fourteenth century. Of his life we have no continuous account, but his name occurs several times in the public records of both kingdoms, as well as in the registers of his own diocese. From various indications it has been inferred that he was born a few years after the battle of Bannockburn, but of his earlier life or training no trace has been discovered. The first glimpse we get of him is in the year 1357 when Edward III. of England grants a safe conduct to "John Barbour, Archdeacon of Aberdeen, with three scholars in his company, going to study at the University of Oxford."[1] Again in 1364 he receives permission to pass through England to "study at Oxford, or elsewhere, as he may think proper;" and in 1365 and 1368, we find him seeking to pursue his studies in France. He was a member of the National Council which procured the release of David Bruce from an English prison; was thrice an Auditor of Exchequer (in 1372, 1382, and 1384), and received from Robert II. by a charter dated 5th December, 1388, an annual grant of ten pounds sterling for the patriotic service of his pen. It is the cessation of these payments which enables us to fix the year 1395 as the date of his death —probably on the 13th of March, as his memory was religiously celebrated on that day in the Cathedral of Aberdeen down to the period of the Reformation. This is all we know about him. As with his great contemporary, Chaucer, a few external and isolated facts make up his biography; but, poor and meagre as they are in themselves, they are invaluable in relation to the historical credit of the *Brus*.

The nature and quality of this poem have not always been fairly appreciated. Englishmen like Mr. Freeman, who denounce the hero "as a traitor in turn to every cause, as a hardened rebel, who at last took to patriotism as his only chance to escape the punishment of a treacherous private murder," naturally cannot

[1] *Rotuli Scotiae*, vol. I. p. 808.

accept as historical the portrait of Bruce which is given in the work, and are easily persuaded that the poem is an ideal romance of knightly fiction. But Scotsmen do not look on Bruce from the same standpoint as Mr. Freeman: they interpret his earlier career less harshly, though they certainly do not hold it up to admiration: they admit that he pursued for a time the selfish vacillating policy of the order to which he belonged, and that he was long a stranger to the national desire for independence; but in the indomitable courage with which he faced the perils of his later enterprise, as well as in his singular power of inspiring confidence and quickening enthusiasm among his friends, they find evidence of something nobler than the desperation of a political gambler and assassin;[1] something that better accords with Barbour's picture than with the view of his character set forth by the new school of English historians.

Though trained at the court of Edward, Bruce was a *suspect* from the first. His bold and ardent spirit excited chronic uneasiness regarding his future policy. His antagonism to Wallace did not imply perfidy to his country but hostility to the house of Baliol. Without assuming on his part a patriotism, which was certainly of later growth, the outcome of that fiery ordeal through which he had to pass after his final rupture with the English king, we may ascribe his dubious conduct to nothing worse than a proud and dissatisfied ambition. The withdrawal of Baliol into France was followed by secret negotiations with members of the national party. Bruce's interview with Lambert, Bishop of Glasgow, at the Abbey of Cambus-

---

[1] Freeman's *Historical Essays*. Lond. 1872.

kenneth in 1304, resulted in a "bond" being drawn up which fell into the hands of Edward. Though purposely vague in its terms, the drift of this document could not be misunderstood. It pointed unmistakeably to an active interference in Scottish affairs, and it was intended to secure the ecclesiastical and military support of the Church for a new national movement, headed by the ablest competitor for the Scottish Crown. No doubt such an arrangement involved duplicity on the side of Bruce. He was an English subject, and an English courtier. He had acknowledged the sovereignty of Edward, and given him feudal help in his later invasions of Scotland; but he was entitled at any moment to withdraw his allegiance from a monarch who had far outstepped the limits of his overlordship, and some other epithet than "infamous" must be applied to the secrecy he was forced to observe in his new policy.

Mr. Freeman is too good a judge of historical character to remain blind to the personal merits of Bruce. He admits that in the end Bruce proved himself "a great captain and a great king"; but his eagerness to maintain the vassalage of Scotland, and the rectitude of Edward's action, makes him speak of the Scottish hero in terms that are incompatible with greatness of any kind whatever. To stigmatize him as "an outlaw and a vagabond" because he was unable for a time to encounter the enemies that had overrun his country and held its strengths, is surely an abuse of language. Read in the fierce light of Bannockburn, the epithets seem absolutely ludicrous. He was not the first nor the last champion of a conquered nation who began his work of deliverance as a "hunted patriot."

The contemporary English chroniclers do not concern themselves with his character, or with the details of his long struggle against the English rule, but their silence or indifference does not make the ampler biography of Barbour a mythical story. What we find in the Scottish poet is the kind of knowledge that would cling to the memory of men who had shared in the unforgotten strife. There is none of the customary symptoms of romancing mendacity in his work. It is pervaded by such a manly frankness of spirit, and shows such a modest simplicity in describing the most thrilling incidents, that no unprejudiced reader can fail to be forcibly impressed with a conviction of its historical reality. There is no crude fervour, no credulous wonderment, no impossible supernaturalism in the tale. It moves on with earnest gravity through all the chequered scenes of the struggle, and even the stirring day of Bannockburn, though its events are detailed with the picturesque minuteness of Froissart, hardly quickens the poet's blood or disturbs the even flow of his verse.

It is of course impossible to prove that the perilous adventures narrated in the poem are as securely vouched for as if Barbour had been the contemporary and friend of Bruce. Such certainty we cannot have; yet when we remember that the author was a scholar and a dignitary of the Church, that he took a prominent part in public affairs, and was likely to be familiar with the most authentic traditions of the previous generation, we need experience little difficulty in accepting as substantially true a narrative that is intrinsically credible, and, except in one point, in no way at variance with earlier authorities. The work is unquestionably a poem as well as a chronicle. When Barbour makes the Bruce who competed with Baliol for the crown, the victor at Bannockburn, it would be absurd to suppose him ignorant of the fact that the latter was the grandson of the former:[1] he deliberately deviates from historical fact to enhance the glory of that national freedom whose praise he has so finely sung. He takes, in short, a poetic license in a somewhat hurried introduction, and avowedly begins his work with the covenant between Bruce and Comyn. All that follows has been for ages in Scotland "familiar in our ears as household words." Granting that popular tradition and the author's patriotism may have given a poetic colour to the story of Bruce's hardships and exploits, no one can rationally doubt that the king and his followers must have led a life very similar to that portrayed in Barbour's tale.

The English chroniclers could not be familiar with the personal feelings, the social friendships, the high hopes, and aspirations of the Scottish leaders, any more than they could know the manner of their life in the stony wastes of Athole and Lorne. They could tell when a march was made, a convoy intercepted, a garrison captured, or a district overrun; but they could not reach those sources of national sentiment and sympathy, where the best and noblest reminiscences of the conflict would survive. Bruce is to them simply a rebel, as Wallace is a robber.[2] In all matters of public notoriety their authority is preferable to that of the later Scottish chroniclers (1201-1346). The chronicle of Lanercost is particularly trustworthy. The events

---

[1] See Cosmo Innes's preface to his edition of the *Brus* (Spalding Club, 1856).
[2] *Princeps latronum* says the Chronicle of Lanercost.

of the reigns of Edward I. and Edward II. are recorded by contemporaries, but we search their works in vain for the faintest perception of the nature of the struggle, or the character of the combatants; and without such pictures as the pages of Barbour furnish, we could understand neither the invincible obstinacy of the Scots nor the heroic temper of their chiefs.

The *Brus* is a poem, but not a fiction. We conceive that the author has worked up into epic shape and form the proud traditions of an emancipated people, the numberless stories of suffering and success that were then floating about in hall and hut, in monastery and burgh. Sometimes he had even conversed with hoary veterans who had survived the agony of the strife. Thus Sir ' Alane off Catkert ' is quoted as his authority for a right fair point of chivalry that happened in the conquest of Galloway by Edward Bruce: and Sir Alane took part in the fray. But we do not mean to assert the rigid accuracy of the annals. Events are not always recorded in their historical connection. They are occasionally arranged for the sake of effect; and when Barbour puts words into the mouths of Englishmen, or ascribes to them motives of which he must have been ignorant, we know that he is merely imitating the fashion of historians from the days of Thucydides and Livy. His description of the death of Edward I. at Burgh on Sands, is an example in point, and stands in striking contrast to the simple and pious account in the Chronicle of Lanercost. But what we contend for is the essentially historic character of the portrait of Bruce drawn by Barbour. It was only such a man who could have borne the burden of the Seven Years' struggle; it was only such qualities as the poet endows him with, which could have conquered despair, turned enemies into devoted friends, subdued the vindictive hostility of the Celts, and restored the sinking soul of the nation. Make what abatements we please for the idealism incident to the mode of treatment, a noble figure must ever remain, in the contemplation of which Scotsmen may legitimately find a perpetual pleasure.

Though temperate in its tone and style, *The Brus* is imbued with a spirit of genuine poetry. The character of the king is clothed with all the graces of chivalry, and his relations to his followers are invariably tender and true. How bold in fight, how fertile in resource, how blithe in cheer when others' hearts are failing, how generous and considerate, how deep his grief when harm befalls his trusty comrades! Neither hope, nor fortitude, nor courtesy, nor humanity ever leaves him. Barbour records, with touches of sweet and simple pathos, many an incident that redounds to the honour of the homeless monarch, even more than the glories of his final triumph. His magnanimous exposure of his life at the ford in Galloway, rather than waken his weary men from their hard-won slumbers, his rare humanity when he stays the march of his host to relieve the sufferings of a poor woman, one of his camp-followers, are examples of the hundred instances of chivalric nobleness that adorn the poem. The parting from the queen and her ladies, when snell winter falls on the Grampians, is told with a tenderness that cannot be surpassed. But perhaps our admiration reaches its climax when we read some of the incidents of the flight to Kintyre and Rachlin. On the way the little band have to cross Loch Lomond, a thing impossible to do till Sir James Douglas discovers a sunken boat, fit to carry three at a time. In the course of a night and a day, by swimming or rowing, all had got to the western shore, the king merrily beguiling the time with the famous stories of Charlemagne and his Paladins. "These men," says Mr. Innes,[1] who is stirred to enthusiasm by the scene, "of high blood and delicate nurture, had long travelled on foot through the wildest mountains in want of all necessaries. The whole country was against them. Starvation urged them from behind; unknown dangers and hunger also might wait them on the other side. At such a time, to find the prince their leader taking such means for entertaining and rousing them, by the examples of those knights of Christian mythology, to deeds of chivalrous daring and endurance, gives us a higher idea of chivalry than any writer of fable has reached."

Another fine feature of the poem is the knightly courtesy shown to adversaries. Barbour is a loyal Scot, and his love for his country is never concealed. He sternly upbraids the English king for his cruelties and oppressions, but he never descends to the fierce vulgarity of Blind Harry, whose Englishmen are generally poltroons, or braggarts, or felons. Many a gallant Southron figures in Barbour's verse, whose valour and worth are recorded in no grudging spirit. Nothing in the Homeric description of Bannockburn affects us more deeply than the death of Sir Giles Argentine. Proudly he bids farewell to his king who is about to gallop from the field, and raising his battle-cry, the terror of the Saracens in more propitious days, he rides

[1] Preface to his edition of *The Brus*, p. xxviii.

unappalled against the invincible ring of Scottish spears, and welcomes death with fiery pride.

> Victrix causa diis placuit, sed victa Catoni.

" Off hys deid " says the generous bard
> " wes rycht gret pité,
> He wes the thrid best knycht, perfay,
> That men wyst lyvand in his day."

Barbour has a singularly keen eye for the traits of knightly character, and his poem is a gallery of noble portraits, but the king towers above them all, like Arthur amid the lesser heroes of the Round Table. Douglas, Randolph, Edward Bruce, Lennox, the Stewart, never obscure his prevailing greatness for a moment. We cannot believe that Barbour's conception of Bruce is merely the fabrication of a patriotic minstrel. His boyhood was passed in the life-time of his hero, whose adventures and prowess would be the theme of many a fire-side tale, and whose wise and prosperous rule he could well remember. No doubt he has heightened and exaggerated the virtues of the great captain. Distance has lent some enchantment to the view. The passionate pride in their independence, which ever marked the Scots after Bannockburn, is visible in the poem. The Bruce of history was probably a less heroic person than the Bruce of Barbour, but he was not essentially different. He was cast in the same mould and wore the same expression. He underwent the same trials, sustained reverses with the same undaunted heart, and won the love of his followers and the confidence of his country by the same evidences of valour and patience and kindliness that have given an immortal charm to the antique verse of his earliest biographer.

In violent contrast to *The Brus* stands Blind Harry's poem on Wallace. All our knowledge of the author is derived from the following passage in Joannes Major's *De Gestis Scotorum:* "In the time of my infancy, Henry, who was blind from his birth, composed the whole *Book of William Wallace*, and committed to writing in vulgar poetry, in which he was well skilled, the things that were commonly related. For my own part, I give only partial credit to writings of this kind. By the recitation of these stories, however, in the presence of men of the first rank, he procured food and clothing, which he deserved." This extract fixes the composition of the work about the year 1460. What was Henry's surname, when he was born, or where he died, we cannot tell. He is mentioned in the Treasury accounts of James IV. as an occasional recipient of the royal bounty, the last of these notices occurring in January, 1492. It is therefore improbable that he survived the close of the fifteenth century. The oldest existing MS. of the poem bears the date 1488, and curiously enough does not name the author; but no critic has thought it necessary to question the universal belief, and we may venture to assume that Blind Harry's right to be considered the author is indisputable. That his origin was humble we have his own testimony. He speaks of himself as a 'bural man'; *i.e.*, a peasant or boor: he frequently apologizes for the rudeness of his literary workmanship.

> "All worthi men at redys this rurall dyt
> Blaym nocht the buk, set I be unperfyt."

But if we could credit his statement that he had only diligently translated into homely Scottish verse the 'fayr Latyn' of Maister John Blair, Wallace's legendary chaplain, there would be less reason for accepting his apology. No human being, however, possessing the faculty of reason, could now be got to believe that any contemporary of the illustrious patriot could by any possibility have penned such a biography as Blind Harry gives us. A Latin work on the exploits of the Scotch patriot does indeed actually exist, and was published by Sir Robert Sibbald under the title *Relationes Arnaldi Blair*. It professes to be the composition of Wallace's chaplain, who (we are told) after his master's death changed his name and became a monk in the Abbey of Dunfermline; but as the 'Relations' are only a crude plagiarism from the *Scotichronicon*, which was composed more than a century after Wallace's death, we are perfectly safe in asserting that this at least is not the original from which Blind Harry borrowed or translated.

The Wallace of the wandering minstrel has become a part of Scottish history, and it is thought to be a kind of profanation to disturb the popular opinion. Although for a century any real or direct knowledge of Blind Harry's poem has been confined to a small number of Scotsmen, the traditions embodied in it have retained their original popularity; and the character of its hero has rather grown in dignity since it has ceased to be associated with the truculent diction of the bard. There is little fear that modern criticism will reverse the verdict of ages or even materially diminish the greatness of Wallace's work; but it may be well to see exactly what in his career is historical, and what in varying degrees of intensity is legendary.

There have been times when men were tempted by the extravagant absurdities of Blind Harry's romance to pronounce Wallace a myth. But his existence is as certain as the existence of Edward I., and rests on evidence that is beyond the possibility of challenge. The oldest authorities on his public career are the English chroniclers; but they know nothing of his private history, of the family to which he belonged, or of the motives which prompted his acts. The obscurity from which he sprung, and his persistent hostility to the foreign yoke, prevented them from acquiring any particulars of his early life, or any genuine conception of his character and genius. To them he is simply a thief or a cut-throat. The Minorite friar who edited the Lanercost Chronicle, and who was probably a younger contemporary of the Scottish patriot, affirms that he was at first a robber chief (*princeps latronum*). Hemingford, following the Harleian MS., which is a transcript from an original drawn up in the reign of Edward I., also speaks of him as a public robber (*quidam latro publicus*) who had often been outlawed. Matthew of Westminster in his *Flores Historiarum* showers upon him a variety of opprobrious epithets. He is an apostate from piety (*refuga pietatis*), a freebooter (*praedo*), an incendiary (*incendarius*), and a murderer (*homicida*). He surpasses Herod in cruelty and Nero in madness, and is guilty of the most shameful indecencies. The Cottonian MS. describes him as an "archer" of base origin (*ignobilis progenie*), who was made a knight by a certain earl, "as a raven is changed into a swan." Langtoft and his translator De Brune are no less complimentary. Not a word falls from any of them that shows the least appreciation of Wallace's personal greatness, and yet their own accounts of his rapid and brilliant successes might have justly rendered them suspicious of their theory of the man—that he was merely a bloodthirsty villain who delighted in robberies, spoliations, and massacres.

What is to be learned regarding Wallace from the English chroniclers and other contemporary sources may be briefly stated as follows:—In the spring of 1296 Edward I. invaded Scotland to punish Baliol for violating his allegiance. His force was irresistible. Every fortress and town in the kingdom from Berwick to the Moray Firth, was in his hands before the close of August. Baliol was dethroned with the most humiliating ceremonies, and imprisoned in the Tower of London. Many of the Scoto-Norman nobles were with the English army on its triumphal march. The Bruce of Bannockburn, his father the Earl of Carrick, and the High Steward of Scotland were there. The *Ragman Roll* (an inventory of names as valuable for ethnological as for political purposes) attests with fatal force of evidence the absolute paralysis of the Scottish nation, and its utter impotence to resist at the moment the most extravagant demands of the conqueror. The nobility, the clergy, the gentry, the chief burgesses, in a word, all orders of the community were driven by necessity to do homage to Edward. English garrisons were placed in all the Scottish strongholds and in all the principal towns. Englishmen carried on the government of the prostrate country. The Earl of Surrey was its military guardian; William Ormesby was its chief justiciar; and a greedy ecclesiastic, Hugh de Cressingham, imposed and collected the taxes required for the maintenance of the foreign host.

Within six months a man suddenly appeared as a leader of outlaws whose numbers were constantly swelled during the winter of 1296 and spring of 1297. The feudal vassals of the Norman nobility then abroad with Edward gathered to his side; the Scottish clergy favoured him, the Lanercost Chronicle rather helplessly asserting that he was instigated to rebel against the English king by the bishop of Glasgow, *semper in proditione primus* ("always foremost in treachery"), because the latter himself lacked courage to break his oath of fealty. His first public and notorious act was the slaughter of Hesilrig, the sheriff of Lanark; but he was soon surrounded by so immense a concourse of "other felons," that he attacked and captured castles and cities in every part of Scotland. An independent movement in Ayrshire headed by Bruce, Douglas, the Steward, and the bishop of Glasgow, collapsed at Irvine in the month of July, and the usual oaths were imposed and accepted; but elsewhere the national cause, under the personal inspiration of Wallace himself, prospered daily. Cressingham's letters in the end of July admit his inability to raise a penny in Scotland, and state that death, sieges, and imprisonments had stripped the land of its English keepers.

Another feudal army was immediately raised and poured into the country, but was overwhelmed at Stirling in the month of September by the military skill of the Scottish leader. So great a disaster had never befallen an English host before in this part of the island. Hemingford gives a full description of the fight, and in one sentence, which he puts into the mouth of Wallace when proudly refusing to come to terms, "Carry back to those who sent you this message, that we are not come here to sue for peace but prepared for battle, to avenge our wrongs and liberate our country," we seem to catch even in a hostile page a momentary glimpse of that sublime spirit that animates the native tradition. The effect of the victory was prodigious. The English garrisons surrendered or fled, and Wallace, armed with the whole power of a liberated and vengeful nation, passed the English borders in the beginning of October. The fury of the invaders knew no bounds. For a month they made utter havoc of the shires of Northumberland and Cumberland. The English chroniclers relate with painful unanimity the dismal tale of slaughter, rapine, and cruelty. At last the ferocious butchery ceased, and the satiated Scots recrossed the Tweed.

Meanwhile Wallace had not lost a moment in seeking to restore the material prosperity of the realm. His letter to the magistrates of Lübeck and Hamburg, first printed by Dr. Lappenberg is dated 11th October, 1297, and must have been despatched on the eve of his march to the Border. It shines out like a ray of light through the darkness that envelops his individual life. We hear the voice of the genuine man, we form some idea of his character and purpose, and in its modest words and humane sagacity, we find no trace of the bloodthirsty brigand who stalks across the pages of the English chroniclers. Along with his letters of protection to the monks of Hexham, it is almost all that has come down to us direct from the hand of the Scottish chief;[1] and not even the most fanatical worshipper of the English supremacy can deny, that these

---

[1] His charter in favour of Sir Alexander Scrymgeour, as Constable of Dundee, is a strictly legal document, but has a political value.

letters are infinitely more in keeping with the character which his countrymen have given him, than with that of the miserable ruffian who figures in Florence of Worcester, or the sacrilegious thief of Hemingford and Knighton.

Edward was not slow to take his revenge. Although personally detained in Flanders by military necessities, he had sent out letters to the Scottish nobles, immediately after the disaster at Stirling, ordering them to co-operate with the new English "governor" (so-called) in suppressing the rebellion; and before Christmas one of the English wardens, Sir Robert Clifford, had made a raid into Annandale, and plundered and burnt to his heart's content for several days. The month of December is crowded with "writs" in reference to Scottish affairs. The most energetic efforts were made. Every baron north of the Trent was summoned to a muster at York on the 20th of January, 1298, and another vast feudal armament was set in motion; but nothing of consequence was attempted till Edward returned from the Continent in the summer following. By the close of June the English king took the field at the head of 90,000 men, encountered a Scottish force under Wallace at Falkirk on the 22nd of July, and, mainly through the cowardice or treachery of the Scottish cavalry, inflicted a ruinous defeat on his enemies. We have detailed and vivid accounts of the battle from English sources, all of which expressly praise the stubborn valour of the Scottish spearmen. Langtoft, in De Brune's version, says: "Als a castelle they stode that was walled with stone." Hemingford admits that it was long before the English knights could pierce the bristling rings of the Scottish infantry, and the others more or less briefly tell the same tale of unavailing heroism. The author of the Cottonian MS., however, asserts with ludicrous animosity, that Wallace himself, when he had said to his men, "I haif brocht you to the ring, hap gif ye cun," turned and fled like a coward! Matthew of Westminster adopts the same fatuous fiction, and satisfies his conscience by denouncing the patriot as a "man of Belial."

From this point Wallace's history becomes dim. He vanishes from the blood-soaked Carse of Falkirk and reappears no more in the national life. Once or twice he seems to hover within our ken, but we never get near him again till the hideous tragedy in London closes with bloody rites a career that his countrymen will never forget. We know that he went to France and perhaps to Rome. The Scottish cause could no longer be upheld by the sword, but it was possible to recover by diplomacy what had been lost by force or fraud. The court of Rome claimed powers that might be turned to the advantage of oppressed and vanquished nations. At what date Wallace left the country is uncertain, but his presence on the Continent is guaranteed by unquestionable evidence. The Cottonian MS. asserts that he betook himself to France to seek help from Philippe le Bel, but was thrown into prison at Amiens, and kept as a present for the English king. But Philippe must have altered his purpose, for a letter of his has recently been discovered[1] in the Record Office in the Tower of London, in which he recommends to the favour of his agents in Rome and of the supreme pontiff, "our loved William the Waleis, of Scotland,

---

[1] By the Rev. Joseph Stevenson, editor of the *Wallace Papers* for the Maitland Club.

knight." There is no actual proof that the great exile ever availed himself of this document; but whether he did or not, nothing came of the negotiations then being carried on at the Papal court on behalf of Scotland, and, disappointed in his dearest hopes, he returned to his native land, to resume under far more unfavourable conditions, but with the same unfailing spirit, the desperate struggle for independence. The Scots had not been wholly inert during his absence. Guardians had been chosen in the place of Wallace, and Edward had found it necessary to repeatedly invade the country. It is plain that the victory at Stirling, and the year of exulting liberty that followed, had not only kindled in the hearts of the Scottish commons an inextinguishable passion for independence, but had shaken the policy of the nobles themselves. Edward could no longer reckon on their fidelity. Their motives, indeed, were still mixed, and their actions dubious. On the one hand, the most stubborn resistance was succeeded by the most abject submission; on the other, men who were deep in the confidence and favour of the English king are suddenly seen in arms against him. Simon Fraser, who triumphed at Roslin, fought against his countrymen at Dunbar and Caerlaverock. Ralph de Haliburton, who hired himself out to assist in the capture of the Scottish chief, bore his part in the splendid defence of Stirling Castle. These are not things of which Scotsmen are proud, but they mark at least the uncertain nature of the hold that Edward maintained over the people of the north.

It does not appear that Wallace, after his return from France, was ever able to offer an effective opposition to Edward. He never again headed an army; he never even took the field with any respectable force; he held no political office; his work in a sense was over. He had made it impossible for Edward to keep Scotland in subjection. The military power of the English king indeed, was irresistible, and he could march in triumph from Roxburgh to Caithness,[1]

"Amazement in his van, with fright combined,
And sorrow's faded form, and solitude behind;"

but his conquests were politically barren. Marked as they were by every circumstance of horror and shame, they only inspired the Scots with sullen rage and implacable hate. Everywhere the gentry and commons were hostile, though their hostility could not again venture to take the shape of a national organization. The feeble "guardianship" of Comyn came to an end early in 1304, and fighting in Scotland was over for a time. With one exception every Scottish rebel was received into the king's peace on more or less liberal terms. But as to "William le Walleys the king means that he be received at his will and subject to his disposal."[2] Edward's letter to Sir Alexander de Abernethy, who was in command on the Forth, makes it clear that, two months later than Comyn's submission, Wallace was still the leader of a "company" of outlawed persons to whom no mercy was to be shown. The "wardrobe accounts" of Edward furnish a few additional facts. A "vallette," Nicholas Oysel, is rewarded[3] for bringing news of a defeat inflicted on Wallace by three of Edward's officers shortly before the king left for

[1] *Campaign of* 1303. See Hemingford.
[2] Palgrave, *Documents and Records Illustrative of the History of Scotland*, vol. 1., p. 284. "Item endroit de William le Waleys: le Roi entent qu'il soit receu a sa volûte et a son ordeinement."
[3] 12th March, 1304.

England; a John de Muskelburgh is paid[1] for acting as guide in an expedition against Wallace and others in parts of Lothian; and finally a document contained in the *Calendarium Genealogicum*, compiled from the Public Records of England, gives an account of an inquest held at Perth in September, 1305, from which we learn that Wallace with a few associates had for some time been reduced to kidnapping single enemies.

A month before this inquest was held, Wallace himself had been captured in Glasgow, according to Langtoft, by Sir John of Menteith, through "the treson of Jak Short his man." The chronicle of Lanercost also makes Sir John Menteith his captor; so does the Arundel MS. (date *circa* 1320), adding that he was "seized in the house of one Ralph Raa"; while Sir Francis Palgrave[2] has published some privy council memoranda of the time, among which we find a reward of land to the value of a hundred pounds assigned to "J. de Menteth" for his services in "the taking of the said William." The *Wallace Papers* published by the Maitland Club include a transcript of the process and judgment on the illustrious prisoner. It recites the acts of his public life; it mentions the slaughter of Hesilrig, and the devastations of the English border; it declares that he summoned parliaments and assemblies, and admits that he had expelled the whole officers of the English king; it alludes to his league with France and his defeat at Falkirk; and in short it conclusively proves that for a time Wallace held as great and commanding a position in Scotland as even the native tradition asserts. There was no trial. The prisoner was not allowed to defend himself or to plead.

---

[1] 15th March, 1304.   [2] *Documents and Records*, etc., p. 295.

He had put himself beyond the pale of mercy. No Scot who rightly understands Wallace should ever stoop to murmur against Edward for that; but what he may justly complain of is the radical falsehood of the charge against him. There is not a fact in Scottish history more certain than that Wallace never swore fealty to Edward, and never acknowledged him as his liege-lord. He was therefore no traitor. He was a mortal enemy of the English king; and the latter was entitled to put him to death, but not to brand him with unmerited epithets, and send him to execution clothed in the shame of a dishonoured criminal. The sentence was revolting in its details, and, if Matthew of Westminster may be trusted, it was carried out with even greater barbarity than the terms required.

Such then is the Wallace of contemporary English history. So much at least we are bound to believe concerning him. What more we may accept rests on another kind of evidence, and must be tried by other tests. The Scottish tradition may be in the main credible, but it is not history. It does not come to us under the safeguards of contemporary record. It was sustained for a century by the romantic enthusiasm of popular idolatry, and when it came to assume a literary form, not a soul was left in Scotland that could personally vouch for its truth. Curious to say there is no mention of Wallace in Barbour's *Brus*. It cannot be urged that such mention was unnecessary. The introduction to the poem goes over the period that intervened between the death of Alexander III. and the coronation of Bruce at Scone, and the career of Wallace deserved notice at least as much as that of Sir William Douglas. It may be that Barbour studiously ignores the soldier who fought for Baliol, and who cared for the honour of his country more than he did for the fortunes of a family. Some have surmised that a jealousy of the popular hero existed among the partisans of Bruce, and we are disposed to consider this intrinsically probable. Whatever the cause may have been, the silence of Barbour is to be regretted, for he must have known much of the genuine history of Wallace, and could have narrated it in a form that would have invited credence.

Wyntoun in his *Cronykil of Scotland*, completed about the year 1426, is really the first Scottish writer to mention him. The Prior of St. Serf's was a man of modest spirit, and his work displays on the whole great moderation and impartiality. Were it not for the interval that separates him from the War of Independence, we should implicitly accept his statements of fact regarding Wallace. It seems to us that no value whatever is to be attached to the hysterical politics of the English chroniclers. When they call Wallace a thief and a robber, when they assure us that he was a base-born outlaw, we instinctively feel that they are not writing history, but merely giving vent to calumnies which are the ignoble offspring of prejudice and hate. During his life-time Wallace could not fail to be well-known in his own land. We have seen, even from the English admissions, how great was the power he wielded, and how close were his relations with the Scottish Church. It is impossible, therefore, to believe that all memory of his kindred and his early career could have died away. Error might creep unconsciously into the living legend; national vanity might exaggerate historic exploits, or even give birth to boastful fictions. Wyntoun himself tells us that "gret gestis" had been made of Wallace's deeds, but these would hardly include his pedigree, of which few of his countrymen could be ignorant. On the whole, therefore, we feel ourselves at liberty to accept the statement of the Scottish chronicler regarding Wallace :—

" he was cummyn of gentlemen.
. . . .
His fadyre wes a manly knycht."
(Wyntoun, b. viii. ch. xiii. l. 7-9.)

The *Scotichronicon* says the same thing. But nothing is said of his family and nothing of his connection with Ellerslie in Renfrew, till we reach the distant age of Blind Harry, nearly two centuries after the hero's death. The tradition may be true: there is much to favour it. The name, though not exclusively Scottish (for it is found in the thirteenth and fourteenth centuries in Wilts, Essex, Norfolk, and York), is connected with the West of Scotland. A Richard Waleuse of Kyle (from whom the little village of Riccarton near Kilmarnock boasts its name) is witness to a charter of Walter, the first Steward of Scotland, in 1174; a Henry Waleuse held lands in Renfrewshire under Walter the Steward, early in the thirteenth century; and for the last four or five hundred years branches of the Wallace family are historically traceable in the counties of Renfrew and Ayr. It is in the west of Scotland that his career opens and closes; and it is impossible to suggest a more likely connexion than with the Renfrewshire Wallaces, but we are not able to confirm the popular tradition by documentary evidence. It may be held as a pious opinion, but must not be exalted to an article of faith.

In trying to ascertain the temper or spirit with which he entered on his stubborn conflict with the enemies of his country, we must forget the vituperative epithets of the English monks, and look carefully at the way in which Edward had made good his authority in Scotland. Before the death of Alexander III. Scotland had long enjoyed a high degree of prosperity. According to Mr. Cosmo Innes, "in a material point of view, it may safely be affirmed that Scotland at the death of King Alexander III., was more civilized and more prosperous than at any period of her existence, down to the time when she ceased to be a separate kingdom in 1707."[1] Elsewhere he says, "the real golden age of Scotland, the time of peace with England, of plenty in the land, of foreign trade flourishing, of internal peace, of law and justice, was the period of a full century following the treaty between William the Lion and Richard Cœur-de-Lion, comprehending the reign of William and the long reigns of the second and third Alexanders."[2] A few years of English tyranny sufficed to destroy this felicity of fortune. It is no wonder that a cry went up from the heart of the Scottish nation in the dark times that followed; a cry of anguish and a prayer for help. Wyntoun closes the seventh book of his *Cronykil* with a "sang" that he says was made after the death of the "peaceable king":—

> "Quhen Alysandyr oure Kyng wes dede,
>   That Scotland led in luwe and le,
> Away wes sons off ale and brede,
>   Off wyne and wax, off gamyn and gle:
> Oure gold wes changyd in to lede.

[1] *Sketches of Early Scottish History and Social Progress*, p. 157.
[2] *Scotland in the Middle Ages*, p. 296.

> Cryst, borne in to Vyrgynyté,
> Succoure Scotland and remede,
> That stad [is in] perplexyté."

The contemporary English writers know nothing of, or care nothing for, the outrages that were perpetrated by a foreign soldiery on a disaffected people; but Barbour has recorded them in language that can still fire the blood of his countrymen. No doubt even his record is traditional. It has passed through the furnace of popular hate, and we cannot assert that it has come out unharmed. It is perhaps overcoloured, though it does not seem to be so, and followed as it is by his thrice famous lines in praise of freedom,

> "A! fredom is ane nobill thing," etc.,

it may help us to understand the passionate enthusiasm with which patriotic Scotsmen in the days of Wallace, took up their country's quarrel. When we see how a studious churchman, long after the struggle was over and the victory won, could still exult in the transcendent glory of national independence, it is not difficult to imagine that when the shameful evidences of bondage were daily before the eyes of brave men, they should be filled with a sacred passion for liberty which would transform them into heroes. The public career of Wallace stamps him as pre-eminently a soldier of this kind. He never wavered in his purpose; in his darkest hour of adversity he never dreamed of submission. There was not gold enough in England to buy his homage to Edward. His was the "nobill hart" that

> "suld think fredom mar to pris
> Than all the gold in warld that is."

On a full consideration of the historical conditions in

which Wallace is found, we absolutely reject the view of his character taken by the English chroniclers, not only as utterly inadequate to explain his public life, but utterly incompatible with its salient features; and while we frankly recognise the traditionary form of the national story, and the absurdity of accepting its details as if they were guaranteed by contemporary authority, we cannot resist the conclusion that the Wallace of the Scottish legend is endowed with qualities of mind and soul that interpret the Wallace of history far more clearly and satisfactorily; and we are therefore forced to believe that, whatever exaggerations and fictions in that legend may veil the simple outlines of the real life, the likeness is truer even in its most extravagant dress than the malignant caricatures of the English monks.

Nothing in the "history" of Wallace is so delightful to Scottish schoolboys as the stories of his wonderful strength. These are probably of great antiquity. They doubtless formed the substance of those "gret gestis" which were current before Wyntoun wrote. That author himself describes with visible relish and full belief the broil in the streets of Lanark, in which Wallace single-handed holds his own 'with his lang swerd' against a crowd of English soldiers, till his 'lemman' opens a friendly door for his escape. In some of the later versions of the *Scotichronicon*[1] the writer exhausts his imagination and his Latin in describing the physique of the Scottish patriot: *Erat enim statura procerus, corpore giganteus, facie serenus, vultu jocundus, humeris latus, ossibus grossus, ventre congruus, lateribus protelus, aspectu gratus, sed visu verus; renibus amplus, brachiis*

[1] See Goodall's edition, vol. II. chap. 28 (Edin. 1759).

et cruribus vigorosus; pugil acerrimus, et omnibus artubus fortissimus et compactus. This is not easily surpassed in its way, but it lacks the charm of illustration; and the Continuator of Fordun does not furnish us with biographical incidents that call for the exercise of these splendid powers. But such preposterous stuff points to the steady growth of a Wallace cult among the Scottish people, who were not content with the public record of a heroic struggle that lasted only eighteen months, but craved more and more as time passed by the coarse excitement of vulgar exploits.

When this cult had reached its acme, Blind Harry appeared and gave it a literary expression, which has more or less moulded the sentiments of every Scot who has since lived. Robert Burns says in his autobiographic letter to Dr. Moore, "The story of Wallace poured a Scottish prejudice into my veins, which will boil along there till the floodgates of life shut in eternal rest." It is difficult from our point of view to approach Blind Harry's poem seriously; but it would certainly be a mistake to consider it a mere fabricated romance of a peasant minstrel. It is much more than that. It is the garner into which has been gathered all that harvest of popular legend about Wallace which had been ripening for nearly two centuries. We do not suppose that the author was at all scrupulous in his treatment of traditions, or that he shrank from contributing his quota to the general sum of patriotic fiction. Everywhere in the work there is evidence of more than poetical license; but we are convinced that in the main it recites and re-echoes the

[1] See Burns, Globe edition, p. 339.

"gests" that had enraptured and amazed successive generations of his countrymen. This, we have seen, was the opinion of the learned and critical Major, in whose boyhood Blind Harry wrote; but no criticism can possibly determine to what extent its "gests" are genuine deeds, or where its history ends and mythology begins. Its outrageous perversions of public and ascertained facts throw a cloud of suspicion over every incident and circumstance in the poem, even when they are of such a nature as not to forbid belief. Nothing can be more worthless, we had almost said more imbecile, than the biographical method adopted by most Scottish writers who have handled the life of Wallace, of whom Mr. Carrick is a favourable specimen. It simply consists in turning Blind Harry into modern prose, and repeating the most minute details of the old minstrel with a solemn gravity of tone, as if everything were as certain and indisputable as the history of Wellington's campaigns in the Spanish Peninsula. It never seems to have dawned on the minds of men like Carrick that the Wallace of Blind Harry is not a hero at all, and that more is lost than gained by filling up the shadowy outline of a great career with exploits that are sometimes mean, often savage, and occasionally impossible.

No one can be sure when Wallace first took arms against the English. Historically he does not appear till the spring of 1297; but if Hemingford's statement may be trusted that he had been outlawed many times, room would be made for that guerilla warfare in which according to Blind Harry his youth was spent. Yet the narrative of the Scottish minstrel at this point is chronologically a hopeless absurdity. He tells us that Scotland was lost when Wallace was a "child," and giving all reasonable laxity to the word, it can only denote early youth, for the hero is afterwards sent to school in Dundee on account of his "tendyr age," and goes through a great variety of adventures before his exploit at Lanark comes off. But only a single winter elapsed between the "loss" of Scotland and the insurrection of Wallace. Carrick and others assert that the "loss" probably referred to the time when Edward, as lord superior, demanded and obtained the right to garrison the Scottish strongholds before deciding on the relative claims of Baliol and Bruce, viz. in 1291-2. This supposition flatly contradicts the order of events in Blind Harry; but even if it were conceded, it would not help the unfortunate biographers, for Lord Percy, the governor of Galloway and Ayr, whose men sought to rob the youthful Wallace of the fish he had caught in the river Irvine, was only appointed in the autumn of 1296, and had no previous connection with the conquered country.

The simple truth is that Blind Harry had no exact knowledge of the duration of the foreign tyranny, and makes it last just as long as it suits his purpose to tell preposterous stories of his hero's prowess. Wallace is introduced to us in a way that his biographer no doubt thought particularly noble. At the age of eighteen, after having long mourned over his country's wrongs, he takes up arms, and begins his patriotic career by quietly assassinating every Englishman he comes across in a convenient spot :

> "Quhar he fand ane *without the othir presance,*
> Eftir to Scottis that did no mor grewance ;
> *To cut his throit or steik hym sodanlye,*
> He wayndyt [1] nocht, fand he thaim fawely." [2]
>
> [1] Cared.   [2] Few in number.

Then we have an encounter with the son of the English "governor" of Dundee, in which the latter is slain, though Wallace is put to desperate shifts to escape detection. Soon after he proceeds in the disguise of a pilgrim to Ellerslie, but when his mother, anxious for his safety, implores her brother, Sir Ranald Crawfurd, sheriff of Ayr, to "purchess pes" of Lord Percy (who was not then in Scotland), Wallace is indignant and goes off to stay with another uncle, Sir Richard Wallace of Riccarton. Here occurs in the month of April his far-famed adventure on the Irvine water, in which, as in all others, he proves in his single person a match for numbers. His enemies are horsed and armed, and Wallace had nothing but the pole of his drag-net. That is of no consequence. In a trice he has struck the foremost on the cheek with such good will that

> "The suerd flaw fra him a fur breid on the land."

Instantly possessing himself of the weapon he cleaves his opponent's skull; a second unfortunate is despatched with the same furious vigour.

> "The scherand suerd glaid to the colar bane";

a third has his sword-hand cut off: the remainder judiciously take to flight, leaving their wounded comrade to be stabbed to death by Wallace at his leisure. This last detail is one of those barbarous touches by which Blind Harry constantly disfigures the character of his hero, though it was probably heard with delight by the bravos who thronged the halls of the Scottish barons. Having informed his uncle of this "worthi werk" he takes refuge with another kinsman at "Auchincruff" in the uplands of Kyle; but as his chief happiness (according to the minstrel) lies in shedding "sothroun blude," he loses no time in paying a visit to the town of Ayr. The market-place swarms with insolent soldiers from the castle, one of whom, a stalwart churl, unwisely offers to stand a blow on the back for a groat from any of the bystanders. With grim liberality Wallace gives him three groats, and then breaks his back-bone with a "steing."[1] The comrades of the dead man rush to avenge him, and Blind Harry is now in his glory. How the hero lays about him! how brains are scattered and necks are broken and steel-basnets are crushed! and all this time, Wallace is not over nineteen years of age! Here we have him engaged in vulgar and meaningless brawls, without followers, dependent on the bounty of a kinsman for the necessaries of life, lurking solitarily in Laglyne wood. Yet historically we are within a few months of the battle of Stirling Bridge! Could absurdity be greater or more complicated? Was this the way the hero fitted himself for his sacred enterprise? Can we trace in the doer of such despicable deeds the lineaments of that thoughtful soldier who revolutionized the military tactics of his nation, or that civilized statesman who wrote the letter to the Lübeck merchants?

But Blind Harry is not content with a single adventure in Ayr. He has something far more marvellous to record. In spite of what has happened, Wallace after a brief interval ventures to re-visit the town on a market day, and is just in time to prevent Percy's steward stealing some fish from the servant of his uncle, Sir Ranald Crawford. Wallace first remonstrates, and gets struck for his pains; then gripping

[1] A pole.

the steward by the throat, he stabs him to the heart
with a " felloun knyff," and throws him aside scornfully
like a dead dog. "Caterer he was no more," says the
minstrel with a touch we fear of what our enemies
call " Scotch wut." Immediately four-score men-at-arms
are upon him. Nothing daunted he draws his solitary
sword, pierces the first to the heart through his steel
corslet, strikes off the leg of a second, " abown the kne,
the bayne in sondir schar," cuts in twain the neck of a
third, in spite of his habergeon, and after hacking
several spears in pieces, makes a wild dash for the sea-
wall, but finding it impossible to escape that way,
rushes once more on his foes, resolved to sell his life
dearly. Unhappily his brand snaps at the hilt with
the fury of his strokes, and after slaughtering three
more with his " knyff," he is borne to the ground and
carried off to prison. Receiving in his " cave " no better
nourishment than " barrell heryng and wattir," he soon
falls ill, and is at last believed to be dead. The gaolers
throw him over the walls into a heap of refuse, where
the supposed corpse is found by his early nurse, who
opportunely makes her appearance and obtains permission to remove it. Extraordinary measures are taken
for his recovery. They need not be described, but
they are successful. When he has regained his
strength he sets out for Riccarton, being still, according
to Blind Harry, a friendless youth, without comrades
or followers. On the way he encounters three Englishmen, who, without any reason assigned, immediately
pronounce him a spy or a thief, and insist on his
returning to Ayr. He refuses, and the customary
slaughter ensues. Our readers now know the style in
which the work is invariably done. Two are cleft

through the brain down to the shoulders, and the third, in the act of flight, is thrust through the ribs with a "seker straik," that exposes his liver and lungs! On his arrival at Riccarton, a gathering of his kinsfolk and friends takes place; and now in July or August, 1297, the minstrel makes Wallace come forward as a guerilla-chief, when contemporary and credible history has already placed him at the head of a large force, and in a position to threaten the whole English garrisons north of the Forth.

But there is worse absurdity to come. The Scottish patriots, after a skirmish at Loudon Hill, find a safe retreat in the forests of Clydesdale. Here they are visited by Sir Ranald Crawfurd, who, under pressure from Percy, induces Wallace to consent to a truce for ten months with the English. It is needless to say that life soon became insupportable to the hero, and taking advantage of his uncle's absence one day, he, with fifteen comrades, paid another visit (in disguise) to the town of Ayr. Of course we know what is going to happen. We can tell it beforehand with the certainty of a Highland seer. An English buckler-player challenged him to a contest, and—

> "Wallace tharwith has tane him on the croune,
> Throuch bukler, hand, and the harnpan also,
> To the schulderis, the scharp suerd gert he go."

The Scots are instantly surrounded. Seven-score men-at-arms set upon the sixteen, but it is all in vain. The sword of Wallace is irresistible;

> "Harness and hedis he hew in sonderys fast,"

and finally the sixteen escape unscathed to the shelter of Laglyne wood, at a time when in reality he is marshalling the feudal power of Scotland, in the absence of its proper leaders, for the decisive conflict on the banks of the Forth.

His subsequent adventures in the Lennox and in Perth, though misplaced in point of time, and distorted in the telling by the most grotesque and vulgar incidents, have some semblance of military purpose and political motive, and are probably a popular, though an utterly untrustworthy, version of those obscure but daring raids on the English quarters, in one of which Wallace and Douglas nearly captured Ormesby the Justiciar at Scone in May, 1297.[1] The rapidity of this guerilla warfare is illustrated by the attack on the Lanark garrison and the slaughter of Hesilrig, to which we have seen reference made in the indictment drawn up at the trial of Wallace. The date of this exploit is also May, 1297. Some fifty years after the death of Wallace, a Northumbrian knight, Sir Thomas de Grey, happened to be captured in the border wars and was confined in the castle of Edinburgh, where he beguiled the tedium of his imprisonment by writing a history of his times. "He tells," says Hill-Burton, "how *in the month of May*, 1297, his father was in garrison at Lanark, and that Wallace fell upon the quarters at night, killed Hazelrig, and set fire to the place. The father had good reason to remember and tell about the affair, for he was wounded in it and left on the street for dead."[2] Both Wyntoun and Blind Harry represent this assault as an act of vengeance on the English governor for putting Wallace's sweetheart to death. Wyntoun does not name her, she is only the hero's "lemman" and a "plesant fayre woman"; but in the later minstrel she

---

[1] See Hemingford and Trivet. [2] *History of Scotland*, vol. II. p. 284.

is said to be a daughter of Hew Braidfute of Lamington, and her relation to Wallace becomes a romance of the purest love, sung with a lyric rapture worthy of a troubadour. Blind Harry's hero is not always immaculate in his amours, but this passion stands out so strong and pure that we are half tempted to believe in its historical reality; though it would be affectation to deny that the stern work Wallace had set himself to do left little room for tender devotion either to a "lemman" or a bride.

It would be tedious to pursue to its conclusion the course of this fabulous poem. Every historical incident is perverted and presented in a ridiculous shape, *e.g.*, the account of the battle of Stirling is a model of extravagant absurdity. The most fantastic misconceptions everywhere abound. Sir Aymer de Vallance, Earl of Pembroke, is supposed to be a recreant Scottish noble, and is usually denounced as a traitor; Sir Richard Lundin figures as a Scottish captain at the bridge of Stirling, when in point of fact he was in the English camp; Sir William Douglas only joins Wallace long after his exploits in Perthshire, though in reality the two conjoined their forces in the raid on Ormesby at Scone. Scores of imaginary encounters are described with amazing enthusiasm and incredible minuteness. Thus, while Edward is still in Flanders, Blind Harry (Book VI.) brings him into Scotland at the head of sixty thousand men, and inflicts on him at the hands of the Scottish leader a crushing defeat at Biggar. Some of the details are exceptionally horrible, but happily for the credit of Wallace they are not true. One herald, son of the king's sister, is beheaded, a second has his tongue, and a third his eyes, torn out!

In the battle which is supposed to have followed this demoniacal cruelty, Wallace slays with his own hand the Earl of Kent, and the English king at last is forced to flee after losing thousands of his men, his brother, Sir Hugh, his second son, and two of his nephews! All this is just as true as anything in Mr. Lemuel Gulliver's voyages to Lilliput and Brobdingnag.

But his version of the invasion of England by the Scots probably exhibits Blind Harry in the profoundest depths of his historical ignorance and stupidity. No one who has not read Book VIII. is in a position to understand how monstrously the Scottish tradition had travestied fact in the course of two hundred years. Here, at least, we should be glad to believe that the audacious minstrel has given his fancy liberty to revel in fiction, and that he is in reality the fabricator of those prodigious lies which he professes merely to rehearse "as I in scriptour fand" (Book VIII. v. 1148). Barbour would have been ashamed to make the renowned English king a coward, but Blind Harry is never disturbed by the compunctions of affronted reason; and when Wallace has devastated Northumberland, Durham, and York to his heart's content (though we have seen Newcastle was the limit of his raid), the minstrel introduces messengers from Edward, "a knycht, a clerk, and a squier of pes," who in their master's name implore Wallace to stay this "felloun stryff," or at least to grant a truce for forty days when battle shall be given him. This is agreed to, but in the meantime the English barons hold a parliament at Pomfrey, and refuse to complete their bargain of battle unless Wallace is crowned king of Scotland. This is, of course, impossible in the case of so pure a patriot, but since a lie will serve the purpose Blind Harry thinks it no dishonour to invent one. The English envoys are informed that Wallace has consented, but when they return with the news consternation seizes the monarch and his advisers. For a time all is confusion and terror. Edward, the first soldier in Europe, flies for safety to London, while the irresistible Scots pillage and burn the whole of the midland counties. At last they reach St. Albans, Wallace having previously sent the English king a message that if he does not fulfil his promise to fight

"At London yettis we sall assailyie sayr."

Edward trembles for his throne; none of his courtiers has the courage to approach the enemies' camp and sue for peace, when the queen herself starts up, and pronouncing a panegyric on the virtues of Wallace, declares that she herself will undertake the perilous mission. All present approve her resolution, and Blind Harry, culminating in audacity, adds that it was rumoured the queen was in love with the patriot chief. The result of the interview (which is told with great dramatic power) convinces the queen that the virtue of Wallace is as invincible as his prowess. To her prayers, her arguments, her blandishments, the incorruptible hero turns a deaf ear, and his royal visitor returns to Westminster baffled in her purpose but glowing with admiration of her husband's foe. By her advice Edward makes peace with his conqueror, and solemnly abjures every right of sovereignty over Scotland, which now enjoys repose for a period of three years, during which time Wallace pays a visit to the king of France who receives him as a demi-god, and for whom he reconquers Guienne from the English.

The whole of this magnificent braggadocio is an impossible fiction. One touch of historic fact, like a wave of Prospero's wand, dissolves the romantic panorama and of the baseless fabric of the vision leaves not a wrack behind. Edward (as we have seen) was on the Continent during the winter in which Wallace harried the English border, and never saw the Scottish leader till they met at Falkirk! Yet books are still written on the absurd supposition that *Blind Harry* contains materials for a life of Wallace. Contrast the outline we have given of the minstrel's story with the real facts of history, and its outrageous absurdity will at once be seen and felt. It is not the mere exaggeration of his narrative that startles us, though that has rarely been surpassed, it is his almost supernatural incapacity to understand the most elementary conditions of historic credibility. When we are told that at a battle near Dunbar, Wallace was accidentally left alone on the field, and for a while successfully opposed with his single sword an entire army, that Edward I. mourned and wept over his misfortunes, that his barons in terror declared England to be lost if peace was not made, that Edward's wife told Wallace she had suffered a good deal at court for his sake, we stand aghast at the effrontery of the Scottish tradition or the minstrel's fable. But in truth the whole groundwork and conception of the poem is fantastically erroneous, whole books are mythical, the character of every notable person, including the hero himself, hopelessly caricatured, the duration of the struggle wildly exaggerated, and the very monarch in whose name it was carried on exchanged for another. After the defeat at Falkirk, Blind Harry carries Wallace in triumph to France, and endeavours to obliterate the stains of his disgrace at home by the lustre of fresh laurels abroad. He wins five great battles and performs individual exploits of unparalleled bravery. Yet history can barely prove his presence in that country, and that he ever signalized himself in warfare is conclusively refuted by the silence of the French chroniclers, to whom his very existence is unknown.

We have now given our readers some idea of the more salient features of Blind Harry's poem, and we venture to think they will agree with us in believing that it has absolutely no value as a historical biography. It does not, however, follow that it is destitute of historical value of another kind. If it tells us nothing of Wallace that is worthy of belief, it throws a powerful light on the age of the minstrel himself. From its fierce and passionate verse, we learn only too well the pernicious result of those desperate attempts, on the part of the English kings, to overthrow the liberties of a proud and obdurate nation. An intense hatred of England (now transformed and mellowed into a gentle jealousy) was the inevitable outcome of a hundred years of bloody and unprofitable strife. The animosities of the poem are those of the fifteenth and not of the thirteenth century. Blind Harry's vision of the past is discoloured by the smoke and flame of the intervening period, when the slopes of the Cheviots continually re-echoed the slogans of the marchers. Through that murky atmosphere neither he nor his countrymen could pierce into the sunshine of a remoter time, when the friendship of Henry and Alexander bound the two realms in prosperous peace. There can be no question but that the struggle for independence on the one hand and for dominion on the other, was marked by deeds of remorseless cruelty on both sides; yet it would be absurd to suppose that it could have engendered those anachronisms of sentiment which bestrew the work, in which Wallace and his associates are represented as hating and distrusting the English, not only for the harm they had recently done, but for their immemorial characteristics of pride, rapacity, and falsehood.

That the brief career of the hero as a guerilla chief was brilliant with picturesque and perilous adventures is more than probable, the opposite is inconceivable; but it was certainly not wasted in the ludicrous exploits recorded by Blind Harry. It took a far nobler form. The English chroniclers, who knew nothing of Wallace's superhuman strength, indicate quite distinctly that he was the centre of a swift national movement. Castles and towns fall into his hands as if by magic; the feudal followers of the absent nobles hasten to his standard. We seem to hear the national heart throbbing with a generous enthusiasm. The words that Burns has put into the mouth of Bruce at Bannockburn:

> "Wha for Scotland's king and law,
> Freedom's sword will strongly draw,
> Freeman stand or freeman fa',
> Let him follow me!"

are far more applicable to Wallace at the victorious beginning of his struggle, than to the successful monarch who was about to crown his triumph over a reckless and incapable adversary.

But with this we must be content. Imagination may fairly enough be permitted to hover over that dark, famine-stricken winter, when the foreign soldiery insult, plunder, and imprison the unhappy Scots at their pleasure,[1] but we cannot venture to give our visionary scenes "a local habitation and a name." It is enough to know that when the light of history falls on the career of Wallace, we can discern with something like certainty a soul valiant, resolute, sincere, and disinterested, beyond the measure of his contemporaries. It is not his victories that make Scotsmen proud of his name, for he is never so loyally loved and honoured by his countrymen as on the fatal field of Falkirk: it is not the wisdom of his rule, for too little time was given him to show his capacity for civil administration: it is the inextinguishable passion of patriotism that glows in his bosom—a passion which shines out as ardent and pure in the melancholy impotence of his latest efforts as in the splendid vigour of his early enterprises, "among the faithless, faithful only he." The very life of the Scottish nation was in his keeping, and he never for an instant betrayed his trust. The military power and ambition of Edward would in all probability have quelled the stubborn temper of the Scottish people, had Wallace not appeared on the scene at the proper moment. A spiritless king and a distracted nobility were not able to inspire even the bravest community of freemen with permanent enthusiasm. It is because Scotsmen recognise that nothing short of the inflexible will and invincible heroism of Wallace, could have saved their country from political destruction, that they cherish his memory with an undying affection.

"At Wallace' name, what Scottish blood
But boils up in a spring-tide flood!"

[1] See Barbour's *Brus* and Edward's orders to Cressingham in Hemingford and the *Foedera*.

All that the Scots are as a distinct and separate nation was bound up in that mighty struggle. We do not say that it might not have been an immediate material gain for them to have come under English rule, but we are certain that the moral effect would have been disastrous. The fourteenth century would perhaps not have shown so miserably in agriculture, commerce, and all kinds of civilized industry;[1] but the race would have lost its bold and hardy traits, that rugged force and firmness of nature which in later ages has enabled it to overcome the most formidable obstacles to its advancement and prosperity, and, alike in the realms of matter and mind, to secure an abundant compensation for its costly devotion to national independence.

[1] See Pinkerton, *History of Scotland*, book V., *Retrospect*.

CHAPTER IV.

HISTORY AND LITERATURE OF FOURTEENTH AND FIFTEENTH CENTURIES.

Rising and Discomfiture of Disinherited Barons.—David.—French Alliance.—Accession of Stewarts.—English Invasions and their Effects.—Literature of the Period.—Barbour, Fordoun, Bower, and Wyntoun, Apologists for Scotland.—Traces of Song and Romance.—Barbour, Arthurian Pieces, Hutchowne, &c.—Fifteenth Century contrasted with Fourteenth.—Freedom from Foreign Aggression.—Miserable Domestic Policy.—Feuds of the Barons.—Reigns of Robert III. and of James I., II. and III.—Brighter Aspects of the Time.—Position of Commons.—Influence of Clergy.—Foundation of Universities.—Literature of the two Centuries contrasted.—Obscure Poets.—Worth of Blind Harry's Work.

IN March, 1328, at a parliament held in York, Edward III. solemnly renounced all claim of superiority over the kingdom of Scotland, and a month later the famous treaty of Northampton decreed among other things that there should be perpetual peace between the two countries. The annals of the fourteenth century form a striking commentary on these declarations. Robert Bruce was scarcely in his grave when events took place that boded ill for the permanence of peaceful relations. The English king had granted Edward, son of John Baliol, permission to return from France and reside in England. Round him gathered a formidable body of malcontent barons, who had been practically "disinherited" of their Scottish possessions for siding with the English in Bruce's wars. Now, when the hero of Bannockburn was dead, and most of his valiant companions were broken with years and the fatigues of war, these men resolved to invade the land from which they had been expelled, and assert their claims by force. The death of the bold and wary regent Randolph, in the very crisis of the movement, was a fatal misfortune for his countrymen. In August, 1332, at Duplin on the Earn, the Scots, though vastly superior in numbers, were routed with immense slaughter, and, in the September following, Baliol was crowned at Scone.

By a secret arrangement with the English king he professed himself the liegeman of Edward. Before the close of the year he was forced to flee across the Border, but in 1333 he was replaced in power by the victory of Halidon Hill, and for the next six years, strove with the help of his English master to rule a broken but turbulent population. At first it almost seemed as if the spirit which Wallace had evoked, and which had carried Bruce to "glorious victory," had mysteriously and inexplicably died away. That patriot monk who passed barefooted before the lines of the Scots at Bannockburn, bearing aloft the crucifix in his hands, and exhorting his countrymen to fight for their liberties, is now found with added dignity sitting in a parliament at Edinburgh (1333-34), which Baliol had summoned to legalize a disgraceful convention with his feudal superior, the king of England. There, too, was seen the once fearless and hardy Bishop Sinclair, who in the days of Bruce had been known for his patriotic courage as the "king's bishop." Soon after, the whole of the southern lowlands was made over to the English crown and placed under English government.

There was no violent outcry at this shameful humiliation, but in reality the Scots were neither dismayed nor disheartened. Events rapidly showed that Baliol had no real power in the realm. The most powerful of the "disinherited" lords, David, Earl of Athole, was defeated and slain by Sir Andrew Moray of Bothwell, son of the colleague of Wallace in the guardianship, at Culbleen on the Grampians (1335). This experienced soldier reverted to the old policy of the Scots in carrying on their wars. When Edward III. marched through Scotland in 1336, at the head of an irresistible force, and wasted the land as far as Inverness, Moray withdrew to the fastnesses of the hills; but no sooner had the enemy retraced his steps than the Scottish leader re-appeared on the scene, and assailed with success the fortresses which Edward had garrisoned in the north. Dunnottar, Laurieston, Kinclaven, Falkland, Leuchars, St. Andrews, and Bothwell, surrendered in succession. The Earl of March, whose family had long been the chief bulwark of the English power in Lothian, joined the national party; and his Countess, a worthy daughter of Randolph, made herself famous by her splendid defence of Dunbar. Ramsay of Dalwolsie and Sir William Douglas, the "knight of Liddesdale," by unceasing raids swept the English out of the southern lowlands; and in 1339 Baliol, finding it impossible to remain longer in Scotland with safety, abandoned the country and became a permanent pensioner of the English crown.

The reign of David II. was inglorious for the monarch and unfortunate for his kingdom, but neither disasters in the field nor perfidy in the crown could change the temper or quell the spirit of the Scots. The carnage at Neville's Cross (1346), the eleven years' captivity of their sovereign, the victorious invasions of the English, their partial reconquest of the southern lowlands, the heavy burden of taxation for the ransom of the royal prisoner; the notorious preference of David for an English residence, his frequent and suspicious visits to the English court, his deliberate suggestion to a Scottish parliament[1] that they should choose Prince Lionel of England as his successor, would have weakened the nerve of a less resolute people; but never once do we find the Scots sounding a note of despair. They distrust their king, but not themselves. With fierce, instantaneous unanimity they spurn the proposal that an Englishman should reign over them.[2] Had they known of the secret agreement under which the traitorous son of Robert Bruce made over to the King of England the succession to the Scottish crown,[3] it may be doubted if even their veneration for his illustrious father would have secured him against the fury of an insulted people. But the agreement never got beyond the parchment on which it was written, and centuries elapsed before the infamy was publicly known.

It was no doubt fortunate for Scotland at this time that Edward III. had involved himself in war with France, and could only devote a small portion of his military skill and energy to the affairs of the northern nation. Probably under no circumstances, however favourable, could he have succeeded where his abler grandfather failed, in reducing to submission a race of men inspired with a fanatical passion for independence; but it is evident he might have periodically ravaged the country at his pleasure, and destroyed even the germs of its future prosperity. Miserable as the social condition of Scot-

---

[1] Scone, 1363. [2] *Scotichron.* xiv. 25; Wyntoun, viii. 45. [3] 1363-66.

land was in the fourteenth century, it might perhaps have reached a point whence no recovery was possible. But it is unprofitable to speculate on contingencies that never became facts. We cannot tell with certainty what their issue might have been. It is enough to see that the English king was hindered by a policy of his own choosing from doing his worst in Scotland.

The same policy may be said to have given birth to that political alliance between France and Scotland which was pregnant with consequences for the latter nation. We can indeed trace that alliance to an earlier date than the reign of David II. When John Baliol was on the eve of his fatal rupture with Edward I., he concluded a league with Philippe le Bel, but nothing came of it, except a certain fluctuating friendliness on the part of the French king, which is more or less visible through the long struggle of the Scots for independence. In the fourteenth century, however, the alliance was renewed and took a practical shape. French gold and armour were distributed among the Scots to enable them to assail the English with greater success. French soldiers even came to their help, though after a time their welcome was none of the warmest, and they were heartily glad to escape from the inhospitable shores and barbarous incivility of their political associates. This alliance continued with interruptions to affect the course of Scottish history down to the period of the Reformation. It never was worth very much in the field of battle; in fact the services of the Scots in France were infinitely more brilliant and useful than any which the French rendered in turn, but in other ways it has left its mark.

In the reign of James IV. it led to Flodden; in the reign of James V., and during the Regencies that followed, it was the source of innumerable evils, the crown of which was the sending back to Scotland, at the gravest crisis in its history, a queen who, in spite of her elegant culture and lively intelligence, neither understood her age nor sympathized with its ideas. The Scottish law-courts and forms of judicial procedure were modelled on those of Paris; the architecture of the northern country during this period shows the influence of her more polished and civilized ally, and the Scottish dialect of the English tongue is tinged in quite a peculiar way with words and phrases of French extraction.

The accession of the House of Stewart to the throne of Scotland in 1370 made no change in the policy of the nation. Robert II. had proved himself in earlier days a trusty guardian of the national honour. Though David Bruce reigned, he could scarcely be said to govern. During his absence in France, a succession of regents had done their best to maintain or restore the liberties of the nation; and among these the Steward of Scotland, if not the ablest, was at least conspicuous by his loyalty and courage. After David's return he still continued to be the leader of the national party, and for nearly thirty years guided and directed the national councils. But age had chilled his ardour, and it was fortunate for his rule that the victor of Creçy and Poictiers was himself no longer able to prosecute war with youthful vigour. The French alliance was again renewed, while a truce with England gave the exhausted land a fourteen years' repose. Border raids went on as usual, but Scotland was not seriously disturbed till Richard II. in 1385 made another grand attempt at its subjugation. The lowlands were wasted to the Forth, and even the French auxiliaries were convinced that all was over, and that Scottish independence was lost for ever. But the Scots themselves were of a different opinion. Their old policy was once more employed. Removing to the hills their cattle and goods, they waited with stubborn patience till famine forced their enemies to retreat, and soon after retaliated with their customary fury. The brilliant fight at Otterburn in 1388 was merely an episode in an avenging invasion of the English borders. Froissart describes it with a knightly relish; and in truth the incidents were marked by a chivalric spirit that has fascinated all later ages.

Robert III. was even a greater lover of peace than his father, but his reign of sixteen years (1390-1406) was neither tranquil nor prosperous. His virtues might have adorned a private station, but his deplorable weakness of character encouraged political intrigue and social turbulence. There was for a time peace with England, but family feuds now begin to disfigure the Scottish annals, and attest the imbecility of the executive power. Wyntoun records several of these—precursors of the still bloodier quarrels of the fifteenth century. The Scots had been at war for generations, and when peace came many of them found it intolerable. The language of the Scottish estates in Parliament reveals clearly the unhappy condition of the country. The law was everywhere disregarded, the labouring population were robbed of the fruits of their toil by bands of marauders, and the king was frankly told that he was unfit to govern. In the *Fair Maid of Perth*, Scott has drawn a graphic picture of a clan duel which occurred in this reign. In itself it was perhaps of no great social importance, for Celtic history is little else than a record of ferocious strife, but it may serve to illustrate the sanguinary violence of the times.

Another English invasion in 1400, though fruitless in results, proved that the dream of conquest and annexation was not yet over. But it was beginning to vanish. Not even the apostacy of March nor the slaughter of Homildon Hill (1402) could inspire Bolingbroke with the faintest hope of ultimate success. The seizure of Prince James on his voyage to France (1405) was a criminal outrage for which no honourable defence can be urged; but the motive for the deed was not to extort from an inexperienced youth a submission that his subjects would have spurned. There is not a vestige of evidence to show that, during his long detention in England, his captor ever sought to entrap him into an acknowledgement of vassalage. Henry IV. knew the real value of his prisoner. He used him to paralyze the alliance between the French and the Scots; and though his expectations in this way were not quite realized—though the Scots at least once harried the English border in the reign of Henry V., and sent the flower of their feudal force to assist the Dauphin of France, yet there can be no doubt that Albany was to some extent kept in check, by the fact that at any moment the English monarch could reduce him to insignificance by restoring James to his kingdom. A far more valuable result of Henry's audacious piracy was that the Scottish prince, while retaining in full measure the spirit of patriotism, which a pleasant captivity is wont to destroy, grew up imbued not only with the best culture of his age, but with a profound admiration of the civilization and vigour of the English government. His reign marks a new epoch in the national history, though its beneficent development was unhappily arrested by the daggers of assassins.

During the century whose political history we have thus rapidly surveyed, Scotland made hardly any progress in material prosperity. Nay, in some important respects it probably fell back. Neither agriculture nor commerce could be carried on with energy or success in days when foreign rapine was so frequent and so fierce. Even in the better times of James I. the country presented few attractions to those familiar with other lands. Æneas Silvius, afterwards Pope Pius II., has drawn a picture of Scotland which he visited in 1435 that is undoubtedly vivid, but on the whole disagreeable; it is, he says, "a cold country, fertile of few sorts of grain, and generally void of trees, but there is a sulphureous stone dug up which is used for firing. The towns are unwalled, the houses commonly built without lime, and in villages roofed with turf, while a cow's hide supplies the place of a door. The commonalty are poor and uneducated, have abundance of flesh and fish, but eat bread as a dainty. The men are small in stature, but bold; the women fair and comely, and prone to the pleasures of love .... The wine is all imported; the horses are mostly small ambling nags, only a few being preserved entire for propagation, and neither curry-combs nor reins are used. The oysters are larger than in England. From Scotland are imported into Flanders hides, wool, salt-fish, and pearls. Nothing gives the Scots more pleasure than to hear the English dispraised. The country is divided into two parts, the cultivated lowlands, and the region where agriculture is not used. The wild Scots have a different language, and sometimes eat the bark of trees."[1]

The poverty and rudeness of the country must have been even worse than is here indicated in the reigns of Robert II. and Robert III. Froissart, who was in Scotland about 1360, asserts in his *Chronicle* that "nothing is to be had in that country without difficulty. There is neither iron to shoe horses, nor leather to make harness, saddles or bridles; all these things come ready-made from Flanders by sea; and should these fail there is none to be had in the country."[2] Both in this and the previous extract there is evidence of exaggeration, but what slender testimony the Scottish statutes for this century furnish, goes to confirm the unfavourable report of the Italian priest and the Picard knight. Horses, kine, sheep and skins of otters, foxes, deer, etc., occasionally figure among the national exports, but the traffic was small, and was almost confined to the Netherlands and France. Very few foreign ships seem to have visited the island. The home-trade was mainly carried on at fairs, which "were commonly held on the day of the saint to whom the parish church was dedicated, and sometimes on Sundays."[3] When we contrast the poor and narrow ways of the Scottish commonalty with the opulent style of the contemporary burgesses in

[1] See Pinkerton, *Hist. of Scotland under the House of Stewart*, vol. I. book v.
[2] Froissart; Johnes' translation (1844), vol. II. p. 36.
[3] Pinkerton, *ut supra*.

Chaucer's Prologue to his Canterbury Tales, we are struck with the vast superiority of English civilization. No doubt the characters in the Prologue are artistic types, but Chaucer was too shrewd an observer to care for hyperbole; and his men and women are true to their order. The faintest approach to such a sketch in the Scotland of the fourteenth century would have been a violent caricature.

Amidst the din of arms the voice of the Muses is heard with difficulty; and yet we are probably indebted to the wars of the fourteenth century for the earliest monuments of the national literature. There are shadowy traces of vanished chronicles in Fordun and Wyntoun that must have been composed in remoter ages than theirs. The church of David I. could not have been utterly sterile in the art of literary composition, but nothing has survived that is worthy of remembrance, and we are forced to speak of Barbour as the "Father of Scottish Literature." His work has already been sufficiently considered, and here we need only advert to the fact that it is one of a group of histories, some in Latin, others in English, some in prose, others in verse, that appeared in the close of the fourteenth and the first half of the fifteenth centuries, as a kind of vindication of the part played by Scotland during the last hundred years.

Fordun, of whom almost nothing is known, except that he was a chantry priest of the cathedral of Aberdeen, and that he wrote between 1384 and 1387, has gathered into his Latin *Chronicle of the Scottish Nation* the monastic fables of the Celts regarding the

Egyptian origin of his countrymen, their wanderings, conquests, and settlements in the west, and he has also made a liberal use of the medieval annalists of England and Wales. He quotes, among others, from Bede and Gildas, from Geoffrey of Monmouth and William of Malmesbury, from Higden and Henry of Huntingdon, from Ambrose, Augustine, Jerome, and Orosius, from Adamnan, Alcuin, and Turgot. Even classical authors are not unfamiliar to him. Ennius, Virgil, Sallust, Seneca, and Suetonius, are laid under contribution. Perhaps he is indebted to Higden for most of his classical allusions; but there is everywhere in Fordun's work evidence of an industry, method, and intelligence, which make him a valuable authority when he reaches the dawn of authentic history in the reign of Kenneth Macalpin. The author is modestly patriotic. In his account of the War of Independence Edward is not vilified, nor Wallace deified. The Scottish priest had an honest and honourable sympathy with his heroic countryman, but he is engaged on a history of the realm, and he cannot sink to personal adulation. Once only he slips into a statement which Blind Harry would have received with rapture, if he could only have allowed that Scots were capable of treachery. Apropos of the battle of Falkirk, he winds up with this amusing generalization: "And it is remarkable that we seldom, if ever, read of the Scots being overcome by the English, unless through the envy of lords or the treachery and deceit of the natives, taking them over to the other side."[1]

Bower, the continuator of Fordun, who died abbot of Inchcolm in 1449, has not only continued but dis-

---
[1] Fordun, chap. 101.

torted him by an extensive series of interpolations, mostly of the pseudo-patriotic sort, and chiefly characterized by exaggeration and crudity. The astonishing description of Wallace's physical endowments, given in the previous chapter, is a specimen of Bower's peculiar workmanship, and contrasts very unfavourably with the temperate eulogy of his predecessor. It is this interpolated work which is usually quoted as the *Scotichronicon*, and wrongly ascribed to Fordun. Students of Scottish history cannot be sufficiently grateful to Mr. Skene for his admirable elucidation of this point in his edition of Fordun.[1]

Andrew of Wyntoun goes over the same ground as Fordun, but prefaces his proper theme of Scottish history by a record of the fortunes of the human race from the creation. Hence he names his work an *Orygynale Cronykil*, i.e., one that starts from the beginning of things. Of him, as of Fordun, hardly anything is known. Born sometime in the reign of David II., he was chosen prior of the monastery of St. Serf's Inch in Loch Leven, before the close of the fourteenth century, for his name appears in the *Chartulary of St. Andrews*, under the date 1395, as "Andreas de Wynton, prior insule lacus de Levin." He was also a canon regular of St. Andrews. The year of his death has not been ascertained, but it is probable he did not long survive the completion of his work, which was finished after the death of Albany and before the return of James I. to Scotland, or between 1420 and 1424. Wyntoun has followed Barbour in the use of the English tongue, and the reason he gives is a thoroughly sound one, "to bring know-

[1] See the *Historians of Scotland*, Fordun, preface to vol. I.

ledge home to every man's understanding." As a piece of literary art we cannot praise the work very highly. The versification is poor, irregular and unmelodious; the narrative is for the most part homely and dull. The Lochleven Chronicler, in spite of his lovely surroundings, had neither the eye nor the ear of a poet; but he has nevertheless many admirable qualities. He is shrewd, sensible, modest, and just in his verdicts. He took great pains to sift and select his material, and he is full of knowledge often drawn from sources that are no longer open to us. If he is in general somewhat garrulous on ecclesiastical topics, and often spins out a story to an immoderate length, through a superfluity of prosaic details, he occasionally rises above this Dutch level, and describes an incident or a scene, especially a battle, with the picturesque felicity of Barbour. His learning is similar in its kind to that of Fordun. The authors to whom he refers are rather more numerous, but they are not of superior merit, and reference to them does not imply on his part the possession of any high intellectual culture. Like Barbour and Fordun he displays no animosity towards the English. He has one severe sentence on Edward I. for his cruelty to the Scots, and another when he recounts the seizure of Prince James, but as a rule he is placidly impartial and bestows an equal meed of praise on the bravery of both countries.

We have called Barbour, Fordun, Bower, and Wyntoun, apologists for Scotland. That appears to us the true explanation of their appearance in literature. All the desperate fighting of the Scots was not to be looked upon as an insane obstinacy. It was rather the stern resolve of a race who could boast of an immemorial antiquity, never to be absorbed by force into another nation. This had now become a sacred tradition : age had deepened and hallowed it : every new generation of Scots was, so to speak, baptized into it as into a national faith ; and at length, when more than a century had passed since the struggle began, it was apparently felt that the time had come when Scotland should give a historical reason for her policy of resistance. Fordun and Bower deliberately set themselves to the work ; Wyntoun was less polemical, but the patriotic purpose is not difficult to see ; while Barbour perhaps only desired, by a crowd of chivalrous incidents, to fan into purer flame the passion for freedom, which the wars of the fourteenth century were fast transforming into lawless ferocity and armed license.

There are also faint traces of song and romance in this sanguinary time. Barbour himself had a knightly spirit, and was familiar with the gests of Arthur and Charlemain. His studious visits to England and France seemed to have opened to him other pages than those of science and theology. No author, not even Froissart himself, is more alive to the charm of chivalry ; it breathes and glows through all his verse, and gives an ideal grace and glory to men who had to fight rough battles with fortune ; but he is nobly free from the narrowness and apathetic indifference to the common weal that mark the famous Frenchman. Patriotism has purified his sentiments, and nothing to him, however lowly, is common or unclean. Fabyan, an English chronicler of the fifteenth century, quotes from a song which he says was long sung by the maidens and minstrels of Scotland in commemoration of the victory of Bannockburn, and adds, "with dyuers other, whiche I ouerpasse." Whether the earlier figure of Thomas of Ercildoune is more than a phantom may still be doubted, and there is no satisfactory evidence for believing him to be the author of the *Romance of Sir Tristrem* which Scott published in 1804. We are not even certain that this romance has any claim to be regarded as a product of Scottish literature; it exists only in a transcript executed in England, and it has no Scottish peculiarities. But the *Gawen and Gologras*, and *Goloran of Galloway*, slips of the great Arthurian epic, probably belong to the fourteenth century, and we need hardly scruple to assign their composition to that "Huchowne" of the "awle ryale" (royal court) whom Wyntoun commends for his curious, eloquent and subtle style. No person of this name is mentioned by Dunbar in his *Lament for the Makaris*, though his list of obscure Scottish poets is remarkably copious; but it has been conjectured that "Huchowne" is a form of Hugh, and that the author may be identified with that "Schir Hew of Eglintoun" who comes first in Dunbar's enumeration, and whose name frequently occurs in the accounts of the great chamberlain of Scotland between 1348 and 1375. To the same writer, Wyntoun ascribes the *Pystyl of Swete Susane*, a version of the well-known tale in the Jewish Apocrypha. These poems are all laboriously alliterative, but not without a certain artificial force of language, while their versification is skilful and correct. It is not at all wonderful that a poor artist like Wyntoun should praise unreservedly their well-turned lines that flow with a musical ease which strikingly contrasts with his own hobbling metre.

There is scarcely any thing in the diction of these poems to mark them as of Scottish origin, but in truth the same may be said of all the Lowland literature of Scotland in this century. Its diction was indistinguishable from that used in the north of England, of which indeed it was only a part. This fact has been clearly demonstrated by Dr. James Murray in a paper of high merit and critical originality published in the *Transactions of the Philosophical Society*, 1870-72.

The Taill of Rauf Coilzear, how he harbreit King Charles, bears the stamp of the same age as the poems just mentioned; it is composed in the same style, and displays the same intricacy of versification, but is a far more graphic and interesting work. Charlemain while out hunting loses his way and is compelled by a storm to take refuge in the hut of a collier named Ralph, whose liberal hospitality is only equalled by his bold and surly manners. Ignorant of the rank of his royal guest, he whacks him at supper with ludicrous violence for his pretence of dandified courtesy. On the morrow the king, who had previously informed Ralph that he is a court servant, invites him to bring a supply of coal to the palace. This his host agrees to do, and Charlemain takes his leave. Next day the collier makes his appearance at court with his load of fuel, and soon discovers the mistake he had made. He is now in great alarm for his life. The king recounts his curious entertainment, and all the courtiers are of opinion that the irreverent rustic deserves death for his outrageous behaviour, but Charlemain thinks otherwise. He remembers only the kindness shown to him, and declares his resolution to make the stalwart churl a knight. This done, Ralph soon proves himself worthy of his new honour, and in due time becomes marshal of France. The tale is full of character and poetic humour. It has a Chaucerian vivacity of sportful incident that gave it a long lease of popularity. Dunbar and Douglas both mention it, and if we could be sure that "Schir Hew of Eglintoun" was the author, it would form not only the earliest, but one of the choicest distinctions of a family whose name is still dear to Scotsmen.

It is pleasant to think that something else than war was going on in Scotland during the fourteenth century, and that here and there in quiet monastic homes, in stately cathedrals, and even in baronial halls, learning and literature had their humble votaries. It makes us feel that the blood-stained annals of the time do not tell us all the story of the national life. Behind the scenes of reeking slaughter, and desolated homesteads and ravaged fields, of cities sacked and castles stormed, we have glimpses of a fairer and humaner life. We behold Barbour and his young companions journeying in search of knowledge to distant shrines, and we are surely not credulous in supposing that others might have wished to join the blameless group. It would be folly to undervalue the importance of the "stern strife and carnage drear" that fill the pages of the early historians. We have seen what it meant for Scotland, but we should gladly have spared a little of the monotonous tale, for some pictures of rural or civic life that would have brought the men and women of those days nearer to us than they are; or some sketch, however meagre, of the literary culture that refined and perfumed the religious houses of the country. But all is sunk in night and shadow save the figures we have named. Others than Barbour and Fordun and Wyntoun there must have been—men who loved peace and the serene service of the Muses, who read and studied if they did not write, who were familiar with the history and romance of the past; and who, in ways no longer visible to us, moulded the dispositions of ingenuous youth, and imbued them with purer tastes than a secular existence could inspire. But we look for their faces in vain, and must content ourselves with dreams.

The fifteenth century in Scotland presents in many respects a striking contrast to its predecessor. The nation has now practically secured its independence and goes its own way. It is no longer menaced by its powerful neighbour, and the French alliance is dormant for a while. The battle of Homildon, with which the century opens, had no political issues, though the slaughter of the Scots was great, and later on the Wars of the Roses gave England full employment at home. But if comparatively free from foreign aggression, Scotland was never more miserable in its domestic policy. The turbulence that began to show itself in the reign of Robert III. and grew worse under the regency of the Albanys, though temporarily checked by the splendid energy of James I., broke out with increased fury after his death and raged unchecked for fifty years. The wars of the fourteenth century are at least dignified by a principle that commands respect, but the intestine conflicts of the fifteenth excite only horror and disgust. Everywhere we behold a barbarous scorn of law, savage insolence, sanguinary feuds, and cruel tragedies. It was the hey-day of unpatriotic feudalism—a feudalism that had thrown to the winds its ancient loyalty, and ravened like a beast of prey over the unhappy land. Again and again the barons were, if one may so speak, summoned by God to assist in the government of the nation during the minority of its kings, and history scarcely affords a parallel (out of France) to their shameful and senseless perfidy. One fancies that he hears a perpetual scream as of vultures hastening to their prey. Never did a nobility prove itself more unworthy of its privileges, or more unfit to guide and civilize a people.

It is quite saddening to look at the reigns of James II. and James III. They are almost meaningless. Both of these monarchs appear to have sincerely desired the welfare of their subjects, but the criminal ambition of the feudal magnates rendered their efforts abortive. Long before James II. had reached his manhood the power of the Douglasses had become greater than his own; while his successor, a prince of cultivated tastes but feeble character, shrank from the rude society of his peers, and surrounded himself with artists of humble origin, whose influence and accomplishments excited the scorn and animosity of the illiterate anarchs. The deeds of the lawless triumvirate composed of the Earls of Douglas and Crawford and Ross, who between them controlled nearly half the country, the audacious murders at Lauder Bridge, and the wretched tragedy of Sauchieburn, are examples of the helplessness of royal authority.

One can pardon and perhaps admire a great ambition when there is an equally great purpose behind it. Historic criticism will be lenient even to the crimes of resolute men, if it can only discern in their policy a clear perception of national wants and a supreme talent for governing. But no trace of this higher spirit shows itself among the great Scottish barons. Not one of them could plead the miserable excuse of doing evil that good might come. Pitscottie, whose quaint and simple narrative[1] is our chief authority for the time, has left, without any malicious intent, a damning record of their guilt. He is continually crying out against "the theft, reif, and slaughter" that everywhere prevail; and in his pages one tale of bloody feud follows another with dismal regularity. Sir Thomas Boyd slays the Lord of Darnley, and is slain in turn by Darnley's brother. The savage islesmen headed by "two notable thieves and murderers," Lachlan Maclean and Murdoch Gibson, invade the Lennox and utterly waste it. The Colquhouns of Luss are nearly cut off to a man on the shores of Loch Lomond in an honourable attempt to beat back the ruffians who, after their victory, "became so proud and insolent that they burnt and herried the country wherever they came, and spared neither old nor young, bairn nor wife, but cruelly would burn their houses and them together, if they made any obstacle; or else, if they made no debate, without consideration and pity would cut their throats and thereafter carry away their gear and wares with their wives and bairns, who, not witting of such incursions, were cruelly murdered and sticked in their beds without any regard of old and young. Thus they raged through the realm without any respect to God or man." The Earl of Douglas orders Sir John Forrester of Corstorphine to attack the Castle of Creighton,

---

[1] *The History of Scotland from* 1436 *to* 1565, by Robert Lindesay, of Pitscottie. The account of the reign of James II. is founded on Hector Boece, but its substantial accuracy is attested by the use which modern historians have made of it. Pinkerton says he quotes it with hesitation, but he constantly quotes it for all that.

belonging to the Chancellor of Scotland; and in revenge the Chancellor collects a great army of his kinsmen and friends who "invaded the Earl of Douglas's land with fire and sword and burnt all the corn and cornyards, villages and towns wherever he came; and sicklike he did in the lands of Abercorn and the town of Blackness with the castle thereof, and carried away great preys of horse, sheep, and nolt out of all their towns." The Lindsays and the Ogilvies quarrel about the bailiary of Aberbrothock, and the neighbourhood of that notable abbey becomes the scene of a ferocious conflict, in which scores of gentlemen disgracefully perish. The unsuccessful attempt of the old Earl of Crawford to prevent the fight is very curiously described by Pitscottie: "A soldier, not knowing what he was and wherefore he came, struck him at the mouth with a spear, and throughout the neck, and he died incontinent in good action, labouring to put Christian men to peace and rest, and conquest a good commendation of all men, *albeit he was very insolent all the rest of his life-time.*" After this (1445) "there followed nothing but slaughter in this realm, every party ilk one lying in wait for another, as they had been setting tinchills[1] for the slaughter of wild beasts." Robert Boyd, captain of Dumbarton, with a company of armed men lies in wait for James Stuart of Auchmynto, murders him and carries off his wife, who in terror "parted with a dead bairn, and died herself the third day thereafter." The Earls of Huntly and Crawford fall foul of each other near Brechin (1453), and when the latter after a long and cruel fight is forced to flee, the only remark he

[1] Scot. "snares," especially the spaces into which deer are driven by a circle of hunters.

makes is that he would gladly have spent seven years in hell to have been victor that day.[1]

These are specimens of the deeds that were constantly being done. Nearly every disorder in the realm can be traced to the intolerable insolence of the Douglasses who, rather than brook the slightest interference with their wanton misrule, made secret alliances with England, and once at least in the plenitude of their power threatened to drive their sovereign from his throne. Had it not been for the loyalty of Sir William Creighton, "a man of great foresight, singular manhood, and a faithful subject, a sicker targe of the commonwealth unto his life's end,"[2] and of Kennedy, Bishop of St. Andrews, whose wisdom, discretion, and probity stand out conspicuous in this age of feudal blackguardism, government would have absolutely ceased to exercise the semblance of authority, and parliaments would have legislated in vain. Pitscottie closes his account of the reign of James II. with a story so wildly horrible that we shrink from believing it, yet does it seem in its very ghastliness to body forth in legendary guise the hideous and unnatural criminality of the times. "About this time (1460) there was apprehended and taken, for a most abominable and cruel abuse, a brigand who haunted and dwelt with his wholefamily and household out of all men's company in a place of Angus, called 'The Fiend's Den.' This mischievous man had an execrable fashion to take all young men and children that either he could steal quietly or take away by any other moyen without the knowledge of the people, and bring them home and eat them, and the more young they were, he held the more

---

[1] Pitscottie's *Hist. of Scot.* p. 79.   [2] Ibid. p. 105.

tender and the greater delicate. For the which damnable abuse he was burnt, with his wife, bairns, and family, except a young lass of one year old, which was saved and brought to Dundee where she was fostered and brought up. But when she came to woman's years she was condemned and burnt quick for the same crime her father and mother were convicted of. It is said that when this young woman was coming forth to the place of execution that there gathered a great multitude of people about her, and specially of women, cursing and warying[1] that she was so unhappy to commit so damnable deeds. To whom she turned about with a wood[2] and furious countenance, saying, 'Wherefore chide ye with me as I had committed an unworthy crime? Give me credit, and trow me, if ye had experience of eating of man's and woman's flesh ye would think the same so delicious that ye would never forbear it again.' And so, with an obstinate mind, this unhappy creature, without sign or outward token of repentance, died in the sight of the whole people for her misdeeds that she was adjudged to."

The reign of James III. is not so marked by the same frantic excesses of feudal misrule as that of his father. The banishment of the Douglasses, which took place in 1454, removed the worst obstacle to the peace and prosperity of the country; but a new evil, that of court favourites, inflamed the passions of a selfish nobility and plunged the commonweal in fresh misfortunes. Bishop Kennedy, who had been the one strong rock of refuge for James II. amid the raging sea of anarchy that surrounded him, died in 1466, when James III. was only fourteen years of age. The eulogy pronounced by

[1] Imprecating. [2] Mad.

Pinkerton on this illustrious prelate and leal-hearted Scot is worthy of remembrance: "A grandson of Robert III., his virtues and abilities conferred a greater glory than his royal descent. His wisdom, his munificence, his public spirit, secured the applause and gratitude of his country: and his fame would diffuse a strong and steady light, independent of the darkness of a barbarous age." . . . He was "eminent in the knowledge of civil law, in the learning of the age, in the experience of men and manners and politics. . . . Nor was the bishop less respectable than the counsellor of state in enforcing the residence of his clergy, their regular preaching and visitation of the sick; and in affording an example, by preaching four times in the year at every church of his diocese, by inspecting the maintenance of the poor, and the education of youth, and by the vigorous punishment of clerical negligence."[1] The influence of the Boyds, who owed their position at court to the kindness of Kennedy, was pernicious, but short-lived. They fell amidst the rejoicings which accompanied James's marriage with Margaret of Denmark (1469), the victims of feudal envy and popular dislike: yet in spite of their folly and presumption, we trace with a certain emotion of pity the obscure and miserable fortunes of the brothers in an exile from which they never returned.

Hitherto James's reign had been outwardly fortunate. He had won Roxburgh and Berwick, he had acquired the sovereignty of Orkney and Shetland, he had wrested the Earldom of Ross from the Lord of the Isles; but he had not the art, nor perhaps even the inclination, to win the favour of his turbulent nobles, and he can

[1] *Hist. of Scot.* vol. I. book vii.

scarcely be said to have secured the affection or respect of the commons, though the Parliaments are sometimes effusive in their expressions of loyalty. When the policy of Edward IV. led him to support the king's brother Albany (who being charged with treason had fled the country) in his attempt upon the Scottish throne, and war broke out between the two kingdoms, the violence of feudal rage exposed Scotland, even in the hour of gravest peril, to the risk of another of those painful humiliations of which the previous century had been prolific. The murders at Lauder Bridge (1482) to which we have referred, were followed by the dispersion of the feudal array and the temporary imprisonment of the monarch. After a brief reconciliation between the brothers, during which they shared one bed and one board, the perfidy of Albany again drove him into treasonable acts, and he again fled to England (1483), to return once more in company with the aged anarch Douglas (1484), whose exile had been spent in perpetual crime against his native land, and who now imagined that he could recover his possessions by force from an imprudent and pusillanimous king. Both were deceived. Douglas's vassals had forgotten him. No one joined the invaders. Surrounded by the gentry of Annandale they suffered ignominious defeat. Albany escaped by the swiftness of his horse, but Douglas was taken prisoner, and with a touch of humane sarcasm, James sent him to spend the remainder of his life in the seclusion of Lindores Abbey. The old earl had been trained for the Church, and he now muttered as he left the royal presence, "He who may no better be, must be a monk."

The last Parliament of this reign issued ordinances

which show that feudal violence and rapacity still continued. The increase of crimes was indeed so great that "justices general are appointed for the divisions north and south of the Forth, to hold courts in every part of the realm with all expedition, supported by their own power and what aid the king could spare, in order to bring transgressors to punishment and to rescue the royal authority from contempt."[1] Even the king was restrained in the exercise of his prerogative of clemency to criminals on account of the evils arising "through treason, slaughter, reif, burning, theft, and open hership, through default of sharp execution of justice, and over-common granting of grace and remission to trespassours."[2] But while Parliament was thus proceeding with a show of diligence in good work, a conspiracy of nobles was being hatched against the throne itself. Its motives are not clear. It was not a mere alliance of lawless chiefs; the conduct of the leaders was that of traitors and rebels rather than of bravos; yet it was calculated to reproduce the worst disorders of an earlier time. The pretext of the conspirators was the favour that James showed to Englishmen, and it is possible they believed it, for there is some evidence to show that the Scottish king sought in this way to lessen the formidable power of his nobles; but it is probable that their chief reason was a profound antipathy to a ruler whose political views and personal sympathies were at variance with their own. In some cases private resentment determined their policy. Most of the northern barons adhered to the royal cause; but Angus (who had succeeded to the

---

[1] Pinkerton, *Hist. of Scot.* vol. I. book viii.
[2] Burton, *Hist. of Scot.* vol. III. p. 191.

possessions of the Douglasses), the Homes, the Hepburns, Huntly, Errol, Glamis, Gray, Drummond, and others, banded against their sovereign. Shaw, the governor of Stirling Castle, placed in their hands Prince James who had been confided to his care, and thus fortified by the presence of the heir to the crown, they gave battle to the king at Sauchie, within a mile of Bannockburn, 18th June, 1488. The unwarlike monarch fled from a scene of slaughter, but, falling from his horse, was carried into a mill close by, where he met his death at the hands of an assassin who pretended to be a priest.

From this gloomy picture of the political and social anarchy of Scotland in the fifteenth century, we gladly turn away in the hope of discovering something else on which the mind can dwell with greater pleasure. The machinery of government must have often been brought to a standstill in all parts of the country, yet we cannot suppose that the king's officers were always unable to execute justice, and that Parliament made statutes which were never observed. The influence of law is everywhere silent and abiding: even when it is broken or defied, it leaves behind it a sense of its greatness and its authority. The feuds of the barons were frightful, but they were intermittent; and there is reason to believe that in spite of the ferocious outrages that disgraced the times, the mass of the urban population and of the peasantry fairly strove to better their position, to secure the fruits of industry, and to lead quiet and peaceable lives. In a poem belonging to this century[1] we get a glimpse of a Scottish burgess, which

[1] Tales of the Priests of Peebles in *Scarce Scottish Poems reprinted* (Lond., 1792), quoted by Pinkerton, *Hist. of Scot.* vol. I. book ix.

is more than interesting. He begins in poverty, but soon by diligence becomes a prosperous pedlar. When his pack is worth forty pounds Scots, he buys a horse and a cart. Then he acquires a shop in town, with counter, chests, and Flemish coffers : he is next a merchant who makes voyages to other countries; he marries a rich wife; his plate is worth three thousand pounds; he dresses in silk on Sundays, and in green or grey cloth on other days, while his spouse glories in scarlet. The sumptuary laws of James II. (1458) imply the existence of a certain comfort and even luxury among the citizens which could only have been acquired by honest and successful industry. Burgesses are forbidden to wear gowns of silk or scarlet cloth, or lined furs unless they are municipal dignitaries. A similar prohibition is enacted for their wives and daughters, who are ordered to wear short kerchiefs with little hoods, as are used in Flanders, England, and other countries. Even the peasantry have to be restrained in their extravagance ! It is enacted that " no labourers, nor husbandmen wear on the workday other than grey or white; and on the holiday only light blue, green, or red; and their wives the same, and kerchiefs of their own making, and that it exceed not the price of forty pence the eln." Sumptuary laws may be a proof of the barbarous condition of political economy; but they are serviceable to the student of history, and help him to form an idea of our social civilization, regarding which the early annals of a country are obstinately silent. There is a statute of James II., of date 1450, which permitted lands to be let in feu, without the obligation of military service. This was a step in the right direction, and seems to indicate that there was at least some desire on the part of the people to pursue industry undisturbed and unmolested. Much practical good may not have come of it, yet we may feel sure it was not a piece of mere theoretical legislation, but rather a response to a felt want. There is evidence that agriculture languished, and that grain had to be imported from England, nor can we wonder at this when we remember the horrible and wide-spread devastations of the century, but the staple exports of skins, hides, and wool had increased, and salmon is now added to the list. We note with satisfaction that the chief imports are cart wheels, wheel-barrows, and haberdashery, all of which suggest a certain growth of peaceable industry and social comfort. A courteous and hospitable reception is recommended to foreign merchants at all Scottish ports, that "they may be excited to return, to the great utility of the whole kingdom."[1] James III. was himself a merchant, and traded abroad in ships of his own; some of the bishops and barons followed his example, while it is clear from various incidental remarks that the burgesses were beginning to display a creditable activity in the same course, stimulated perhaps by the wholesome rivalry of strangers.

Politically the Scottish commons were not of much account. No doubt they had representatives in Parliament, but these were few in numbers, and powerless to affect legislation. Through nearly the whole of the fifteenth century they are dumb, and we can only conjecture from one or two manifestations where their sympathies lay. Thus it was the fierce cry for vengeance rising from the citizens of Perth that so speedily

[1] Acts of Parl. of 1487, cap. 114.

brought the assassins of James I. to justice; and three years after the murder of James III., the estates were still busy with plans "for the ceasing of the heavy murmour and voice of the people" in reference to that deed; while in the general amnesty passed by the victorious party forgiveness is specially accorded "to all the burgesses, merchants, and unlanded men" who had fought for their king at Sauchieburn. But the Scottish democracy was only growing in the dark. It had neither political weight nor public influence; it had no natural cohesion, and no artificial confederation. The peasants and villagers of one part of the country remained ignorant, we might almost say, of the very existence of those in another, except when the savage feuds of their masters brought them together in mortal strife. The burgesses of the larger towns and seaports were a more independent and important class; but even they, though they seem to have loyally stood by their kings, were not yet sufficiently organized or numerous to break up the leagues of the barons, or extirpate the caterans of the Hebrides.

The only order of the community capable of restraining in some degree the excesses of the nobles was the clergy. A third—some writers reckon a half—of the land in Scotland belonged to them, while in addition to their territorial power, they were the sole interpreters of the mysteries of religion, and wielded the thunderbolts of the church. Moreover, many important civil offices requiring a knowledge of law, historical precedents, foreign languages, etc., were of necessity in their hands; but except that on the whole they were more humane in their dealings with their tenantry than the mass of secular landlords, it cannot be shown that they earnestly sought to grapple with the disorders of the times. The great prelates were themselves members of aristocratic families, and were swayed by ambitions as worldly as those that raged in the hearts of the Crawfords and the Douglasses. In connection with the newly established universities,[1] the cathedral chapters, and the great abbeys, there would always be a certain number of cultivated and enlightened men; but there is sufficient evidence to show that monastic piety had lost its original ardour, and that the fatal rule of celibacy was corrupting to the core the manners both of the friars and the secular clergy. The noblest name in the ecclesiastical history of Scotland during the fifteenth century is that of William Elphinstone, Bishop of Aberdeen, yet even he was the offspring of priestly concubinage. His father was rector of Kirkmichael and archdeacon of Teviotdale. That the church winked at such unlawful connexions, and that society tolerated them, may have lessened the disgrace, but it did not lessen the iniquity. It saved the offspring perhaps from the cruel reproach that in ordinary cases follows bastardy, but it seared the conscience and sensualized the appetites of those who gave themselves the unhallowed license. The literature of the century throws hardly any direct light on the moral condition of the church; but, in the first half of the sixteenth a flood of satire is let loose, which tells of evils that must have been of ancient growth. Chaucer has drawn portraits of an Oxford clerk and a " pore Persoun of a toun " that show us how religion was not all the scandalous farce that his jolly monks, and flattering friars, and cunning pardoners tried to make it. There were doubt-

---

[1] St. Andrews founded in 1411; Glasgow in 1450-51; Aberdeen in 1494.

less in Scotland also good and true men, who spent their lives in works of charity and devotion, and in the pursuit of wisdom and learning.

The character of Bishop Kennedy has been already sketched. In a later and more auspicious period of the same century, after nine years of laborious study and honourable distinction abroad, William Elphinstone returned to his native country with the highest reputation. He was successively Official General of the Diocese of Glasgow, Rector of the University of that city, Official of Lothian, Bishop of Ross, and Bishop of Aberdeen; and his biography, written by Hector Boece, gives us a delightful picture of a man in whom strength and grace and wisdom and purity were happily combined. He stands out the centre of a society of priests and gentlemen that loved music and learning and wit, himself ever gay and cheerful, of the most extraordinary vigour and spirit, discussing affairs of state with acuteness and vivacity in his eighty-third year, and retaining to the last the exquisite charm of his manner. "We know him," says Mr. Cosmo Innes,[1] "in the history of the time as the zealous churchman, the learned lawyer, the wise statesman; one who never sacrificed his diocesan duties to mere secular cares, but knew how to make his political eminence serve the interests of his church; who, with manners and temperance in his own person befitting the primitive ages of Christianity, threw around his cathedral and palace the taste and splendours that may adorn religion; who found time amidst the cares of state and the pressure of daily duties to preserve the Christian antiquities of his diocese, and collect the

[1] *Sketches of Early Scotch History*, pp. 87, 88.

memories of those old servants of the truth who had run a course similar to his own; to renovate his cathedral service, and to support and foster all good letters; while his economy of a slender revenue rendered it sufficient for the erection and support of sumptuous buildings, and the endowment of a famous university." That a man of this high quality should flourish in the days of the Borgias, and in a land where impurity and coarseness were so rampant among the clergy, is a proof that the Scottish Church, even at its worst, could boast of men who may favourably compare in learning, culture, and piety with the choicest spirits of the Reformation.

The foundation of three Universities in so small a state and in so distracted a century, is a surprising phenomenon, and tempts us to believe that a stream of pure intellectual life may have flowed on unperceived beneath the turbid surface of feudal misrule. It would be easy no doubt to exaggerate the importance and dignity of these new homes of learning. They were for a long time poor in resources, and some of them, *e.g.* Glasgow, had a hard fight to maintain their existence, but almost from the first they produced famous scholars, and in the sixteenth century, as Mr. Burton says, "foreign universities swarmed with learned Scotsmen."[1] When we think of the rapid decline of the Church in faith and morals during the fifteenth century, let us not forget that we owe to the zeal and munificence of its bishops those great institutions, which have conferred lasting renown on the nation and incalculable benefits on the people. It was no longer necessary to wander abroad in search of a

[1] *Hist of Scot.* vol. IV. p. 115.

liberal education, which could be got without trouble or danger at home. Enterprising and ambitious youths then as now frequently sought the more ancient and illustrious seats of arts and philosophy on the Continent, but it is abundantly clear that they carried with them a solid foundation of scholarship acquired in their native schools. They rose to posts of distinction with ease, and gave Scotland as great a name in wit as it had ever obtained in arms. Though it is not to the universities that we must look for examples of the vernacular literature, which as a rule flourishes best under open skies and not in cloistered halls; nevertheless the mental culture and refinement of taste that are the natural fruits of liberal studies, make university scholars the best and most sympathetic critics even of vernacular literature; and it can hardly be doubted that they were an influential part of that small community who in the fifteenth century formed the Republic of Letters in Scotland.

In an earlier part of this chapter we have alluded to the striking contrast between the political history of the country in the fourteenth and fifteenth centuries. There is an equally great contrast in the literature of the two periods. Some anonymous pieces, such as *Cockelbie's Sow*, are marked by the same curious blending of humour and romance that we have seen in *Rauf Coilzear;* while others whose authorship is known repeat the metrical peculiarities of the Arthurian poems ascribed to Huchowne of the "awle ryale." To the latter class belongs Holland's *Buke of the Howlat*, composed about 1450, before the fall of the Douglasses, to whose party the writer, probably a priest, belonged. It is one of those elaborate allegories which the poets of the middle ages apparently found so delightful, but which to modern minds seem unspeakably dreary and absurd. The Howlat (owl) ashamed of his form and plumage begs the Peacock as the pope of birds to use his influence with Nature in getting him changed; the Peacock refers him to the Eagle, who is emperor of the winged tribes and an emblem of the temporal power. His prayer is granted, and he is decked out in all the splendour of borrowed feathers, but becomes so insolent in his new attire that a complaint is laid against him by the other birds, and he is compelled to resume his original form. The poem is obviously a warning against pride, needed by none more than by the noble house of which Holland was a follower to the bitter end; but as a literary performance it cannot rank high. The allegory is spun out to a tedious length, the characters are not conceived with artistic congruity, the incidents are often ludicrous, and in one place the didactic fable is superseded by a historical discourse on the exploits of the Douglasses. Another poet, Sir Gilbert Hay, who was contemporary with Holland, and was long in the service of King Charles VI. of France, translated a French metrical romance on Alexander the Great. Both he and Holland were once popular. Sir David Lyndsay says, in the Prologue to the *Complaynt of the Papingo*, that their books were "levand" in his time and had still the power of delighting readers; but the satirist was probably thinking more of Henryson, Mercer, and Quintyne, whom he names in the same connection, than of these less gifted authors.

In his *Lament for the Makaris*, composed in 1507-8, Dunbar has a long list of Scottish poets, all of whom with one exception were then dead. Of "Schir Mungo Lokert of the Lé," "Schir Johne the Ross," "Guid gentill Stobo," "James Afflek," "Etrik," "Heryot," and "Sandy Traill," absolutely nothing has survived, and the absence of historical sequence in the mention of the names makes it impossible for us to fix their age with certainty, but they are believed for the most part to belong to the latter half of the fifteenth century. Two or three are still extant in fragments. *Roull's Cursyng*, we learn from a casual allusion, was written in the pontificate of Alexander VI (1492-1503). It is an amusing specimen of that awful indignation that is wont to seize clergymen when they happen to be victimized. Schir Johne Roull has had his geese, capons, hens, and other fowls stolen, and in consequence he proceeds to curse the thief in the most elaborate and minute style, and with a heartiness that is peculiarly refreshing to read in these degenerate days. Dunbar mentions two Roulls, one of " Abirdene " and the other of Corstorphine. The latter he describes as " gentill," from which we infer that he was *not* the clerical humourist. Of " Patrik Johnestoun " there survives a poem entitled *The Three Deid Powis* ("The Three Deathsheads"). It is a piece of fine poetic moralizing on the vanity of life, after the fashion of Henryson, and might have proceeded from his pen. It breathes the same pure and serious spirit, and has the same charm of sweet and cultured melody. " Merseir " is an author of whom we would gladly have known more. Dunbar bestows more praise on him than on any other name in his catalogue. His theme was love, and his pictures were full of life. His words were terse and vivid and strong. Only a small fragment of one of his poems has come down to us. It illustrates his favourite subject, and if it does not quite justify the high eulogy of his brother bard, the verses are graceful, and the images stand out clear and distinct. He warns maidens of the peril that lies in paramours, with a kindly sympathy that seems to suggest an honest man. The Bannatyne MS. contains a poem by one "Clerk," and another by "Broun," who are probably the persons of that name mentioned by Dunbar.

We might easily enlarge the number of Scottish poets who have either wholly perished or survive in insignificant fragments; but enough has been said to show that the reproach of literary barbarism could no longer be justly urged against the nation. When we read Pitscottie, we see nothing but base intrigues and brutal outrages; yet it is certain, in spite of his omissions, that civilization and culture were slowly asserting themselves in the distracted land. The influence of Chaucer is felt more powerfully and yields richer fruit in Scotland than in England. Towering high above the group of lay and clerical poets whom we have just named, stand out the splendid figures of King James, Henryson, and Dunbar, whose genius would shed a lustre on any literature, and who are in fact the only great English poets of the fifteenth century. They and their successors in the sixteenth form a real connecting link between the age of Chaucer and that of Spenser, and enable us to measure in some degree the sovereign sway exercised by the great. " Father of English poetry." In the following chapter we propose to examine the character of their genius and work.

Blind Harry who belongs to the same period stands

apart. He does not represent the culture of his time. He is the oracle of the unlettered crowd, high and low, to whom the legends of classical antiquity and the new world of romantic allegory were alike unknown; but who listened with rapture to the record of Wallace's miraculous exploits in the cause of national freedom. Blind Harry is the rude embodiment of a national feeling, which only an ignoble cynicism will despise. We have already dealt with his work from a historical point of view, and have unsparingly criticized its portentous absurdities; but when we remember the political turpitude of the century that gave it birth, we can forgive much to a man who was inspired with the strongest passion of patriotism. Whatever the moral defects of the *Life of Wallace* may be, it is throughout a graphic and picturesque poem; and in particular passages it even reaches an exquisite beauty. The growth of Wallace's love for Marion Braidfute of Lamington is told with a sweetness and idyllic grace, that prove the minstrel to have been capable of something finer and more poetic than the celebration of those superhuman adventures, in which his hero slaughters his foes with the fury of a Hun. The maiden herself, lovely, modest, pensive, and discreet, living under a perpetual fear of outrage from Hesilrig, and therefore "wary and wise," "weyll-rewllyt off tong," forms a picture full of vivid charm; while her frank but virtuous passion, blent with sad reminiscences of her country's miseries, is expressed with a force of simple and tender pathos that is singularly dramatic. Hardly less admirable is the description of the interview between Wallace and the Queen of England. If it were possible to conquer the amazement which the story excites, we could hardly fail to be struck with the splendour of the accessories and the grace and courtesy of the dialogue. But the literary merit of the work is in general insufficient to constitute it a great poem, and the popularity it has enjoyed for centuries, in one form or another, is mainly due to the fascination which the subject has always possessed for Scotsmen of every degree.

CHAPTER V.

KING JAMES, HENRYSON, AND DUNBAR.

Period of James's Captivity—The Dukes of Albany—The King's Return—Arrest of the Regent and his followers, and of the Highland Chiefs—Conspiracies against the King—His Murder—Character of his Administration—His Poems, "The Kingis Quhair," &c.—Robert Henryson—His Life—His shorter Poems—Robene and Makyne—Fables—Testament of Cresseid—William Dunbar—Characteristics of his Time—New Era of Scottish History—Features of the Reign of James IV.—Decline of Feudalism—Commerce—Increase of Wealth—Compulsory Education—Lollards of Kyle—Corruptions of the Church—Dunbar an Image of his Time—His Poems, Allegorical, Satirical, and Moral—His Place in Scottish Poetry—His Verse characterized by Distinctive Features of the National Character.

When James, Prince of Scotland, was captured by an English ship off Flamborough Head in 1405, he was eleven years of age. Nineteen years passed before he obtained his freedom, and returned to his native country. The interval was, on the whole, a deplorable period in Scottish history. Though it was marked by two memorable and happy events, the foundation in 1411 of the first Scottish University, St. Andrews, and the repulse in the same year of Donald, Lord of the Isles, in his devastating march through the lowlands of Moray and Aberdeen, at "the sair field o' Harlaw," yet its prevailing features are disagreeable and repulsive.

What kind of man the Duke of Albany really was, it is rather difficult to say. Wyntoun and Bower laud him for his virtues and the graces of his person; and there is some reason to think that he was possessed of gifts which win confidence and inspire respect. His brother, King Robert III., does not seem to have distrusted or disliked him ; and it is not certain that the proposal to send Prince James to France, arose from a dread of the criminal ambition of the regent. Others who read him perhaps more profoundly than the facile monarch, may have cherished suspicions of his sinister intents. The Bishop of St. Andrews was probably one of these; but Albany was a staunch churchman, and signalized his regency by the first martyrdom for religious heresy that blackens the annals of the kingdom. No one, even of his enemies, could doubt that but for him the anarchy of the country would have been much greater than it was, during the reign of his incapable brother. But his policy after the seizure and imprisonment of James in England is peculiarly crooked, and leaves on the mind a strong impression that he was not at all anxious that his sovereign should ever be released. Scott has drawn a picture of him in the *Fair Maid of Perth*, which embodies the unfavourable view of his character and motives taken by the historians of the sixteenth century; and it is more than probable that he will continue to be remembered by the dark but vivid portrait of the novelist, rather than by any representation based on temperate and judicial criticism.

When Albany died in 1419 he was succeeded in the regency and dukedom by his son Murdach, who did not possess a spark of his father's genius. Even in his own family he could not command respect or obedience. Hector Boece records an incident which may or may not be historical, but which at any rate illustrates the feebleness of his parental authority. The regent had a favourite falcon which his son Walter had long wished to possess. The latter repeatedly begged that it might be given to him. At last, enraged by refusal, he tore it from his father's hand and twisted its neck in his presence; whereupon Murdach feeling his own impotency exclaimed, "Since you pay me so little respect I must invite him whom both must obey." No one will seriously believe that so trivial a circumstance determined him to procure the return of his sovereign; but there can be little doubt that a consciousness of his own weakness induced him to give effect to the national desire.

James's position was every year growing more anomalous. There was no longer a political reason for retaining him in captivity. The Scots still adhered to the French alliance. The flower of their soldiery were in the service of the Dauphin, and not even the presence of their captive king in the English camp could abate the ardour of their courage, or induce them to desert their companions in arms. It was clear that James would be more useful to England on the throne of his fathers than ever he could be as a prisoner at the English court. Negotiations were entered into. Commissioners from both nations met at Pomfret in July, 1423; two months later the terms of release were settled at York; and in April, 1424, the Scottish monarch re-entered the realm to which he had so long been a stranger, amidst an outburst of enthusiasm that proved the sincerity and depth of the national joy.

Of James's life during his residence in England we cannot be said to know much. He had been well trained for his years by Wardlaw before he left for France, but in his captivity he received an education

as liberal and varied as ever fell to the fortune of any
king. No one can reasonably refuse credit to the
accounts that have come down to us of his marvellous
accomplishments. Bower's panegyric may be rose-
coloured, but it is at least the work of a writer who
was a contemporary of James, and the very minuteness
of its details forbids us to believe that it is greatly
exaggerated. Universal tradition confirms it. The
fame of the Scottish monarch reached as far as Italy in
later generations. During the earlier years of his
captivity he was confined in the Tower of London and
the Castle of Nottingham, but soon after the accession
of Henry V. to the throne he was removed to Windsor.
The order for his transference is given in Rymer's
Foedera, and is dated 3rd August, 1414.

Although strictly guarded, the royal prisoner suffered
no personal hardships. Under the care of Sir John
Pelham, he was trained to all knightly exercises, and
disciplined in almost every branch of medieval learning. To the more elegant forms of culture, such as
poetry, oratory, and music, he added the graver studies
of theology and law. He was not excluded from the
society of his countrymen, and Burton is even of
opinion that from his prison chamber in the south he
made his influence felt on the politics of his native land.
Of this influence it must be confessed there is little
trace in the history of the times; but on the other hand,
it is hardly credible that a prince of his energy and
intelligence could have been altogether a cipher in the
frequent negotiations carried on between the govern-
ments of the two countries. What stands out distinctly,
however, is the magnanimity of the English king. "In
the treatment of his captive guest," says Burton,

"Henry V. showed a nature in which jealousies and crooked policy had no place. Had he desired to train an able statesman to support his own throne, he could not have better accomplished his end. The King of Scots had everything that England could give to store his naturally active intellect with learning and accomplishments; and he had opportunities of seeing the practice of English politics, and of observing and discoursing with the great statesmen of the day both in England and France, where Henry had also a court. He would be sent back all the abler governor of his own people and more formidable foe to her enemies, for his sojourn at the Court of England."[1]

The great event that marks the later years of James's captivity is his passion for Lady Jane Beaufort, whom he married in February, 1424, a month or two before his return to his own dominions. It was a pure, tender and romantic affection, which glowed with undiminished ardour through all his fierce struggle with treason, anarchy, and barbarism; and it gave birth to a poem which displays an imaginative grace and power that no other European monarch has even distantly approached. The nature and merits of the *Kingis Quhair* will be afterwards considered; here it may be enough to say that, apart from his beneficent labours as a king, its quality is such as to entitle the author to a conspicuous and permanent place in the history of English literature.

The public career of James is really the history of his time. He came back to Scotland sternly resolved to take vengeance on the house of Albany, which was responsible for his protracted imprisonment, and to repress the turbulence and savagery which threatened to

[1] *History of Scotland*, vol. III. p. 106.

destroy the civilization of the realm. His reign is a dramatic succession of startling incidents, culminating in a scene of tragic horror which will for ever excite the pity of mankind. Hardly eight months after his restoration, he arrested the late regent with one of his sons and two leading followers.[1] Murdach and

[1] Dr. Ross had accepted the statement of Scottish historians, that in addition to the persons specified in the text, twenty-six of the leading nobles of Scotland were arrested. The true state of the case was pointed out by Sir J. H. Ramsay in a communication to the *Scotsman*, dated 12th July, 1883. An examination of the ancient chronicles to which Sir James refers has led us to accept his "historical correction," and to alter the text into accordance with it. We are permitted to give his words :—" The arrest of such a body of men, practically the whole of the Scottish House of Lords, would no doubt have greatly 'astounded the country.' Such a *coup d'état* would have exceeded the powers not only of a new-fledged King of Scotland, but of any king that ever sat on the throne of England or France. The list in question is merely that of the men who were knighted by James at his coronation, and the confusion has arisen from mistaking an awkward parenthesis in the *Scotichronicon* for part of the text. The passage may be given in English as follows :—' And on the ninth day he (King James) let arrest the Lord Murdach, Duke of Albany, and his younger son the Lord Alexander Stewart, whom, on his coronation day, he had knighted, with six-and-twenty others, namely, Archibald, Earl of Douglas,' etc. In Goodall's text it will be seen that the parenthesis is made to include only the words corresponding to 'whom, on his coronation day, he had knighted' (vol. II. p. 482). That the parenthesis ought to include all the twenty-six names appears from the text itself, which, after the close of the list, resumes thus :—' And on the same day he arrested the Lord Montgomery,' etc. If the preceding list was that of the persons arrested, why should the writer begin again like that? He would simply have added the name to the list. In the 'Liber Pluscardensis,' and the 'Extracta e Cronicis Scotiæ,' the facts are given without ambiguity. The list of the supposed six-and-twenty is given under the coronation, in its proper place, in 1424; and the persons arrested in 1425 are given as the four above-named, and no more. The *Scotichronicon* makes no allusion to the trial or emancipation of these six-and-twenty gentlemen, though it follows up the careers of the four who really were arrested. There is no lack of corroborative evidence in support of the view here set forth. One of the six-and-twenty was Sir John, the Red Stewart of Dundonald. But he was killed on the 3rd May following, fighting for James I., at Dumbarton. A man so recently suspected of treason would never have been placed in such a position. Again, another of the men is Sir Walter Ogilvy of Lintrathen, the founder of the house of Airlie. But he was treasurer of the king's household all the time, and we find him quietly holding an audit in May

Alexander Stewart suffered death as a warning to all who sought to oppose or conspire against the royal authority. James meant to govern his kingdom and not to reign on sufferance. Wherever insubordination or usurpation of his sovereign rights showed itself, his vengeance fell like a thunderbolt, sudden, swift, and scathing: nor was he ever baffled in his conflict with the desperadoes of his realm, till the perfidy of a minion, and the chance of an hour, made him the victim of a band of unimportant assassins.

The condition of the Highlands was a source of constant worry and trouble to a monarch who in England had learned to appreciate the blessings of

(Exchequer Rolls, Scotland, IV. 379). A treasurer might be arrested on suspicion of treason, but a treasurer who had been so arrested could hardly be sent back to his duties within two months, as if nothing had happened. Lastly, I may point out that some seven or eight of the twenty-six were picked out by James to sit in judgment on Murdach." That our readers may be in a position to judge for themselves we append the passage from the *Scotichronicon*. It is clear that the parenthesis should not end at "Militem," but be made to include all that remains of the paragraph and terminate after the words " Willelmum Crechtoun, ejusdem." Bower manifestly means to emphasize the fact that the regent and his son now arrested had, on the coronation day, been knighted, along with the other great nobles of the kingdom. The passage is as follows :—"Eodem anno, xiii. die Martii, tenuit rex apud Perth, secundum suum parliamentum, et in die nono ejusdem arrestari fecit dominum Murdacum ducem Albaniæ comitem de Fife et Menteth, ac etiam dominum Alexandrum Stewart filium juniorem ejusdem (quem die coronationis suae praecinxit in militem), cum viginti sex aliis, videlicet Archibaldum tertium comitem de Douglas, et Willelmum Douglas comitem de Angus, Georgium de Dunbar comitem de March, Alexandrum Lindesay, Adam Hepburn de Haliz, Thomam Hay de Zester, Walterum de Haliburton et de Ogilby, David Stewart de Rossyth, Alexandrum de Seton de Gordon, Patricium Ogilby de Ochtirhous, Johannem Red Stewart de Dundonald, David Murrave de Gask, Johannem Stewart de Cardine, Willelmum Hay de Errol constabularium Scotiae, Johannem Scrimgeour constabularium de Dundé, Alexandrum de Irvyne de Drum, Herbertum Maxwel de Carlavcrok, Herbertum Herrice de Terreglem, Andream Gray de Fowlis, Robertum Conyngham de Kilmauris, Alexandrum Ramsay de Dalwonlsy, Willelmum Crechtoun, ejusdem.

" Quo etiam die arrestavit dominum Johannem de Montegomorie ejusdem, et Alanum de Otterburn secretarium ducis, et incontinente misit et accepit castra de Faukland et Doun in Menteth," etc.—[ED.]

civilization, justice, and order. The Lords of the Isles were the greatest offenders against law and authority. They were wont to assert an intolerable position. Claiming to be independent of the Scottish crown, they formed alliances with England, and were ever ready to waste the fertile straths of the north, when the feudal force of Scotland was called to the Border, or when political confusions made them an easy prey to the spoiler. In the spring of 1427 James assembled a parliament at Inverness, summoned the Celtic chieftains to attend, and then with his usual quick, decisive energy, arrested about fifty of them. Some were put to death, others were imprisoned in strong castles, and in distant parts of the kingdom. The Lord of the Isles himself suffered a year's captivity, and was then released after the most solemn admonitions to become a loyal and peaceable subject, but immediately gathering his savage hordes, he attacked and burned the town of Inverness. James instantly collected an army of ten thousand men, overtook the Islesmen in a marsh of Lochaber, and routed them with bloody slaughter in June, 1429. Most of our readers will remember the abject submission which this anarch was forced to make two months later in the chapel of Holyrood, when, attired only in his shirt and drawers, he fell upon his knees at the high altar, and presented a naked sword to the king. His life was spared, but after his release from Tantallon Castle he appears no more in the history of this reign.

The next great blow that James struck at the power of the nobles fell on the house of March. That house had never been sincerely loyal. It was not of Scottish origin. The first Cospatrick was an English exile to whom Malcolm Ceannmor had given an asylum and lands in

Lothian. His descendants had repeatedly showed their lack of patriotism since the days of Wallace. In James's youth it was an Earl of March who revenged a private affront by renouncing his allegiance, and fighting on the side of England at Homildon Hill. Albany had condoned his offence, allowed him to return to Scotland, and received him into favour; but the forfeiture of his estates in the reign of Robert III. remained legally unrecalled, and in January, 1434, a parliament held at Perth unanimously decided that they ought to revert to the Crown. Unfortunately it was not the traitor himself who experienced the relentless justice of the king, but his son, against whom personally nothing could be urged, though James probably suspected that in his hour of peril he could hope for no help from any member of an unfaithful house. Yet we can trace a certain shrinking from the consequences of the decision at which his parliament had arrived. He would not have the proud and powerful noble sink down into a "nameless outcast," and offered him the titular Earldom of Buchan with an annual pension of four hundred marks; but March scorned to accept the paltry compensation, and withdrew to England in rage and disgust.

No one can say exactly when the malcontent nobility began to draw together, and secretly discuss the dangers which threatened them. Probably from the first year of the king's restoration, there were many who disliked and distrusted his policy. All who had been intimately associated with the regents, and who had profited by half a century of license and outrage, were sure to be alarmed and indignant at the stern measures employed for the suppression of anarchy. One parliament after another was held, in which laws mainly of the most just and beneficent character were passed, and which embraced nearly every matter of interest and importance in the national life. New courts of justice were established, which sat thrice a year in different parts of the country; old laws were revised and amended; and the acts of Parliament were ordered to be registered, and copies made for the prelates, barons, and burgesses at their expense. In a word, though James was unquestionably the moving power of the whole political machinery of the kingdom, his object was to infuse into his parliaments a sense of responsibility. His administrative energy was in no sense that of an enlightened despot. Every act of his reign, however fierce and sanguinary it may seem, was performed under legal sanction and in a constitutional manner. He strove in this way to carry the nation with him in his multifarious reforms, and, in spite of the malignant hostility and fatal triumph of his personal foes, I see no reason to believe that he failed in his great intent.

But that he had from the first a number of disloyal subjects among the nobility is certain, and that he increased this number by the Draconian severity of his justice is no less certain. It is probable that, even before the fall of March, conspiracy was beginning to work. In James's first Parliament it was decreed that the sheriffs should ascertain what lands belonged to the crown during the reigns of his three predecessors, and that the present holders of these must show their charters when the king chose to demand their production. Such orders were calculated to inspire fear in many a breast conscious of ill-gotten gains; and this fear must have been intensified and aggravated by a later statute, which declared that all alienations of lands made during the regencies "in consequence of the demise of a bastard," were "revocable by the crown, although the transaction had been completed by feudal investiture."[1] The second Parliament of James passed laws to prevent leagues among the king's subjects, condemning to death and confiscation all who propagated falsehoods between the king and the people. We have here evidence of some traitorous discontent; and perhaps a suspicion or a knowledge of this feeling dictated the closing act of the Parliament of 1428, by which all the prelates, barons, their heirs and successors, together with the commissaries of burghs, were required to take an oath of fidelity to the queen. It has also been conjectured, not unreasonably, that the sudden disbanding of his army at the siege of Roxburgh in 1436, when the fortress was on the point of capitulating, was caused by the discovery that a large party of his nobles were not only disaffected, but were prepared for armed resistance to his power.

James had received startling proof of this the year before. At a parliament held in January, 1435, Sir Robert Graham had been deputed by the malcontent barons to represent their "grievances." He made a passionate and powerful speech, but his fury carried him beyond all bounds, and he demanded the immediate arrest of the monarch. His allies trembled at this unforeseen audacity, and remained silent. James instantly ordered the daring orator to be seized and hurried off to prison. The only authority for this scene is *The Contemporary Account of the Murder of*

---

[1] Tytler, *Lives of Scottish Worthies*, vol. III. p. 32.

James I., published by Pinkerton, who dates the MS. about 1440, but it is not intrinsically improbable. Sir Robert Graham was the uncle of the Earl of Strathearn, whom James had deprived of his title and estates in 1427, and he may have been dissatisfied with the recompense that his nephew received, viz. the Earldom of Menteith. It is clear from the desperate and revengeful character of the man, that he needed small provocation to entertain and nourish the most ferocious animosity. He was one of those truculent spirits to whom feudal privilege was the very breath of life, and who could not endure a government that was bent on making the most arrogant noble as submissive to the law as the poorest serf on his lands. This was an insufferable disgrace and humiliation to men like Graham who, brought up to the love of license in the evil days of the regency, were easily goaded into mutiny by the inflexible policy of the king. The document to which we have just referred informs us that Graham was soon after banished, and his heritages and goods forfeited to the crown. Retiring into the country of the wild Scots (*i.e.* the Highlands), he renounced his allegiance, in a letter full of the bitterest complaints, and swore that if ever he could get the chance he would slay the tyrant with his own hands.

Probably about this time Graham drew the Earl of Athole, uncle of James, into a plot to murder the king, which he had planned in his savage retreat. The bait offered to the aged noble was nothing less than the crown itself. There is no reason to believe that any other person of distinction was privy to the design. A plot, especially a plot to murder, is most likely to succeed when it is known only to a few, but Graham may have thought that many would rejoice at its success who would shrink from taking part in its execution. In any case he himself would drink the sweet wine of revenge. Fortune favoured him. James resolved to keep Christmas at Perth. As he rode northward with his attendants, an Ersch spae-wife[1] warned him if he valued his life not to cross the Forth; but doomed men are proverbially deaf to warnings, and James passed on to his destruction. He took up his residence in the monastery of the Black Friars, outside the city of Perth, and there held a succession of splendid festivities. Meanwhile the conspirators were at work. Athole and Stewart, the king's chamberlain, had communicated with Graham, and the time was now fixed for the horrible deed. The outlaw drew near with three hundred caterans from the hills. The evening of the 20th of February had been passed in playing chess, reading romances, singing, piping, and harping, "and in other honest solaces of grete pleasance and disport." Once more that Ersch spae-wife flits across the scene. She forces her way into the monastery, reaches the door of the king's apartment, and implores speech of him, but is told by the usher to come back on the morrow, and vanishes with words of mournful omen on her lips. It is needless to repeat the details of the assassination, which are stamped on every memory. The rush of the savage Highlanders at midnight over the planks laid across the garden moat, the gleam of torches, the clatter of harness, the dread suspicion of the king, the broken locks of his chamber, his momentary escape into a vault beneath by an exercise of

[1] Prophetess.

superhuman strength, his accidental discovery, the agonizing struggle with his murderers, and his pitiless butchery (his body was almost hacked to pieces), are the chief incidents in a night the ghastly horror of which has no parallel in the annals of Scottish kings.

We have sketched merely the sharp outlines of James's career as a ruler. His reign is in reality crowded with action. Nobly did he keep the promise which, according to Bower, he made on his return from captivity:[1] "By the help of God, though I should myself lead the life of a dog, I shall make the key keep the castle, and the bush secure the cow." His Parliaments were incessantly at work. It would take pages even to enumerate the statutes they enacted. Nothing escaped their vigilant attention; and it is certain that during the life-time of the monarch, the most turbulent barons were afraid to openly resist the authority of his officers. Bower exults in the recollection of those happy days: "The people then sat in the opulence of peace, secure from ravagers, elate in heart, and tranquil in mind, because the monarch had wisely expelled quarrels and rapine from the state, had appeased discord, and reconciled enmity."[2] There is here no doubt something of the fiction that is inseparable from panegyric, but the language could only have been applied to one who had subdued for a time the evils of disorder and the outrages of barbarism.

[1] *Scotichronicon*, vol. II. p. 511 :—"Si Deus mihi vitam dederit, ipso auxiliante, et vitam saltem mihi caninam praestante, faciam per universum regnum clavem castrum, et dumetam vaccam . . . custodire."

[2] *Scotichronicon*, vol. II. p. 510 :—"Sedebat igitur tunc populus in opulentia pacis, a raptoribus securus, in jucunditate cordis, serenitate mentis, et tranquillitate animi ; eo quod rex sapienter e regno pepulit simultates, compescuit rapinas, discordes sedavit, et inimicos concordavit."

K

We do not believe that James's toils made his life miserable. No ruler could possibly be unhappy who saw peace and prosperity come back to a land that had suffered wretchedness for a hundred years. He had, it is true, much grim justice to perform; but to James who loved justice with a fierce passion, the execution of criminals was not in the least degree painful. We rather imagine that it made him feel "life was worth living" when he was able to punish a ruffian as he deserved. Bower has a case in point.[1] He tells us of a poor "Shunamite," *i.e.* a widow, who was plundered in the "transalpine" parts of the kingdom (the Highlands, it is to be suspected) by a robber who was notorious for his crimes. She swore in his presence that she would never wear shoes again till she had laid her complaint before the king. "You lie," said the spoiler, "I shall take care that you are shod before you see him," and instantly had two horse shoes nailed to her feet. She survived the agony of pain, made her way to court, told the king her story, and showed him the cruel wounds, yet unhealed. James was transported with indignation, and ordered the savage miscreant to be hunted down. When taken he was carried to Perth, and condemned to death. A shirt was thrown over him on which was painted a picture of his crime. For two days he was drawn through the streets of the city to excite the abhorrence of the people, then he was dragged at the tail of a horse, and finally hanged. It is reasonable to believe that James felt a glow of happiness amounting to rapture when his sheriff (*Vicecomes*) sent him the news that this cateran was in his power, and that he fixed his doom with a stern but most real joy.

[1] *Scotichronicon*, vol. II. p. 510.

But apart altogether from the high satisfaction that accompanied or followed the discharge of his duty, there is evidence that James's life was full of the vivid happiness that belongs to bright and cultured genius when placed in a brilliant sphere. Bower in the two chapters of the *Scotichronicon*[1] devoted to a description of the " virtues " of the Scottish king, gives us a very minute account of his personal appearance, his skill and strength in all manly and graceful exercises, and the rich and various resources of his leisure. In wrestling (*ad colluctandum*) he feared none; he was a first-rate archer (*optimus arcitenens*), dextrous in spear-play (*hastiludiator gnarus*), could throw the stone or the hammer farther than most (*ultra communem usum hominum*), could run as if his feet had wings (*alipes*), and excelled in horsemanship and walking (*eques strenuissimus et viator*). But the old chronicler becomes rapturous over the king's skill in music. Not only was he a fine singer, but there was scarcely an instrument of which he was not master: organ, psaltery, flute, lyre, drum, trumpet, pipe, and harp, the last of which he played like another Orpheus (*tanquam alterum Orpheum.*) When the cares of public business allowed, he delighted in the pursuits of literature and in elegant penmanship (*operi artis literatoriae et scripturae*), in drawing and painting (*protractioni et picturae*), in the cultivation of the garden and the orchard (*in jardinis herbarum et arborum fructiferarum plantationi et inserturae*), and in all honest sports and solace that could enliven the spirits of his followers (*honestis ludis et solatiis ad refocillandum suorum sequacium animos*). Bower also

---

[1] Book xvi. cap. 28 and 30.

speaks of "mechanical arts" which James learned in England, and ascribes to him an "incredible ardour for scriptural knowledge," of which unhappily there is no evidence in his life, unless the martyrdom of the Bohemian physician, Paul Crauar, for secretly teaching the doctrines of Wiclif, presented itself in that light to the orthodox Abbot of Inchcolm. Enough has been quoted to show that James had made the most ample provision for the tranquil yet genial enjoyment of his leisure hours: and some sprightly efforts of his genius still remain, to show what joyous humour and human sympathy dwelt in the breast of this remorseless devotee of justice.

The *Kingis Quhair*[1] is generally supposed to have been written during James's captivity, and there can be little doubt that the poem was conceived and mainly composed before he left England; but it may have been retouched about the time of his return to his native country, for in the sixth stanza of canto II. he speaks of his imprisonment as past, while in the epilogue he pours out his profuse thanks for the happiness which his marriage has brought him. The epilogue may well have been added on the occasion of his marriage. It is a kind of epithalamium, and the verse has the rosy bloom of bridal hours. The framework of the poem is an example of that fantastic allegory which enchanted the fancy of the Middle Ages, and which was essentially an incongruous mixture of romantic sentiment and classical fable. This form of allegory was a peculiar product of chivalry—of that vague yet ambitious spirit which sought to surround the poverty and rudeness of medieval life with the glory and grandeur of antiquity.

[1] "Book," a Chaucerian word.

It preceded the revival of learning, which indeed put an end to its daring anachronisms, its grotesque perversions of ancient myths and characters, and its uncritical jumble of crude knowledge. But genius forces its way through every obstacle; and though we can no longer find much pleasure in the phantom world of impossible personages, and in the adventures and pilgrimages of the poet from sphere to sphere, we still delight to trace the presence of imaginative energy in those wonderful descriptions of nature, which seem to us more true and picturesque than anything in our later literature. Chaucer was the first Englishman to give the romantic allegory a home in this country; Gower laboriously seconded the brilliant efforts of his friend and contemporary; and King James became an enthusiastic disciple of both. He calls them his "Maisteris dere," and declares them to be "superlative as poetis laureate." But he is by no means a feeble imitator. He goes his own way, invents his own story, and paints his own pictures with a distinct and original touch. Chaucer and Gower familiarized him with a new form of poetry, which he admired. But he did not copy their productions; he created for himself. In fact, James is a much greater poet than Gower. He did not write so much, but he wrote a great deal better. Nothing in the *Confessio Amantis* is comparable in point of vigour or beauty to the best parts of the *Kingis Quhair*. None the less is it creditable to the king's modesty that he spoke with such honest reverence of the twain, whose renown began to fill all England at the time.

A brief outline of the *Kingis Quhair* may not be superfluous. The poet, awaking at midnight out of his sleep, takes up the *De Consolatione Philosophiæ* of Boethius, a favourite work of the Middle Ages, of which and of its author we have some account. At last his "eyne 'gan to smert for studying," and he lay down again, revolving in his mind the uncertainty of Fortune, and finding a sad illustration in his own history. Wearied out with his "thoughtis rolling to and fro," he gladly hears "the bell to matins ryng." The "fantasye" took hold of him that the bell was a living voice, and that it commanded him to relate what had befallen him. As he had often before "ink and paper spent" to little purpose, he now resolved to write something new. His strange and woeful lot presses upon his recollection, but he fears that he has not ripeness of wit to describe it properly. The images he uses are taken from the sea. His "feble bote" is steered with doubting heart amid the waves and rocks. All through the dark winter night he waits a favouring wind to fill his sails, and invokes with equal piety the help of Calliope and the Virgin Mary. Resolved, however, to proceed, he asks the Muses to let their "brycht lanternis" shine upon him, and guide "my pen to write my turment and my joye." So ends the first canto.

The second is the gem of the poem. Many of its stanzas are hardly inferior to Chaucer's best work of the same kind, and we read them with heightened feelings of surprise and wonder, that a youth of James's rank could under any circumstances have drunk so deeply of the Pierian spring. In the springtime of the year, when the tender flowers are opening under the sunlight, the young prince amid many friendly farewells sets sail for France. His violent capture and his "strayte ward" in an English prison are then touched upon. He paints his long imprisonment as a season of dolour and pain, that he may more poetically contrast it with the sweet relief of love that is coming. Bird, and beast, and fish all live in freedom; why should he suffer such cruel enthralment? Long days and nights he thus bewails his fortune, "despeired of all joye and remedye." But one bright May morning, when he is gazing in listless mood from the window of his prison-chamber on the fair garden below, girdled with hedges of hawthorn and juniper, he listens to the song of the "lytil suete nyghtingale" as it sat on the "small grene twistis" of the "herbere," and finds himself able by some subtle sympathy to interpret it. It is an amorous chant, calling upon lovers to rejoice in their new-born bliss. The royal captive is bewildered by this rapture. "Quhat lufe is this that makis birdis dote?" While he muses over what he has read in books regarding the power of love, he is insensibly drawn to express a wish that he too might be allowed to enter the service of a god who can "maken thrallis free." At that moment his eye falls upon the fairest flower of womankind he had ever seen. His whole blood starts to his heart, and in an instant he understands the magic mystery of love.

His description of the lady's charms is in the highest style of courtly and chivalrous panegyric. Her sweet face, in which there was no menace, her golden hair, her rich attire, loose and open, yet sparkling with pearls and precious stones, her brilliant head-dress with its spangled love-knots, her white enamelled neck, adorned with a chain of delicate gold work, from which, shaped like a heart, there hung a flawless ruby, that glowed like fire upon her ivory throat, are all descanted upon in a strain of innocent admiration and delight. But above and beyond all this splendour of ornament, there was

"Beautee eneuch to mak a world to dote."

But the graces of her mind surpass even those of her person. Here James perhaps anticipates a later knowledge, but the point is a trivial one; it is poetically finer that all her perfections should be set forth in one dazzling picture, than that they should be noted in the mere order of their discovery. The result is an almost ideal image of maidenly sweetness, prudence, dignity, and grace. Yet the fidelity of the king to his accomplished consort through all his troubled life might lead us to believe that he had not greatly exaggerated the virtues of her character.

Now that he knows the secret of bliss, James pours forth his prayers to Venus, and in his immeasurable joy calls upon the "lytil nyghtingale" again to repeat its gladsome song. In bright and vivid verse, in airy and quaint fancies, he eagerly expostulates with the winged minstrel for delaying its amorous notes. At last the gush of melody bursts forth, to which the impassioned prince sets happy words. All the other choristers of the garden become jubilant, in praise of the tender season of the year and the pastimes of loving hearts. At last the lady retires from the garden, and gloom and despair immediately take possession of the prisoner. He lingers at the window till "Esperus his lampis gan to light," and, according to the fantastic imagery of the times (which was itself a Virgilian reminiscence), weeps and wails piteously. At last, "ourset" with sorrow, he falls into a half sleep, half swoon, during the lapse of which wonderful things happen to him in a vision.

The third, fourth, and fifth cantos are devoted to his adventures in allegorical realms, and may be more briefly sketched. Raised mysteriously into the air, he finds himself "clippit in a cloude of crystall clere and faire," and so passes from sphere to sphere until he reaches " the glad empire off blissful Venus," whose court is described at once with minuteness of detail and vivacity of fancy. All kinds of martyrs and confessors of love are presented to us; the true and the false, the happy and the unhappy; those that would fain have loved, but who were forced into a cloistered life; princes famous for their gallantry, and the poets who recorded their deeds. In a soft retreat he finds the "goddesse of delyte" herself, reclining on her couch, attended by her usher "Fair Calling," and her thrifty chamberer " Secretee." He salutes her in his finest and most copious rhetoric, " sterre of benevolence! Pitouse princesse, and planet merciable!" "suete well off remedye,"

> "And in the huge weltering wavis fell
> Off lufis rage, blissful havin, and sure,"

and implores her help in his suit. If it were possible for us to take a lively interest in this antiquated form of poetry, we could not fail to be moved by the passionate enthusiasm that here animates James's verse. As it is, we are forced to feel that a true and genuine love fires his bosom, though the literary fashion of his age required a dreary pedantry of expression that chills all modern sympathy.

Venus explains to him at considerable length that the help of more than one goddess is needed in his difficult case, and sends him to the sphere of Minerva under the guidance of "Gude Hope," by whose advice he may "atteyne unto that glad and goldyn floure." He soon reaches "Minerve's Palace, faire and bryt," is admitted by the master porter, "Pacience," and, after admiring "the strenth, the beautee, and the ordour digne" that mark her court, is presented to the wise goddess by his guide. Once more he tells the story of his love. Minerva listens patiently, and when he has finished explains to him that if his passion be founded on virtue and not on "nyce lust," she will lend him her aid. She dilates with great earnestness on the merit of fidelity in love, denounces profligate wooers who employ their wits "the sely innocent woman to begyle," and laments that so few men are true and honourable in their courtship. James declares that the "gude fame" of his lady is dearer to him than all the gold in the world. When Minerva is finally satisfied that his affection is "set in Cristin wise," she promises her most cordial help. It does not seem to amount to much after all, as it chiefly consists of a metaphysical discourse on free will and necessity, winding up with a recommendation to her visitor to seek the help of her whom clerks call Fortune.

His journey in quest of this famous deity is described with Chaucerian richness of imagery and melody of verse. Again and again the pupil in his graphic and graceful pictures imitates and equals his mighty master. The "lusty plane" through which a pleasant river ran, murmuring musically on its lucid course, the flowers fragrant and bright, the glancing motions of the little fishes, the long rows of trees loaded with delicious fruits, the brilliant array of beasts of divers kinds that he passed on his way, are all touched off with the most artistic beauty. At last he spies "Fortune, the goddesse, hufing¹ on the ground." Her great wheel is right before her, and multitudes are clambering upon it. Underneath lay an ugly pit, "depe as ony helle." Whoever fell into it as he climbed, "com no more up agane tidingis to telle"; and very few could keep their footing or their seat on the revolving spokes. The vicissitudes of human life are finely symbolized. When the poet has told her why he has come, she encourages him to step on to the wheel, rallying him kindly on his faint-heartedness. At this critical moment he awakes from his swoon, and the vision comes to an end.

The sixth and last canto is very brief, but it is exquisitely tender and sweet. Opening with an apostrophe to man's "besy goste," that is ever restless till it finds rest in that Heaven from which it came, it goes on to tell how miserable the royal lover felt when he discovered that his happiness was only a dream; but suddenly a white turtle-dove—the bird of Venus—alights on his hand, and looks at him so softly that the "kalendis of confort," or dawn of hope, begins to rise in his heart. In her bill she holds a stalk of "red jeroffleris,"² on whose leaves are written in golden letters the blissful news that his cure is decreed in Heaven, and that Fortune has smiled upon his suit. Then follows the epilogue, of which we have already spoken—a thanksgiving ode, ringing with notes of manly joy, and inspired with a chivalrous devotion that might almost be considered a romantic exaggeration, but for the witness furnished by the king's domestic life.

The *Kingis Quhair* marks a new epoch in the history of Scottish poetry. The plain, unadorned, semi-prosaic

---

[1] Dwelling.   [2] Gillyflowers

style of the metrical chronicles gave place to a delicacy and refinement of imaginative feeling, a richness and elegance of diction, and an artistic melody of verse hitherto unknown. The revolution in the national literature was as great as the revolution in the national policy, but it was more benign in its operation and more lasting in its effects. Henceforth Scotland has a share in the culture of western Christendom. All that Chaucer learned from the trouveurs of France and the poets of Italy, who heralded the Renaissance of letters, passed into the spirit of the Scottish prince, and was transmitted by him as an impulse and inspiration to the most gifted of his successors. To what extent his work was read or studied in his own country, we cannot say. There is a singular absence of precise or definite allusion to the influence exercised by James on the development of Scottish literature. Historians dwell almost exclusively on his personal accomplishments, and we can only trace the impress of his genius in the character and quality of the subsequent poetry of the nation. But it is hardly possible to doubt that to him we mainly owe the new direction that Scottish poetry took, and which it continued to maintain, till the passionate desire for reform in religion absorbed into itself all other enthusiasms, literary and moral. Chaucer is the great emperor to whom the lesser kings and princes of verse pay homage. They walk in his light, they imitate his style, they celebrate his praise ; some delight in his brilliant and courtly allegories ; some in his fresh and fragrant landscapes ; some in his graphic portraits of men and women ; some in his sly and subtle humour, or coarse and scandalous drolleries—all in that art of bright, vivid, and graceful expression which literature invariably acquires when it begins to understand the charm of classic antiquity. This was an English conquest to which no exception could be taken by the most patriotic Scot. The victories of civilization inflict no wounds on national pride, and no shame follows in their wake. They are twice blessed—in the nation that bestows, and in the nation that receives, the boon of a higher culture. Nothing is lost that is worth preservation. The old traits of national character are as marked as ever under the new forms. In no Scottish monarch is the *perfervidum ingenium Scotorum* more nobly conspicuous than in James. The fiery energy, the passionate earnestness, the stern tenacity that have distinguished the greatest Scots, from Columba to Chalmers, are in his case only placed in more striking relief by the splendid accessories of his English education.

When he turned from the airy realms of romantic allegory to the humble scenes of common life, we see with what admirable skill he used the Doric pipe. *Christis Kirk of the Grene* and *Peblis to the Play* are instinct with the most genuine spirit of nationality; and to this day the vivacity of the description, the blytheness of the humour, the geniality of the satire, and the merry music of the verse, have an indescribable charm for his countrymen. It may be admitted that a shade of suspicion rests on the authorship of these poems. No contemporary evidence ascribes their composition to the Scottish king; but the whole weight of traditional authority is in his favour. Major[1] says that he wrote *et jucundum artificiosumque illum*

---

[1] *De Gestis Scotorum.*

cantum ("that blythe and skilfully composed song,") beginning, "At Beltayn," which are the opening words of *Peblis to the Play*; while in George Bannatyne's MS. collection of old Scottish poems written before 1568 (the date of his manuscript), *Christis Kirk of the Grene* stands first in the order of antiquity, and has at the end of it these words—"Quod King James I." There is absolutely no external evidence of the slightest importance in favour of James V. The internal evidence also points to the age of the earlier ruler as the date of its composition. James I. knew the value of the bow in war. Most of the famous victories of the English in France and Scotland had been won by the deadly skill of their archers. His own countrymen trusted too much in their ring of spears, and neglected the practice of archery. Among his earliest enactments on his return from captivity, was one ordaining "that every person after twelve years of age busk himself as an archer; that bow-marks be maid near every paroch kirk, wharin on holidays men may come and schutte at least thrice about, and have usage of archerie; and wha sa uses not the said archerie, the laird of the land or the sherriff sall raise of him a wedder." *Christis Kirk of the Grene* is a jocund skit upon the ludicrous incapacity of the Scottish rustic to handle a bow; and the king may have wished to fortify the statutes of law by the aids of ridicule and satire. But the poem is far more than a satire; it is the work of a man who delights in the society of his fellow-creatures, and in the bright world about him; who has a heart for simple, homespun, pleasures, a kindly sympathy for wooers and maidens in their holiday moods, a quick eye for pretty faces and for the coy ways of sprightly damsels, and an overflowing appreciation of the fun and drollery of rustic strifes. If James was the author of this inimitable piece, he must rank among Scots as the earliest of those graphic humourists who have sought the sources of their inspiration in the common life of the people, as the originator not only of the learned and ornate poesy of his country, but of that humane and joyous realism which attained its perfection in the verse of Burns.

Robert Henryson, the most exquisite of the Scottish Chaucerians, is little more than the shadow of a name. He has no place in the history of his times, and his personal biography is almost a blank. Mr. Laing, whose edition of the poet's works[1] leaves nothing to be desired, conjectures that he was born not later than the year 1425. "That he received a liberal education, and proceeded 'in the schools' through the usual course till he had taken the degree of Master of Arts, might be inferred from the circumstance that he is uniformly styled MASTER ROBERT HENRYSON, a title given in those days exclusively to persons who had received this academical distinction. At that period there existed only two Universities in Scotland—that of St. Andrews, founded in the year 1411; and of Glasgow, in the year 1451; but his name does not occur in the existing registers of either; and we may conclude that he pursued, or at least completed, his studies at Louvain, Paris, or some other foreign University, where prelections in canon and civil law were given."[2] On the 10th of September, 1462,

---

[1] The Poems and Fables of Robert Henryson, now first collected, with notes and a memoir of his life. By David Laing. (Edinburgh: William Paterson. 1865.)

[2] *Ibid.*, Memoir, p. xi.

"The Venerable Master Robert Henrysone, Licentiate in Arts and Bachelor in Decrees, was incorporated or admitted a member of the newly-founded University of Glasgow."[1] He settled in Dunfermline, where he practised as a notary public, his name occurring thrice in that capacity as a witness to deeds dated March, 1477-8, and July, 1478. Absolutely nothing more is known for certain regarding him. There is no record of his death, which Mr. Laing is disposed to place " a few years before the close of the fifteenth century," and he is first called "scholemaister of Dunfermeling" in the Edinburgh edition of his "Fabilis" published by Henry Charteris in 1570. It is not at all unlikely that he held this office, and if we accept the tradition, he may be safely pronounced the greatest poet that his order has yet produced—at least in Scotland.

The greater part of Henryson's life is embraced under the reigns of James II. and James III. His boyhood witnessed the firm rule of the poet-king, and his closing years the vigorous administration of the gallant prince who fell at Flodden; but all between was occupied by those scenes of turbulence and treason which we have already tried to sketch; and their shadow seems at times to rest upon his verse. He does not cry aloud against oppressors and demand reform; he is in no sense a moral satirist like Lyndsay, inflamed with righteous rage; but as he looks out from the peaceful cloisters of Dunfermline Abbey on the wild confusions of feudal strife, on the havoc made of men's lives and fortunes, there falls upon his heart a deep conviction of the vanity of earthly possessions and pleasures; he takes refuge in religious

---

[1] *Ibid.*, Memoir, p. xii.

meditation, in a faith that conquers the world and opens the gates of the Kingdom of Heaven.

Such poems as *The Abbay Walk, The Prais of Aige, The Ressoning betwixt Deth and Man*, are fine examples of the grave, serious, and thoughtful spirit of the writer. Their didactic tone is not that of a cold philosophy, but of a warm and living Christianity. As he paces alone the cloisters of an abbey "fair to se," and muses on the changeful fortunes of men, the divine truth is brought home to him that nothing in this world comes by chance, that all happens by the great provision of God, and that the supreme duty of man is loyal obedience to the mysterious Will.

"Obey, and thank thy God of all."

The Prais of Aige is distinctly coloured by the public calamities of his time. In the following lines we can read the protest of a meek and gentle and pious nature against the brutal license and greed of the feudal magnates :—

"Now trewth is tynt,[1] gyle hes the governance,
And wrachitness hes turnyt al fra weill to wo ;
Fredoume is tynt, and flemyt[2] the Lordis fro,
And cuvattyce is all the cause of this."

The burden of the poem is

"The moyr of aige the nerar hevynnis blis."

It is supposed to be sung in a garden of roses by a man, old and decrepid, but with a clear and sweet voice. He is full of joy at the thought of parting with this false world, where nought is certain but uncertainty.

[1] Lost.   [2] Banished.

> "This day a King, the morne na thing to spend!
> Quhat haif we heyr bot grace us to defend?
> The quhilk God grant us till amend our myss,
> That till His joy He may our saullis send;
> The moyr of aige the nerar hevynnis bliss."

Still more solemn and impressive is the dialogue or "Ressoning" between Death and Man. The former proclaims his resistless power. None can withstand him, "paip, empriour, king, barroun, and knycht." Man, for a moment boastful of his youth, refuses to yield to the stranger; but when the dread name of the latter is announced ("Thay call me Deth"), his arrogance vanishes in confession of sin and humble acceptance of his fate:

> "Jesus, on thee, with peteous voce, I cry,
> Mercy on me to haif on domisday."

Beautiful in its way is *The Bludy Serk*, a version in ballad-metre of one of those curious allegorical tales in the *Gesta Romanorum*, in which religious doctrines are expounded through exploits of chivalry. The deliverance of the soul from the power of Hell was, perhaps, never more quaintly or poetically told than in this piece, where each thing seems a part of some mortal adventure in real life, till all is moralized at the last into theology. *The Salutation of the Virgin* is a devotional lyric, full of sweetness and grace.

> "O lady, lele and lusumest,
> Thy face moist fair and schene is!
> O blosum blith, and bowsumest,
> Fra carnale cryme that clene is."

The strictest Protestant will readily forgive its Mariolatry for the sake of the deep spiritual feeling that pervades and sustains it. There is no evidence that

Henryson had taken priest's orders. He is nowhere styled *clericus* or *presbyter;* but his heart is tuned to heavenly music, and he lives " as ever in his great Taskmaster's eye."

Henryson's piety, however, has nothing austere or ascetic about it. It is sweet and natural, and is compatible with sympathies and interests from which a monk would shrink as from sin. An instance in point is the ballad of *Robene and Makyne,* one of the loveliest pastorals in all literature. Every stanza has its own particular charm. The green hill with its belt of wood, and flock of sheep, the summer night warm and dry, the yearning passion of the maid, the cruel repulse by the cold-hearted youth, his quick remorse, and unavailing efforts to win the love he had slighted and scorned :

> " Robene, thow hes hard soung and say,
>   In gestis and storeis auld,
> ' The man that will nocht quhen he may,
>   Sall haif nocht quhen he wald.'
> I pray to Jesu, every day,
>   Mot eik thair cairis cauld,
> That first preissis with thee to play,
>   Be firth, forrest, or fauld : "

—all stands out, even in the antique dialect, as clear and vivid as if Burns or Tennyson had penned the verses. How pathetic the sad assurance of these lines —

> " Robene, that warld is all away,
>   And quyt brocht till ane end,
> And nevir agane thairto perfay
>   Sall it be as thow wend."

The note here struck is of the truest. The poet

leaves Makyne going home "blyth anneuche" "attour" the forest grey, while Robene sits down in dolour and care at the foot of a steep bank to mourn his inexpiable folly. Scotsmen may reasonably be proud that in the department of pastoral poetry their mother tongue is at least the rival of Greece, and the superior of Rome; for there is nothing in the Thyrsis or Amaryllis of Theocritus that can excel, nothing in Virgil that can equal, in point of sweetness and fidelity to nature, Ramsay's *Gentle Shepherd* or Henryson's *Robene and Makyne*.

The fables ascribed to Æsop have found their way into every European tongue, but they have never been illustrated with such wealth of descriptive imagery and fulness of incident, humorous and sentimental, as in the forgotten version of this gifted Scot. Lord Hailes has censured the prolixity of these renderings and pronounced them tedious; but though they lack the terseness of the classic originals, few will agree with his lordship's criticism. They have the genuine character of such works. The animals are clothed with all the attributes of humanity, and are presented in the guise of the poet's own time. Thus we have, as it were, unintentional delineations of contemporary manners and institutions that are as fresh are they are valuable. Take for example one or two circumstances from *The Taill of the Uplandis Mous and the Burges Mous*. While the former lived solitarily like an outlaw, the latter is "gildbrother" and "ane free burges." When she goes to visit her upland sister, she passes out of town barefooted, with pikestaff in her hand like a poor pilgrim. At their meeting they embrace and kiss each other, now laughing and now crying for joy. The rustic dinner is brought from the "butterie," and excites the scorn of the city-bred "madame." By and by we have an elaborate civic feast "with all the coursis that cuikis culd defyne." In fact take away the element of fable and in every case these poems resolve themselves into pictures of real life by an artist who has a fine eye for "the outward shows of sky and earth," for social usages, and traits of character; and whose shrewdness of observation is sweetened by a kindly humour that makes us love the writer.

In no essential respect does the literary skill of the workmanship seem to us inferior to Chaucer's; but Henryson most nearly approaches the master in his *Testament of Cresseid*. It is a continuation of Chaucer's *Troilus and Creseide*, and is inspired by a keener moral sense. The English poet leaves the infidelity of the Trojan maid unpunished. While the noble Troilus perishes on the field of battle, his false bride remains in the possession of the treacherous Diomede. Henryson thought her story should have a different ending, and hence his novel episode, a masterpiece of melodious versification and pathetic sentiment. The introduction is charming. It is a frosty night in early spring. A keen north wind is whistling through the air. Henryson draws near the fire, for he is now old and his blood is thin, and after making himself comfortable with a "drink," he sits down with the poem of "worthie Chaucer glorious," "to cut the winter nicht and mak it schort"; but by and by he takes up another "quhair" (his own, of course), in which he finds "the fatall destenie of fair Cresseid that endit wretchitlie." Deserted by her paramour, she sinks into a slough of vulgar vice, "sa giglotlike, takand thy foull plesance"; but at last, apparently from want rather than remorse, steals home to the house of her father, Calchas, who is "keeper" of the temple of Venus and Cupid. He receives her kindly, but she does not venture to face the people going to the "kirk." She conceals herself in a "secreit orature," where she gives full utterance to her anguish, upbraiding Cupid and his mother as the cause of her misfortune. She then falls into an ecstasy, during which the seven planets or deities descend from their spheres and sit in judgment on her sin. Their portraits are sketched with the free and picturesque touch of one who is a master in the art of vitalizing abstractions. We do not indeed recognise the forms of Grecian mythology and art, though here and there a classic feature has been preserved. They are original creations of a northern and medieval fancy, and may rank with the best allegorical figures in *The Fairy Queene* or *The Mirrour of Magistrates*. Take these of " Saturn " and " Mercury " as specimens :—

"His face frosnit, his lyre was lyke the leid,
   His teith chatterit, and cheverit with the chin,
His ene drowpit, how, sonkin in his heid,
   Out of his nois the meldrop fast can rin,
   With lippis bla, and cheikis leine and thin,
The iceschoklis that fra his hair doun hang,
Was wonder greit, and as ane speir als lang.

. . . . . .

With buik in hand, than come Mercurius,
   Richt eloquent and full of rethorie,
With polite termis, and delicious,
   With pen and ink to report all reddie,
   Setting sangis, and singand merilie ;
His hude was reid heklit atouir his croun
Lyke to ane poeit of the auld fassoun.

> Boxis he bair with fine electuairis,
>   And sugerit syropis for digestioun,
> Spycis belangand to the pothecairis,
>   With mony hailsum sweit confectioun,
>   Doctour in phisick cled in skarlot goun,
>   And furrit weill, as sic ane aucht to be,
>   Honest and gude, and not ane word culd lie."

Their sentence is, Cresseid shall be punished with leprosy. When she awakes she finds to her horror that the dream has come true. Calchas takes her to the "spittail hous"; and here, as she lies alone at night in a dark corner, she pours forth a lament on her fearful fate, contrasting her present misery with the splendour and happiness of the days when she was the star of beauty and pleasure. The pathos throughout is so sweet and tender, the imagery so rich and various, the word-painting so felicitous, in spite of an excessive alliteration, that we venture to pronounce this part of the poem the highest achievement of Henryson's genius, and unsurpassed by anything in the whole range of Chaucer's works. The interview between Cresseid and Troilus is a most affecting incident, and is admirably managed. The hapless lady, with her companion lepers, is one day sitting by the wayside, begging for alms, when Troilus rides past in triumph to his native city. Something in the miserable face and form of Cresseid reminds him of his lost darling, and an agony of vague remembrance shakes his frame. He drops a purse of gold and a heap of jewels at her skirt, and then rides on without a word. When she learns the name of her generous benefactor (for she had not dared to lift her eyes), there bursts from her lips a storm of self-upbraiding and a passionate eulogium on her former lover, after which she makes her "Testament," and dies. When Troilus hears of her dread fate and death his pity subdues all sense of wrong. Over her remains he reared a temple of grey marble, with this simple inscription in golden letters:—

> "Lo, fair ladyis, Cresseid, of Troyis town,
> Sumtyme countet the flour of womanheid,
> Under this stane, late lipper, lyis deid."

No one can read this beautiful poem without a deep admiration, both of the imaginative genius and the moral discernment of the author. We have said that Henryson had no place in contemporary history. Outwardly, that is true; yet we may learn from his writings something that the political annals of his time do not teach. Such men as he are never isolated phenomena. They mark the existence of invisible currents of thought and feeling. They have an audience fit, though few, even in a barbarous age, when might is the only right, and they exercise an influence that is none the less powerful because it is unseeen. Though the fifteenth century produced only one Henryson, we have seen that it was prolific in poets of lesser fame; and we may rest certain that, scattered among the universities, and abbeys, and schools, and cathedral chapters of Scotland, were some who shared his literary sympathies, though they were not endowed with his diviner mind, and whose own powers were enriched and strengthened by the splendid efforts of his muse. These men were all engaged in diffusing a higher culture and a more humane spirit. Humble though they might appear from a secular point of view, they were really irresistible, for the God of Civilization was on their side. Poetry is, indeed, not the only nor always the chief factor in human progress; but in the dismal reigns of James II. and James III. we mark with peculiar interest its radiant and beneficent presence.

William Dunbar, "the darling of the Scottish muses," and incomparably the greatest poet of Britain between Chaucer and Spenser, was a native of Lothian, and probably a cadet of the disgraced and impoverished family of March. He can hardly have been born later than 1460, for in 1477 his name figures among the *Determinantes* or Bachelors of Arts in St. Salvator's College, St. Andrews, and that degree could not be taken by students till the third year of their attendance. But of every circumstance of his youth we are absolutely ignorant. In 1479 he proceeded to the degree of M.A., sometime after became a Franciscan friar, and in that capacity (by his own confession) travelled over the greater part of England, and even crossed the Channel to Picardy; but at an early date he renounced his Franciscan habit, and entered the service of James IV. He tells us that he had been employed not only at home, but in France, England, Ireland, Germany, Italy, and Spain; and he sharply complains of the royal ingratitude. What was the nature of his service we can only conjecture. He was probably a clerk to some of those foreign embassies which were so numerous in the reign of this monarch; but his name does not occur in any public record connected with the Court till the close of the century, when he had reached the age of forty. On the 15th of August, 1500, it is directed that a sum of ten pounds be paid out of the royal coffers to "Maister William Dunbar for all the dayis of his life, or untill he be promoted by our sovereign lord to a benefice of the value of forty pounds or more yearly." By this time we must believe he had reached the maturity of his powers. His brother bard, Gawin Douglas, in his *Palace of Honour* (1501) mentions him among the illustrious poets of his country, and he himself, under date 1503, speaks of songs that he made in years gone by. From the books of the Lord High Treasurer we learn that on the 17th of March, 1504, he performed mass in the king's presence—an incident which seems to refute the notion suggested by the occasional license of his verse, that his conduct was such as to prevent James from bestowing on him any ecclesiastical preferment. In November, 1507, Dunbar's pension was increased to £20 a year. In August, 1510, under a warrant of the Privy Seal, we find it raised to £80, " until he be promoted to a benefice of £100 or above "—a promotion eagerly desired and repeatedly implored, but which, for some cause now unknown, was never obtained.

His poems enable us to fix one or two more dates in his obscure history. He accompanied Queen Margaret on her visit to the North of Scotland in 1511; and he lived long enough to lament the recurrence of feudal anarchy after the calamity of Flodden in 1513; but there is no further reference to him in the contemporary records, and it is only by inference that his death is supposed to have happened about 1520. The external circumstances of his history are hardly better known to us than those of Henryson's, but his character, and the conditions of his life, are so graphically portrayed in his works, that we scarcely feel the need of a detailed biography. As the shadow of poverty constantly attended him, as his marvellous genius never won a dignified recognition or secured for its possessor any social distinction, it may be doubted if much that is interesting or edifying could be obtained from a closer inspection of his sordid struggles to extract a livelihood from a prodigal and embarrassed Court.

Dunbar flourished at a time when the old world was passing into the new, when the clouds of ignorance and superstition that had gathered round the human mind during the Middle Ages were rolling off, and lights were rapidly shooting over the whole horizon of European life. The flight of the Byzantine scholars to the West, both before and after the capture of Constantinople by the Turks in 1453, had given a brilliant impetus to the revival of letters; and the new devotion to the literature of Greece had awakened a spirit of criticism and liberal speculation to which Christendom had long been a stranger. Dunbar was born only seven years before Erasmus, and he lived to see the dawn of that vast revolution in religious opinion which received its earliest impulse from the wit and scholarship of the Dutch humanist; but he was in his grave before even its first vibrations were felt on the shores of Britain, and the changes that were to be are not foreshadowed in his verse. Still, though we cannot claim him as in any sense a product of the Renaissance, though he is essentially a Medievalist and a Chaucerian, there is a daring freedom of spirit and speech in his satire that distinctly separates him from all his predecessors, and points to new conditions of life in Scotland.

The reign of James IV. is in truth a new era in Scottish history. The long anarchy of the nobles came to an end for a time. The new king was their favourite, but not their minion. He had prematurely obtained the crown by their successful conspiracy against his father; but his presence in the camp of the rebels at Sauchieburn was involuntary, and as he never displayed the vindictive spirit of a partisan, he was never exposed at home to the malice of foes or the machinations of traitors. Since the age of Robert Bruce, no monarch of equal popularity had occupied the throne. His court was a perpetual revel; and his nobles strove with each other for social distinction. Some of his success was undoubtedly due to that magical charm of manner in which no royal dynasty ever equalled the Stewarts; but James IV. was in fact one of the most accomplished sovereigns that ever swayed the sceptre.

Don Pedro de Ayala, Spanish Ambassador at the Scottish Court in James's time, sent to his master an elaborate description of the Scottish king, his subjects, and his country, which has been preserved in the archives of Simancas, and of which Bergenroth has made an abstract in his *Calendar of Spanish State Papers*. The sketch, it should be remembered, is the work of a foreigner, who had no motive for flattery; who wrote what James was never to see, and who happened to be removed from Scottish influence when he penned his despatch, which bears date London, 25th July, 1498:—

"The king is twenty-five years and some months old. He is of noble stature, neither tall nor short, and as handsome in complexion and shape as a man can be. His address is very agreeable. He speaks the following foreign languages—Latin, very well; French, German, Flemish, Italian, and Spanish; Spanish as well as the marquis, but he pronounces it more distinctly.

He likes very much to receive Spanish letters. His own Scottish language [1] is as different from English as Aragonese from Castilian. The king speaks, besides, the language of the savages who live in some parts of Scotland and on the islands. It is as different from Scotch as Biscayan is from Castilian. His knowledge of languages is wonderful. He is well read in the Bible and in some other devout books. He is a good historian. He has read many Latin and French histories, and profited by them, as he has a very good memory. He never cuts his hair or his beard. It becomes him very well."

"He fears God and observes all the precepts of the Church. He does not eat meat on Wednesdays and Fridays. He would not ride on Sundays for any consideration, not even to mass. He says all his prayers. Before transacting any business he hears two masses. After mass he has a cantata sung, during which he sometimes despatches very urgent business. He gives alms liberally, but is a severe judge, especially in the case of murderers. He has a great predilection for priests, and receives advice from them, especially from the Friars Observant, with whom he confesses. Rarely, even in joking, a word escapes him that is not the truth. He prides himself much upon it, and says it does not seem to him well for kings to swear their treaties as they do now. The oath of a king should be his royal word, as was the case in bygone ages. He is neither prodigal nor avaricious, but liberal when occasion

---

[1] This is the first instance of the term "Scottish" being applied to the Anglian dialect of the Northern Lowlands. Hitherto, and even later, the term "Scottish" meant Gaelic; and even Don Pedro, by what he says in the latter part of the sentence, shows that he recognised Lowland Scotch to be only a dialect of English.

requires. He is courageous, even more so than a king should be. I am a good witness of it. I have seen him often undertake most dangerous things in the last wars. I sometimes clung to his skirts, and succeeded in keeping him back. On such occasions he does not take the least care of himself. He is not a good captain, because he begins to fight before he has given his orders. He said to me that his subjects serve him with their persons and goods, in just and unjust quarrels, exactly as he likes; and that, therefore, he does not think it right to begin any warlike undertaking without being himself the first in danger. His deeds are as good as his words. For this reason, and because he is a very humane prince, he is much loved. He is active and works hard. When he is not at war he hunts in the mountains. I tell your highness the truth when I say that God has worked a miracle in him, for I have never seen a man so temperate in eating and drinking, out of Spain. Indeed, such a thing seems to be superhuman in these countries. He lends a willing ear to his counsellors, and decides nothing without asking them; but in great matters he acts according to his own judgment, and in my opinion he generally makes a right decision. I recognise him perfectly in the conclusion of the last peace, which was made against the wishes of the majority in his kingdom.

"When he was a minor he was instigated by those who held the government to do some dishonourable things. They favoured his love-intrigues with their relatives, in order to keep him in their subjection. As soon as he came of age, and understood his duties, he gave up these intrigues. When I arrived he was keeping a lady with great state in a castle. He visited her from time to time. Afterwards he sent her to the house of her father, who is a knight, and married her. He did the same with another lady by whom he had had a son. It may be a year since he gave up, so at least it is believed, his love-making, as well from fear of God, as from fear of scandal in this world, which is thought very much of here. I can say with truth that he esteems himself as much as though he were Lord of the world. He loves war so much that I fear, judging by the provocation he receives, the peace[1] will not last long. War is profitable to him and to the country."

Here and there in this remarkable letter we can detect a conventional note. It was, in fact, the custom in early times to exaggerate the virtues and attainments of popular monarchs, nor has the practice quite disappeared; but every one must be struck with the absence of hyperbolical diction in Don Pedro's portrait of the Scottish king. He puts down plainly and pithily the results of his observation, and leaves on our mind the impression that he was a man of shrewd discernment and liberal spirit, whose judgment was not likely to be warped by national prejudice. There can be little doubt that the James of Don Pedro's letter is the James of history. We may remember him best by the field of Flodden, and in the page of Scott, but he was a much greater prince than he appears in *Marmion*. The modern poet has only shown us a single phase of his character, his gallantry in love and war, but his reign had features incomparably more significant than his casual amours or his Quixotic invasion of England.

First of all there was in his time a rapid advance in the material prosperity of the country. If we except

[1] *i.e.* with England.

the slight expedition to the border in 1496 in support of Perkin Warbeck's adventure, no English war arrested the course of agricultural and commercial industry during James's reign until its close. Irritations and discontents, it is true, had sprung up even before Henry VIII. succeeded his prudent father. The new Scottish marine which had been created by James III., and greatly enlarged and improved by James IV., was accused of piratical enterprises; and one thing at least is certain, that England, now becoming a great naval power, looked with alarm and jealousy on the extraordinary efforts of her smaller neighbour to become her rival on the sea. The bold exploits of Sir Andrew Wood are recorded by Pitscottie with great minuteness of detail, and though no mention of them occurs in English sources, their historical character must be regarded as above suspicion, since Pitscottie drew his information from the brave and honest seaman himself. The "Michael" built for the Scottish king in 1511 was the largest ship of her time. She "took so mekil timber that she wasted all the woods in Fyfe except Falkland wood,"[1] besides much that came from Norway. Native and foreign shipwrights wrought at her for a whole year. She was 240 feet in length, ten feet thick in her hull, "so that no cannon could doe at her, she cumbered all Scotland to get her to the sea," and cost James £40,000. But like the Great Eastern of our day she turned out a failure, and after a noteless career was sold to the French. Barton's fame as a naval commander was not inferior to that of Wood. He cruised the narrow seas with singular audacity, but in the eyes of the English he was simply a buccaneer. When at

[1] Pitscottie, 237.

last he met defeat and death in the Downs in 1512, the government of Henry refused compensation on that ground. But probably international jealousies would not have led to war had not continental politics lent their fatal aid. These maritime collisions, however, were intermittent, and did not materially affect the peaceful relations between the two countries. The marriage of James in 1502 with the Princess Margaret, daughter of Henry VII., helped to prolong the period of tranquillity.

But, in fact, his energetic administration of justice had, almost from the beginning of his reign, restored confidence, and re-awakened in his subjects an industrial activity, that had slumbered since the death of Alexander III. Everywhere he set his barons the novel task of keeping their territories in order. The Huntlys in the North, the Argylls in the West, were made virtual viceroys of the Highlands; the Douglasses were charged with maintaining the peace of the Borders; and at length the formidable Lordship of the Isles, which had been the source of all the Celtic troubles of Scotland since the days of Somerled, was broken up in 1504, after a series of fierce revolts, and the claim to an independent sovereignty abandoned for ever. Henceforth the chieftains of the Hebrides held their lands of the Crown, and were made responsible for the conduct of their clans. All over the kingdom the harvests were gathered in peace, and foreign trade expanded with the great increase of the native produce. The Spanish ambassador has, in the despatch from which we have quoted, some valuable notes on this point. "I am told," he says, "that Scotland has improved so much during his (James's) reign, that it is worth three times more than formerly, on account of foreigners having come to the country, and taught them how to live. They have more meat, in great and small animals, than they want, and plenty of wool and hides." Again: "Spaniards who live in Flanders tell me that the commerce of Scotland is much more considerable now than formerly, and that it is continually increasing. It is impossible to describe the immense quantity of fish. The old proverb says already *piscinata Scotia*. Great quantities of salmon, herring, and a kind of dried fish (stoque fix) are exported. The quantity is so great that it suffices for Italy, France, Flanders, and England. They have so many wild fruits which they eat, that they do not know what to do with them. There are immense flocks of sheep, especially in the savage portions of Scotland. Hides are employed for many purposes. There are all kinds of garden fruits to be found, which a cold country can produce. . . . The corn is very good, but they do not produce as much as they might, because they do not cultivate (*i.e.* skilfully) the land." Not less significant of the increase of wealth is the following: "The towns and villages are populous. The houses are good, all built of hewn stone, and provided with excellent doors, glass windows, and a great number of chimneys. All the furniture that is used in Italy, Spain, and France is to be found in their dwellings." Some of the Acts of the Scottish Parliament point in a similar direction: one of 1504, for example, ordains "all landed proprietors to form parks with deer, fish ponds, rabbit warrens, dove cots, orchards, hedges; and to plant at least one acre of wood, where there were no great woods nor forests."[1]

[1] Pinkerton, *Hist. of Scot.*, vol. II. p. 409.

Dunbar's poems furnish abundant and valuable evidence of the growth of the nation in wealth and luxury. The wives of merchants can clothe themselves in the costliest fashion when they please. In the *Freiris of Berwik*, Symon Lawder's spouse awaits her lover in a kirtill of silk, embroidered with silver; her other garments shine like gold; her fingers are loaded with rings; her table is covered with cloth of costly green, and all her napery is of the finest quality. In *The Twa Maryit Wemen and the Wedo* the same splendour is visible. The Wedo has gay silks, gowns of engrained cloth, great golden chains, rings royally set with rubies, and she busks her bairns like the sons of barons. When Queen Margaret visits Aberdeen, the burgesses stream out to meet her, in rich apparel, with caps of gold and silk. Four of their number, clad in velvet gowns, bear a pall of "cramasé" above her head. Four and twenty maidens of marvellous beauty, with white hats bravely ornamented, play on timbrels before her; the streets are all hung with tapestry; and the magistrates present her with a large golden bowl full of coins of the same precious material. The king himself set an example of lavish expenditure, which even his father's hoards could not sustain, and which sometimes forced him to practise extortions that a less popular ruler would not have ventured to attempt. His court was thronged with all sorts of needy adventurers. Dunbar's heart was embittered by the favour shown to them. In his *Remonstrance to the King* they are described with an acrid humour that not even the quaint and half-obsolete diction can quench. After a list of the honourable servitors of the king:

> "Kirkmen, courtmen, and craftismen fyne;
> Doctouris in jure, and medicyne;
> Divinouris, rethoris, and philosophouris,
> Astrologis, artistis, and oratouris;
> Men of armes and valyeand knychtis;
> And mony uther gudlie wichtis;
> Musicianis, menstralis, and mirrie singaris;
> Chevalouris, callandaris, and flingaris;
> Cunyouris, carvouris, and carpentaris,
> Beildaris of barkis, and ballingaris;
> Masounis, lyand upon the land,
> And schip wrichtis hewand upone the strand;
> Glasing wrichtis, goldsmythis, and lapidaris,
> Pryntouris, payntouris, and potingaris"—

all of whom he admits to be worthy of the royal patronage, though he proudly asserts that his own work will last as long as the best of theirs:

> "Als lang in mynd my wark sall hald!
> Als haill in everie circumstance,
> In forme, in matter, and substance,
> But wering, or consumptioun,
> Roust, cankar, or corruptioun,
> As ony of thair werkis all"—

he proceeds to stigmatize, with all his wealth of vituperative expression, the ignorant herd of "fantastik fulis, bayth fals and gredy," who fatten on the favours of the king:

> "Fenyeouris, fleichouris, and flatteraris;
> Cryaris, craikaris, and clatteraris;
> Sonkaris, gronkaris, gledaris, gunnaris:
> Monsouris of France, gud clarat cunnaris;
> Inopportoun askaris of Yrland kynd;
> And meit revaris, lyk out of mynd;
> Scaffaris and scamleris in the nuke,
> And hall huntaris of draik and duik;
> Thrimlaris and thriftaris, as they war woid,
> Kokenis, and kennis na man of gude;
> Schulderaris, and schowaris, that hes no schame,
> And to no cunning that can clame."

The accounts of the Lord High Treasurer amply bear out the angry accusations of the poet. Happily they do more. They show us almost the daily life of the monarch in all its aspects. "They enable us to accompany the prince to his chapel royal at Stirling; we see the boys of the choir bending down to remove his spurs, and receive their accustomed largesse; we follow him in his progresses through his royal burghs, and listen to the thanks of the gudewife of the king's lodging, as the generous prince bestows his gratuity; we climb the romantic crag on which St. Anthony's Chapel is situated, and almost hear his confession; we can follow him into his study, and find him adding to the scanty library which was all the times permitted even to a king, the works of Quintilian and Virgil, and the sangbuiks in which he took so much delight; his shooting at the butts with his nobles; his bandying jokes with his artillerymen; his issuing to the chase or the tournament, from his royal castles of Stirling or Falkland, surrounded by a cavalcade of noble knights and beautiful damsels; his presence at the christening of the Earl of Buchan's son, and the gold piece which he drops into the caudle—all are brought before us as graphically as at the moment of their occurrence. And whilst our interest is heightened and our imagination gratified by the variety and brilliancy of the scenery which is thus called up, we have the satisfaction to know that all is true to nature, and infinitely more authentic than the pages even of a contemporary historian."[1]

To the reign of James belongs one memorable statute which may be considered the first imperfect attempt at

[1] Tytler's *Lives of Scottish Worthies*, vol. III. pp. 97-98.

a system of national education, of which we have any record in any country. Schools of course had existed, in one form or another, from the earliest establishment of the Christian religion. The monks undertook with pleasure the instruction of those who had chosen a religious life, and burghal schools endowed by the community are probably as old as the days of the later Alexanders. We read of one Master Thomas of Bennum who writes himself *Rector scholarum de Aberdeen* in the year 1262. In the reign of James I. the alderman and the community of the same town induct a schoolmaster into his office; and in the reign of James III. the "master of the grammar schules of Abirdene" receives a salary out of "the common gude of the toune."[1] But attendance in all such schools was voluntary. We now come upon a compulsory act. In 1496 it was ordained that all barons and substantial freeholders in the realm put their eldest sons and heirs to the schools "fra thai be aucht or nyne zeires of age," and to remain there "quhill they be competentlie foundit and have perfyte Latyne." The statute further provides that afterwards they shall remain three years at the schools of "art" and "jure." The object of this legislation was that justice might reign throughout the realm, and that all sheriffs and judges might know how to do justice, so that the poor people should not need to see the king's principal auditors for every little injury. The penalty for failing to obey this statute is twenty pounds. We have no means of ascertaining with what degree of rigour it was en-

[1] Cosmo Innes's *Sketches of Early Scottish History*, pp. 255-256. The question is more exhaustively handled by Grant in his *History of the Burgh Schools of Scotland; Part I., Schools before the Reformation.*

forced. Mr. Burton thinks the act was mainly hortatory; but even if this were conceded, it can be shown that the exhortation was not in vain. Early in the sixteenth century the famous grammarian, Andrew Simpson of Perth, had at times no fewer than "three hundred scholars under his charge, including sons of the nobility, gentry, yeomen, and burgesses."[1] In fact we may fairly conclude that under the operation of this act something like a national intelligence was gradually awakened, and the gentry and burghers of the Lowlands fitted to receive with enlightened ardour the doctrines of the Reformation.

James's predilection for priests was, we have seen, noted by the Spanish ambassador. His youthful excesses must have often driven him to confession, for his conscience was quick if his blood was warm; but a most singular incident happened in the early part of his reign which shows that he was not in the least degree priest-ridden. In 1494 when he was only twenty-two years of age, some thirty men and women, chiefly belonging to the gentry of Ayrshire, and known as the "Lollards of Kyle," were brought up before him and his council on a charge of heresy. Knox in his *History of the Reformation in Scotland*[2] has given a list of the articles of accusation, which he extracted from the " Register of Glasgow," an ecclesiastical courtbook no longer in existence. They are thirty-four in number, and some are of startling audacity. They denounce the worship of images and saints' reliques, and assert that the consecrated bread remains bread, that every faithful man and woman is a priest, that the

---

[1] Grant's *Burgh Schools of Scotland*, p. 27.

[2] Woodrow Society's edition, by David Laing, vol. I. pp. 8-10.

Pope is head of the Kirk of Antichrist, that he deceives the people with his bulls and indulgences, that he cannot forgive sins, nor remit the pains of purgatory, that the excommunication of the kirk is of no consequence, that the Virgin Mary ought not to be worshipped, that we are not bound to pray in the kirk more than in other places, nor to believe all that the doctors of the kirk have written; that in fine the Pope and his ministers are murderers, and that the chiefs of the kirk are thieves and robbers. The spirit and even the language of Wiclif is recognisable in some of these propositions, but we can hardly resist the suspicion that Knox has given them a Reformation tint. Be that as it may, the king allowed the accused (some of whom "war his great familiaris") freely to defend themselves both by argument and ridicule, and finally quashed the prosecution.

This incident, we may remark in passing, throws an unexpected light upon the religious condition of the country. It has been already mentioned that, early in the fifteenth century, one or two disciples of Wiclif found their way into Scotland, and were burned at the stake for preaching heresy; but, during the confusions that followed the murder of James I., all memory of their work seems to have perished. Hardly a trace of their presence is visible in the reigns of the next two monarchs. Yet suddenly in the reign of James IV. there flashes out of the spiritual darkness of the land, a beam of light as pure and piercing as ever shot from Wittemberg or Geneva. No man can tell its source for certain. There was no stir in England at the time. The German Reformation was still unborn, and Martin Luther but a boy of eleven toiling through his Donatus at the

Latin school of Mansfeldt. The singularity of the phenomenon lies in the fact that it does not appear as something imported from abroad, or called into existence by the agency of priests: it was a native heresy deep-rooted and wide-spread among at least a section of the laity in those western parts of Scotland where two centuries later the Covenanting ardour was hottest. That its chief supporters were found among the gentry or smaller landholders of Scotland, may be taken as a proof that this class, preserved by its political inferiority from the coarse ambition that agitated the lives of the feudal magnates, was unconsciously preparing for the noble position it afterwards assumed when Knox went forth to battle for the truth.

The Church itself at this time as a religious institution was in a bad way, and was fated to become worse. The parish priests had grown utterly indolent and worldly. They almost never preached, contenting themselves with mumbling the service, after which they were wont to join their rustic congregations in the gross frolics of the churchyard or the noisy debauchery of the alehouse. Concubinage was only varied by the seduction of their female parishioners. The friars who strolled about the country, Franciscans and Dominicans, had here, as elsewhere, a great reputation for pulpit oratory, and no doubt in their pristine days, their zeal and eloquence were of a high order; but they fully shared in the general corruption of ecclesiastical morality which spread with shocking swiftness in the fifteenth century, and in the pages of Dunbar and Lyndsay they figure as profligates of the basest sort. The sale of benefices had reached a scandalous height; so had the offence of pluralities. "The great dignitaries of the

Church," says Dr. Cunningham,[1] "set the example, and besides their bishoprics, held abbacies, priories, and parishes, for the sake of their revenues. Forman and Beatoun were notorious for this. Every one grasped as many livings as he could; and if the teinds were got hold of, there was little thought of the cure of souls. Another sacrilegious practice had arisen—bestowing abbacies and priories *in commendam*. The commendator need not be a man of learning and piety; he need not be in holy orders at all; he drew the revenues without being able to discharge the duties of the office. If the abbot was a commendator, the prior did the work; if the prior was a commendator, the sub-prior was at hand. In a previous part of our history we have adverted to yet another evil—the appropriation of parishes, patronage, teinds, everything, by religious houses, who appointed a vicar to serve the cure, or perhaps had the duties perfunctorily discharged by one of their own sodality. The parish priest in this way lost much of his respectability, independence, and income, and the tenth sheaf and the tenth lamb went to fatten the useless inmates of some distant monastery. These things might be tolerated in times of mental stagnation; but it was certain that so soon as men began to think, and inquire, and judge, and condemn, the system must perish. The tree stands stately and erect in the summer's calm, though there be rottenness at the heart; but with the first breath of the hurricane it goes crashing to the ground."

The purity, devotion, and munificence of Elphinstone; the literary fame, the charity and the benevolence of Douglas; all the learning, elegance, and ardour of the

[1] *Church History of Scotland*, vol. I. pp. 270-71.

pre-Reformation scholars could not save the church: they could not even change it for the better; mortification had set in, and the issue was inevitable. The splendour and social license of James IV.'s reign were probably injurious to the morals and habits of the clergy: in Scottish literature, at least, we first come across the wanton and sensual priest in the verse of Dunbar. In the days of James V. he wears a still uglier aspect: he is sodden in vice and drowned in superstition, though already the echoes of the new faith are heard across the Tweed, and Lyndsay's burning scorn is beginning to inflame the popular imagination. In the hour of its final trial the old Latin Church found no friends in Scotland. The commons turned with loathing from rites that had lost their sanctity, and the lords were hungering to seize the wealth that had been so unscrupulously acquired.

This then was the character of the age in which Dunbar lived and wrote; material and intellectual progress strangely blent with ecclesiastical corruption and social license. The poet himself is in many ways an image of the time. His anxieties are all of the earth, earthy; no spiritual passion consumes his dross and etherealizes his soul; nor does he see any fairer future in which priests and laymen shall lead purer lives. His religion, such as it is, lingers round the ancient altars and feeds on the ancient forms of faith; but so long as he was in the vigour of his manhood, it does not appear to have excited much devotion in his breast. He looks upon the church as a great collection of benefices from all enjoyment of which a malignant fortune has excluded him. In his *Dream* he records with envious satire that a "Schir Johne Kirkepakar" is "possest in kirkis sevin," and hopes to have more before one is bestowed on a wretched "ballet maker." And he frankly confesses that a little favour on the part of the king would cure him of his melancholy and make him blind to the scandals that now provoke his rage. In short, he is not in any sense a religious reformer. Pinkerton has compared him to Langland; but the author of the *Vision of William concerning Piers the Plowman* was a stern moralist, and his satire is inflamed with a sacred zeal that never once fires the verse of Dunbar.

The humour of the Scottish poet is often licentious and rarely earnest. His story is that of a French fableur or an Italian novelist. Chaucer, it is true, has composed a good deal in the same coarse and sensual strain, but he has moral and spiritual ideals which are wholly unknown to Dunbar. The "Pore Persoune of a Toun," the studious "Clerk of Oxenford," the wise, valiant, and modest knight, the shy, well-mannered, gentle, and pure-minded "Prioresse," the sweet and stainless Constance, and the Tuscan wife Griselda, that miracle of all meekness and long-suffering love, are examples of a class of characters of which Dunbar apparently never had a thought: at least he never attempted similar creations. No doubt as he grew older he became more pious. Such pieces as of *Luve Erdly and Divine, The Merle and the Nychtingaill, The Maner of Passyng to Confessioun, The Tabill of Confessioun, Of the Nativitie of Christ, Ane Ballat of Our Lady* (a most extraordinary jingle of rhymes), *Of the Passioun of Christ*, and *Of the Resurrection of Christ*, may be taken as evidence that with him (as with Chaucer) advancing years had induced him to review his past life somewhat remorsefully. He acknowledges the sin of his "thochtis jolye," by which we may perhaps understand poems like *The Twa Maryit Wemen and the Wedo*, deplores his former indulgence in fleshly lusts, and prays to be kept from all "cursit company" in future. Worldly disappointments, in all probability, contributed to produce this religious mood in which, however, he is neither so genuine nor so unaffected as his predecessor Henryson, though the fire of his genius still glows through his superstitious devotions and his fantastic confession of sins that he never had a chance of committing.

Dunbar's poems are of a very miscellaneous character, and it is not possible to classify them with any precision. They have been grouped under the heads of allegorical, satirical and moral; but single poems, such as *The Dance of the Sevin Deidly Synnis*, exemplify all the three kinds, while a number of interesting pieces could not be placed in any of the divisions. Still this classification is on the whole perhaps the best, certainly the most convenient, that could be adopted, and allows us to survey in a sufficiently comprehensive manner the more conspicuous efforts of his genius.

His most brilliant and beautiful, but not his most original or powerful, poems are *The Thrissill and the Rois*, and *The Goldyn Targe*. Although allegorical, they are not inane. We forget the unreal fantasy in the splendour and vivacity of descriptions. The first is an epithalamium in honour of the marriage of the English princess, Margaret Tudor, daughter of Henry VII., to James IV. The poet is awakened one morning by Aurora "with hir cristall ene." Fresh May, a sweet benignant nymph, stands before him in all her wealth of floral loveliness, and urges him to write something in her praise. He does not think the season genial enough to deserve a song, but May reminds him of his promise to describe "the Rois of most plesance." He follows her into a garden "dulce and redolent off herb and flour, and tendir plantis sueit." The dawn is painted with a Spenserian richness of colour and music, which is all the more wonderful when we remember that Dunbar preceded the author of the *Faery Queene* by a whole century.

> "The purpour sone with tendir bemys reid,
>   In orient bricht as angell did appeir,
> Throw goldin skyis putting up his heid,
>   Quhois gilt tressis schone so wondir cleir
>   That all the world tuke confort, fer and neir,
> To luke upone his fresche and blisfull face,
> Doing all sable fro the hevynnis chace.
>
> And as the blisfull soune of cherarchy [1]
>   The foulis song throw confort of the licht :
> The birdis did with oppin vocis cry,
>   O luvaris so, away thow dully nycht,
>   And welcum day that confortis every wicht :
> Haill May, haill Flora, haill Aurora schene,
> Haill Princes Nature, haill Venus luvis quene."

After this melodious prelude, "Dame Nature," as universal sovereign, commands serene skies and smooth seas to herald the great pageant. Every beast and bird and flower is summoned by appropriate messengers to compear before her highness and do her reverence. As by a sorcerer's charm "all present wer in twynkling of an é." The lion is crowned king of his order. In his description of the noble animal the poet has contrived to suggest the Scottish king by a heraldic allusion :—

[1] The angelic host.

> " On feild of gold he stude full mychtely
>   With flour-de-lycis sirculit [1] lustely ; "

and Dame Nature dismisses him to his rule "in woddis and schawis" with this admirable advice, the political meaning of which shines clearly though its quaint allegorical form :—

> " Exerce justice with mercy and conscience,
>   And lat no small beist suffir skaith na scornis,
>   Of greit beistis that bene of moir piscence ; [2]
>   Do law elyk [3] to aipis and unicornis,
>   And lat no bowgle [4] with his busteous [5] hornis
>   The meik pluch-ox oppress, for all his pryd,
>   Bot in the yok go peciable him besyd."

We have seen that in James's reign the "wild oxen" of feudalism not only ceased to oppress "the meek pluch-ox" of lowly industry, but even shared in its peaceful toils. Some of the nobles for example had a pecuniary interest in the commercial adventures of the time. A similar exhortation is addressed to the eagle when crowned king of birds. He is to be as just to curlews and owls as to peacocks and parrots, and "to mak a law for wycht [6] fowlis and for wrennis."

But the third coronation, that of the "Thrissill" and "Rois," is the *raison d'être* of the poem, and here Dunbar is seen at his best in point of spirit and style. When the "awfull Thrissill" comes forward "kepit with a busche of speiris," [7] he is addressed in words of the noblest frankness, that redound to the honour of the struggling courtier, and deservedly procured for him the friendship of the

---

[1] Encircled. [2] Puissance. [3] Alike. [4] Wild ox. [5] Boisterous.
[6] Strong. [7] The national weapon of the Scots.

English princess. James's wild youth is hinted at quite plainly, and he is enjoined to be a true and faithful spouse:

> "Nor hald non udir flour in sic denty
>   As the fresche Rois, of cullour reid and quhyt :
> For gife thow dois, hurt is thyne honesty ;
>   Considering that no flour is so perfyt,
>   So full of vertew, plesans and delyt,
> So full of blissful angeilik bewty,
> Imperiall birth, honour and dignitié."

When the "Rois" receives her crown there is an outburst of praise and salutation from all the birds, with which as with a marriage peal the poem ends. The passage is a fine specimen of Dunbar's brightness of fancy, his force and luxury of words, and the rich and resonant music of his verse:—

> "Thane all the birdis song with voce on hicht,
>   Quhois mirthfull soun wes mervelus to heir ;
> The mavyis sang, Haill Rois most riche and richt,
>   That dois up flureiss undir Phebus speir ;
>   Haill plant of yowth, haill Princes dochtir deir,
> Haill blosome breking out of the blud royall,
> Quhois pretius vertew is imperiall :
>
> The merle scho sang, Haill Rois of most delyt,
>   Haill of all flouris quene and soverane :
> The lark scho sang, Haill Rois both reid and quhyt.
>   Most plesand flour, of michty cullouris twane :
>   The nychtingaill sang, Haill Naturis suffragane.
> In bewty, nurtour, and every nobilness,
> In riche array, renown, and gentilness.
>
> The commoun voce up raise of birdis small,
>   Apon this wyis, O blissit be the hour
> That thow wes chosin to be our principall :

> Welcome to be our Princés of honour,
> Our perle,[1] our plesans, and our paramour,
> Our peax,[2] our play, our plane[3] felicité;
> Chryst thé conserf frome all adversité."

Like *The Kingis Quhair*, *The Thrissill and the Rois* has a charm of which every allegory cannot boast. It is based on a historic fact, and our interest in the poetic fantasy is heightened by the knowledge that a nation's fortunes were concerned in the nuptials thus quaintly celebrated. For this perhaps as well as for its intrinsic merits "time still spares the Thistle and the Rose." The want of reality is fatal for instance to the *Romaunt of the Rose*, in spite of its gay and shining pictures, and all the fluent sweetness of its lines. We follow listlessly the adventures of *L'Amant* and view with indifference the phantoms that encircle him. Yet it must be allowed that in *The Goldyn Targe*, Dunbar has shown that a mere allegorical vision, destitute of all personal or historical significance, and only designed to prove in the abstract the irresistible power of love, is capable of exciting his imagination to the highest pitch. It is his masterpiece in that style of poetry, and it may challenge comparison with anything of the same sort in the whole literature of romance. All the beauties of *The Thrissill and the Rois* are here seen in rarer and more sparkling perfection. The scenes and figures are painted in brighter colours, and the music of the verse has a more voluptuous swell. Something almost of a lyric rapture runs through his elaborate descriptions. Here are the opening stanzas:—

---

[1] A translation of the name Margaret.
[2] Peace.   [3] Full.

"Bryght as the stern of day begouth[1] to schyne,
   Quhen gone to bed war Vesper and Lucyne,
      I raise, and by a rosere[2] did me rest ;
   Up sprang the goldyn candill matutyne,
   With clere depurit bemes cristallyne,
      Glading the mery foulis in thair nest ;
      Or Phebus was in purpur cape revest
   Up raise the lark, the hevyns menstrale fyne
      In May, in till a morow myrthfullest.

   Full angellike thir birdis sang thair houris
   Within thair courtyns grene, in to thair bouris,
      Apparalit quhite and red, wyth blomes suete ;
   Anamalit was the felde wyth all colouris,
   The perly droppis schuke in silvir schouris ;
      Quhill all in balme did branch and levis flete[3]
      To part fra Phebus, did Aurora grete ;
   Hir cristall teris I saw hyng on the flouris,
      Quhilk he for lufe all drank up with his hete.

   For mirth of May, wyth skippis and wyth hoppis,
   The birdis sang upon the tender croppis,
      With curiouse notis, as Venus chappel clerkis :
   The rosis yong, new spreding of thair knoppis,[4]
   War powderit brycht wyth hevinly beriall[5] droppis,
      Throu bemes rede, birnyng as ruby sperkis ;
      The skyes rang for schoutyng of the larkis,
   The purpur hevyn oure scailit in silvir sloppis
      Ouregilt the treis, branchis, leivis and barkis."

The poet, who is lulled asleep by the murmur of streams and the music of birds, sees in the fantasy of his dream a ship swiftly hastening like a falcon to the shore. It pours forth a wealth of beauty on the blooming meads.

   "Ane hundreth ladyes, lusty in to wedis,
      Als fresch as flouris that in May up spredis,

[1] Began.   [2] Rose-bush.   [3] Float.   [4] Buds.   [5] Beryl.

> In kirtillis grene, withoutyn kell[1] or bandis:
> Thair brycht hairis hang gletering on the strandis
> In tressis clere, wyppit[2] wyth goldyn thredis,
> With pappis quhite, and mydlis small as wandis."

The famous goddesses of ancient mythology are there — Venus, Diana, Juno, Proserpine, Aurora, Minerva, etc.; the Seasons too send their tribute of graces. Nature is queen of all. Birds salute her with their merriest notes; flowers bend in reverence before her, and shed their balmiest fragrance on her path. The dreamer now sees another court where Cupid rules as king, and is surrounded by a host of incongruous deities, "Mars, aufull and sterne," "crabbit Saturn," "Mercurius, wise and eloquent," Priapus, Faunus, Janus, Neptune, Eolus, Bacchus, "the gladdir of the table," and Pluto, "the elrich incubus." In spite of their dignity they play merrily on harp and lute,

> "And sang ballettis with michty notis clere."

Then they join in a dance with the "ladyes." The poet is enraptured, and draws nearer to the scene. Venus espies the rash spectator and bids her archers arrest him. He is dragged before the Court of Love, where Dame Beauty vainly seeks to pierce his heart with her arrows, Reason defending him successfully with his Goldyn Targe (whence the poem has its name). All manner of cunning auxiliaries now come to the help of Beauty in her assault, and the conflict waxes hot. At last a magic powder is thrown into the eyes of the poet's champion by "Perilouse Presence"; he reels like a drunkard in his blindness, and is befooled and banished into the woods. The defenceless prisoner is instantly transfixed. For a brief space

---

[1] Cap.   [2] Girt, encircled.

he rejoices in his wounds. Dame Beauty seems lovelier than before, and he imagines himself in Paradise, but soon strange and forbidding forms gather round him. "Dangere" becomes his constant attendant, and when she takes her departure, she delivers him over to "Hevynesse." His Paradise becomes a Hell. Suddenly a bugle blast from Eolus summons the visionary company to their mystic ship. In a moment the landscape is a solitude.

> "Thare was bot wilderness,
> Thare was no more bot birdis, bank, and bruke."

As the vessel vanishes over the flood she fires off cannon whose echoes fill the skies. The poet starts from his slumber to find a sweet May morning shining around him as brightly as anything in his dream, and closes with a eulogy on Chaucer and his successors, who, in his opinion, could have handled the theme more worthily than himself.

> "O reverend Chaucere, rose of rethoris all,
>   As in oure tong ane flour imperiall,
>   That raise in Britane evir, quho redis rycht,
>   Thou beris of Makaris the tryumph riall;
>   Thy fresch anamalit termis celicall
>   This matir coud illumynit have full brycht:
>   Was thou noucht of oure Inglisch all the lycht,
>   Surmounting eviry tong terrestriall,
>   Alls fer as Mayes morow dois mydnycht.
>
> O morall Gower, and Lydgate laureate,
> Your sugurit lippis and tongis aureate,
>   Bene to oure eris cause of grete delyte;
> Your angel mouthis most mellifluate
> Our rude langage has clere illumynate,
>   And faire oure-gilt our speche, that imperfyte
>   Stude, or your goldyn pennis schupe to write;

> This Ile before was bare and desolate
> Off rethorike, or lusty fresch endyte."

One admirable feature of Dunbar's allegories is their brevity. The *Thrissill and the Rose* extends only to 189 lines; the *Goldyn Targe* to 279. There is no room for prolix adventures in which personified phantoms laboriously imitate the manners of human life. The visions are indeed of a glorious brightness, but they pass swiftly like the splendours of an evening sky, though their celestial sheen never fades from our memories. Yet we do not consider these poems, in spite of their marvellous workmanship, the most genuine or spontaneous efforts of Dunbar's genius. Their landscapes, for instance, never betray a trace of the country in which the poet lives. The imagery, in spite of its magnificence, is purely conventional and general; it would suit Kent, or Normandy, or Provence, as well as the Lothians—or even better. For the rose gardens, the parks of pleasance, the meadow dances, the lavish profusion of flowers, the praise of May, are all borrowed from the romance poets of the south, or from their English disciples, and we can hardly believe that his own "land of brown heath and shaggy wood, land of the mountain and the flood," was ever present to Dunbar's mind, or gave a solitary impulse to his imagination, when shaping his visionary scenes. This holds true of all the Scottish Chaucerians; but it is somewhat surprising that a man of Dunbar's force and originality should have been so completely in bondage to the formalism of allegorical poetry, and able to show the superiority of his genius only by surpassing his predecessors in the pomp and beauty of his style. Not till the age of Allan Ramsay, do we find Scottish poets drawing their inspiration from the scenery of their native land.

But the real strength of Dunbar lies in his satirical humour, which was fed and nourished by his sour experience of life. Here he is thoroughly independent, and portrays the aspects of the society about him with incomparable vigour and pungency. He has no shame, no scruples, no reticence; he shrinks from no foulness of language or grossness of incident. Some of the *Canterbury Tales* are as coarse, *e.g.*, that of the *Miller*, and some intrinsically more lewd, *e.g.*, that of the *Marchaund*, but the Scottish poet has a vocabulary of vulgar ribaldry that has never been equalled. But there is really no limit to the variety of his humour. It is by turns mirthful, mocking, sarcastic, grotesque, profane, stern and intense; and it even shows its Protean character by the multiplicity of its metrical forms.

The Fenyeit Freir of Tungland is a rare specimen of burlesque spiced with gay malice. A certain John Damian, from Lombardy, had established himself at the court of James IV. as a physician and alchymist. He soon became a great favourite with the king, and in 1504 was made Abbot of Tungland in Galloway. Three years later he undertook to fly with wings from Stirling Castle to France, and actually made the attempt. The result was a broken thigh and universal ridicule. Dunbar was no doubt delighted to get the chance of satirizing the exploit of a fortunate quack who had reached the high places of the Church. He turns the adventurer into a Turk of Tartary, who after a vagabond career in Lombardy, where he kills a priest to escape baptism, passes into France and pretends to be

a leech. Under the same character he finally settles in
Scotland. Dr. Hornbook was not more fatally successful in his practice. But he is a poor prelate. He
cares nothing for the rites of religion. The alchymist's
"smithy" is his only haunt. When his experiments
fail and his popularity begins to wane he resolves to
seek his original home by a flight through the air.
Dunbar now gives full swing to his exuberant fancy
which pours forth a torrent of ludicrous images. All
the fowls of heaven gather about the feathered
monster in amazement, and begin to assail him with
savage glee. The disaster is exquisitely comic. He
sinks into mire out of sight, and the exasperated
rooks and crows seek for the vanished impostor in vain.
But no partial quotation could do justice to the
strength and terseness of the language, or to the racy
humour of the incidents.

In *The Justis betuix the Tailyeour and the Sowtar*
there is a Rabelaisian extravagance of dirt, but nothing
really impure. A tournament is held "in presence
of Mahoune" between "a pricklouse and a hobbill
clowtar." It might as well have taken place on earth,
but there is a profane audacity of humour in the
selection of hell as the scene, and in the outrageous
circumstances of the fight, which stamp it as one
of Dunbar's most startling performances. From the
first line to the last it is faultless in execution. Not
one weak word or halting verse occurs; and rhymes—
though this in truth holds good of all his satirical
poems—come to him with Hudibrastic ease and
patness. If we are not indelicately squeamish we may
still venture to enjoy an honest laugh at its broad but
harmless fun. Dunbar followed it up by an ironical

apology in which he tells how an angel from heaven came to him and sang the praises of *Tailyeouris and Sowtaris.*

> "Sowtaris, with schone[1] weill maid and meit,[2]
> Ye mend the faltis of ill-maid feit,
>   Quhairfoir to Hevin your saulis will flie :
> Tailyeouris and Sowtaris, blist be ye.
>
> .   .   .   .   .   .
>
> And Tailyeouris with weill-maid clais,
> Can mend the werst maid man that gaiss,
>   And mak him semely for to sé :
> Tailyeouris and Sowtaris, blist be ye.
>
> .   .   .   .   .   .
>
> In Erd ye kyth[3] sic mirakillis heir,
> In Hevin ye sal be Sanctis full cleir,
>   Thocht ye be knavis in this cuntré :
> Tailyeouris and Sowtaris, blist be ye."

But *The Dance of the Sevin Deidly Synnis* is the most powerful of his poetic creations. It is an allegory both grim and grand, grotesque and horrible. The scene is laid in no imaginary fairyland of sensuous beauty, where mythological figures are grouped together in "most admired disorder," and take part in vain and ridiculous exploits. Hell is rudely opened to our view, and the vices that make havoc of our nature are shown disporting in a ghastly revel under the leadership of "Mahoun." It is the night before Lent, when the Carnival-riot is at its maddest. Everything is morally real though presented in such farcical guise. A dance in hell may seem a contradiction in terms; but the wild humour of the idea has a weird fascination for the mind, and Dunbar never till just at the close seeks by light-heeled levity to mitigate the horror of the infernal

---

[1] Shoes.   [2] Fit.   [3] Show.

vision. Pious souls, as a rule, will shrink from the
poet's daring license of imagination in thus handling
a supernatural mystery, nor do we say that they are
wrong. It is a perilous feat to attempt, and it is rarely
a complete success. The feeling of reverence is apt to
be outraged, especially where (as in the case of Dunbar)
there is no spirit of religious devotion to sustain and
sanctify the humour. But let us be just. The visions
that are conjured up by the poet excite no profane
laughter. We look on spell-bound with a kind of awe,
as each vice comes forward in fit attire and with appropriate followers, who leap through scalding fire and
pursue their freaks with dismal hilarity. Campbell in
his *Specimens of the British Poets*[1] says it would be
absurd to compare it (Dunbar's poem) with the beauty
and refinement of the celebrated *Ode on the Passions*
by Collins. Not a doubt of it. No human being, we
should suppose, ever thought of instituting such a comparison. "Beauty" and "refinement" are not the qualities for which we look in a picture of the Seven Deadly
Sins; but on the other hand there is an intense dramatic
power and vitality, both in the principal figures and in
the acts and circumstances of the rabble rout that
accompany them, to which the exquisite creations of
Collins can make no pretension. Chaucer himself never
showed more force and distinctness of imagination. No
minstrelsy enlivened the dance of the foul phantoms,
for gleemen were not admitted into hell; but at last a
Highland coronach is shouted by a "Makfadyane" and
kindles such an eloquent fury in the bosom of the
Gaelic crowd down below,

"The Devill sa devit[2] wes with thair yell,

[1] Vol II. p. 68.   [2] Deafened.

> That in the depest pot of hell
> He smorit[1] thame with smuke."

Dunbar was a Lothian Angle—a Lowlander of the purest type, and to gratify his antipathy to the Celt he breaks the grim charm of his own vision, and dissolves the phantasmagoria in a crackling squib of satire.

Another and an uglier phase of Dunbar's satirical humour is seen in *The Tua Maryit Wemen and the Wedo*. It is the only unrhymed poem of the author's that is known, or rather it is the only poem of his that adopts the alliterative rhyme of the oldest English verse, and which Langland had striven to revive in his *Vision*. In this, as in every other metre that he attempted, Dunbar displays the most astonishing facility and skill. Indeed no Scottish poet except Burns can compare with him in metrical art. The piece, too, is one of the most powerful and piquant of his productions. Each of the married women is invited in turn by the widow to state

> "Quhat mirth ye fand in maryage, sen ye war menis wyffis,"

and when their stories have been told, and she sees that they lack cunning to be properly successful in their vicious desires, she comes to their help like an old campaigner, and describes her own method of cheating and befooling husbands with incredible frankness:—

> "Quhen endit had her ornat speche this eloquent wedo,
> Lowd thai leuch all the laif,[2] and loiffit[3] hir mekle;
> And said, thai suld exampill tak of hir soverane teching,
> And wirk eftir hir wordis, that woman wes so prudent.
> Than culit thai thair mouthis with comfortable drinkis;
> And carpit[4] full cummerlik,[5] with cop[6] going round."

[1] Smothered. [2] Rest. [3] Praised. [4] Chatted. [5] Gossip-like. [6] Cup.

The pictures set before us are incapable of reproduction in modern times, and they could not even be described except in the most general terms; but there is such an extraordinary exuberance of detail in the poem that we can form a pretty correct idea of the manners, usages, and sentiments that prevailed in the Scottish Court when the "champion of the dames" was king. A love of luxury and ostentation is visible throughout; a fierce hunger for sensual pleasures, and a corresponding heartlessness and hypocrisy. It is not a wholesome satire; it lacks moral bitterness and scorn. Dunbar labours to invest his subject with every allurement and grace, and in spite of the mild query with which he ends—

"Of thir thré wantoun wiffis, that I haif writtin heir,
Quhilk wald ye waill[1] to your wif, gif ye suld wed one?"

we cannot help feeling that his sympathies are not on the side of chastity. The setting of the piece, however, though brilliant, is extravagant and unnatural. Women in rich attire would not in any age sit carousing all night in green arbours, while the dew makes the vales dank; nor would their "glorius gilt tressis," even in a midsummer midnight, cast a gleam on the grass, or the colours of their dresses glitter as in morning sunshine. But there is something worse in the setting than this. Though their language and sentiments are of the most vicious and licentious character, such as even common courtesans might shrink from, the "ladies" are represented as endowed not only with the rarest beauty, but the sweetest modesty of mein:—

[1] Choose.

> "Off ferliful ¹ fyne favour war thair *faceis meik*,
> All full of flurist ² fairheid, as flouris in June;
> Quhyt, seimlie, and soft, as the sweit lillies."

In all this there is a certain depravity of ethical feeling that robs the satire, if it be a satire, of force and dignity. But we prefer to regard the poem as a comedy such as the Restoration might have inspired, in which profligacy is portrayed but not condemned. Yet, if we could sever the setting from the dialogue we should be free to praise without stint the idyllic grace of the description. In the following lines the summer morning stands out in fresh and living beauty:—

> "The morow myld wes and meik, the mavis did sing,
> And all remuffit the myst, and the meid smellit;
> Silver schouris doune schuke, as the schene cristall,
> And birdis schoutit in schaw,³ with thair schill notis;
> The goldin glitterand gleme, so gladit thair hertis,
> Thai maid a glorious glé amang the grene bewis.
> The soft souch ⁴ of the swyr,⁵ and soune of the stremys,
> The sueit savour of the sward, and singing of foulis,
> Myght confort ony creatur of the kyn of Adam."

A far more admirable specimen of moral satire is *The Devil's Inquest*. Dunbar in a dream sees the fiend passing among men, and everywhere finding his own. All swear by the most holy oaths that they speak the truth, and imprecate perdition on their souls if it be not so, and yet they all lie and cheat. To each in turn, priest, courtier, minstrel, merchant, soutar, tailor, baxter, flesher, browstar, maltman, smith, thief, and fishwife, he whispers with grim solemnity—

> "Renunce thy God, and cum to me."

---

[1] Wonderful. [2] Blooming. [3] Wood. [4] Sigh. [5] Hillside.

One cannot but be struck in this poem with the shocking abundance and variety of the modes of swearing, which, in truth, continued to be a shameful distinction of our countrymen long after the Reformation, and which has been explained by philosophical critics as a morbid development of the *pervervidum ingenium*. The different characters are set before us with that picturesque terseness of touch in which Dunbar excelled all his predecessors, except Chaucer. One or two stanzas will give the reader an idea of the style and quality of the piece :—

> " Ane goldsmyth said, The gold is sa fyne
> That all the workmanschip I tyne;[1]
>   The feind ressaif me gif I lie.
> Think on, quoth the devill, that thow art myne,
>   Renunce thy God, and cum to me.
>
> Ane tailyour said, In all this toun,
> Be thair ane better weil maid goun,
>   I gif me to the feynd all fre,
> Gramercy, tailyour, said Mahoun,
>   Renunce thy God, and cum to me.
>
> Ane baxstar sayd, I forsaik God,
> And all his werkis, evin and od,
>   Gif fairar stuff neidis to be.
> The devill luche,[2] and on him cowth nod,
>   Renunce thy God, and cum to me.
>
> Ane fleschour swoir be the sacrament,
> And be Chrystis blud maist innocent,
>   Never fatter flesch saw man with e.
> The devill said, Hald on thy intent,
>   Renunce thy God, and cum to me."

It will be seen from these quotations that human nature—especially the human nature of tradesmen—is

[1] Lose.   [2] Laughed.

much the same in all ages. Loud advertisements have superseded loud oaths, but the vice stigmatized is still rampant.

Tydingis fra the Sessioun is a singularly felicitous sketch of the ups and downs, the movements and motives of suitors at the old Scotch Court of Session, or at the Court of Daily Council or Committees of Parliament, established in the reign of James IV. In every line we have a separate picture, a distinct phase of character or of action; and a bit of keen malevolent satire aimed at "religious men of divers placis," gives the requisite sting to the tail of the poem.

There are many other satiric or quasi-satiric poems of Dunbar which deserve notice for their lively humour, descriptive vigour, or clever versification, *e.g.*, *The Testament of Mr. Andro Kennedy*, an extremely amusing specimen of macaronic verse, *The Complaint to the King* and *The Remonstrance*, from which a quotation has been already made, *The Visitation of St. Francis*, which, besides its other merits, has a biographical value, *To the Merchantis of Edinburgh*, a most graphic and interesting sketch of that city, in fact the oldest that exists, and *The Flyting of Dunbar and Kennedy*, perhaps one of the most astounding instances of verbal scurrility to be found in all literature, yet probably nothing more than a mere *jeu d'esprit*, or a friendly boxing-match between two famous pugilists, "who give each other plaguy knocks, with all the love and fondness of a brother." But our limits compel us to pass them by without further reference. If *The Freiris of Berwik* is not the work of Dunbar, then Scotland has a nameless poet of the same age, who, in comic humour, richness of invention, knowledge of human nature, skill in the arrangement of detail, and a charming vivacity of narrative, rivals the author of the *Canterbury Tales*.

That section of Dunbar's poems in which a moral element predominates is also of great interest, both personal and literary. Most, though not all, of them belong to the later period of his life, and show us the real character of the man better than the more splendid or amusing products of his genius. Disappointment gave a keener edge to his satire, a more reckless license to his humour; but it did not transform him into a cynic. In these poems we see him revolving the different phases of life, and there is no bitterness in his mood. Now and again a repining note is heard when he thinks of the shabby treatment he has received. It runs through all his verses to the king, especially those beginning, "Sanct Salvatour send silver sorrow," in which he tells us how he "wald blythlie ballattis brief," but for the chilling effect of penury; "Off benefyce, Schir, at everie feist;" and "Schir, yit remembir as of befoir," a most touching plea to be remembered in his old age for the service he had given in his youth. But on the whole he dwells far more on the general instability of human fortunes than on his own want of success. Experience has taught him prudence, moderation, justice, and sincerity. He knows how to value things aright; he sees the folly of worldly ambition, greed, avarice, discontent; and with Horatian conciseness and ease he puts into words his wise and sober reflections. The pieces on *Discretioun in Asking, Discretioun in Geving*, and *Discretioun in Taking*, are admirable examples of the best kind of didactic poetry. In the last of them the blundering and injustice that men commit are placed before us in a succession of sombre pictures drawn from the times in which Dunbar lived :—

> "The clerkis takis beneficis with brawlis,[1]
> Sum of Sanct Petir, and sum of Sanc Paullis;
>   Tak he the rentis, no cair hes he,
> Suppois the devill tak all thair sawlis :
>   In taking sowld discretioun be.
>
> Barronis takis fra the tennentis peure,
> All fruitt that growis on the feure,[2]
>   In mailis[3] and gersomes[4] raisit ouir hie,
> And garris thame beg fra dure to dure :
>   In taking sowld discretioun be.
>
>   .   .   .   .
>
> Sum takis uthir mennis takkis,
> And on the peure oppressioun makkis,
>   And nevir rememberis that he mon die,
> Quhyll[5] that the gallowis gar him rax :
>   In taking sowld discretioun be.
>
> Some takis be sic,[6] and sum be land,
> And nevir fra taking can hald thair hand,
>   Quhyll he be tyit up to ane tré;
> And syne thay gar him undirstand,
>   In taking sowld discretioun be."

The verses on "Covetyce" make it quite clear that one of the evils springing from the new-born luxury of James's court life was a spirit of extravagance and greedy ambition. Both gentle and simple appear to have been in some respects demoralized. No doubt

---

[1] So Hepburn stormed St. Andrews, and Douglas Dunkeld.
[2] Furrow.   [3] Land-dues.
[4] Sums paid at the entry of a lease.   [5] Until.
[6] Perhaps an allusion to the piracies of the new fleets of England and Scotland.

there is exaggeration in the picture. Vices that were probably local are represented as national. Scotland, as we have seen, was making progress and not falling back in James's time; but it was also undergoing great internal changes in its social organization, and these never occur in any nation without causing some temporary disorder and mischief. It would be absurd to take the poet's sketch for more than a single aspect of the new order of things; but on the other hand it would be still more absurd to suppose that the most shrewd and sagacious poet that Scotland has yet produced, imagined evils that did not exist. Cards and dice most certainly led to gambling and the ruin of many honourable households. But we need not accept too literally the following lines :—

> "In burghis to landwart and to sic,
> Quhair was plesour and grit plentie,
> Vennesoun, wyld-fowill, wyne, and spice,
>   Ar now decayid thruch Covetyce.
>
> Husbandis that grangis had full grete,
> Cattell and corne to sell and ete,
> Hes now no beist bot cattis and myce;
>   And all thruch causs of Covetyce.
>
> Honest yemen in every toun,
> War wont to weir baith reid and broun,
> Ar now arrayit in raggis with lyce;
>   And all thruch causs of Covetyce."

But he is not soured by the spectacle. Life is still worth living — not, indeed, the false court life, but another, simpler, purer, and happier :—

> "Man, pleiss thy Makar, and be mirry,
> And sett nocht by this world a chirry;
> Wirk for the place of Paradyce,
>   For thairin ringis[1] na Covetyce."
>
> [1] Reigns.

In some poems, as *Gude Counsale, Rewl of Anis Self, Of Deming, How Sall I Governe Me*, we see Dunbar stirring as it were to attain an independence of fortune by the help of serious and solemn thought; in others, as *Best to be Blyth, Of Content, No Tressour availis without Glaidnes*, he is as cheery as if the world had always gone well with him; in others again, as *Advice to Spend Anis Awin Gude*, he advises men, since life is short, to take all the enjoyment out of it they can get. One of the finest and most animated of these ethical productions is that entitled *None May Assure in this Warld*. Here he reviews with melancholy resignation the triumph of injustice, falsehood, flattery, and deceit, and comforts himself and all other unfortunates with the remembrance of the judgment to come:

> "Oh! quha sall weild the wrang possessioun,
> Or the gold gatherit with oppressioun,
>   When the Angell blaws his bugill sture,[1]
> Quhilk unrestorit helpis no confessioun:
>   In to this warld may none assure.
>
> Quhat help is thair in lordschippis sevin,
> Quhen na house is bot Hell and Hevin,
>   Palice of licht or pitt obscure,
> Quhair youlis ar hard with horreble stevin:[2]
>   In to this warld may none assure."

The *Lament for the Makaris*,[3] the last of his poems that we propose to notice, was written during an illness when he thought his own end was near. The reflections are simple and obvious. "This fals warld is bot transitory." All estates of men are swept away by death. There is no security in youth, or beauty, or wit,

---

[1] Loud or strong. [2] Sound. [3] Poets.

or prowess. Even the poets for all their bright magic are not spared.

> "I see that makaris amang the laif
> Playis heir thair padyanis,[1] syne gois to graif."

Then begins the chief interest of the piece, viz. an enumeration of the poets who have flourished in Scotland, with now and then a touch of criticism in passing. In a previous chapter we have given some account of such as are otherwise known or who have left any memorial of their genius, but there are not a few of whom the only record in existence is contained in the catalogue of Dunbar. There is one surprising omission from his list, the name of King James I. Probably this is due to mere inadvertence. After the evidence that has been adduced, no one could be so sceptical as to doubt the historic basis of that monarch's literary reputation, but still it is difficult to imagine by what lapse of memory so illustrious a figure could have been overlooked. Sadness fills the heart of the poet, as he thinks of the gay brotherhood who have all passed "from sunshine to the sunless land," except his friend Kennedy who lay at the point of death.

> "Sen he[2] hes all my Brether tane,
> He will nocht lat me leif[3] alane,
> On forse I mon his nyxt pray be;
> Timor mortis conturbat me.
>
> Sen for the Deid remeid is non,
> Best is that we for deid dispone,[4]
> Eftir our deid that leif may we;
> Timor mortis conturbat me."

---

[1] Pagents.   [2] Death.   [3] Live.   [4] Prepare.

When we consider the originality, strength, and richness of Dunbar's genius, we have no scruple in assigning him the highest place after Burns in the ranks of Scottish poets. Both are distinguished for their force and intensity, their command of terse and graphic language, their daring humour, and their keen insight into the workings of the human heart. Both were galled by poverty and discontented with their lot. Both assailed the favourites of fortune with mingled ridicule and rancour. In Burns, the rich merchant or the haughty noble—in Dunbar, the church-pluralist, is represented as a creature of hateful stupidity and pride. In his *Second Epistle to J. Lapraik*, Burns thus gives expression to his spleenful scorn:

> "Do ye envy the city gent,
> Behind a kist[1] to lie and sklent [2]
> Or purse-proud, big wi' cent. per cent.,
>   And muckle wame,
> In some bit brugh to represent
>   A bailie's name?
>
> Or is't the paughty,[3] feudal Thane,
> Wi' ruffled sark and glancing cane,
> Wha thinks himsel' nae sheep-shank bane,
>   But lordly stalks,
> While caps and bonnets aff are taen,
>   As by he walks?"

Again in his *Epistle to Davie:*

> "It's hardly in a body's power
> To keep, at times, fra being sour,
> To see how things are shar'd;
> How best o' chiels[4] are whyles in want,
> While coofs[5] on countless thousands rant,
> And ken na how to wair't."[6]

[1] Chest or counter. [2] Prevaricate. [3] Supercilious.
[4] Fellows. [5] Fools. [6] Spend it.

Compare these with the indignant grumblings of the older bard, in one of the series "To the King":

> "Jok that wes wont to keip the stirkis [1]
> Can now draw him ane cleik[2] of kirkis,
> With ane fals cairt into his sleif,[3]
> Worth all my Ballatis undir the birkis: [4]
> Excess of thocht dois me mischeif.
>
> Twa curis[5] or thré hes upolandis Michell,
> With dispensationis bund in a knitchell;[6]
> Thocht he fra nolt[7] had new tane leif,
> He playis with totum,[8] and I with nichell![9]
> Excess of thocht dois me mischeif."

Both are bitter at the way things are divided; but here the likeness ends. There is no trace in Dunbar of that glowing humanity which warms the verse of Burns, and makes the friendship of honest men an abundant consolation for all the miseries of his lot. Dunbar cares nothing for the joys and sorrows, the toils and hardships, the pastimes and pleasures of common life. Nor has he any tenderness, and therefore he never approaches the fountain of tears or the furnace of passion. Love to him, when it is not allegorical moonshine, is simply lust, and he thinks of women with the impurity of a priest. Moreover, he lived far too early in history to be touched by that democratic ardour of sentiment, which has given birth to some of the noblest poetry of Burns, and made him the oracle of freemen in every land where English is the national tongue. But he has merits almost of the highest kind. His humour is as deep as that of Burns, some would even venture to assert that it was deeper, and more imaginative.

[1] Young bullocks or heifers. [2] Heap or haul. [3] Sleeve.
[4] Birch trees. [5] Curacies. [6] Wallet.
[7] Cattle. [8] A game of chance. [9] Nothing.

"Tam o' Shanter" is not so marvellous a creation as *The Dance of the Sevin Deidly Synnis*, though we may find it easier to appreciate the modern poem, in which the tipsy hilarity of the hero gives a familiar aspect to the devilry of the witches, and robs it of the weirdness and horror that should mark the spectacle of a supernatural world. Burns's humour plays most freely round the incidents of human life, though none can deny the boldness with which it now and again makes a sweep into the realms of superstition; but Dunbar leaves on our mind an irresistible conviction of the reality of his hideous pageant—a decisive proof of the imaginative unity of his effort. His humour is not sceptical, it is only wildly grotesque, uncontrollable. But, in fact, we can form no just idea of his merits by dwelling on the qualities of any single work, however wonderful. We have to remember the range and variety of his principal poems, from the visionary splendours of allegorical scenery down to the licentious gallantries of humble friars, from the pitiless satire of courtiers and churchmen to sober and serious surveys of mortal existence, before we can properly realize the extraordinary wealth of his genius.

Dunbar is the first Scot in whose literature we recognise the distinctive features of the national character. That character had, it is true, been formed and established long before. We have traced its growth from the age of Malcolm Ceannmor, when the process of Teutonizing began, and we have seen how secular and ecclesiastical politics in different ways contributed to its vigorous development. But it cannot be said that this character ever found literary expression before the days of Dunbar. Barbour is patriotic, but there is nothing

Scottish in his spirit of thought; *The Kingis Quhair* is a purely English composition, the fruit of a purely English culture; Blind Harry, perhaps, in his rude way shows some national traits, but he is too ridiculous a fanatic to possess much character at all; the fables of Henryson display not a little of the shrewd and serious sense which has been thought to mark his countrymen in a peculiar degree; but Dunbar is the first Scottish poet—indeed the first Scottish author who strikes us not only with a sense of originality, but of dissimilarity from all his predecessors on both sides of the Tweed. Everything he has written, at least everything of moment, has a certain unique intensity of feeling and pith of language that give it a peculiarly national stamp. This quality of passionate or indomitable force, ever tending to extravagance and one-sided zeal, distinguishes and differentiates the people of the North from their Southern neighbours, and is particularly conspicuous in all their foremost men, whether in literature or public life. Not to speak of those spiritual heroes in the dim dawn of Scottish history, Columba, Kentigern, and Cuthbert, it blazes out fiercely in Wallace, King James I., Knox, Melville, Buchanan, the Covenanters, Burns, Chalmers, Carlyle. It does not always take a religious or poetical direction, nor is it always "perfervid." We recognise it in Hume, Scott, Hamilton, Brewster, Livingstone, Colin Campbell, as clearly as in the others we have mentioned. That its origin is partly due to the excess of Celtic blood in Scottish veins, cannot, we think, be rationally doubted; but since it shows itself the same in all parts of the country—Knox, its most potent embodiment, was an East-Lothian Angle—its chief cause must be sought in that desperate and protracted effort to repel the English claims, which strung to the highest pitch the passions and energies of the people, and infused into their souls for all time to come a self-reliant, self-asserting vehemence, which has enabled them to reach all but the highest excellence.

Dunbar has this quality of intensity in a remarkable degree. It gives a richer glow to his landscapes, a grimmer humour to his satire, a more fearless license to his language, a deeper gravity to his reflections, and a more nervous vigour to his verse than other poets of equal or even superior genius can boast. It has tempted critics of high respectability to exalt him above Chaucer; and it has led Scott, whose literary judgment is generally sound, into a panegyric that requires abatement. "This darling of the Scottish Muses has been justly raised to a level with Chaucer by every judge of poetry, to whom his obsolete language has not rendered him unintelligible. In brilliancy of fancy, in force of description, in the power of conveying moral precepts with terseness, and marking lessons of life with conciseness and energy, in quickness of satire, and in poignancy of humour, the Northern Maker may boldly aspire to rival the Bard of Woodstock."[1] Whatever Dunbar attempted, he did as well as Chaucer, often, indeed, with greater animation and lavish wealth of words; but if he has the national vigour, he has also the national narrowness. Chaucer has an immensely wider vision, and, therefore, immensely broader sympathies. All forms of life, all types of character, all modes of feeling attract and interest him. He loses himself, like a

[1] *Memoirs of George Bannatyne*, p. 14. Printed for the Members of the Bannatyne Club.

genuine dramatist, in his stories and his personages; but Dunbar is full of himself; of his own misfortunes and other people's unmerited luck. He rarely gets clear of the atmosphere of court, of its ambitions, its intrigues, and its scandals. When he looks abroad upon society it is not with the genial and sympathetic humour of his great master, but with an intolerant scorn that everywhere finds matter for reprobation or mockery. He has nothing to suggest in the way of reform, for he is bitter rather than earnest, and this is, perhaps, the reason why in the austere and religious times that followed he was almost forgotten in spite of his transcendant powers.

"During his own age," says Mr. Laing,[1] "he received the homage due to his genius, and his writings for a time continued to be admired and imitated by succeeding poets; yet he was doomed to such total and absolute neglect during the long period which elapsed between the year 1530, when Sir David Lyndsay mentions him among the poets then deceased, and the year 1724, when Allan Ramsay published a selection of his poems, that, with one solitary exception, no allusion, not even so much as the mere mention of his name, can be discovered in the whole compass of our literature!" The men of the Reformation found nothing in his verse that accorded with their own spirit and aims. The subjects of his satire were too personal, local, or temporary, to excite the interest of those who were engaged in a mightier controversy; and his wild and free humour was too much that of a monk or a friar to suit the temper of Genevan divines; nor did his countrymen ever give him a thought till the ardour

[1] Dunbar's *Poems*, vol. I. p. 4.

of Presbyterian zeal had begun to wane, and a love of secular culture had sprung up on the ruins of the covenant. Succeeding generations have striven to atone for the long oblivion to which he was consigned. Critic after critic has arisen to proclaim the greatness of his genius. What made his work insignificant and mean to the disciples of Knox, is its main charm and value to us. The pictures that he paints have a historical if not a polemical importance : they exhibit in some measure the temper and character of the times in which he lived; they brighten the dusty records of legislation and government; and clothe with flesh and blood the phantoms of a distant past.

CHAPTER VI.

THE EARLIER HALF OF THE SIXTEENTH CENTURY.

Comparative Interest of the Sixteenth Century for England and Scotland.—Need for Reformation greater in Northern Kingdom.—Severance from the Past more complete.—Approach of the Crisis.—Literary Culture and Scholarship in Earlier Half of the Century.—Group of Academic Authors.—Hector Boece.— Lives of Bishops of Aberdeen.—Scotorum Historiæ a Prima Gentis Origine.— Joannes Major.—His Residence abroad and Earlier Works.—Professorship in Glasgow and Publication of his Historia.—Characteristics of the Work.— Removal of Major to St. Andrews.—Relations to Knox.—John Bellenden.— His Translations of Boece and of Livy the Earliest Examples of Prose in Scottish Literature.—His Poetry.—James Inglis, etc.—The Complaynt of Scotland.— Conjectures as to Authorship.—Analysis.

For Scotland even more than for England the sixteenth century possesses a transcendant interest and importance. In the southern kingdom the middle ages were more brilliant and civilized than in the northern. We have already noted their vast superiority in literature, but in truth there is scarcely a department of intellectual activity in which the same superiority is not visible. The moral need for reformation was probably not quite so great in England as in Scotland; but in any case the same terrible severance from the past was not made. The old Church of Augustine and Dunstan, of Lanfranc and Anselm, of Thomas à Becket and Robert Grossetete, had indeed suffered severely at the hands of secularists like Cromwell, but its outward framework remained almost untouched, and much of the medieval spirit survived in its medieval rites. But in Scotland " old things passed away." A new religious world arose. Even those who are most deeply imbued with a reverence for the sanctities of the past, whether Roman or Genevan, recognise in the work of Knox a spiritual revolution so intense, unsparing, and remorseless, as to place an almost impassable gulf between the two periods of Scottish history, the period that preceded and the period that has followed the destruction of the medieval Church. There is, perhaps, no country in Christendom where the historic sentiment in religion is so weak, where the religious imagination of the people is so thoroughly restricted, in its backward flight, to the age of the Reformation. All before the days of Knox is regarded with the same pious contempt that Mussulmans bestow on the centuries that elapsed before the birth of Mohammed; and even now the ecclesiastical leaders who most effectively represent the traditional feelings of the Scottish people, view with suspicion and alarm all attempts to revive a human and sympathetic interest in the older forms of Christian life. They fear lest the great results of Knox's work should be undone.

The Scots were always a stern and serious people; but the new faith gave an elevation and dignity to the national temper which it had never displayed before. Mr. Carlyle, with his rare power of grasping, even while exaggerating, the real character of an epoch, speaks of his native country as first receiving a *soul* at the Reformation. "A cause, the noblest of causes kindles itself, like a beacon set on high; high as Heaven, yet attainable from Earth;—whereby the meanest man becomes not a Citizen only, but a Member of Christ's visible Church; a veritable Hero, if he prove a true man!"[1] It is this immense advance in

[1] *Heroes and Hero Worship*, Lect. IV.

spiritual energy and freedom which gives an unspeakable preciousness to the work of Knox. He first brought the great mass of his countrymen into direct and living contact with the purest and most divine thought the world has seen; and, from that day till now, the moral strength of Scotland has been solely due to the Christian faith and principle which he rooted forever in the hearts of the people. It is not wonderful, therefore, that Scotsmen, who realize what Knox has done for his nation, should be somewhat jealous of that historical latitudinarianism which seems to minimize the significance of the Reformation. But there is in reality no cause for alarm. All reverent and catholic treatment of the past will only bring into greater prominence the sublime heroism of the Reformers; nor is it any diminution of their glory that the Celtic church of Columba, or the Norman church of David I., was the exponent of a devotion as deep and spiritual, if not as rational and pure, as that which flourished in the kirk of Knox. Scotland gains by recognising the fact that "many brave men lived before Agamemnon." We may rest assured that the time is hopelessly past when the children of the Reformation require to maintain its truth and worth by an ignorant indifference to the successive phases of medieval piety. The corruption of manners that marked the decline and fall of the older form of religious life, may have justified the fierce and contemptuous assaults of the Reformers on the system as it stood before them in all its glaring iniquity, but it does not justify us in carrying the truculent spirit and unmeasured speech of combatants into the serener region of historic exposition. In a previous chapter we have tried to set forth some of the fairer aspects of the primitive ecclesiastical life of Scotland; and in later scholars and authors we have seen that saintly spirit and enlightened intellect continued to grace and adorn the Scottish church even in the age of the Borgias; but we now approach a period in which these are to disappear, and the whole fabric of the ancient religion is to be hurled into irretrievable ruin by a storm of popular fury, the like of which never raged in any other country of Christendom.

Meanwhile, however, we may briefly notice the literary culture and scholarship of Scotland in the first half of the sixteenth century. By far the greatest names are those of Douglas and Lyndsay, in connection with which the political and ecclesiastical history of the time naturally falls to be discussed, but there is also a group of academic authors whose learned labours were long renowned, and still entitle them to honourable notice. Perhaps the most famous of the number is Hector Boece, whose *History of the Scots* has in modern times been assailed with more ridicule than almost any work we know. A native of Dundee (whence the epithet of *Deidonanus* applied to him by Ferrerius), and a member of an ancient Angus family, he went abroad to prosecute his studies, and took the degree of bachelor of divinity in the University of Paris. Theology, philosophy, and history were his favourite subjects, and in 1497 he was appointed professor of philosophy at the College Montaigre, where he taught with distinction for three years, and became the friend and associate or correspondent of not a few of the most gifted scholars of his age. His admiration for Erasmus was unbounded, and Erasmus in turn spoke of Boece with cordiality and high respect. In

1500 Bishop Elphinstone invited him to return to Scotland as *Primarius* or Principal of his newly-founded University at Aberdeen.

We have already seen that Elphinstone was the centre of a highly accomplished society in the north. Boece found in particular a great amount of learning among the Canons Regular, and most of the professors in the new institution were chosen from this order. The names of Arthur Boece, the Principal's brother, of John Vaus, of William and Alexander Hay, of Guthrie, of Ogilvie, of Spittal, of Galloway, rector of Kinkell, and many others, are now almost or quite forgotten; but their virtues and their gifts are eulogistically recorded by Boece in his *Lives of the Bishops of Aberdeen*,[1] a work designed as a monument to the memory of the illustrious churchmen to whom he owed his academic dignity. The studious, earnest, and exemplary men who figure in these biographies strikingly contrast with the sordid, vicious, and illiterate priests at whom Dunbar rails or jests. Yet both were contemporary, and both were real, though the first were a mere handful in comparison with the second. These scholars of the old faith had nothing in common with the profligate herd of monks and seculars, or the greedy prelates, to whom religion was a selfish and ambitious policy: they were children of the Renaissance, who loved the clear light of knowledge and the face of truth. Boece, the friend of Erasmus, was essentially a humanist, a lover of literary art and elegant scholarship; a man of irreproachable character, who had a genuine admiration for what was true, pure, and classical; and who probably

---

[1] *Vitæ Episcoporum Murthlacensium et Aberdonensium* (Par. 1522). Printed for the Members of the Bannatyne Club.

thought the enlightened study of the masterpieces of antiquity would purge the priesthood of its grossness, and imbue it with chaster and more refined sensibilities. His ideals were those of a scholar, not of a theologian; and he was content to live a life of honourable industry and blameless morals, under the shelter of a venerable system, whose sacred traditions could not be tarnished even by the vices of a degenerate age.

Boece's great work, *Scotorum Historiæ a prima Gentis Origine*, first published at Paris in 1526, under a slightly different title, came down as far as the death of James I.; but in 1574, Joannes Ferrerius, a Piedmontese, who had lived some years in Scotland, published a second edition, containing two new books, that brought it down to the reign of James III. The first edition was translated into the vernacular for the use of James V. in 1530-31, by John Bellenden, afterwards archdeacon of Moray. Boece has invested the mythical history of his country with all the picturesque ornament that a lively imagination, tempted by the example of Livy, could devise. But he is in no sense responsible for the great polemical fable that vindicates the antiquity of the Scottish nation. That had been developed and accepted long before his time. Dissatisfied with the Cymric tale of Brutus the Trojan, which made them the progeny of a younger son, the Scots began as early as the thirteenth century to hint at a grander and more august origin. The claim of superiority which the English kings put forward on all convenient occasions, especially in matters ecclesiastical, seems to have finally stirred the northern clergy to an audacity of invention that was probably successful in staggering their opponents. They discovered that their ancestors were not

Trojans at all, but were of Græco-Ægyptic descent, and could trace their name and lineage to Scota, daughter of that Pharaoh who perished in the Red Sea. This startling story first appeared in a chronicle (*circa* 1280) quoted in the *Scalacronica*, and the violent aggressions of Edward I. soon gave it a hold on the national imagination. It became an indisputable truth which every patriotic Scot was bound to believe and maintain. At the Court of Rome during the frequent negotiations carried on after the defeat of Wallace, and before the revolt of Bruce, it was urged and argued with all possible effect; and when Fordun began to compose his history it had already become familiar to Christendom, and had left on the mind of Continental nations an impression that Scotland was a kingdom of immemorial antiquity and renown. Fordun fortified the fable by his mode of treatment, which imparted a greater unity and consistency to the story than it had hitherto possessed; and as England had now practically abandoned its claim of feudal lordship over Scotland, it had no longer an interest in controverting the preposterous fictions by which the Scots sought to shield and protect their country's independence, and the latter were consequently left to the full enjoyment of their glorious traditions. Boece, like every other Scot, was brought up in the firmest conviction of their historic character. He would as soon have thought of challenging the authority of the Pope, as the veracity of the national legend. But he was a scholar and an artist, who appreciated the beauty, freedom, and fine details of the Roman story; and he did not consider himself guilty of vulgar mendacity when he draped anew in classic garb the early annals of his country, and heightened the interest of his narratives by all the artifices of exaggeration and invention that a credulous age permitted or approved. No doubt his method is that of a romancer. We cannot trust him whenever a point is in dispute. But he did not write to settle points. He wrote to celebrate in heroic fashion the far-descended fame of the Scottish kingdom, and his picturesque touches and full-blown fictions probably seemed to him only the appropriate decorations of his splendid theme. Something may be due to personal credulity and national vanity, but in the main we do not think that these were the chief causes of the peculiar features of his work; and while we frankly admit that he has no claim to a place among trustworthy historians, we repudiate the idea that he is an impostor and a cheat. His aim was epic, though his genius and his taste were insufficient for his ambition. Europe for a time thought highly of his *History*, but its fictions have been too much for the patience of modern writers, who have seldom remembered the age in which it was written, the ideas of historic literature that then prevailed, the new-born love of rhetoric and ornament, the unique position of the Scots on the Continent, and the total absence of all criticism of ancient authorities.

The Scottish Government seems to have appreciated the patriotic labour of Boece. In 1527, only a year after the publication of his *History*, he received a pension of £50 Scots, which was to be paid by the Sheriff of Aberdeen out of the king's casualties. Two years later the pension was confirmed "until the king should promote him to a benefice of 100 merks Scots," and the record of the payments appears annually in the treasurer's books till 1534, when it is probable he obtained the rectory of Fyvie which he held at his death in 1536. Against the intemperate abuse of Pinkerton and the cynical malice of Lord Hailes, may be set the respectful admiration of his contemporaries, who knew his virtues as a man and his erudition as a scholar.

Another Scottish historian of a very different spirit and character was Joannes Major or Mair, who was born at Gleghornie near North Berwick, probably about 1470. After completing his *tyrocinia* in the schools of his native country, he is supposed, on the authority of a passage in his *Historia*,[1] to have gone to Cambridge; but the language is indefinite as to time, and we may almost say that the first certain fact in his career is his connection with the University of Paris. He joined the college of St. Barbe about 1493, where he perfected his knowledge of the liberal arts, and then passed to the college or gymnasium of Montacute, where he began the study of theology. Of the latter seminary he speaks in high terms in his commentaries on the sentences of Petrus Lombardus. He calls it "domum suam nutricem et cum veneratione semper nominandam." In 1496 he took the degree of M.A., and in 1508 was made D.D. in the Sorbonne. The incidents of his life are not well known and their sequence cannot be very clearly traced, but there is abundant testimony to show that in Paris his reputation as a philosopher and divine was of the highest. He was reckoned one of the best scholars and one of the best teachers of his day. While acting as a professor in his favourite college he published the Com-

---

[1] *Christi Collegium in quo olim trimestris auditor fueram.* Lib. I. cap. v.

mentaries to which we have alluded above, at intervals between 1509 and 1519, dedicating them to distinguished countrymen of his, viz., George Hepburn, then Abbot of Aberbrothock, who was afterwards made Bishop of the Isles and fell at Flodden, Gavin Douglas, Bishop of Dunkeld, and Robert Cockburn, Bishop of Ross. His *Introductorium in Aristotelicam Dialecticen, totamque Logicam*, appeared at Lyons in 1514, and must have increased his fame and authority. In 1518, when Martin Luther was just beginning his iconoclastic work, Major sent forth a little treatise with a significant title, *De Auctoritate Concilii supra Pontificem Maximum Liber*, which seems to be taken from a larger volume devoted to an exposition of the Gospel of St. Matthew published in the same year. In writing and printing such a work at such a time, Major explains his own position. He is not a religious reformer; he is an academic churchman, jealous of scholastic liberty of thought, but probably indifferent to the discontent and murmurings of an ignorant laity. Such a theory of the man best explains his uneventful life and his peculiar reputation.

Major returned to Scotland not later than 1518, for in that year he was incorporated a member of the University of Glasgow, and in the records of that university figures thus: "Egregius vir Magister Joannes Maior, doctor Parisiensis, ac principalis regens collegii et pedagogii dicte universitatis, canonicusque capelle regie, ac vicarius de Dunlop."[1] According to the same authority he was professor of theology in 1521, and had John Knox for a pupil. It is impossible to doubt that

[1] *Munimenta Universitatis Glasguensis*, vol. II. p. 134. Printed for the Members of the Maitland Club.

he exercised a considerable influence on the mind of the great Reformer. Knox was then an impressionable youth of sixteen, and would have all a student's admiration of a bold, keen-witted teacher who came before him clothed in the glory of a Continental renown.[1] While lecturing in Glasgow his famous history was being published in Paris. Its exact title is *De Historia Gentis Scotorum Libri sex, seu Historia Majoris Britanniæ, tam Angliae quam Scotiae, è veterum monimentis concinnata*. The author's preface or dedication to James V. is extremely interesting. He is quite aware of his inelegant style, "better fitted for a theologian than a historian";[2] even friendly critics called it *stylus Sorbonicus*, but he reckons the fault a minor one, for "the first duty of a historian is to tell the truth";[3] and he is strongly of opinion that a theologian conversant with the high ethics of religion is peculiarly qualified to pronounce just and weighty judgments on historical actions. This opinion is not fashionable in the nineteenth century. Politicians and journalists are never weary of affirming the incompetence of divines to interpret the lessons of history; but we confess to a strong sympathy with the view of the old churchman, and we think that his handling of the national story justifies his contention.

The work, composed or finished in 1518, bears unmistakable traces of a foreign, and particularly of an English, influence. His authorities are largely English. Bede he holds in the profoundest respect, like every genuine student. As the title shows, a considerable

---

[1] See M'Crie's *Life of Knox*, Period I.
[2] *Magis theologo quam historico congruum*.
[3] *Historiographi prima lex est rerum scribere*.

part of his history is devoted to English affairs, and there runs through it in particular places a certain distrust of "our annals" (*nostros annales*). Major rejects the Graeco-Aegyptic "figment" regarding the origin of the Scots, which his countrymen revered, affirming what is unquestionably true, that it was invented to out-do the Cymric fable of Brutus the Trojan.[1] He ignores those imaginary kings who flourished between the fictitious and the real Fergus; and though he does not quite give up the story of the "primus Fergusius," son of Ferchard, who ruled 700 years before Fergusius, son of Erc, he speaks of him in a dubious, semi-sceptical way. Major was apparently not well versed in the Celtic legends and literature of the Scots, and probably had a Lothian Angle's contempt for the wild Scots (*Scoti sylvestres*) of the Caledonian forest; but it is surprising to notice how shrewdly and sensibly he writes on ethnological questions which had long passed into the domain of romance. He knows exactly the relations of the Irish and Scots, of the Angles north and south of the Tweed; and if he follows Bede in regard to the Scythian origin of the Picts, it is only because no records of that Celtic race survived from which, in Major's time, an independent conclusion could have been formed. He is singularly dispassionate for a Scot of those days, and will not allow himself to be carried away by national prejudices. In the chapter *De Scotorum Moribus*,[2] after telling us how the Scots and the English are characterized by each other, the Scottish as "basest of traitors",[3] and the English as "cowards who can only succeed in their schemes by fraud and cunning,"[4] he goes

---

[1] See lib. I. cap. ix. [2] Lib. I. cap. vii. [3] "Traditores esse pessimos.
[4] "Sed dolo et astutia omnia perficere."

on to say: "But I am not wont to credit either the abuse of the English by the common Scots, nor, on the other hand, of the Scots by the English."[1] And this principle runs through the whole work. It marks his treatment of the War of Independence. He recognises fairly enough the genius of Wallace, and his strong republican sentiment is evident in his condemnation of the Scottish nobility;[2] but he loses no opportunity of expressing his contempt for the popular legends which the national patriotism had fostered or created. He argues against Blind Harry's version of Wallace's career in France, and points to the significant silence of the French historians as an evidence of its falsehood; but he goes a step too far when he adds: "I am, therefore, of opinion that he never visited France."[3] It is curious to note that one who generally shows a judicious scepticism on doubtful points, has partly accepted the groundless fiction that Edward I. declined battle with Wallace at Stanmuir during a second and mythical invasion of the English border. The 8th book of Blind Harry is the high water mark of Scottish credulity, but even so unflinching a critic as Major could not altogether escape the influence of the popular fable. On the whole Major cannot make up his mind whether or not Wallace was justified in his opposition to the English king.[4] But, on the other hand, he repudiates vigorously in many parts of his work the Eng-

[1] "Ego autem nec Scotis vulgaribus in Anglorum, nec e diverso Anglis in Scotorum vituperatione, fidem praestare soleo."

[2] In that chapter from which we have quoted above, De Scotorum Moribus, he has some plain words that may be given: "Nulla est prorsus vera nobilitas nisi virtus et ejus actus. Vulgaris nobilitas non est nisi ventosus hominum loquendi modus."

[3] "Ergo reor eum nunquam Gallias visitasse." Lib. IV. cap. xv.

[4] "An probe egit Edwardo Anglo resistendo non insisto." Lib. IV. cap. xv.

lish claim of superiority both on moral and historical grounds, and asserts, what is only too obvious, that it was the cause of dreadful misery to the one country, and of fruitless cost to the other; though he is not blind to the fact that a union of the crowns would have allowed the growth of a peaceful civilization centuries before it became possible.[1]

By far the most striking and characteristic feature of Major's history, however, is its bold and free treatment of ecclesiastical acts, and of matters in which the Church was deeply concerned. Not that there is any trace of Protestantism in the author's attitude. He is a scholastic theologian and jurist to the core, but he invariably exercises the freedom of an academic thinker, and his sense of what is just and right never suffers obscuration. The chapters on David I. and Alexander II. are examples of this. The virtues of the "sair sanct" are recorded in the most generous and ungrudging spirit, but his reckless and pernicious liberality to the Church is emphatically condemned. Major had a scholar's horror of lazy monks; and in his day learning had departed from the monasteries, in which ignorance and vice found undisturbed retreats. He criticizes the pious foundations in the light of their later corruptions, and declares that if David could only have foreseen their future condition, he would have been less lavish of his gifts. He denounces the sensuality, worldliness, rapacity, and lack of devotion which now prevail, and in spite of his grave and serious style we are reminded that he was a contemporary of Dunbar. No doubt it is a cheap "philosophy of history" to disparage institutions that have done their work and become antiquated.

[1] Lib. IV. chap. xviii. passim.

Major was probably incapable of appreciating the exalted temper of David I., or the civilizing effect of the great monastic institutions in their pristine vigour and purity; but his remarks, though valueless as regards the twelfth century, throw a light on the early part of the sixteenth. We see from them what was the attitude of the scholars of the Scottish Church, towards the abuses that were hurrying it to its ruin. In their own calm way, they would have saved it, if they could: and though we know that they proved powerless to stem the current of evil, we must always feel a kind of pathetic interest in the beaten men, who followed the ways of Erasmus and not the ways of Luther.

In his account of the reign of Alexander II., Major has a remarkable passage on the value of ecclesiastical censures. Here he argues after the fashion and with the dexterity of a schoolman. Scotland had been laid under an interdict by the papal legate for outrages perpetrated on the English border, and particularly for the seizure of Carlisle. Alexander in terror ("fortasse plus aequo," says the cautious historian) restored the city to the English, and paid a large sum of money to the representative of the Pope. Whereupon Major proceeds to discuss the question, When are church censures to be dreaded; and decides that they are to be dreaded only when they are just. "An unjust excommunication is no more an excommunication than a dead man is a man."[1] He thinks many people who are excommunicated are in a state of grace, and no "sophistica excommunicatio" can hurt any body, whether he lies in consecrated ground or not.[2] All through the work, in the most unex-

[1] "Excommunicatio injusta non magis est excommunicatio quam homo mortuus sit homo." Lib. IV. cap. vii.
[2] "Sive in terra sancta, sive prophana sepeliatur." Lib. IV. cap. vii.

pected places, a spirit of free criticism shows itself, the product partly of Major's mental temperament and partly of his scholastic discipline. There is not a great deal of the Renaissance spirit in him, in spite of his attacks on monasticism. He has no flowery elegance of diction, and, in truth, small literary merit of any kind, but he is a shrewd, logical, hard-headed Scot; and his frankness, honesty, and vigour give a certain intermittent vivacity to his narrative, which partly atones for the absence of rhetorical charm. Although not a profound historian, he is eminently sensible in his ideas of government, and argues against the "divine right" of kings in the coolest fashion. When discussing in his formal scholastic style the relative claims of Baliol and Bruce to the crown, he gives expression to the boldest political sentiments: *e.g.,* " A free people confers power on the first king, whose authority is derived from the whole community; for Fergus, the first King of Scotland, had no other right, and so is it everywhere, and commonly has been from the beginning of the world."[1] Again: " The people may depose a king for his offences, and exclude his family from the throne, just as it possessed the right at first to appoint him;"[2] and once more, "As to kings, that should be done which is most for the good of the commonwealth: for example, if a state is attacked by the enemy in such a way that a king A cannot defend it, but allows it to be crushed, and if B wrests it from the grip of the enemy and holds it with a strong hand; then A ought

---

[1] " Populus liber primo regi dat robur, cujus potestas a toto populo dependet; quia aliud jus Fergusius primus Rex Scotiae non habuit; et ita est ubi libet, et ab orbe condito erat communiter." Lib. IV. cap. xvii.

[2] " Regem et posteros pro demeritis populus potest exauthorare sicut et primo instituere." Lib. IV. cap. xvii.

to be deposed and B put in his place."[1] The same opinions are even more boldly stated in his commentaries on Petrus Lombardus.[2] In such passages as we have quoted we recognise the teacher of Knox and Buchanan, and are of opinion, with Christopher Irvine, that he deserved better treatment at the hands of the latter than to be made the subject of a paltry sneer, "solo cognomine Major."

In 1522 his patron, Archbishop Beaton, was translated from Glasgow to St. Andrews, whither Major followed, probably in the following year, and was appointed professor of theology. At any rate he was incorporated into the University of St. Andrews, 9th June, 1523, under the designation *Doctor Theologus Parisiensis*. Buchanan studied under him in 1525, and is understood to have afterwards accompanied him to France. His motive for returning to the country in which he had first acquired a celebrity as a scholar and teacher is not known, but the political confusions of the time are supposed to have been the chief cause of the step. Between the "Erection," *i.e.*, the investiture of James V., then a boy of twelve, with sovereign authority, and the fall of Angus in 1528, there were four years of the most false and treacherous statecraft ever witnessed in Scotland. It is possible enough that Major found little comfort in the situation. His patron had been once imprisoned, and though he had recovered all his power, Major may have experienced the incon-

---

[1] "Illud circa reges faciendum est quod maxime ad reipublicae utilitatem conducit : sed sic est quod in casu quo ab hoste respublica sic invaditur, quod eam A rex tueri non potest, sed in ejus subversionem consentit ; et B eam tuetur et de manu hostis surripit et bene manu tenet : A deponi et B imponi meretur." Lib. IV. cap. xvii.

[2] See M'Crie's *Life of Knox*, period I.

venience of shifting fortunes; but it is also possible that difficulties arose in connection with the spread of the new heresy. As we have stated before, he was not in the least a Protestant in his theology, but his attitude was that of a philosophical disputant and not of an intolerant fanatic. Calderwood[1] tells a story of a certain Friar William who, in the year 1528, preached a sermon in Dundee, in which he inveighed "more liberallie against the licentious life of bishops than they could weill beare, and against the abuse of cursing and false miracles." For this he was buffeted by the jackmen of the Bishop of Brechin and branded a heretic. "The Frier," continues Calderwood, "went to Sanct Andrewes, and communicated the heads of his sermoun with Mr. Johne Maior, whose word was then holdin as an oracle in maters of religioun. Mr. Johne said, his doctrine might weill be defended, and conteaned no heresie." The poor friar had in fact said nothing which the "oracle" itself had not uttered over and over again in books and lectures. It is not at all unlikely that Major found himself out of sympathy with the policy that sent his pupil, Patrick Hamilton, to the stake; and yet it would be unsafe to assume so much, for in the sentence pronounced against the youthful martyr, it is expressly stated that the archbishop arrived at his decision "with the counsell, decree, and authoritie of the most reverend Fathers in God, and Lords, Abbots, *Doctors of Theologie, Professours of the Holie Scripture, and Masters of the University* assisting us for the time." Whatever part, if any, circumstances may have forced him to take in the evil policy of the Church, he was, after his fashion, a fearless censor of her abuses; and

[1] *Historie of the Kirk of Scotland*, vol. I. p. 82. (Woodrow Society Edition.)

although not a heretic himself, he was singularly successful in breeding heretics. Major did not remain long abroad. About 1530 he returned to Scotland, and in 1533 was made provost or principal of Salvator's College, St. Andrews, an office which he held till his death in 1550.

One would like to know whether in his old age he preserved the courage and independence of his earlier years, or whether the progress of the new doctrines had cooled his ardour and stiffened his orthodoxy. But history is silent on the point, and the remainder of his life is almost a blank. Only once does he become visible again in any real way, but the occasion is memorable. Among the audience who listened to John Knox when he preached his first public sermon in the parish church of St. Andrews, in 1547, was his aged preceptor. The words are worth quoting: "Yf any here (and thare war present Maister Johne Mayre, the Universitie, the Suppriour, and many Channonis, with some Freiris of boyth the ordouris) that will say, That I have alledgeid Scripture, doctour, or historye, otherwyise then it is writtin, lett thame come unto me with sufficient witness, and by conference I shall lett thame see, not onlye the originall whare my testimonyes ar writtin, but I shall prove, that the wrettaris ment as I have spokin."[1] What did the venerable provost think of the ex-priest whose daring infinitely exceeded his own? Many and diverse criticisms were passed on the discourse; but among those which Knox records there is none that looks as if it *might* have been Major's. It is possible that Major, whose liberalism did not touch the

[1] Knox, *History of the Reformatioun of Religioun*, vol. I. p. 192. (Woodrow Society Edition.)

dogmas of religion, may have been altogether hostile to a movement which regarded the Roman Church as the "Babylonian harlot" and "synagogue of Satan," and which spoke scornfully of the whole structure of medieval faith and practice. He had his own clear sharply defined, restricted notions of ecclesiastical reform, and he may have felt indignant and alarmed at the revolutionary violence that threatened to overwhelm in a common destruction both the good and the evil. The church could never seem to him what it seemed to Knox. It must have stood before his mind as a divine institution, hallowed by centuries of illustrious saints and scholars and prelates. His deep learning made him familiar with hosts of great names, the memory of whose virtues and talents gave it an irresistible claim to his reverence and affection. He had all a scholar's indifference, if not antipathy, to the opinion of an illiterate populace; and strongly as he had himself denounced the corruptions of his own and preceding ages, it is almost certain he could never have given his voice for the subversion of a system, that had nourished and maintained for a thousand years men, to whose learning and speculations he owed nearly all the distinction and delight of his professional career. The very latest mention of his name occurs in connection with a Provincial Council of the Scottish Church, held at Edinburgh, in 1549, when "M. Johannes Mayr, decanus facultatis theologicae Universitatis Sancti Andreae, et Martinus Balfour, Doctores in theologia, *annosi, grandaevi, et debiles, comparuerant per procuratores.*" [1]

Here we may close our account of a man, who in his own generation was probably considered the most

---
[1] See Wilkins *Concil.*, vol. IV. p. 46.

weighty and authoritative thinker in the Scottish schools, and one of the greatest ornaments of the Latin Church, but on whose literature the Reformation fell like a frost or a blight, so that to all later ages he has been known merely by name. His Logic and Theology were perhaps doomed to die, for after a certain time books survive only in virtue of their style, and Major's was "*exile, aridum, conscissum, ac minutum*"; his History did not appeal to national prejudice or conceit, though it contains matter that is not to be found in Boethius, Buchanan, and other authors: but his political and ecclesiastical opinions mark him out as a characteristic product of that transition period when the Renaissance was exercising a subtle and disintegrating influence on medieval society, and when even the champions of the Church were moved by a zeal for reform. The spirit of the time had breathed upon the rigid schoolman; it did not imbue him with the picturesque eloquence of Boece, but it gave him a boldness and freedom of sentiment that even yet invite our admiration and respect.

John Bellenden[1] is a prose stylist of the highest merit. Like Dunbar and Major he was a native of Lothian, and was born towards the close of the fifteenth century. He entered the University of St. Andrews in 1508,[2] and completed his studies at the Sorbonne, where he took the degree of Doctor of Divinity. On his return to Scotland during the minority of James V., he found employment at court as clerk of accompts, but after a time lost his situation through the malice of enemies. He seems, however, to have recovered the

---

[1] The name is also spelt Ballenden, Ballentyne, Ballentyn, etc.

[2] At least a "Jo Ballentyn nactus Loudoniae" matriculates in that year.

royal favour, probably after the fall of the Douglasses, for in 1530 at the command of the king, he began a translation of Boece's history into the Scottish vernacular, for the benefit of those who had "missed their Latin." The work was finished in 1533, and was probably printed soon after, but the exact date of its publication has not been ascertained.[1] About the same time Bellenden executed a translation of the first five books of Livy—a work printed for the first time in 1822 by Mr. Maitland from a MS. in the Advocates' Library. The great value—we might also say the great charm—of these versions is that they are the earliest examples of prose in Scottish literature. Political circumstances in the long run made the successful cultivation of this form of literary expression impossible, but the monuments of it in the sixteenth century are really admirable for their quaint simplicity and racy vigour. Bellenden in particular is a master of style. By little happy touches of his own, idiomatic turns and graces, he gives an original freshness to his narrative that makes one quite forget it is a translation. With regard to Boece, he does not merely translate; he revises, and re-edits him as it were; correcting his mistakes, filling in omissions from his own researches, and adding passages of which there is no trace in the original. The following is a good specimen of his English :—

"Nocht lang eftir, hapnit ane uncouth and wounderfull thing, be quhilk followit sone, ane gret alteration in the realme. Be aventure, Makbeth and Banquho wer passand to Fores, quhair King Duncane hapnit to be

[1] The History and Croniklis of Scotland with the cosmography and description thairof, compilit be the noble clerk, Maister Hector Boece, Channon of Aberdeene. Translatit laitly in our vulgar and common langage by Maister Johne Bellenden, Archedene of Murray and Channon of Ross.

for the time, and met be the gait thre wemen, clothit in elrage[1] and uncouth weid. Thay wer jugit, be the pepill, to be weird sisteris. The first of thaim said to Makbeth, 'Hale, Thane of Glammis!' the secound said, 'Hale, Thane of Cawder!' and the thrid said, 'Hale, King of Scotland!' Than said Banquho, 'Quhat wemen be ye, sa unmercifull to me, and sa favorabil to my companyeon? For ye gaif to him nocht onlie landis and gret rentis, bot gret lordschippis and kingdomes; and gevis me nocht.' To this, answerit the first of thir weird sisteris, 'We schaw more felicite appering to the than to him; for thoucht he happin to be ane king, his empire sall end unhappelie, and nane of his blude sall eftir him succeid; be contrar, thow sall nevir be king, bot of the sal cum mony kingis, quhilkis, with lang progressioun, sall rejose[2] the croun of Scotland.' Als sone as thir wourdis wer said, thay suddanlie evanist out of sicht. This prophecy and divinatioun wes haldin mony dayis in derision to Banquho and Makbeth. For sum time Banquho wald call Makbeth, King of Scottis, for derisioun; and he on the samin maner, wald call Banquho, the fader of mony kingis. Yit, becaus al thingis succedit as thir wemen devinit, the pepill traistit and jugit thame to be weird sisteris. Not lang efter, it hapnit that the Thane of Cawder wes disherist and forfaltit of his landis, for certane crimes of lese majeste; and his landis wer gevin be King Duncane to Makbeth. It hapnit in the nixt nicht, that Banquho and Makbeth wer sportand togiddir at thair supper. Than said Banquho, 'Thow hes gottin all that the first two weird sisteris hecht.[3] Restis nocht bot the croun, quhilk wes hecht be the

---

[1] Elvish, wild. [2] Enjoy, possess. [3] Promised.

thrid sister.' Makbeth, revolving all thingis as thay wer said be thir weird sisteris, began to covat the croun ; and yit he concludit to abide quhil he saw the time ganand [1] thairto, fermelie beleving that the thrid weird suld cum, as the first two did afore.

"In the mene time, King Duncane maid his son Malcolme Prince of Cumbir, to signify that he suld regne eftir him. Quhilk wes gret displeseir to Makbeth : for it maid plane derogatioun to the thrid weird, promittit afore to him be thir weird sisteris. Nochtheles, he thocht, gif Duncane wer slane, he had maist richt to the croun, becaus he wes nerest of blude thairto, be tennour of the auld lawis maid eftir the deith of King Fergus, ' Quhen young children wer unabil to govern the croun, the nerrest of thair blude sall regne.' Als, the respons of thir weird sisteris put him in beleif, that the thrid weird suld cum as weill as the first two. Attour,[2] his wife, impacient of lang tary, as all wemen ar, specially quhare thay ar desirus of ony purpos, gaif him gret artation[3] to persew the thrid weird, that scho micht be ane quene; calland him, oft timis, febil cowart, and nocht desirus of honouris ; sen he durst not assailye the thing with manheid and curage, quhilk is offerit to him be benivolence of fortoun ; howbeit sindry otheris hes assailyeit sic thingis afore, with maist terribil jeopardyis, quhen thay had not sic sickernes to succeid in the end of thair laubouris as he had.

"Makbeth, be persuasion of his wife, gaderit his freindis to ane counsall at Innernes, quhare King Duncane happinnit to be for the time. And becaus he fand sufficient oportunite, be support of Banquho and otheris his freindis, he slew King Duncane, the VII.

---

[1] Fitting. [2] Moreover. [3] Instigation, incitement.

yeir of his regne. His body was buryit in Elgin, and efter tane up and brocht to Colmekill, quhare it remanis yit, amang the sepulturis of uthir kingis; fra our redemption MXLVI. yeris."[1]

We have chosen the foregoing passage because the subject is familiar to all who possess even an elementary acquaintance with English literature, but it is by no means among the finest in the work. The story of Caractacus (bk. iii. chap. xvi.) is a masterpiece, but in fact the whole of the prehistoric narrative has a poetic freedom and dignity of expression, which entitle Bellenden to be considered the most perfect artist that ever worked in Scottish prose. He is the first and the greatest of his kind.

Let the classical reader compare the following with the original in Livy (bk. i. chap. viii.), and he will see how naturally Bellenden delivers the Roman story.

"The justice and relligioun of Numa Pompilius was of singulare renowne in thir dayis. This maist resolute and prudent man dwelt in ane place callit Curis of Sabinis, and had, sa far as ony creature micht have into thay dayis, full cognossance baith of devine and humane lawis. Sindry belevit, that Pythagoras was preceptour and auctor of his doctrine; for thay can nocht imagin, that ony uthir man micht have sic erudicioun in thay dayis. Bot thair opinioun is vane; for it was cleirlie knawin, that Pythagoras was more than C yeiris eftir the empire of Numa; that is to say, in the time of Servius Tullius; and held ane scule of young childrin [2] in the remote and last boundis of Italie, beside the landis of Metapont, Heraclea and Crotona. Attoure,

[1] Bellenden's *Cronikli* of *Scotland*, bk. xii. chap. iii. (Edinb., 1822.)
[2] Livy has *juvenum*.

howbeit the said Pythagoras had bene equale of aige with Numa, quhat fame suld have drawin him out of sa remote and fer cuntre, to have cummin amang the Sabinis? be quhat langage micht he have drawin sa mony young childerne to desire of letteris? be quhat way or supple micht ane man have travellit throw sa mony uncouth pepill, different fra uthir in maneris and langage? Be thir ressouns I can nocht affirme that Numa was lerned ony maner of way be Pythagoras; but erar, that Numa, of his awin ingine, temperat his liffe in vertewe, and *nocht alanerlie was instruckit in strange and uncouth science, but als in the tetrik and sorrowfull science usit amang the Sabinis; of quhilkis na kinde of science was mair corruppit in this erde.*[1] The Romanis herand the name of Numa Pompilius rehersit afore thaim, howbeit it apperit that all thair riches suld cum in the Sabinis handis gif he war king, yit becaus thair was nane amang the pepill, nor Faderis, nor citeyanis of the toun, that micht prefer thaimself, or ony uthir of thair opinioun, to the said Numa, thay condiscendit to maik him king."

The epistle to James V. at the conclusion of Bellenden's work, gives us a favourable impression of the author's character. It reads like the utterance of an honest man, who wished to speak the truth to his sovereign, and to point out to him what lessons he ought to learn from the record of the national history. He contrasts the tyrant and the true king with spirit and discernment. And one passage, instinct with that patriotic ardour which never deserts a Scot, is still worth quotation :

[1] The words italicized are rather a failure as a translation. Livy says : "Instructumque non tam peregrinis artibus, quam disciplina tetrica ac tristi veterum Sabinorum : quo genere nullam quondam incorruptius fuit."

"Quhat thing may be mair pleasand than to se in this present volume, as in ane cleir mirroure all the variance of tyme bygane; the sindry chancis of fourtoun; the bludy fechting and terrible berganis sa mony yeiris continuit, in the defence of your realm and liberte; quhilk is fallen to your hieness with gret felicite, howbeit the samin has aftimes been ransomit with maist nobill blude of your antecessoris. Quhat is he that will nocht rejoise to heir the knychtly afaris of thay forcy campions, King Robert Bruce and William Wallace? The first, be innative desyre to recover his realme, wes brocht to sic calamite, that mony dayis he durst nocht appeir in sicht of pepill; but amang desertis, levand on rutes and herbis, in esperance of better fortoun; bot at last, be his singulare manheid, he com to sic pre-eminent glore, that now he is reput the maist valyeant prince that was eftir or before his empire. This other, of small beginning, be feris curage and corporall strength, not only put Englishmen out of Scotland, but als, be feir of his awful visage, put Edward King of England to flicht; and held all the borders fornence Scotland waste."

But we must not forget that Bellenden was also a poet. Many, perhaps most of his compositions have perished, which is certainly matter for regret, since what are extant, though not of the first order of merit, display a liveliness of fancy and an ease of versification that make them not unworthy of remembrance. As early as 1530 he had acquired a high poetical reputation. In *The Testament and Complaynt of our Soverane Lordis Papingo*, by Sir David Lyndsay, written in that year, he is thus mentioned :—

> " Bot, now of lait, is starte up haistelie,
>   Ane cunnyng Clerk, quhilk wrytith craftelie,
>   Ane plant of Poeitis, callit Ballendyne,
>   Quhose ornat workis my wytt can nocht defyne :
>   Gett he into the courte auctoritie
>   He wyll precell Quintyn and Kennedie."

Several of his pieces are still unpublished, but in his translation of Boece are two proems : " The Proheme of the Cosmographe " and " The Proheme of the History " ; and another in his translation of Livy, all of which may still be read with at least that degree of languid pleasure which the flowery allegorical Renaissance poetry can give, but which do not call for special criticism.

Shortly after he had finished his two historical works, Bellenden was appointed archdeacon of Moray and canon of Ross. As far as we can learn he seems to have been a zealous and conscientious churchman, vehemently averse to the " new heresy " which he opposed in every way, yet conscious that the morals of the clergy required a thorough reformation. When he found that the new heresy was likely to prove irresistible, and that the fires of martyrdom were kindled in vain, he quited his native land and withdrew to Rome, where he died about 1550.

James Inglis, abbot of Culross, deserves a passing notice. Fate has been unkind to his memory. Not a vestige of his literature has survived, yet in his day he ranked with the foremost of his contemporaries, and in that poem of Lyndsay's, which we have just quoted, he is extolled as unsurpassed by any of the poets of the Scottish court.

> " And, in the Courte, bene present, in thir dayis,
>   That ballatis brevis lustellie, and layis,

> Quhilkis tyll our Prince daylie thay do present.
> Quho can say more than Schir James Inglis sayis,
> In ballatis, farses, and in plesand playis ?
> Bot Culrose hes his pen maid impotent."

His ecclesiastical promotion seems to have paralyzed his poetic faculty, or perhaps he thought it unbecoming the dignity of an abbot to continue ballad-mongering. At any rate his lusty verse has vanished, and he himself has become *nominis umbra*. If he ceased to sacrifice to the muses, when he became a prelate of the church, they were quickly avenged, for on the 1st March, 1530, he was assaulted and murdered by Blackadder, Baron of Tulliallan, in consequence, it is thought, of a dispute about their respective temporal rights.

One or two additional authors, such as Kyd, Stewart of Lorne, Galbraith and Kinlouch, might be mentioned, but their "ornate werkis" have also perished, and even their names but dimly survive in the *Complaynt of the Papingo*.

An anonymous work, called *The Complaynt of Scotland*, possesses a singular interest, both political and literary. Its authorship has been variously assigned to a Schir James Inglis, who was chaplain of the Abbey of Cambuskenneth from 1508 to 1550; by Leyden in his edition of the *Complaynt* to Sir David Lyndsay; and by no less an authority than David Laing, to a certain Robert Wedderburn, who held the vicarage of Dundee as late as 1553; but it seems to us that Dr. J. A. H. Murray[1] has conclusively shown that none of these three can be

---

[1] *The Complaynt of Scotlande.* Edited for the "Early English Text Society" by James A. H. Murray. Lond., 1872.

reasonably accepted as the probable writer. For the first, hardly anything can be urged except the untrustworthy statement of Mackenzie in his *Lives of Scottish Writers* (Edin., 3 vols, 1708), who confounds the chaplain of Cambuskenneth with his namesake, the abbot of Culross; as regards the second, it may safely be asserted, in spite of numerous literary similarities, that the political and religious standpoint of Lyndsay was widely different from that of the author of the *Complaynt*; while the third, one of three brothers all deeply involved in the Lutheran heresy, was still more incapable of composing a work in which not a whisper is uttered against the doctrines or even the institutions of the church. Dr. Murray further contends—and on this point no living scholar is a greater authority—that the dialect of the *Complaynt* is that of the Southern Lowlands. If this be conceded, the claims of Wedderburn and Lyndsay at once fall to the ground; while those of Inglis are too shadowy to demand examination. "The only things," says Dr. Murray, "that I consider certain as to the author are (1) that he was a distinct and thorough partisan of the French side; (2) that he was a churchman, still attached to the Catholic faith; (3) that he was a native of the southern, not improbably of the Border counties." The force of these conclusions will be seen from the following description and analysis of the work.

The *Complaynt*, as we learn from a passage in Chap. V., was composed in the year 1548 or the beginning of 1549,[1] and in its present form consists of twenty

---

[1] "Nou, to confound the opinione of Socrates, ande to confound al them that vil nocht beleue that the varld is neir ane final ende, i vil arme me vitht the croniklis of mastir Ihone Carion, quhar he allegis the prophysye of Helie, sayand, that fra the begynnyng of the varld on to the consummatione of it, sal

chapters, though there is clear evidence that it underwent revision and enlargement at the hands of the author before it was printed.[1] It is dedicated to the "Excellent and Illvstir Marie, Quene of Scotlande, the margareit and perle of princessis," by whom is meant the Queen-Mother, Mary of Guise, and not her more famous daughter. She is extolled in rhapsodical diction as "ane immortal ande supernatural medicyne, to cure and to gar conuallesse al the langorius desolat and affligit pepil, quhilkis ar al mast disparit of mennis supple, ande reddy to be venquest ande to be cum randrit in the subiection ande captiuite of our mortal ald enemeis, be rason that ther cruel inuasions aperis to be onremedabil." The special causes of Scottish affliction at this time are three in number: "the cruele inuasions of oure ald enemeis, the uniuersal pestilens and mortalite, that hes occurit mercyles amang the pepil, ande the contentione of diuerse of the thre estaitis of scotlande, throucht the quhilk thre plagis, the vniuersal pepil ar be cum distitute of iustice policie ande of al verteus bysynes of body ande saul." But Mary of Guise, whose "heroyque vertu" surpasses that of "Valeria the dochtir of the prudent consul Publicola, or of Cloelia, Lucresia, Penelope, Cor-

be the space of sex thousand zeir, the quhilk sex thousand sal be deuydit in thro partis. . . . . . the third tua thousand zeir sal be betuix the incarnatione and the last aduent, quhilk sal be the cōsummatione of the warld. Bot thir last tua thousād zeir (as mastir Ihone Carion allegis in the prophesye of Helie) sal nocht be completit, be rason that the daye of iugemint sal be antecipet, be cause of them that ar his electis, as is vrityn in the xxiii. chapter of Sanct Mathou . . . . . ther for, eftir the supputatione of Helie, as mastir Ihone Carion has rehersit, the varld hes bot four hundretht fyfty tua zeir tyl indure," etc.

[1] Probably at Paris, 1549. See Dr. Murray's "Introduction" to the *Complaynt*, pp. cvi-cviii.

nelia, Semiramis, Thomaris, Penthasillie, or of ony vthir verteouse lady that Plutarque or Bocchas hes discriuit," has been raised up to deliver the Scottish realm from the ravages of the wolves of England, like another Esther or Judith! She nobly exiles herself from the society of her young and only child, " our nobil princes, and rychteous heretour of Scotland : quha is presentlye veil tretit in the gouernance of hyr fadir of lau, the maist illustir potent prince of the maist fertil and pacebil realme, vndir the machine of the supreme olimp," in order that she may restore freedom and prosperity to her daughter's heritage. The roll of her glorious ancestors from Godfrey of Bouillon, down to her father, the hero of St. Quentin, is recited with devout admiration. To whom could a leal Scot more fitly present his work than to a lady of such high renown and patriotic spirit? None could be more deeply touched by a rehearsal " of the onmersiful afflictiōe of the desolat realme of Scotland." His gift may be a small one, but she will receive it graciously as the Persian king did the handful of water from the poor man who could offer him nothing more, or as Christ commended the widow's mite more than the great contributions of the rich.

It is amazing that a scholar like Leyden should have supposed it possible that in 1548 Sir David Lyndsay could have expressed such sentiments, or that at any period of his literary history he could have adopted such a florid and hyperbolical style.

The Dedication or " Epistil to the Qvenis Grace," as it is also called, is followed by a " Prolog to the Redar," in which the author denounces idleness. He quotes from Diodorus an edict of Amasis II., King of

Egypt, ordering every man to show how he earned his living, refers to that "institute" of the Indian Gymnosophists which forbade "corporal refectione" to any man till he could prove that he had worked for it, and also to the decree of Sesostris, that none of the "zong princis and gentil men of his court .... suld tak ther refectione quhil thai hed gone and run the tyme of fife or sex houris." Such ordinances are still "verray necessair to be vsit in al realmys, be rason that the maist part of the pepil, throucht ther natural fraigilite, consumis the maist part of ther dayis in ydilnes." He then vindicates himself against such an accusation. The labour of the pen is no pastime. From of old it has been a potent instrument for advancing the greatness of nations. "The romans var mair renforsit in curageus entreprisis be the vertu of the pen, ande be the persuasions of oratours, nor thai var renforsit be the sourdis of men of veyr." He then goes on to illustrate by examples drawn from antiquity the propositions that every craft is necessary for the public weal and equally honourable "gyf ane craft or sciens be gude, than it is as gude as ony craft can be," and that no man can be master of every craft. Cicero is freely quoted, but the most vivid story is that of Hannibal and Antiochus visiting the school of Phormio, the philosopher, and hearing a discourse on the art of war, the delivery of which by one inexperienced in battles, is condemned by Hannibal. The writer of the *Complaynt* apologizes for his own boldness in venturing to come forward as an author: "My dul rude brane suld nocht hef been sa temerair as to vndirtak to correct the imperfectione of ane comont veil, be cause the maist part of my knaulage is the smallest part of my ignorance: zit nochtheles i hope that vyise men vil reput my ignorance for ane mortifeit prudens, be rason of my gude intentione that procedis fra ane affectiue ardant fauoir that i hef euyr borne touart this affligit realme quhilk is my native cuntre." No one who reads the *Complaynt* can doubt the sincerity of this apology. What follows is equally sincere but much more surprising: "Nou heir i exort al philosophouris, historigraphours, ande oratours of our Scottis natione, to support and til excuse my barbir agrest termis: for i thocht it nocht necessair til hef fardit ande lardit this tracteit vitht exquisite termis, quhilkis ar nocht daly vsit, bot rather i hef vsit domestic Scottis langage, maist intelligibil for the vlgare pepil. There hes bene diuerse translatours and compilaris in ald tymis, that tuke grite pleseir to contrafait ther vlgare langage, mixand ther purposis vitht oncoutht exquisite termis, dreuyn, or rather to say mair formaly, reuyn fra lating, ande sum of them tuke pleiseir to gar ane vord of ther purpose to be ful of sillabis half ane myle of lyntht." The fact is that the language of the *Complaynt* from beginning to end justifies the broad statement of Dr. Murray "that no Scottish writer of his own or any other age has left us a work so groaning under the burden of its foreign words." Probably want of literary experience, the dominant influence of the French tongue on the written Scotch of the sixteenth century, and the strong French sympathies of the writer may account for his extraordinary hallucination regarding his "barbir agrest termis."

The first five chapters of the *Complaynt* form a kind of moral or philosophical introduction to his special subject, and do not excite a lively interest in the reader. The "actor" (author) discourses on the "mutations of monarches," on the "thretnyng ande menassing of Gode contrar obstinat, vicius pepil," and on the "diuers opinions that the pagan philosophours held of the conditions ande induring of the varld." He recalls the fate of ancient empires and commonwealths, finds in them a principle of growth and decay, and piously recognises in their vicissitudes the presence of a divine power and justice whose ways are inscrutable. "The iugement of Gode (quhilk virkis al thyng) is ane profound onknauen deipnes, the quhilk passis humaine ingyne to comprehende the grounde or limitis of it." The recent disaster of Pinkey[1] (which seems to have been the immediate motive of the work) was not owing to "the mal talent of dame fortoune, the quhilk ymaginet opinione suld be detestit; for fortune is no thyng bot ane vane consait ymaginet in the hartis of onfaythtful men." Deep study of the holy scriptures has convinced him that national calamities are the fruit of national sins. He fortifies his position by quotations from Leviticus, Deuteronomy, and Isaiah. No greater sorrow than his is recorded in history. It rivals that of Anchises when the Greeks took Troy: of Rosaria when her husband Darius was vanquished by Alexander; of the prophet Jeremiah, when he bewailed the captivity of Israel; of David, when Joab slew Absalom; of Cleopatra, when her "love" Marcus Antonius was overthrown by " the empriour Augustus"; of Marcellus, when he saw Syracuse in flames; of the patriarch Jacob, when he heard of the loss of his son Joseph, and so on

[1] "The grite afflictione quhilk occurrit on oure realme in September mvxl vii zeirs, on the feildis besyde Mussilburgh."

with singular indifference to chronology; but since he acknowledges the sins of the Scottish people, he is not without hope that the " auful scurge of aperand exterminatione sal change in ane faderly correctione." Though the English have been permitted by God to punish the Scots, it does not follow that they are his favourites, for did God not allow Satan to scourge that holy man Job? "Ane boureau or hangman" is not a favourite of the prince who employs him to execute justice on transgressors; and the English are simply God's hangmen! " Quhar for i treist that his diuine iustice vil permit sum vthir straynge natione to be mercyles boreaus to them, ande til extinct that false seid ande that incredule generatione furtht of remembrance, because thai ar, ande alse hes beene, the special motione of the iniust veyris that hes trublit cristianite thir sex hundretht zeir by past."

The fourth chapter is devoted to a comparison of the calamities that Isaiah predicts shall befall Judah[1] and those that now afflict Scotland. God in his righteous anger has taken from the Scots their lords and barons, that might have defended them from their "ald enemeis"; as to the "iugis ande iustice that ringis presently in oure cuntre, Gode maye send vs bettir quhen he pleysis. Ande as to the precheours, i reffer that to the vniversal auditur of oure realme." When the author has to apply the verse: "As for my people, children are their oppressors, and women rule over them," he is extremely anxious to explain that this passage is not to be understood literally. It would have borne rather hard on the lady to whom he dedicated his *Complaynt*, and in whose praise he is so pro-

[1] Isaiah, chap. iii.

fuse; but he is indignant with all envious calumniators and secret detractors who refuse to find a bit of Scottish history in the prophecies of Isaiah.

The fifth chapter is a fit conclusion to its melancholious predecessors. Human weakness in all ages of Christianity has found a curious consolation in misfortune by indulging in the belief that the world is coming to an end. Probably nothing seemed to account more satisfactorily for the state into which Scotland had fallen than this transcendent expectation, which raises the author for a moment into a Pauline mood. Since the world is near an end, "haue it in detestatione," and "haue premeditatione of the future eternal beatitude ande felicite, that Gode hes promeist til al them that haldis it in abhominatione."

The sixth chapter, entitled "Ane Monolog of the Actor," is now the most precious part of the *Complaynt*, and is full of such literary beauties as the Euphuistic diction of the writer will allow. Wearied with the labour of the pen, he seeks recreation in the open air, and "past to the greene hoilsum feildis, situat maist comodiusly fra distemprit ayr ande corruppit infectione, to resaue the sueit fragrant smel of tendir gyrssis, ande of hoilsum balmy flouris maist odoreferant. Besyde the fut of ane litil montane, there ran ane fresche reueir as cleir as berial, quhar i beheld the pretty fische vantounly stertland vitht their rede vermeil fynnis, ande there skalis lyik the brycht siluyr. On the tothir syde of that reueir, there vas ane grene banc ful of rammel[1] grene treis, quhar there vas mony smal birdis hoppand fra busk to tuist, singand melodius reportis of natural music in accordis of mesure of diapason prolations,

[1] Branchy.

tripla ande dyatesseron. That hauynly ermonyie aperit to be artificial music." All day he lingered in the fields, refreshing himself with the sweet sights and sounds; and even when night fell, he could not leave the happy scene, but wandered up and down the green woods, till he "persauit the messengeiris of the rede aurora, quhilkis throucht the mychtis of titan hed persit the crepusculyne lyne matutine of the northt northt est orizone, quhilk vas occasione that the sternis and planetis, the dominotours of the nycht, absentit them, ande durst nocht be sene in oure hemispere, for dreddour of his auful goldin face." The return of day and re-awakening life is described with a lavish wealth of detail that is positively bewildering. It is not, however, genuine poetical description. No definite picture is presented to the eye. Fancy scatters her treasures profusely, but the shaping spirit of imagination that gives the unity of life to an inorganic mass of details is awanting. After telling us how horse, cattle, sheep, dogs, and swine sent forth their various din, "Actor" goes on in this elaborate fashion: "The chekyns began to peu quhen the gled[1] quhissillit. The fox follouit the fed geise, ande gart them cry claik. The gayslings cryit quhilk quhilk, ande the dukis cryit quaik. The ropeen[2] of the rauynis gart the crans[3] crope. The huddit crauis cryit varrok varrok, quhen the suannis murnit, be cause the gray goul mau[4] pronosticat ane storme. The turtil began for to greit, quhen the cuschet zoulit. The titlene[5] follouit the goilk,[6] ande gart hyr sing guk guk. The dou croutit hyr sad sang that soundit lyik sorrou. Robeen ande the litil vran var hamely in vyntir. The iargolyne of the suallou

[1] Kite. [2] Hoarse cry. [3] Cranes [4] Gull mew. [5] Hedge-sparrow. [6] Cuckoo.

gart the iay i angil. Than the maueis¹ maid myrtht, for to mok the merle.² The lauerok³ maid melody vp hie in the skyis. The nychtingal al the nycht saug sueit notis. The tuechitis⁴ cryit theuis nek, quhen the picttis⁵ clattrit. The garruling of the stirlene gart the sparrou cheip. The lyntquhit⁶ sang cuntirpoint quhen the oszil⁷ zelpit. The grene serene⁸ sang sueit quhen the gold spynk⁹ chantit. The rede schank¹⁰ cryit 'my fut my fut, and the oxee¹¹ cryit tueit. The herrons gaif ane vyild skrech as the kyl hed bene in fyir, quhilk gart the quhapis¹² for fleyitnes flee far fra hame."

When "Actor" had sufficiently enjoyed this multitudinous music, he sought the sea shore, and sat down under a cliff to listen to the rush and roar of the waves. Here he becomes a spectator of a naval engagement, which gives him an opportunity of going round the whole circle of nautical phraseology; and for this purpose apparently the scene has been introduced, since it is in no way connected with the slender "action" of the story. The ever-increasing importance of maritime enterprise after the discovery of the New World, and the great efforts made by recent Scottish kings to develop a powerful navy, may help to account for the prominence given to this incident. "Actor" does not wait to see the end of the fight. "The reik, smeuk, and the stink of the gun puldir, fylit al the ayr maist lyik as plutois paleis hed bene birnand in ane bald fyir, quhilk generit sik mirknes ande myst that I culd nocht see my lyntht about me." So he retraced his steps inland, and lighted upon a company of shepherds, whose "mornyng bracfast" was being brought to

¹Thrush. ²Black-bird. ³Lark. ⁴Pee-wits or lapwings. ⁵Magpies. ⁶Linnet. ⁷Ouzel. ⁸Greenfinch. ⁹Goldfinch. ¹⁰Redshank. ¹¹Ox-eye tomtit. ¹²Curlews: mod. Scotch "whaups."

them by their wives and children. It consisted of "euyrie sort of mylk baytht of ky mylk and zoue mylk, sueit mylk ande soure mylk, curdis and quhaye, sourkittis,[1] fresche buttir ande salt buttir, reyme,[2] flot quhaye[3], grene cheis, kyrn mylk, ry caikis, and fustean[4] skonnis made of flour." After the "disiune"[5] the principal shepherd delivers a marvellous oration on the "hie stait and dignite" of pastoral life. No analysis could give an adequate idea of the harangue, into which the author pours, with fantastic incongruity, the whole resources of his learning. "The maist anciant nobilis that hes bene in ald tymis, tha detestit vrbanite, and desirit to lyue in villagis and landuart tounis to be scheiphirdis, or to laubir rustic ocupation on the hoilsum feildis, as diuerse historigraphours hes maid mentione. For in ald tymis pastoral and rustical ocupatione vas of ane excellent reputatione, for in thai dais quhen the goldin varld rang, kyngis and princis tuke mair delyit on the feildis and forrestis to keip bestialite and to manure corne landis, nor thai did to remane in pretoral paleeis or in tryumphand citeis." Then follows the usual string of heterogeneous examples. We are told that the "riche kyng Amphion vas verray solist to keip his scheip, and at enyn quhen thai past to there faldis, scheip cottis and ludgens, he playt befor them on his harpe;" that David loved more to be a shepherd than to be governor of the people of Israel; that Apollo, though reckoned a god by the poets, kept the flocks of Admetus; that the noble Romans in old times were not ashamed to labour and manure their barren fields with their own hands, of whom Cincinnatus was a shining example; so too were

[1] Clouted cream. [2] Cream. [3] Whey brose. [4] Soft, fluffy. [5] Breakfast.

Porcius Cato, Romulus, Fabricius, Numa Pompilius, Paris son of Priam, Scipio Africanus,[1] Lucullus, Diocletian and Pericles. Were not Abraham, Isaac, and Jacob, the princes and prophets of Israel, herdsmen and shepherds? He next contrasts the corruption and intemperance of city life with the health and innocence of rural occupations. He repudiates with disdain the notion that shepherds are "ignorant, unciuil, and rude of ingyne"; and affirms that they were the earliest teachers of science with " natural mecanyc " and the " speculatione of supernatural thingis."

This leads to a most exhaustive exposition of the cosmography of the universe, which proves the writer of the *Complaynt* to be at least familiar with the astronomy of his age. It would serve no purpose to give an outline of an obsolete and erroneous system, but we are not surprised that the shepherd's wife is at length driven to exclaim : " My veil belouit hisband, i pray the to decist fra that tideus melancolic orison, quhilk surpassis thy ingyne," and to propose less solemn recreation, viz., that " cuyrie ane of vs tel ane gude tayl or fabil, to pas the tyme quhil enyn." This suggestion is received with delight, and for a moment we entertain the hope that the lowland Scotch dialect is to be enriched with a rival of the *Canterbury Tales*. But it immediately turns out that the author, fearing to be accused of prolixity, has resolved to content himself

[1] The *elder* and *younger* Scipio are rolled together in a way that will surprise more exact students of Roman history : " Nobil Scipio, quhilk vas vailzeant ande no les prudent, he conqueist Affrica, and pat Cartage to sac, and subdeuit Numance and vanqueist Annibal, and restorit the liberte of Rome, than in his age of lij zeir, he left the toune of Rome, and past to remane the residu of his dais in ane landuart village betuix Pezole ande Capue in Ytalie, ande there he set his felicite on the manuring of the corne land, and in the keping of bestialite."

with the enumeration of the titles of his stories. Even this, however, is information of the greatest value. We see on what literature the little reading world of Scotland was nursed in those days. Besides the Chronicles of the Lives of Saints, with here and there a Patristic treatise, we find that educated Scots before the Reformation had for their pleasure and profit a rich library of romance in prose and verse. The list embraces nearly fifty works. It begins with Chaucer, and ends with Ovid, whose *Metamorphoses* are laid under frequent contribution. Barbour's *Brus* and Blind Harry's *Wallace* are mentioned; so are Mandeville's *Travels*, Douglas's *Paleis of Honour*, Dunbar's *Goldin Targe*, and the story of *Rauf Coillzear*, which we have already noticed. Most of the Arthurian tales, and one or two of the Carolingian cycle are named; besides a considerable number intended specially for popular consumption, as: *The tayl of the reyde eyttyn*[1] *vitht the thre heydis; The tayl of the volfe of the varldis end; The tayl of the giantis that eit quyk men; The tayl of the thre futtit dog of Norrouay;* and *Robene hude and litil Ihone*.[2]

When the shepherds had finished their tales, "than thay ande ther vyuis began to sing sueit melodius sangis of natural music of the antiquite." Their art is wonderful. They surpassed the "foure marmadyns that sang quhen thetis vas mareit on month Pillion," and rivalled the "musician Amphion quhilk sang sa dulce quhil that the stanis mouit, and alse the scheip and nolt, and the foulis of the ayr, pronuncit there bestial voce to sing vitht him." Only the names of the songs

---

[1] O.E. *eoten*, a giant.

[2] For a critical notice of these stories see Furnivall's Introduction to "Captain Cox, his Ballads and Books," edited for the Ballad Society in 1871.

are given, but some are familiar to us, and even famous. *Pastance vitht gude companye* is ascribed to Henry VIII.; *Stil vndir the leyuis grene*, printed by Pinkerton from the Maitland MS., is a beautiful lyric; *Cou[1] thou me the raschis grene* is printed in Ritson's Ancient Songs, vol. I., p. 75, with the music; *The frog cam to the myl dur*, which according to Pinkerton was sung on the Edinburgh stage shortly before 1784; *O lusty maye vitht flora quene*, first printed by Chepman and Myllar in 1508; *The battel of the Hayrlau*, now extant only in Ramsay's version, the genuineness of which is more than doubtful; *The huntis of Cheuet*, obviously, from the title, the older and finer form of the ballad of *Chevy Chase*; and others which were afterwards metamorphosed into "godlie ballatis" by too zealous reformers.[2] The songs are succeeded by dances. "Euyrie ald scheiphyrd led his vyfe be the hand, and euyrie yong scheiphyrd led hyr quhome he luffit best." The names of the musical instruments and of the dances are given. The former comprised a "drone bag pipe," a "pipe maid of ane bleddir and of ane reid," a "trump," a "corne pipe," "a pipe maid of ane gait[3] horne," a "recordar," a "fiddil," and a "quhissil"; and it is perhaps almost needless to add that neither Amphion nor Apollo, nor Orpheus nor Pan, nor "al the scheiphyrdis that Virgil makkis mention in his bucolikis" played more sweetly than those northern minstrels. Few of the dance tunes can now be recognised, but we may hazard a selection from the list: *Al cristyn mennis dance; The northt of scotland; Huntis up; Lang plat[4] fut of gariau;[5] Robene hude; Thom of lyn; The gosseps dance*

[1] Pluck or cull. [2] See Laing's *Gude and Godlie Ballatis* (Edin. Paterson, 1868).
[3] Goat.   [4] Flat.   [5] Garioch.

Freris al; Schayke leg fut before gossep; Rank at the rute; Ihonne ermistrangis dance; The alman haye;[1] and *Schaik a trot.* At last the merriment is over, and the shepherds go about their daily tasks. "Actor" leaves the scene, and enters an unmown meadow full of "al sortis of holisum flouris, gyrsis, and cirbis maist conuenient for medycyn," whose virtues are described with amusing naïveté. He now thinks of returning home "to proceid in the compiling of my beuk," but, overcome by drowsiness, he lies down on "the cald eird," and is soon fast asleep. In this condition he dreams a dream which he professes to rehearse "as neir the verite as my rememorance can declair to my rude ingyne."

This dream or vision forms the "complaynt" proper, and occupies the remaining chapters of the work. In these the character and political sentiments of the writer are clearly revealed. He figures as an ardent and narrow-minded Scot, whose heart is inflamed by the outrages perpetrated on his country by the English armies after the death of James V., and by the infamous submission of the Border clans to the English Government. He thinks the two nations ought to cherish an implacable hostility to each other; and with honest zeal he urges the various orders of his countrymen to cease their discords and quarrels, and by the reformation of their manners and a display of disinterested patriotism, to strengthen themselves against a cruel, treacherous, and irreconcilable foe. Blind Harry is not a more thoroughgoing partisan than this nameless ecclesiastic, whose voice is still for war. Most of the historical matter is cast in a

[1] The German "Hay" or country dance.

polemical mould, and possesses little value, though the illustrations from biblical, classical, and modern European history are profuse and quaint to a degree; but the descriptions of the social condition of Scotland, even if we allow them to suffer from the exaggerations of an unchaste rhetoric, are singularly graphic and interesting.

In his "dullit dreyme" is seen a lady of excellent extraction and ancient genealogy. She is in sore terror and distress because of the violence she has suffered. "Hyr hayr, of the cullour of fyne gold, vas feltrit[1] ande trachlit[2] out of ordour, hingand ouer hyr schuldiris. Sche hed ane croune of gold, hingand ande brangland,[3] that it vas lyik to fal doune fra hyr hede to the cald eird. Sche bure ane scheild, in the quhilk vas grauit ane rede rampand lyon in ane feild of gold, bordoryt about vitht doubil floure delicis." Her mantle was "of ane meruelouse ingenius fassoune." The upper part, which symbolized the nobility, contained many precious stones, and had engraven on it "scheildis, speyris, sourdis, bayrdit[4] horse harnes, ande al vthir sortis of vaupynis ande munitions of veyr"; the middle part, which symbolized the spirituality, had images of "beukis and figuris, diuerse sciensis diuyne ande humain, vitht mony cheretabil actis ande supernatural miraclis"; while the lower part, with its representations of "al sortis of cattel ande profitabil beystis, al sortis of cornis, eyrbis, plantis, grene treis, schips, marchantdreis, ande mony politic verkmanlumis for mecanyc craftis," was of course emblematic of the commons. The condition of the mantle, however, shows the condition of the three orders. It was

[1] Dishevelled. [2] Bedraggled. [3] Waving. [4] Caparisoned.

all torn and ragged; the first part wanted many of the shields and spears that originally adorned it; the second was so altered from its primitive fashion, and so separated from the rest, that "na man culd extract ony profitabil sentens nor gude exempil furtht of ony part of it"; the third was in the worst plight of all, " for it aperit that al the grene treis, cornis, bestialite, mecanyc craftis, ande schips, and marchandreise, that hed bene curiouslye vrocht in ald tymis in the bordour of the tail of that mantil, vas spilt ande distroyit, ande the eird vas becum barran ande stirril, ande that na ordinance of policye culd be persauit in it, nor esperance of releif."

But a more living and natural image of the three orders is given to us in the pictures of the lady's three sons, the oldest of whom is brought before us, "traland ane halbert behynd hym, beand al affrayit ande fleyit for dreddour of his lyue"; the second sits in a chair, "beand clethd in ane sydegoune, kepand grite grauite, heffand ane beuk in his hand, the glaspis var fast lokkyt vihht rouste"; while the youngest lies in rags on the ground, "makkand ane dolorus lamentatione ande ane piteouse complaynt." On inquiry, he learns that the lady is called Dame Scotia; that she had once enjoyed great prosperity and renown, but that she is now overcome and afflicted by her "ald mortal enemeis" (*i.e.*, of course, the English) owing to the ingratitude and cowardice of her three sons, whom she now proceeds to upbraid with maternal vehemence. We may briefly pass over her solemn reproaches. Her children are destitute of patriotism; they will not fight for their native land, though "the foulis of the ayr vil deffende ther nestis vitht there nebbis ande feit; the beiris, lyons, voluis, foxis, dogis vil deffende there cauerne ande there quhelpis, vitht there tethe ande feit." They are selfish and distrustful of each other. Some have even committed the unpardonable sin of making terms with their foes, remaining in their own houses, "on the Inglis mennis assurance," while others are become neutral, "lyik to the ridars that dueillis on the debatabil landis." But even this degradation does not secure them peace. They are still subject to insult and injury by their cruel allies, and when they cross the Border " al the gude treittyng that Scottis men gettis in Ingland changis in ane vile seruitude." The "afflicted lady" next exhorts her degenerate offspring to take an example from those nations and individuals whom God has delivered at sundry times from persecution, when they have put their trust in Him. This affords the author great scope, and he enlarges to his heart's content and with his usual disregard of chronology. We are reminded of the glorious wars of the Maccabees; of the fortunes of Joseph and David ; of the miraculous preservation of Shadrach, Meshach, and Abed-nego in the Babylonian furnace, and of the prophet Daniel in the den of lions; of the splendid victory of Gideon over the Midianites ; the discomfiture of Darius and Xerxes in Greece ; the expulsion of the English from France within the last hundred years, and, finally, the memorable triumphs of Robert Bruce after "he tint threttyne battellis contrar Inglismen," and was forced to flee to Norway to save his life! Moreover, "the famous historiographours and croniklis of al cuntreis" show that outrageous tyranny and pride always come to a miserable end. Witness the fate of Semiramis, Hercules,

Mithridates, Philip of Macedon, Alexander the Great, Xerxes, Cyrus, Hannibal, and others. "There for I hope in God that vitht in schort days the protectour of Ingland, ande his cruel counsel, sall be put in the croniklis in as abhominabil stile as vas Philaris, Dionysius, Nero, Callugala, or Domician, the quhilkis maid ane mischeuous ende, for the violent inuasions of vthir princis cuntreis but ony iust titil."

The tenth chapter, though brief, has great political interest. The writer—for Dame Scotia seems rather to fall out of sight for a time—refers to certain English "oratours," who, at the instance of the Protector, have put forth a book to prove that Scotland was originally an English colony; but "realmis," he proudly declares, "ar nocht conquest be buikis, but rather be bluid." No book of the kind here described is known to exist, but a number of pamphlets have been preserved which prove that efforts were being made to convince the Scots that the welfare of both nations demanded their union, as in the beginning. It is probable that the author of *The Complaynt* mixes up these pamphlets with the prophecies of Merlin, which he tells us in the same chapter, were much credited in England, because they foretold the union of the crowns. It is amusing to see how his patriotism leads him to speak of the great magician as an "ald corruppit vaticinar"; then, as if not quite satisfied with his own contempt, he adduces examples to show that men in past times have misinterpreted prophecies to their own confusion, and he hopes "in God" that this will turn out to be the case with Englishmen now, who are so impious that they put more faith in the "ald corruppit vaticinar" than in Isaiah, Ezekiel, Jeremiah, or even the Evangel itself. In fact, he is sure that the union of the crowns will come to pass, but not in the way Englishmen look for it. He has read in the English chronicles "in ane beuk callit polichornicon," a prophecy which says that England shall be first conquered by the Danes, then by the Saxons, and then by the Normans; "and there last conquessing sal be conquest be the Scoitis quhome Inglismen haldis maist vile." The two nations shall form one monarchy under one prince; "and sa Inglis men sall get there prophesie fulfillit to their awen mischeif."

The eleventh and twelfth chapters illustrate the stubborn conviction of the Scots that, in spite of a common language, they are quite a distinct people from the English. The latter are represented as foreigners in Britain, the false brood of Hengist who overpowered and subdued the genuine natives, and tyrannously established themselves in the realm, while it is hinted that the former are a race that have been immemorially settled in the isle. In this view there is of course a certain amount of truth. The Scots, politically so-called, are, as we have seen, far more deeply Celtic in their pedigree and history than the English. Great movements, both religious and political, took rise among them before the slightest Teutonic influence made itself felt; but what the author of *The Complaynt* did not perceive, and what the mass of his countrymen do not yet very distinctly realize, is, that after the time of Malcolm Ceannmor, the whole aspect of Scottish history is changed, and new agencies are continuously at work remoulding the national character, and giving prominence to elements that had no place in the kingdom of Kenneth Macalpin. Yet the early chroniclers of the North delighted themselves with the figment that the term Scots had always the same extension of meaning; and that descendants of the Cymri of Strathclyde, the Angles of Lothian, the Norman baronage, and the Flemish burgesses of the seaboard, might somehow regard as their ancestral rulers the Gaelic chiefs who sprung from the daughter of Pharaoh. In this way the English become "the ald mortal enemes" of the Scots, "tuelf hundretht yeiris by past," though, as a matter of fact, any English who were foes of the Scots at that remote period must have been ancestors of the men of Lothian, who had been for centuries loyal subjects of the Scottish kings. The causes that led to the growth of the later Scottish nationality have been indicated in an earlier part of the volume, and it is unnecessary to repeat them here; but the author is extremely bitter against the English, "ald subtil doggis," on account of their inveterate hatred of his native land, and their perpetual efforts to foster dissension and perfidy. History is again ransacked for proofs of the fatal results of civil discords. It would be tedious to recount his illustrations, but he makes Dame Scotia warn her three sons that worse and more shameful punishment than the Samnites inflicted on the Romans at the Caudine Forks, shall befall those Scots who forget the glorious patriotism of their fathers, and are vile enough to participate in the English invasions of the Borders. He asserts that thousands of his countrymen have passed into England to better their fortunes, or to escape the penalties of rebellion; that they have thriven wonderfully by their own industry and the favour of the English king, but that they dare not own their northern origin, and try to palm themselves off as natives of Kent, or York, or London. Probably there is a good deal of exaggeration in such statements. The Scottish immigration into England on any great scale is of much later date; but it is quite true that after the fate of the Douglasses political malcontents in considerable numbers found an asylum in the South. Nevertheless, we may accept without difficulty his graphic statement that "quhon beit that the kyng of Ingland garris tret Scottis men vitht gold and siluer as thai var his frendis, yit doutles he vald be rycht glaid sa that euerye Scottis man hed ane vthyr Scottis man in his bellye." He uses them as instruments for his wicked purposes, but he does not love them any more than Augustus Cæsar loved the Thracian captain Rhymitalkes, who betrayed his master Antony.

In the thirteenth chapter the author seeks to show how this base regard for England has originated. It is all owing to the fatal familiarity of the Scottish borderers with their Southern neighbours "in marchandeis, in selling and bying hors, and nolt, and scheip" —a thing that ought to be stopped, for " in the dais of Moises, the Jeuis durst nocht haue familiarite vitht the Samaritanis, nor vitht the Philistiens, nor the Romans vitht the Affricans, nor the Grekis vitht the Persans." The old laws of the Marches forbade all such intercourse between Scots and English; but for the last seven years or thereby these laws have been a dead letter, and the King of England has taken advantage of the circumstance to tamper with "diuerse gentil men of Scotland," as Hannibal and Jugurtha were wont to do with their adversaries in olden times. In this way it has come about that some traitor reveals the secret plans of the Scottish Council to the King of England, so that "as sune as the lordis of the counsel hes determit ony guide purpos for the deffens and veilfair of the realme, incontinent vitht in tuenty houris thereftir, the sammyn counsel is vitht in the toune of Beruik, and vitht in thre dais there eftir the post of Beruik presentis it in London to the counsel of Ingland, quhilk is occasione that the Inglismen hes there deffens reddy contrar our purpos, or ve begyn to exsecut the counsel that vas determit." The writer of *The Complaynt* thinks, and rightly too, that such secret perfidy deserves severer punishment than the bold treason that openly shows itself in arms on the enemy's side. He was probably unaware himself of the extent to which it existed; but the publication of the State papers of this period makes it painfully clear that most of the Scottish nobles and gentry were perfectly willing to sell themselves for gold to the English king. Their avarice had so blinded their reason and hardened their heart that one could no more expect fidelity from them than one could expect "ane fische of the depe flude speik hebreu or greik." In chapter fourteenth the author, speaking for Dame Scotia, winds up his long discourse with the customary array of "proofs" from history that conspirators invariably suffer punishment at the hands of those princes who profit by their treason. Here, as everywhere in this singular book, we have conclusive evidence of classical knowledge without classical culture, which is one of its most marked features. It would be difficult to find a writer more profoundly familiar in one sense with the life of antiquity. The biographies of its great men, or at least the striking incidents of their history, are all at his finger ends; but grace of expression and symmetry of form are unknown to his style, nor is there the faintest perception of the distinctive peculiarities of the ancient world. Somehow we feel as if his Greek and Roman narratives might have been part of the history of Scotland or Judea.

The next chapter merits close attention. It is the cry of the Scottish labourer against his twin tyrants, the lairds and the clergy. We often hear it in the literature of the first half of the sixteenth century—nowhere more distinctly than in the verse of Sir David Lyndsay. But Lyndsay was a reformer and an implacable foe of the priests. Let us listen for a moment to the voice of one whose sympathies were with the old historic church of the nation, who was himself a minister at its altars, but whose patriotism was a more ardent passion than his religion, and who remembered with pride that the commons of Scotland in the brave days of Wallace and Bruce were not the betrayers of their country's liberties.

The third son of Dame Scotia admits at once the reasonableness of his mother's complaint, but thinks it "wondrous bitter" that he who has been the chief sufferer from the crimes of his two brothers should also be scourged with undeserved reproaches. "I may be comparit to the dul asse in sa far as i am compellit to bayr ane importabil byrdyng, for i am dung and broddit to gar me do and to thole the thing that is abuif my power." He is a mark for all the arrows of tribulation: the most remorseless extortions are practised upon him. Day and night he labours with his hands for lazy, idle, useless men who requite him with hunger and the sword. They live through him and he dies through them. "My tua brethir, nobilis and clergie, quhilk suld defend me, tha ar mair cruel contrar me nor is my ald enemes of Ingland." His corn and cattle are reft from him. But not only is he subject to wanton hership, he is as pitilessly rack-rented as an Irish farmer used to be. "I am exilit fra my takkis and fra my steddyngis. The malis and fermis of the grond that i laubyr is hychtit to sic ane price, that it is fors to me and vyf and bayrns to drynk vattir. The teyndis of my cornis ar nocht alanerly hychtit abufe the fertilite that the grond maye bayr, bot as veil thai are tane furtht of my handis be my tua tirran brethir." Nor is this the limit of his misery and wrong. If he betakes himself to merchandise or some mechanic craft to better his condition, he is forced to lend his gains to his lavish and improvident brothers, and if he ventures to crave payment of his loans he is bullied and kicked and often killed. Nor can he think of any way of relief. He sees nothing before him but "arrage, carage, taxationis, violent spulze, and al vthyr sortis of aduersite."

Even the war that is proclaimed against England resolves itself into the desolation of the homesteads of the poor. He reminds his mother that the labouring class is "ane notabil membyr of ane realme, vitht out the quhilk the nobillis and clergie can nocht sustene ther stait nor ther lyif," and that the Romans in old times instituted "ane nobil man of office, callit *tribunus plebis*, quha deffendit the fredum and liberte of the comont pepil contrar the crualte of the hie senat, or ony vthir grit man of grit stait." He laments the want of such a champion in Scotland who might stand between him and his unnatural oppressors. Therefore he is constrained to cry to God for vengeance, nor does he believe he will cry in vain. "For it is to be presumit that the lamentabil voce and cryis of the affligit pepil complenant to the hauyn, vil moue to pitie the clemens of the maist merciful and puissant diuyne plasmator,[1] the quhilk throcht his eternal iustice vil succumb in confusione al violent vsurpatours quhilkis parpetratis sic cruel iniquiteis on the desolat pure pepil. Therfor (o thou my mother) sen i am in dangeir of the deitht, and disparit of my lyif, necessite pulsis and constrenzes me to cry on god, and to desire vengeance on them that persecutis me, in hope that he vil relief me, or els to tak me furtht of this miserabil lyif, for the ingratitude of my tua brethir, their dissolutione, and the misknaulage of god, and ther disordinat misgouernance is the cause of my impatiens, and cause of all my afflictione; for as ther euil conquest reches multiplies, ther disordinat pompe and ther delicius ydilnes, vitht misknaulage of god augmentis, quhilk is occasione that tha ar ambitius in ther stait, couetics of gudis, and desirus to be gouernouris of the realme."

Yet in spite of his murmurings the two brothers persist in their extortions. He again implores his mother to be more just and generous to himself. There is a Latin proverb which says *parce sepulto* ("spare the dead,") and the Scottish peasant is as good as dead. All through the expostulation hitherto there has been visible a certain democratic spirit, but it now flames up into fierce contention. The labourer denies that he is the youngest son: on the contrary he is the eldest. "The begynning of nobillis and spiritualite hed bot pure lauboraris to ther predecessouris." "My tua

---

[1] Maker.

brethir professis them to be gentil men, and reputis me and al lauberaris to be rustical and inciuile, ondantit, ignorant, dullit slauis. Thai vil nocht consider that al there gentreis hes procedit and discendit fra me." Adam and his children were all simple labourers by whose industry, foresight, and policy the later framework of human society was built up. But instead of feeling proud of their descent from the " grand old gardener and his wife," ignorant vanity of the higher orders tempts them to draw their origin from angels and archangels.

Then follows a roll of the illustrious poor—David, king of Israel, son of an obscure shepherd, Tulius Hostilius, " the sone of ane pure lauberar of the grond," Tarquinius Priscus, whose father was a humble merchant, Varro, Perpenna, Marcus Cato, Socrates, " jugit to be the maist prudent man in the vniuersal varld," Euripides, Demosthenes, " that prudent duc of athenes, the sone of ane pure marchant that sellit ald knyuis," Agathocles, and Cicero. He treats with scorn the haughty fiction of noble blood; "for I trou that gif ane cirurgyen vald drau part of there blude in ane bassyn, it vald hef na bettir cullour nor the blude of ane plebien or of ane mecanik craftis man;" and so he prays God to open the eyes of his arrogant brothers and give them grace to "ken themselfis." Then he pleads once more with his mother "to considir the verite of my innocens." Treason never has its birth among the commons; they are too weak, helpless, and ignorant to plot successfully against a despotic prince. History proves that conspiracies have invariably been formed by the great; and even they have found it difficult to preserve secrecy in their designs in spite of the advantages of their position. All that the poor can do is to make their wives and bairns pray covertly to Heaven for deliverance from the cruel tyranny under which they groan, for in strange company they must with feigned heartiness cry out, "God save his Grace, and send him long life and prosperity." If ever they are sincere in their expressions of good will it is only like the old wife of Syracuse who prayed for the tyrant Dionysius on the ground that his successor was likely to prove worse than himself, as he had proved worse than either his father or grandfather. Nor can the commons be blamed if they take "assurance" of the English. Their natural protectors, the nobles and clergy, have failed in their duty, and not even a cow or an ox will they give to help a wretched peasant who has been plundered of all his goods by English rievers. If the leaders of the nation would only show a spirit of patriotism, the commons of Scotland would not be slow to follow; but as things stand at present, prudence constrains them to dissimulate like Junius Brutus, nor can they be charged with treason so long as they lack the force to resist the violent dominion of their enemies.

To this plea of her youngest son Dame Scotia will not listen. The sixteenth chapter is her answer to the democratic vehemence of the fifteenth. Cicero is quoted to show that no man should be admitted as a witness in his own case, nor must the guilty accuse others of guilt, as the Pharisees did with the woman taken in adultery. People should take the beam out of their own eye before they attempt to take the mote out of their neighbours' eyes. Perseus, the Roman satirist, tells us that every man carries two wallets, one before and one behind. The former contains his neighbour's vices, the latter, his own. The first is quite visible to his view, the second he cannot see at all. Dame Scotia is therefore not much convinced by the invective of her youngest son against his two brothers, though it is not surpassed in "calumniations" by the fifteen philippics of Cicero against Antony. The labouring or working class—husbandmen, merchants, and craftsmen—deserve " punition " no less than the nobles and clergy. In their revolts against authority they have ever shown themselves " mair cruel nor the vyild beystis of the desertis of arabie." "There for none of you suld haue liberte, bot rather ye suld be daly dantit and haldin in subiectione, be cause that your hartis is ful of maleis, ignorance, variance and inconstance. For the maist part of you al gyffis louyng tyl vicius men, and ye hald verteous men abhominabil, and quhen ye are al convenit to gydthir for the auansing of ane gude purpose, ye cry and berkis ilk ane contrar vthirs, that nocht ane of you knauis quhat ane vthir sais. Ande quhen ye hef flyttyn ande berkit but ryme or rason al the lang daye, ye accord nocht nor condiscendis prudently on ane substancial constant purpose, and he that is the maist cummirsum[1] cryar, ande maist obstinat contrar raison, ye reput hym for the maist prudent man of the realme. Then quhen he gois, al the leaue rynnis and follouis hym, lyik the brutal scheip that vil nocht pas throucht the slop of ane dyik for the mannessing of there hyrd, quhil ane of the verst of the flok mak foir gait, than al the leaue follouis."

In this way Dame Scotia goes on, chiefly by the help of Cicero, to set forth the vices of the commons. Better is the judgment of ten wise men than of a whole populace of ignorant fools. The civil law recognises

[1] Troublesome.

the incapacity of the common people and forbids them to form combinations among themselves. They are cowardly, intemperate, lustful, unbridled—worse than the beasts that perish; for "the ondantit brutal beystys that hes there liberte on feildis and forrestis, none of them eytis, drinkis, nor sleipis, bot quhen ther natural appetit requiris, nor the mail vitht the femmel committis nocht the verkis of natur, bot in the saison of generatione." The "dolorous mother" does not seem to understand that the commons are what bad laws and bad government have made them. Much of her accusation is artificial and conventional. It is in part a reflex of the patrician scorn of the plebs which stamps the early ages of Roman history and re-appears in the fastidious elegance of the Augustan literature, and in part an expression of that coarser and more cruel contempt for their serfs which centuries of feudal barbarism had engendered in the breasts of the nobility. In so far as the charges against the commons are well founded, they are still graver charges as against the governing classes who saw no need for a change in the social conditions from which such vices sprang. But one can hardly tell if the author of *The Complaynt* is quite in earnest here. Perhaps he is only playing the part of devil's advocate. If he is absolutely in earnest, he does not see his way very clearly, and does not know how to censure the multitude with justice or discretion. By and by, however, he makes Dame Scotia the mouthpiece of some shrewd observation which the parvenus even of the nineteenth century might profitably ponder. Some of the commons, he notices, work hard and grow rich. What then? Why, "thai be cum mair ambicius ande arrogant nor ony gentil man sperutual or temporal, that ar discendit of the maist nobil barons of the cuntre. Ande there childir, distitut of ciuilite, throucht the ignorance of there fathers, ande for falt of educatione and eruditione, thai be cum vane, prodig, ande arrogant, be cause thai succeid sa eysilie to reches vitht out the suet of there brouis, or pane of there body, nocht heffand regarde to the fyrst pouerte of there predecessouris, nor of the cald, hungir ande punirite[1] that there fathirs and mothers indurit in the conquessing of sic reches." In fact it is the nature of low-born churls when the accident of fortune exalts their station "to mysken them selfis, their friendis, ande there familiaris." Nor is there anything in the world more odious than such a spectacle of "myskenning." It leads "mecanye pepil heffand superflu prosperite" to deny their parentage and genealogy, and to claim connection with noble houses. They prove their ancient blood by their haughty bearing and their ruthless treatment of the poor, but their prosperity is of short duration. The heirs of wealthy burghers thrive not to the third generation. And the reason is not far to seek. "Ane person that hed neuyr aduersite and hes veltht that procedit neuyr of his auen industrie, and syne hes liberte, and hes neueir knauen education, eruditione, nor ciuilite, it is onpossibil that he can be verteous, and he that heytis vertu, sal neuyr thryue."

So ends Dame Scotia's answer to her youngest son. It is not satisfactory: it is over-charged, cynical in tone, and partly false. After all has been said, the cry of the poor still rings in our ears, and we remember with emotion the tale of their wrongs. But the author of *The Complaynt* was making an appeal to his country-

[1] Penury.

men at large. It was not his business or his aim to set class against class. He wished to bind them together in a common bond of patriotism against the English alliance, and he may have thought it prudent to expose with severity the vices of the commons before proceeding to denounce the baseness of the nobles.

The seventeenth chapter contains a great deal of what in our day would be called Radicalism. Every one knows that the Church has always had democratic sympathies. Its prelates and other high officers might care nothing for the poor; but the monks sprang from the people, and the monastic literature is sometimes inspired with a political audacity that would have been dangerous to the feudal fabric if it had passed from sentiment and theory into the sphere of popular agitation. The author of *The Complaynt* scouts the pretensions of the nobles to superiority. He makes Dame Scotia indignantly declare, "There is nocht ane sperk of nobilnes nor gentrice amang the maist part of you." What is real nobility and how did it originate? he asks. "In the gude anciant dais, quhilk sum men callit the goldin varld, there vas na defferens of staitis at that tyme amang men, nothir in pre-eminens, dignite, superiorite, nor honour, for at that tyme al men var egal, and nocht partial nor deuidit, for the pepil lyuit al togydthir in ane tranquil and louabil communite, ande thai left no thing to there posterite bot regrettis for the alteratione of that gude varld." The classic dream of a golden age in the spring-time of the world was the basis of medieval Radicalism, but this political creed was certainly re-inforced by the practical doctrines of the Christian religion. Men did not perceive the irreconcilable antagonism between the two, and wrote and thought about the golden age with a sincerity of belief that the ancient poets themselves did not share. In that happy time "the pepil eit nor drank nocht bot quhen hungir constrenyet them, and than there maist delegat refectione vas acquorns, vyild berries, green frutis, rutis, and eirbis, ande thai drank the fresche vattir."

There is something very quaint and graphic in many details of the picture. "At that tyme ther vas no ceremonial reuerens nor stait, quha suld pas befor or behynd, furtht or in at the dur, nor yit quha suld have the dignite to vasche ther handis fyrst in the bassine, nor yit quha suld sit doune fyrst at the tabil. At that tyme the pepil var as reddy to drynk vattir in ther bonet, or in the palmis of ther handis, as in ane glas, or in ane tasse of siluyr. . . . Than ane lang tyme there eftir, nature prouokit them to begyn sum litil police. For sum of them began to plant treis, sum to dant[1] beystis, sum gadthrid the frutis and kepit them quhil on to the tyme of necessite, and sum neurist ther childir. At that tyme the pepil drank nothir vyne nor beir, nor na vthir confekkit drynkis. At that tyme straynge cuntreis var nocht socht to get spicis, eirbis, drogis, gummis, and succur[2] for to mak exquisite electuars to prouoke the pepil til ane disordinat appetit. At that tyme there vas no sumpteous clethyng of fyne claytht and of gold and silk of diuerse fassons. At that tyme, in the begynnyng of ther police, coppir, bras, and yrn, and vther mettellis var meltit to mak vtensel veschel necessair to serue ane househald, and var nocht meltit to be gunnis ande cannons to sla doune the pepil." But that is all past long ago. The golden

[1] Tame.   [2] Sugar.

age has vanished for ever. We are now in the midst of an iron world where meekness has given place to malice, peace to war, ease to pain, love to hatred, charity to cruelty, justice to extortion, faith to hypocrisy. How this came about is explained with extreme simplicity. It was caused by the evil dispositions of men who began to oppress their neighbours. To protect themselves the people chose "the maist robust and maist prudent to be there deffendouris," who "gat for ther panis and laubyr, the butin[1] and spulye[2] that thai conqueist fra the tirran oppressouris." Hence arose the order of nobles—brave men who fought victoriously for the good of their neighbours. On the other hand, "thai that var vicius and couuardis var reput for vilainis ande carlis!" This he goes on to "prove" after his fashion by references to the customs of the Carthaginians, Macedonians, ancient Germans, Scythians, and others. True nobility is therefore not something hereditary but personal. It demands "virtue" in its possessor. The proper use of armorial bearings, he finely asserts, is to remind the present race of nobles of the brave deeds their fathers had done for the commonwealth: they do not so much confer a privilege or an honour, as they impose an obligation on those who bear them to follow in the footsteps of their illustrious predecessors, and whoever among them fails in virtue ought to be summarily degraded from his rank. The order of knighthood is an example of true nobility. It is like the laurel crown and triumphal palm of antiquity. "Bot allace," says Dame Scotia, "(O ye, my eldest sone, nobilis ande gentil men) there is nocht mony of you that meritis to veyr the ensenye of the fleise,[3] of the

[1] Booty. [2] Spoil. [3] Fleece.

cokkil,[1] nor of the gartan,[2] nor yit there is nocht mony of you that meritis to be borne in ane charriot to resaue the tryumphe of the palme tre nor of the laure tre; for your imbecilite, auereis, ande contentione that ringis amang you, rather deseruis degrading fra your pretendit gentreis, nor ye deserue louyng or commendation for vertu."

This opinion the author makes the Dame repeat several times and in various ways, as if he could not sufficiently emphasize it, showing how strongly he was impressed with the sordid and faithless character of the Scottish nobles. He even goes so far in his ethico-political republicanism as to declare that "the sone of ane prince beand distitut of vertu is no gentil man; ande in opposit, ane sone of ane mechanyc plebien, beand verteous, he is ane gentil man." His great countryman who more than two hundred years later in history wrote those lines, which are the death-knell of flunkeyism,

> "The rank is but the guinea's stamp,
> The man's the gowd for a' that,"

could hardly have supposed that his democratic sentiment had been anticipated at so early a date by a nameless priest of the Roman Church. Antiquity, as usual, is invoked to furnish proofs of the statement that "no man can succeid to gentreis nor to vertu." The same family may exhibit the most striking contrasts of character. But, after all, it is a foolish pride that leads men to glory in their genealogy, since the race originated in mud and clay. "Al men," says the Preacher, "ar eird and alse."[3] So it would be a wiser course, if they would have these for their armorial

[1] Cockle.   [2] Garter.   [3] Ashes.

bearings. Death is the great leveller. "Quhen the corrupit flesche is consumit fra the banis, no man can put defferens betuix ane prince and ane begger." Besides, "the crop [1] ande rute of our gentreis ande genologie hes succedit fra adam. Ande quhen we entrit in this mortal lyif ve var naikyt and vepand, and quhen ve depart ve sal be vile and abhominabil, ande ve sal carye no thing furtht of this varld bot the coulpe [2] of our synnis, or the meritis of our vertu." Let the Scottish nobles earnestly reflect on these things! Virtue lies buried in the graves of their ancestors, and nothing is left to them but "the stile of there gentreis." When Dame Scotia looks round her she sees " no thing amang gentil men bot vice. For honestee is maculat, ignorance is prisit, prudens is scornit, chestite is banneist; the nychtis ar ouer schort to gentil men to commit there libedencus lust, and the dayis ar ouer schort to them to commit extorsions on the pure pepil. Ther blasphematione of the name of God corruptis the ayr. The prodig pride that ringis amang gentil men is detestabil, nocht alanerly in costly clethyng abufe their stait, bot as veil in prodig expensis that thai mak on horse and doggis, abufe ther rent or reches. Ane man is nocht reput for ane gentil man in scotland, bot gyf he mak mair expensis on his horse and his doggis nor he dois on his vyfe and bayrnis." The Greek poets tell us that Diomede's horses devoured men, and that Actaeon was torn to pieces by his dogs. These stories, says the writer, are not idle fables: they are wise parables. The horses of Diomede were not literally men-eaters, " but the superflu and prodig expensis that he (Diomede) maid on corne to feid ane grit numir of onutil

[1] Top. [2] Lat. *culpa*, guilt.

horse, gart the victualis be deir and skant, quhilk vas occasione that the pure pepil deit for hungir." Nor was Actaeon really worried to death, but he was "ane vane gentil man that set al his felicite on doggis for hunting, on the quhilkis he maid ouer prodig expensis abufe his faculte, quhilk vas occasione that he sellit his heretage til entretenc his vane pleseir, and ther eftir he fel in pouertie. Ther for the poietis fenyeis that his doggis distroyit hym." There are far too many horses and dogs of this sort in Scotland. Let the nobles put a curb on their extravagance, which is the root of their baseness, and generally spend their energies in virtuous pursuits, and not in rancorous animosities, or before long the English will inherit their lands, and their name will pass into forgetfulness.

The next chapter of *The Complaynt* deals with the faults of the clergy. It originally and properly formed the eighteenth chapter, but the condition of the MS. shows that in the recension of the work the author had made great alterations on the text, and had entirely suppressed its successor, the nineteenth, whose number it now bears. The clergy, according to Dame Scotia, deserve greater punishment than either the nobles or the commons, for they have not the excuse of ignorance. God's law has been put into their mouth. But not only do they excel the other orders of the community in divine science, they are also superior in humanity, liberal science, moral and natural philosophy. Now these advantages are not meant for their private gratification. The clergy are the messengers of God, and the dispensers of knowledge among an ignorant people. To what better use could they put their talents than to bring about national unity and concord.

And first of all let them set a good example by a life that conforms to their profession and doctrine. The ancients were very severe in their punishment of malefactors in high position on account of the greater influence they exercised. Much is said in the chapter about abuses in the Church, and the need for reformation, but the language is very general. No particular fault is laid to the charge of the clergy, except a disposition to quarrel with the government. " Ye tua ar lyke cattis and doggis berkkand on vthers." Probably more was meant. The writer could not have been ignorant of the vices that were demoralizing the priesthood and the monastic orders, but he tenderly veils them under phrases that could not inflict a pang. To their "abusione" and the "sinister ministratione" of their office he traces the "scisma" and the "diuers sectis that trublis al Cristianite." The root of these may be in Germany, Denmark, and England, but the branches have spread into other realms, and everywhere laymen are casting greedy eyes on the patrimony of the Church. Nor shall this plague of schism ever cease, no matter what laws are passed, no matter what banishments, burnings, and other tortures may be practised, till the clergy mend their lives. A "gude conuersatione" on their part would more quickly extinguish heresy than "al the punitione that al Cristianite can exsecut." Persecution of schismatics by an unreformed Church is in fact utterly useless, " for, as sune as ther is ane person slane, brynt, or bannest, for the halding of peruerst opinions, incontinent ther rysis up thre in his place." There are only two ways in which schism could be extinguished, either "gyf al the heydis of the uniuersal Cristianite be strikkyn fra them, or ellis bot gyf the ministers reforme and correct ther auen abusione."

This passage settles the religious standpoint of the author. It is not the language of a Lutheran, of a rebel against the doctrine and authority of Rome. " Schism " is in his eyes a monstrous evil with which no good man could have the slightest sympathy, and he deprecates persecution only because the " sklanderous abusione that ringis" among the clergy has made it a failure. He is on the side of Boece and Major, not of Wishart and Knox. The Renaissance has reached him. At every pore his classical learning oozes out. He may not have been a Greek scholar; there is no evidence that he was: but the spirit of literary culture pervades his work, and finds expression in flowery rhetoric, and a diction that exhausts the resources of the Latin tongue. His sacerdotal office and perhaps a lowly origin explains his sympathy with the poor, but the freedom and boldness of his political opinions are mainly due to his wide knowledge of Roman history.

What gives a unique character to *The Complaynt*, however, is its pugnacious nationalism. The writer uses all his stores of learning, all his powers of pictorial description, all his ardour of moral enthusiasm, to inflame his countrymen against England. He preaches unity and concord that the Scots may cope successfully with their "dissaitful and incredule ald enemies." In the remainder of this nineteenth chapter the clergy are warned to be vigilant in their work of reformation, for if the King of England prospers in his unjust wars he will show them no mercy. He will treat them as he has treated their brethren across the Border. " Fyrst he tuke the patrimone and the temporal landis of the kyrkis of ingland, and anext ane part of them to the proprite of his croune, and ane vthir part he distribut amang ane certan of grit personagis of his realme, quhilkis adherit til his tirran opinion, and syne he chesit furtht ane certan of the hiest genologie of ingland that hed bene promouit to cathidral digniteis, and til vthir sperutual beneficis, quhome he gart his flaschar[1] lay ther craggis[2] on ane stok and gart heyde[3] them, and syne, he gart hyng ther quartars on potentis[4] at diuerse comont passagis on the feildis quhar the maist confluens of pepil passit and repassit, and thridly he compellit pure speritual men, baytht regular and religiouse preistis, monkis and freris, to pas to leyrn mecanyc hand laubyrs, sum to be cordinaris,[5] sum to be tailyours, sum to be marynalis,[6] and sa to proceid to diuerse vthir craftis; and thai that var obstinat and disobedient tyl his cruel statutis he gart bannes ane part of them, and presone[7] the bodeis of ane vthir part in perpetual captiuite."

Here also the sympathies of the author are visibly with the historic Church. There is an entire absence of that scornful animosity that marks the Protestant reformer. He denounces the spoliations and cruelties of Henry VIII.; he speaks tenderly of the religious orders; he laments the hard fortunes of the monks after the dissolution of the monasteries. None the less is he convinced of their negligence and "sklanderous abusione" of their office. The remedy he proposes is remarkable, and shows the fervour of his patriotism. It takes us back to the fighting ages of the Irish Church, when clans had their monastic fraternities who took part in the conflicts of their secular kinsmen.[8] He

---

[1] Flesher, or butcher. [2] Necks. [3] Behead. [4] Stakes. [5] Shoemakers. [6] Sailors. [7] Imprison. [8] See chap. II., pp. 24 and 25.

urges them, if they love their country and wish to preserve "the liberte of ther faculte," to pass "in propir person in battel vitht my lord gouuernour and vitht the nobil lordis and barrons of scotland contrar the cruel invasions of [ther] ald enemies of ingland." It may be an evil, but it will deliver them from a greater evil, and as Cicero writes to his brother, "in duobus malis fugiendum majus, levius est elegendum." Therefore, let the clergy change their "sperutual habitis, bayth coulis[1] and syde gounis,[2] in steil jakkis and in cotis of mailye"; if they are aged and infirm, but have the means, let them "furneis pure preistis, monkis and freris, vitht al necessair thingis conuenient for the veyris." They need have no scruple in the matter. The law of God, the law of nature, positive law, civil and canon law—in a word all law, divine and human, binds every order and condition of men to fight if need be for the defence of the commonwealth to which they belong. He has no difficulty in proving his case from the Old Testament, but the canon law does not lend itself so readily to the support of his contention. However, by the help of a patriotism that despises logic, he comes off victorious here too. Blind Harry could not have done better. The canon law says: "Saraceni bellantes contra Cristianos, juste a Cristianis impugnantur," and the author of *The Complaynt* is prepared to "reffer the expositione of this text to the vniuersal Cristianite to juge quhidder that Inglismen be Sarrasyns or Cristin men." Again, the canon law declares: "Bella sumpta contra excommunicatos et infideles meritoria sunt," and he is willing to leave it to the judgment of all Christian princes, "quhiddir that

---

[1] Cowls. [2] Long robes.

inglismen be excommunicat and denuncit goddis rebellis be al lauis for ther infidilite, incrudilite, crualte, tirranrye, sacreleige, and for the vsurpatione of vthir princis dominions vithout ony occasione or just titil." Nothing could be fairer than this, and on the strength of the interpretation, the clergy are thus exhorted: "put al cerimonial scrupulnes furtht of your hartis," and "pas in propir person contrar your ald enemeis." If they do this, then their "faculte sal nocht be spulyeit fra the liberte that it possessis."

The twentieth and last chapter of *The Complaynt* is an exhortation to concord addressed by Dame Scotia to all her three sons, and partakes to some extent of the nature of a recapitulation. We are told again how intestine strife has done more hurt to Scotland than the great armies of England have done. Scotsmen behave to each other like barbarians and not like Christians. Why should God deliver them from their foes, since they have lost their own honour, become "sodiours and pensionaris" to England, and can show their valour only in "berkyng" on each other like dogs and cats? Christ's word is true, "omne regnum in se divisum desolabitur." The detestable wars that ruined the commonwealth of ancient Rome are repeated in modern Scotland, where envy, rancour, and greed exercise universal sway. The border wars, the social wars, the civil wars, the servile wars of antiquity have all their fatal counterparts at home. Our author's evidence of this may excite a smile among the students of Roman history, but it would easily pass muster in his own day. He also alludes to the insurrection of the Peasants in Germany as an example of a servile war, where men assembled for violent ends without the authority of their " dukis and superioris." This often happens in Scotland. " I hef sene," says Dame Scotia, " nyne or ten thousand gadyr to giddir vitht out ony commissione of the kyngis letteris, the quhilk grit conuentione hes bene to put ther nychtbours furtht of ther steding and takkis on vytson veddyinsday,[1] or ellis to leyd auaye ane pure manis teynd in heruyst; bot thai vald nocht be half sa solist to conuene thre hundretht at the command of the kyngis letteris to pas to resist our ald enemeis of ingland." In fact the dissensions that rage among her children are so bitter that it seems to Dame Scotia as if "sum sorseris and vytchis, quhilkis ar instramentis of the ald enemye of mankind," had tempted them and subdued their reason. If Heraclitus and Democritus were now alive, the state of the Scottish realm would furnish matter enough for the tears of the one and the laughter of the other. This point is dwelt upon at great length, and is handled in verse as well as prose. There is a deep earnestness in the tone of this part of the exhortation. All preachers, of course, are given to extravagance. The power of rhetoric, especially of moral rhetoric, lies in its vehemence and one-sidedness. It must exaggerate evils in order to vanquish them. Men's blood does not boil till their imaginations are inflamed; their conscience is not pierced till they feel themselves in the presence of an offended Deity.

It is impossible to accept literally the language of *The Complaynt*. Scotland was in a bad enough condition after the death of James V., but it was not a pandemonium; it was not a scene of universal anarchy, rapine, and hatred. The great mass of the people went

[1] Whitsun Wednesday.

about their daily work with more or less content. Fields were ploughed and harvests gathered; crafts were followed; men bought and sold; houses and palaces and churches were built; here and there schools were quietly busy; knowledge was spreading, and the dawn of the Reformation reveals to us not a few lairds' homes where serious piety and intellectual culture ennobled life. But we never get a glimpse of this in *The Complaynt*. It is not present to the vision of the author, whose imagination dwells upon the disorders of the realm till everything else disappears. His great weakness is his lack of historical prescience. He has not the remotest conception of what the future of his country is to be. He longs for an old-world Scotland, in which all classes of the community will be united in an indissoluble bond of enmity to England, and in which the fierce fire of patriotism will burn up the corruptions of social and individual life. It was an utterly unwise policy he favoured, and one that could not have secured the ends he desired. Had it been adopted in the sixteenth century, Scotland would have sunk into one of the most insignificant nations in Europe, and been lost to civilization for ages.

No one can doubt the honesty and zeal of the writer. He is filled with a sort of righteous indignation at the treachery and baseness of the Scottish nobles, but this indignation loses its moral character when it drives him to proclaim a policy of eternal hostility to a neighbouring state. All his religious adjurations to repentance and concord wind up with this war-whoop, "than ye sal triumphe contrar your enemeis." It was quite right that he should denounce the evils of the commonwealth in the strongest language. They existed; and they were alike a dishonour and a weakness to Scotland. So long as any considerable number of her nobility were in the pay of England, and a still larger number were willing to be bought, the nation could not politically prosper, because it could not hold an independent position, but the prudential "alliances" of the Borderers with the English were merely a consequence of the distracted councils and selfish ambitions that marked the regency, and were not properly a subject for censure at all. Had the government been strong, and its policy vigorous and independent, they would have been unnecessary; but as matters stood, no other *modus vivendi* was open to the Scots. Again, the abuses of the church had nothing in common with the treason of the nobles. They were of older origin; and were not peculiar to Scotland. They flourished in states where patrician traitors were unknown, and where the whole conditions of life were utterly dissimilar to those of Scotland. Their cessation would certainly have been a blessing both to the church and the country. A church that had purged itself of gross vice, and had become imbued with a high sense of its religious duty, could scarcely have failed to exercise a powerful influence on the actions and the character of the laity, but it is very doubtful if the result would have been the violent and morbid patriotism that inspires the author of *The Complaynt*.

CHAPTER VII.

GAVIN DOUGLAS.

His Descent and Earlier History.—Becomes Provost of St. Giles' and a prominent Ecclesiastic.—Period of his Literary Activity.—The Years after Flodden.—Marriage of Queen Margaret to the Poet's Nephew.—Her Letters to the Pope in behalf of Douglas.—Plots against the Queen.—Albany recalled and made Regent.—Douglas becomes Bishop of Dunkeld.—Absence of the Regent.—Broils between Douglasses and Hamiltons.—Margaret's Quarrel with her Husband.—She joins the Regent on his Return.—Douglas becomes the Envoy of Angus and his Party to the English Court.—His unpatriotic Conduct.—Deprived of his Bishopric.—His Death.—Criticism and Analysis of his Works.—The Palice of Honour.—King Hart.—Translation of the Æneid.

GAVIN DOUGLAS, Bishop of Dunkeld, is one of the most conspicuous names in Scottish poetry, yet his celebrity is not wholly due to his literature. Something must be ascribed to the fact that he was a member of the foremost family in the state, took part in the political intrigues of his kinsmen, and was involved in their ruin. Dunbar had a far more powerful and trenchant genius, yet his whole outward life was one ineffectual struggle to emerge from obscurity. Douglas, on the other hand, was destined to distinction, and his merits received from the first the amplest recognition.

He was the third son of Archibald, Earl of Angus, known in the national history as the "Great Earl," and more familiarly as "Bell-the-Cat." The exact date of his birth cannot be ascertained, but when examined before the Lords of the Council on the 6th of June

[July], 1515, touching the means he had used to obtain the bishopric of Dunkeld, he stated that he was "ane man of 40 yeris of age or therby," from which we may infer that he was born about the year 1475. From 1489 to 1494 he studied at the university of St. Andrews, and it is probable that he afterwards spent a year or two abroad. The diction of his poems, at any rate, favours the supposition of a residence in France, of which, however, we have no external evidence.

Douglas did not require to wait long for ecclesiastical preferment. In 1496, when he had barely reached his majority, he obtained a grant of the teinds of Monymusk in Aberdeenshire; two years later the king gave him a presentation to the parsonage of Glenquhom, when it should become vacant by the resignation of Sir Alexander Symson. Family influence also appears to have secured for him the parsonage of Lynton and rectory of Hauch (Prestonkirk), and about the year 1501 he was appointed dean or provost of the collegiate church of St. Giles, in Edinburgh. "This church, which was on a more extensive scale than any other of the kind in the country, except the chapel-royal at Stirling, supported a provost, a curate, sixteen prebendaries, and seven other officers, on the original foundation, to which was superadded a vast number of altars and chaplainries, some of them richly endowed."[1]

Up to this date Douglas's life, so far as we know, had been passed in lettered ease and rural seclusion. We cannot trace him in the history of the time, and probably his pastoral duties did not severely tax his energies; but, as we shall see when we come to examine

[1] The Works of Gavin Douglas, Bishop of Dunkeld: edited by John Small, Biographical Introduction, pp. vii.-viii.

his poetry, his leisure hours must have been assiduously devoted to scholarship and literature. Henceforth he becomes a prominent and influential ecclesiastic. He is present at meetings of Lords of the Council; he is active in the celebration of the religious services of St. Giles; he visits the Continent that he may advance his interest at the papal court (for this genuine poet and gentle-hearted man has a steady eye to the main chance); he gets the freedom of the city of Edinburgh *gratis*, during the provostship of his father, the Great Earl. The actual notices of Douglas between his appointment to the deanery of St. Giles, and the death of James at Flodden, may not be numerous, but they all indicate a leading position. Circumstances forced Dunbar to speak about himself and others with singular frankness and fulness. The king, his courtiers, parasites, and servitors; the poet himself, his penury, neglect, and shame, all stand out, presented in the bitter humours of his verse; but in spite of Dunbar's numberless pictures of court life, no one can doubt that the high-born and dignified Douglas was far more intimate with his sovereign than the Rabelaisian priest, whose satire did not spare even the crown itself.

The period to which we have referred is also the season of Douglas's literary activity. Its opening year witnessed the completion of his earliest extant poem, *The Palice of Honour*, and less than two months before "red Flodden," he finished his latest and most enduring work, the translation of Virgil's Æneid. He was now in his thirty-eighth year. Probably no man then living in Scotland had a more enviable fortune or a fairer fame. Of the noblest lineage, rich in the friendship of powerful kinsmen, possessed of a liberal revenue, graced with the highest culture of his time, happy in the inspirations of his own poetic fancy, and honoured with the esteem of illustrious contemporaries, he seems placed almost beyond the malice of fate.

But Flodden proved as fatal to his peace—one might almost say, to his honour—as to that of his country itself. The nine remaining years of his life are a pitiful spectacle of ignoble intrigue, baffled ambition, and inglorious exile. We need not accuse him of any personal baseness, but he was an unscrupulous partisan of his house; he thought far less of the welfare of the realm than of the power of the Douglasses; he used their temporary ascendancy to promote his private interests; and amidst the cares and worries of political warfare his singing robes were laid aside never to be donned again. We may admit that nature did not intend him for a schemer. The picture that Scott draws of him in *Marmion* is probably true:

> "A bishop[1] by the altar stood,
> A noble lord of Douglas' blood,
> With mitre sheen, and rocquet white;
>   Yet showed his meek and thoughtful eye
>   But little pride of prelacy;
>   More pleas'd that, in a barbarous age,
>   He gave rude Scotland Virgil's page,
> Than that beneath his rule he held
> The bishopric of fair Dunkeld."[2]

Yet even if a certain chivalrous loyalty to his house entered as a motive into his political action, he cannot be acquitted of the charge of seeking too keenly his

---

[1] Douglas, as will be seen from the sketch of his life here given, was not a bishop, however, till three years after Flodden.
[2] Canto vi., st. 11.

own advantage. He may have done violence under pressure of circumstances to a naturally sweet and serious disposition, but the fact remains that he deliberately associated himself with a policy that was not patriotic, and not even respectable.

Let us glance at this period of his history of which we know much, and would rather know nothing. Margaret, the widowed queen of James IV., was at first greatly distressed by the loss of her husband, but soon consoled herself. In less than eleven months after his death she was married in the church of Kinnoull to Archibald, Earl of Angus, grandson of "Bell-the-Cat," and son of George, Master of Angus, who had fallen at Flodden with upwards of 200 gentlemen of the house of Douglas.[1] She had been appointed regent of Scotland during the minority of her son (afterwards James V.), and it may be that she felt the need of a protecting power in her dealings with a fierce and factious nobility. This apology at least has been offered for the indecent haste with which she rushed into a new matrimonial connection; but if she wished to create or strengthen an "English party" in Scotland, she took the worst possible way of doing it. Her own sympathies were naturally English, and if her domestic conduct had been prudent and dignified, and her policy marked by as great a regard for the country over which she ruled, as for that from which she was sprung, it is almost certain that she would have succeeded in her wishes, and that Scotland would have had a brighter and happier history in the first half of the sixteenth century. But her selection of a powerful noble like Angus

---

[1] The "Great Earl" was so stricken with the news that he withdrew to St. Mains, a religious house in Galloway, where he died early in 1514.

for her second husband alarmed and incensed his peers. It was investing the house of Douglas with almost royal dignity, and the experience of the last hundred years had shown only too well how insolent, daring, and ambitious that house could be.

The Scottish lords therefore set to work to checkmate Angus, and the result of their action was to draw still closer the alliance between Scotland and France, to greatly increase the hostility to England, of which *The Complaynt*, written more than thirty years later, is a striking evidence, and to drag the house of Douglas into a policy that ended in its destruction. There is no doubt that the Provost of St. Giles actively approved of his nephew's marriage. He was one of those who had been named by the Lords of Council to remain with the widowed queen when the news of Flodden reached Edinburgh, and he appears to have enjoyed her confidence and favour from the first. As early as June, 1514, he was nominated Abbot of Aberbrothock by the queen, who, in accordance with the usage of the times, wrote a letter to the Pope (Leo X.), requesting his consent to the appointment. The letter is extremely interesting. It could only have been written on behalf of a warm partisan. The Provost of St. Giles is described as a man "who is worthy not only of the abbacy, but of the highest ecclesiastical authority, even the primacy," and, again, as "foremost in rank among the nobles of this kingdom, second to none in literature and morals," to which there is discreetly added the following : "who already presides over the monastery by our ordinary authority as œconomus [or administrator of its revenues], nor would his family permit him to be deprived of that office ; in fact his extrusion could only be accomplished by superior force, or, if accomplished at all, could only be so at no small risk."[1]

On the 5th of August, the day before her marriage with Angus, she wrote from Perth in the name of her infant son, another letter to the Pope on the practice of the papal see in reference to ecclesiastical vacancies in Scotland. These vacancies were very numerous at this time. Among the notable churchmen slain at Flodden were the Archbishop of St. Andrews, who was also Abbot of Aberbrothock and Dunfermline, and Prior of Coldingham; the Bishop of the Isles; and the Abbots of Kilwinning, Inchaffray, Cambuskenneth, and Glenluce. The queen makes her son strongly impress on his Holiness the desirableness of giving effect to her recommendations. "We implore you in the most urgent manner, by your paternal goodness to your son, for the sake of the quiet of the kingdom, and especially by your regard for our safety, that our foster father, the present Bishop of Aberdeen,[2] a prelate distinguished for judgment and experience, be transferred to the Archbishopric of St. Andrews; that George, Abbot of Holyrood, of the order of St. Augustine, be appointed Bishop of Aberdeen; that Patrick, Abbot of Cambuskenneth, of the same order and diocese, be promoted to the Abbey of Holyrood; that the foresaid Abbey of Cambuskenneth be given, *ad commendam*, for life, to the reverend father, Andrew, Bishop of Caithness; and that the other monasteries be given in terms of our letters, as follows, in this manner, Arbroath to Gavin Douglas, Dunfermline to James Hepburn, Inchaffray to Alexander Stewart, Glenluce to the Bishop of Argyle, Coldingham to David Hume, who are among the chief

[1] Small's Douglas, vol. I., Biog. Introd. p. xiii.   [2] Elphinstone.

nobility of the kingdom."[1] So far everything looked well for the Provost of St. Giles.

But the marriage of his nephew was neither a political nor a domestic success, and Douglas soon found that he was likely to reap more humiliation than honour by the friendship of the queen. About six weeks[2] after the marriage, the Lords of the Council in consequence of that act deprived her of the regency, ordered Angus to appear before them to answer for his unconstitutional conduct, and resolved to invite the Duke of Albany (grandson of James II., and cousin of James IV.), to return from France, and become governor of Scotland. Eight months elapsed before Albany arrived, and the interval marks the beginning of that deplorable anarchy which prevailed all through the minority of James V., and renewed itself with equal violence after his death.

The queen was determined to fight for her position. She withdrew from Edinburgh, took up her residence at Stirling and Perth, and looked for aid to her brother Henry VIII., who suddenly stept forward in the suspicious character of protector and governor of Scotland. His right to such an office was disclaimed by the Lords of Council with all the vehemence that Scots were wont to show when the independence of their country was threatened, and nothing ever came of his claim. Meanwhile confusion increased. Angus seized Archbishop Beaton, chancellor of the kingdom, who was a strong opponent of the royal marriage, and forced him to surrender the great seal, which was then placed in the hands of Gavin Douglas; and in spite of minutes of the Lords of Council, the latter seems to

---

[1] Small's Douglas, vol. I., Biog. Introd. p. xv.   [2] 18th Sept., 1514.

have held the office or at least the title of "chancellor" for some considerable time.

The plot now thickens. Henry, finding his notion of a protectorate hopeless, thought that he might still become master of the situation in Scotland, if he could induce his sister and her children to take refuge in England. Secret negotiations were entered into through the medium of a certain Adam Williamson, a Scottish priest in the English interest and resident in London. Williamson's letters to the queen and Douglas, which have been printed by Small from the original MSS. in the British Museum, furnish decisive proof that the poet allowed himself to be tempted with promises of preferment in the church. Thus in a letter endorsed 20th January, 1515, we read, " My Lord Dacre has delyueryt to Schir James iij. letteris wiche var direct to fals Panter the sacrittary, wherein yee may see that Murray has gettyn the gift off all the best benifices of Scotland. Yff the Quene folow the kynggis consell, as I haff vrittyn, Murray shal be prevyt a tratour, *and yee shall haue what benefices that yee desyre in Scotland.*"[1] There is more to the same purpose, but a single example may suffice. A letter of the queen to Williamson makes it no less clear that Douglas was at this time ready to assist the traitorous scheme of flight. In it she states that it would have been "rycht plesant" to her "yff it hadd bene possible to doo efter the said counsell," but laments that she cannot find an opportunity, because the " folk of this land ar sa inquisitife that sic thing may nocht be performit without grete knawledge to sindry folkis, and *there is nane that I may trust bot my husband and his uncle quhilk ar rycht glad thereto yf it mycht be.*"[2]

[1] Small's Douglas, vol. I., Biog. Introd. p. xxiii.   [2] *Ibid.* p. xxviii.

During her brief period of trust in her husband, the queen did what she could for his uncle, whose nomination to Aberbrothock had come to nothing. The archbishopric of St. Andrews still remained vacant owing to the death of Elphinstone,[1] and she at once exerted herself to secure the appointment of Douglas to the primacy of the Scottish Church. Not only did she nominate him herself, but she also got her brother Henry to write to the Pope in his favour. The letter of the English king is obviously an "inspired" production. The laudation of "Mr. Gavin" may pass without challenge. It represents Margaret's estimate of her privy counsellor, whose personal merits are not overstated, though we may reasonably doubt if his appointment would have had the effect stated, of "laying the foundation of peace and concord" in the country. But it is extremely amusing to read the following bit of false prophecy. "In regard to the Bishop of Moray,[2] he not only is wholly unlike the said Gavin in nature and temperament, *but we know for certain that he will never be admitted to the foresaid Archbishopric of St. Andrews.*"[3] As a matter of fact, not only did the Bishop of Moray obtain the primacy, but also all the other benefices held by his predecessor, including the Abbey of Aberbrothock to which the unfortunate poet had been "postulated."

The next incident in Douglas's history is his presentation by the queen to the bishopric of Dunkeld.[4] But before he could be consecrated to his office he had to undergo the most acute mortifications. Of course

[1] 25th Oct., 1514.
[2] Andrew Forman, ambassador of Scotland at the French court.
[3] Small's Douglas, vol. I., Biog. Introd. p. xxix.
[4] Rendered vacant by the death of Bishop Brown in Jan., 1515.

he had a rival. This was Andrew Stewart, Prebendary of Craig, and a brother of the Earl of Athole, who was the most powerful nobleman in that part of Perthshire. Through the earl's influence Stewart was installed in the episcopal palace. Meanwhile the queen followed up her nomination by the same procedure as in the case of the Aberbrothock appointment. She wrote [1] in favour of Douglas to the Pope, and she again induced the English king to assist her in the same way. His Holiness confirmed her nomination, acknowledging in his reply [2] the virtues and celebrity of the poet. The queen's patronage, however, was not at that moment the pathway to success. A party among the nobles adhered to her, but she had been deprived of the regency, and any authority she might exercise depended on the amount of force she could command.

Before steps could be formally taken to put Douglas in possession of the bishopric, Albany arrived in Scotland,[3] and within two months summoned a Parliament to meet at Edinburgh. One of the main subjects discussed was the negotiation of Scottish benefices at the court of Rome. It is quite clear that Douglas's action had excited great suspicion in Scotland, not so much from his having sought the papal sanction (for that was an ecclesiastical necessity) as from his employment of foreign and, above all, of English influence to obtain his promotion. The violent arrest, near Moffat, on the 4th of July, of a messenger of Lord Dacre's,[4] who was carrying a packet of letters to the Scottish queen, shows that his enemies were eager to procure evidence that would justify a judicial punishment.

[1] 17th Jan., 1515.   [2] 18th Feb., 1515.   [3] May, 1515.
[4] Dacre was warden of the English marches.

These letters were four in number,[1] and every one of them contained matter that compromised the poet. Each stated that Douglas's success at Rome was owing to the kind offices of the English king ; and that addressed by Dacre to Douglas pointed out a line of policy which he was recommended to pursue, and which it was not within the right of any Englishman to urge upon any independent Scot. Albany laid the letters before the Lords of the Council. Douglas made a stout defence, but his friends were in a minority, and some of them in the hour of trial did not even prove staunch. The result was a sentence of condemnation : " The Lordis decretis and deliueris that the Actis of Parliament maid apoune Clerkis purchessing placiis at the Court of Rome without the kingis license sal be put to execucioun apoune Master Gawin Douglas, Postulate of Arbroth, in all poyntis efter the forme and tenour of the samin ; because he has brokin the said Actis and Statut in the purchassing of the Bischoprik of Dunkeld without the kingis licence or my Lord Gouernouris of commendacioune or laudacioune to the Papis Halynes for the sammin, as was clerlie vnderstand to the saidis Lordis."[2] The poet was imprisoned for about a year—first in the Castle of Edinburgh, and afterwards in the Castles of St. Andrews and Dunbar, and finally in Edinburgh again.

But Albany's own position was not improved by his severity. The Pope sent him a letter of solemn menace for his conduct towards Douglas; and the

[1] (1) A letter from Lord Dacre to the Queen ; (2) a letter from Lord Dacre to Douglas ; (3) a letter from Alexander Turnbull, Douglas's agent at the court of Rome ; and (4) a letter from Williamson, already mentioned.

[2] *Acta Dom. Concilii*, XXVII. foll. 38, 39.

queen fled from Scotland to the court of her brother, who had all along warmly upheld her cause, and who might now be induced by her presence to support it with arms. The regent therefore opened up a correspondence with Margaret, which ended in the liberation of the poet, whose name figures in July, 1516, in a sederunt of the Lords of Council, and who was soon after consecrated to the bishopric of Dunkeld. He did not, however, easily obtain possession of the see. His rival, Stewart, held the palace and steeple of the cathedral with an armed force, and for a time it seemed as if a bloody contest was unavoidable, but a threat of excommunication on the part of Douglas finally daunted the defenders, and induced them to yield. After some litigation at court, Stewart withdrew his opposition on condition that he should be allowed to retain all the episcopal rents he had already collected, together with the churches of Alyth and Cargill.

The poet had now apparently reached a haven of rest, and had he not been a Douglas, the remainder of his public life would in all likelihood have been marked by a serene grace and dignity that would have encircled his poetic fame with a halo of religious beauty. For his official duties were well discharged. His private life was exemplary; he was a faithful, zealous, and munificent bishop; and we may fairly suppose that in leisure hours, of which no record has been left, he frequently forgot his miserable ambition in the purer charms of ancient literature, and the lovely scenes of his Highland home. Unhappily he could not give himself wholly to the service of the muses. The world had a strong grip of his heart, and his political career up to the hour of his death is intensely selfish.

There is only one incident in that career which we can remember with pleasure. In 1517 Albany returned to France, ostensibly to sign a treaty [1] which had been drawn up between that country and Scotland—a renewal in fact of the ancient league of friendship; but in reality because he was heartily sick of his vexatious office and the eternal broils of his subjects. During his absence the regency was entrusted to a council composed of the Archbishops of St. Andrews and Glasgow, and the Earls of Angus, Arran, Huntly, and Argyle. But there was no patriotic concord between the members of the regency. None cared for the nation; each schemed to aggrandize himself. Forman, Archbishop of St. Andrews, was jealous of the pretensions of Beaton, Archbishop of Glasgow, and his new rival in ecclesiastical dignity; while the lust of predominance made Angus and Arran implacable foes. The ferocious brawls between their retainers (the Douglasses and Hamiltons) were the terror of the country. One of them has become memorable under the title of "Cleanse the Causeway." It happened in the year 1520.[2] A Parliament had been summoned to meet at Edinburgh on the 29th of April. The Hamiltons mustered in great force, and it was soon apparent that they meant mischief. Their chiefs held private consultations in the house of Beaton, and the rumour got abroad that an attempt was to be made to arrest Angus. Gavin

---

[1] The Treaty of Rouen.

[2] Pitscottie assigns it to the year 1515, but he is not a good authority in chronology.

Douglas was employed by his uncle to mediate between the rival factions and prevent bloodshed. His efforts were unsuccessful. He found the Hamiltons in arms, and when he implored Beaton to remember his duty as a churchman, the archbishop (who had already a coat of mail under his ecclesiastical robes) " answered him again with an oath (clapping on his breast), 'By my conscience, I know not the matter.' But when Mr. Gavin heard the bishop's purgation, and how he clapped on his breast, and perceived the plats of his jack clattering, thought all was but vain that he had spoken; and answered, and said unto him, 'I perceive, my lord, your conscience is not good, for I hear it clatter.'"[1] He then withdrew to his lodging to pray for the safety of his nephew. The contest soon began, and the High Street of Edinburgh, from St. Giles to the Castle, became a scene of fell and furious encounters. Buchanan says that Beaton flew about "like a firebrand of sedition,"[2] but victory remained with the Douglasses, who had been reinforced at the last moment by a band of fierce borderers. The archbishop sought sanctuary in the church of the Blackfriars,[3] but was dragged from the precincts of the high altar, and was only saved by the kindly offices of the poet, who flew to his rescue. In this incident we get a glimpse of the real nature of Douglas, in keeping with the impression of tenderness and gentleness that Scott's lines leave on our minds—an impression that

---

[1] Pitscottie, pp. 218, 219 : Glas., 1749.

[2] *Qui cum maxime pacis auctor esse debuisset, velut seditionis fax, volitaret armatus.* Buch. *Hist. Rerum Scoticarum,* lib. XIV.

[3] Occupying the site of the Old Infirmary.

harmonizes with the finest qualities of his verse. But he is never again presented in the same favourable light. All that history has preserved is a record of unhappy intrigues which have thrown a shadow on his honour and his fame.

Upwards of four years elapsed between Albany's departure for France and his return to Scotland. He had promised to be back in almost as many months, but political complications made it impossible for him to keep his word. During his absence Scottish history is nothing but a series of bloody disorders. De la Bastie, commander of the French auxiliaries, and one of the ablest soldiers of his age, seemed for a moment likely to quell the license of the feudal bravos, but he was surprised by an ambuscade of border ruffians and slain only four months after the regent had sailed. As the murderers, the Humes of Wedderburn, belonged to the Douglas faction, the Lords of Council appointed Arran, warden of the marches, an act which still further inflamed the animosity of the rival chiefs.

Meanwhile the conduct of Angus had cost him the affection of his royal wife. In October, 1516, Margaret, who had become practically a prisoner in the hands of the regent, effected her escape to England, and was joined at Wooler by her husband and some of his adherents. But while she was lying at Morpeth, prostrated by an attack of typhus fever, Angus made terms for a time with Albany, and basely left her to recover as best she could from her dangerous malady. She never forgave his heartless cruelty, and when rumours afterwards reached her at her brother's court of his flagrant amours in Scotland, the idea of a divorce seems to have rooted itself in her mind. But seven years passed before she was able to carry out her purpose.

A week after the regent sailed, Margaret re-entered Scotland, having obtained restitution of all the dowries she had formerly possessed as the widow of James IV., on condition that she would attempt no plots against the authority of Albany. At first she either veiled or suppressed the resentment she felt at her husband's conduct: she even sought to strengthen his influence in the council of the regency by the sale of her jewels and plate, but this apparent cordiality lasted only for a short time. The extravagance of Angus was so great that she was forced to deprive him of the control of her private revenues, and appoint a commission to collect her rents. Her threat of a divorce however alarmed Henry, who was then seeking to establish his influence in Scotland; and although he himself was destined to become in after years the scandal of Christendom for the license he gave himself in his matrimonial connections, he vehemently denounced the step she proposed to take. His letters did not shake her purpose, but they probably postponed the catastrophe, and they unquestionably helped to bring about that singular change in her policy when she became for a time the ally of Albany, and a supporter of the French party.

That Margaret meant to permanently abandon the English interest need not be supposed; but she was determined to force her brother to pay more regard to her wishes and personal interests than he was then disposed to do. She secretly urged the regent to return to Scotland, and in different ways strove to weaken the influence of Angus, whom she now treated with undisguised contempt. Gavin Douglas had heard a rumour of the queen's plot—if it may be so called—early in 1521, for we have a letter of his to Cardinal Wolsey, dated "at Edinburgh this penult day of Februar," in which he says: "Pleis your lordschipe to wyt that x or xii dais syne their com ane schip furth of Franche, quhairin come ane Gonsailis, ane seruand of the Dwik of Albancis, and hes brocht diuers writingis to syndrie of this cuntre assurand thaim that within schortt tyme he salbe within this ralme, quhilk will nother cum for honour nor proffeit to the Kingis Hienes of this realm."[1] There are one or two sordid touches in the letter sadly characteristic of the poet—e.g., "And I beseik your Graice that the Kingis Hyenes and your Graice haif me and my afferis recommendit in Royme."

On the 19th of November, Albany landed at the Gareloch in Dumbartonshire. The queen joined him at Linlithgow, and a crowd of nobles, including the whole of the Hamilton faction, rapidly gathered round them. Ships laden with artillery and engineers arrived from France. The coalition was obviously irresistible, and Angus in alarm fled to the Borders, accompanied by Lords Home and Somerville. They took refuge in the Kirk of Steyle,[2] where they were soon after joined by the Bishop of Dunkeld on his way to Rome, probably to look after his own weary "afferis." Douglas was at once utilized by the fugitives, and despatched to London with a letter from his nephew to Wolsey, and a set of "instructions" to be shown to Henry. These instructions were designed to blast the character of

[1] MSS. Brit. Mus., Cal. B. I., fol. 77, quoted by Small.
[2] Probably now Ladykirk in Berwickshire.

the queen,[1] and to excite suspicions of Albany's motives. Albany is accused of aiming at the crown; the young king's life is not safe; all the servants about him are creatures of the regent, who ought not to be allowed to come within thirty miles of his sovereign. Nor can the queen be trusted to do her duty as a mother. She is infatuated with Albany, "mekill inclynyt to the plesour of the Duke in all maner of thingis"; the two are "neuer syndry bot euery day togidder, owther forrow none or efter." Dacre, an old friend of Douglas, was a strong supporter of the Angus party. He repeated the charge of scandalous intimacy in a letter to Wolsey, and referred him to Douglas for details. There is no doubt that Margaret's conduct at this crisis was equivocal, but not a vestige of evidence has ever been adduced to show that she was guilty of criminal intercourse with the regent. In any case the part that Douglas played was not noble. Margaret had been a staunch friend to him, and it says as little for his judgment as for his generosity that, in her quarrel with her husband, he deliberately threw in his lot with his vain and profligate kinsman.

Several letters of Douglas to Wolsey, belonging to this period, are extant. None of them is very important, but they exhibit the bishop as extremely afraid of the hostility of Albany, and extremely anxious that the statements of his messengers should receive no credence at the English court. Douglas knew that his position was perilous. He had voluntarily joined the exiles, and had even turned aside from an ecclesiastical mission to become the oracle of their complaints and

---

[1] Pinkerton has no scruple in believing the "instructions" to have been drafted by the bishop himself.

calumnies. As Bishop of Dunkeld he was answerable to the government of Scotland for his machinations or misdeeds, and from the first must have feared the fate that befell him. Meanwhile he sought such protection and favour as the English king could give. Pinkerton "abstracts" from a memorial presented to Henry at this time, a series of formidable charges against the administration of Albany.[1] He believes Douglas to have been the author of the paper, and adds that it is in the handwriting of his secretary.[2] There is certainly no other person from whom it was so likely to have proceeded. Some of the accusations were well-founded (for Albany was neither a wise nor a vigorous ruler), but others are manifestly the product of partisan zeal and credulity. Henry hardly required such a document to prejudice him against the regent, with whom he was soon to be at open war, but it would no doubt be agreeable to him to listen to so elaborate and damnatory an arraignment.

On the other hand Margaret had not been slow to defend herself. On the 6th of January, 1522, she sent a messenger to Henry with a series of instructions entirely drawn up by herself. Among them occurs the following in reference to Douglas:—"Item, ye sall geve his Grace to vnderstand of the guid bering that he [the Regent] dois towart me, and how he has put in my handis the disposition of the Bishopryc of Dunkeld, now vacand for the delict of hym that had it, and hes geuine me the profittis tharof, and hes gevine to my seruandis ane Abaysy and other benefices for

---

[1] *Hist. of Scotland*, bk. XIII.

[2] It is given in *extenso* by Small, who affirms that it is in Douglas's own handwriting.

my help and favor, quhar for I pray his Grace richt effectuoslie that he help not the said Dunkeld, *considdering the gret evill that he has done to this realm be his evill counsall, for he has been the caus of all the dissention and trobill of this realme,* and has maid fals and evill raport of me baitht in Ingland and Scotland, and for that effect the lard of Wedderburn bruder was send to your Grace to that effect: and sen I helpit to get hyme the benefice of Dunkeld, I sall help hyme to want the saymn." But her brother was implacable. Both he and Wolsey pretended to believe the worst of her. Margaret replied to Henry's reproaches with great dignity and spirit. To Dacre, who had written her a censorious communication at the request of Wolsey, she addressed an able vindication of her policy and character. It is printed by Pinkerton in the appendix to the second volume of his history, bears the date 11th March, and is noteworthy for the keenness with which she repels the charge of scandalous behaviour urged against her by the Bishop of Dunkeld, and the vehemence with which she declares nothing will ever induce her to live with Angus again.

Margaret was in a position to use such language with effect. Her husband had once more displayed his customary impulsiveness. Alarmed by the regent's seizure of his estates, he suddenly abandoned his own cause and made his peace with Albany, obtaining pardon on condition of withdrawing to France for a time. Margaret arranged the terms, and Angus left for the Continent in the month of March. But his uncle remained, and on him the final blow was now to fall. The desertion of Angus had filled him with grief and dismay. In a letter to Wolsey, dated "the In of Carlyle,[1] the last day of Januar," [1522], he says that the dolorous news he has received have made him weary of life, but asserts his own unshaken fidelity to the English king in language that repels our sympathy when we read it. Every true Scot should have felt it to be dishonourable. "I promittis to God and your noble Grace, as your humle seruand and ane true Christis priest, that I sall neuir have nor tak way with the Duke of Albany, the vnworthy Erl of Anguse, nor na vtheris that assistis to the said Duke, but your express commande and avise; nor neuer sall pass in Scotland but at your plesour, so lang as this wikkyt Duke is thairin or has rewle thairof." The "meek" bishop is savagely contemptuous towards his nephew. "Albeyt yon young wytles fwyll has runnyn apoun his avne myscheyf be continewall persuasioun of wylye subtile men, and for lak of good counsale, schewing to him, I dowte not, mony fenzeit lettres and wounderful terouris: that the Lord Hume and vtheris wald pass in and lefe him allane, and that I wald be takin and haldin heyr, and that Galter the Dukis secretar had appoyntit with the Kingis Hienes for his distructioun, and the Duke to mary the Quene." A little farther on he adds: "And I beseyk God that I may see him really punyst for his demerittis and promyssis brokyn mayd to the Kingis Hienes and me his vncle, and sall be glad to sollist the Kingis Hienes and your Grace to this effect at all my powere." Towards the close he expresses a resolution not to leave England: "furth of this Realme will I not depart so lang as I may remane thairin with the Kingis plesour and youris

[1] Apparently some place in London.

quhat penurite and distress so euir I sustene."[1] A peculiar interest attaches to this letter. It is the last of Douglas's that has come down to us, and it gives us almost our last glimpse of the writer. He vanishes from our sight with accents of anguish on his lips. His long inglorious struggle for preferment and power is over. Baffled in his policy and broken in his spirit, he sinks into an obscure and hopeless exile made all the more bitter by the pinch of poverty.[2]

The death of Forman, Primate of Scotland, seemed (but only seemed) for a moment to give one more chance to the unhappy bishop. Dacre tried to get Wolsey to use his influence with the Pope in his behalf. But even before the English warden had written, Douglas had received his *coup de grace*. Beaton, Archbishop of Glasgow and Chancellor of the kingdom, a prelate whose greed and ambition surpassed even his talents, meant to be himself the successor of Forman, and he now exerted his whole power to make Douglas an impossible candidate. The truce between England and Scotland had expired on the 2nd of February, and the two nations were really at war. Both were preparing for a spring campaign. The Bishop of Dunkeld was consorting with the enemies of his country, and must therefore be dealt with as a traitor. Through Beaton's influence, a formal proclamation was drawn up in the name of the boy-king, James V., in which Douglas is declared guilty of high treason, and solemnly deprived of the government and revenues of the diocese of Dunkeld. "And lest the man, persevering in a malevolent

[1] State Papers, Scotland, MSS., vol. I., No. 85, quoted by Small.
[2] In his will, dated 10th September (and still extant), he speaks of some of his plate as "impignorated."

intention, should from time to time devise new plots, as in past times he added fuel to the flames of civil discord, and now has voluntarily withdrawn from the kingdom, nor shews any disposition to return to reason, in terms of the said act, and proclamation following thereon, all and several the lieges of the kingdom of whatever condition, degree, ecclesiastical or secular rank, are prohibited under the penalty of high treason, from assisting or supporting him by money, or from holding communication with him by letters or messengers."[1] From a measure like this there was no recovery, except through the overthrow of his enemies, and Douglas did not live to witness the return of his party to a temporary triumph.

It would be pleasant to think that the complete ruin of his earthly hopes had purged his soul of earthly ambition, and that the brief remainder of his mortal career was devoted to religion and literature. Polydore Vergil, the only person who lifts for an instant[2] the veil that hides his exile, presents Douglas in this favourable light. But we must remember that he had become an inveterate intriguer. His rupture with his kinsman and his treatment by the Scottish government forced him to adhere more tenaciously than ever to the English alliance. For Albany he entertained the strongest antipathy, and we are afraid that, all through the summer of 1522, he followed with hungry expectation the mustering of forces on the Border. It is improbable that he lived to hear of the extraordinary truce drawn

---

[1] Translated by Small from the original *Epist. Reg. Scot.* I. p. 328.

[2] See his *Historia Anglica* (7th ed. Lond. 1651) or Ellis's edition of the old MS. translation into English in the British Museum, for the Camden Society, vol. I. p. 105.

up between the Regent and Dacre, at the Chapel of Salom (near the Solway or Solam Moss), on the 11th of September, for he died sometime between the 10th of that month, when his will was made, and the 19th, when probate was granted. His remains were interred by his own desire in the Hospital Church of the Savoy. According to his friend Vergil the plague carried him off; perhaps the miserable turmoils and anxieties of his later years made him an easy victim to a passing epidemic. It is with a feeling of deep relief that we turn at last from the factious and scheming ecclesiastic to the lover of learning and the votary of the muse.

We are entirely in the dark as to the earlier and better part of Douglas's life, the time when he was smitten with the love of song, when books were more to him than men, and his imagination, still untainted with low ambition, revelled in the civilized literature of antiquity. It is hazardous, perhaps idle, to indulge in conjectures that can never be verified, and may possibly be vain, but the contrast between the poet and the politician is so strong that we find ourselves almost irresistibly led to draw upon our fancy for a picture of his youth. But in truth, whether his boyhood was spent where

> "Tantallon's dizzy steep
> Hung o'er the margin of the deep,"

or amid the rural solitudes of Douglasdale, or in some other of the stately homes of his father, is really a matter of no moment. Wherever he grew up, he learned to love nature—"the outward shows of sky and earth," with all the tenderness of a true poet, and perhaps "impulses of deeper birth" also came to the studious youth in solitude. In those wonderful pieces, the

Prologues to his translation of the books of the Æneid, there is abundant proof of a direct and original sympathy with the phenomena of nature in his own rough northern clime. No mere book-lore, no mere susceptibility to the charm of Virgilian or Chaucerian verse, could have enabled him to paint the vivid pictures of a Scottish winter that form the substance of his superb introduction to the seventh book. Every line gives evidence of a genuine personal insight—the independent vision of a new poet, not the reflected light of scholarship and mimetic art.

It is natural to suppose that this power—one of the rarest and divinest which Heaven confers on man—was gradually developed in that shadowy period of his history before he was called from his rural parsonage in East Lothian to the provostship of St. Giles. His two earlier poems, *The Palice of Honour* and *King Hart*, do not indeed show much trace of it, and are strictly conventional in their descriptive style; but Douglas is not the only poet who has required the discipline of time to teach him the art of being natural. It was perhaps more difficult for him than for most of his contemporaries to resist the influence of his predecessors in poetry. He was a deeper student than Dunbar, and his genius was less bold and aggressive. The very richness of his culture tempted him to walk in the old ways when he began to write, but his native genius at last broke out in a flush of luxuriant beauty that even yet makes obsolete diction glow and shine.

The Palice of Honour and *King Hart* are both allegorical poems, and the first has certainly a claim to rank among the most singular examples of that style of composition. It was finished by Douglas at the age of twenty-six. We have his own authority for the date. In the "Dyrectioun" or "Dedication" of his Virgil to Lord Sinclair he says :—

> "To you, my Lord, quhat is thar mair to say?
> Ressaue your wark desyrit mony a day;
> Quharin also now am I fully quyt,
> As twichand Venus, of myn ald promyt
> Quhilk I hir maid weil *twelf yeris tofor*,
> As *wynessyth my Palice of Honour.*"

This proves that it was composed in the year 1501. In the verses addressed to James IV. at its close, Douglas speaks of it as a piece of "roustic rurall rebaldrie," and as a "buriall quair,"[1] clad in "russet weid," terms which, if they mean anything at all beyond the customary self-disparagement of authors, point to the parsonage of Linton as the place where it was written.

The poet enters a garden on a bright May morning, and falls into an "extasie or swoun." In this condition he has a wondrous dream. He finds himself far away in a desert place,

> "Amyd a forest by a hyddeous flude."

While he is trembling at the terrors of the scene, he hears a loud noise, and soon a noble cavalcade sweeps past. It is the Queen of Sapience with her court, on their way to the Palace of Honour. Minerva is attended by one of the most incongruous crowds ever assembled even in an allegory, of which the Sibyls, Deborah, Circe, Judith, Jael, Solomon, Aristotle, Sallust, Livy, Socrates, Averroes, Enoch, Job, Ulysses, Cicero, and Melchisedek, are conspicuous members.

[1] Rustic book.

Hardly have they disappeared when Diana with her vestal train approaches. The goddess rides aloft on an elephant " in signe that scho in chaistetie incressis." Her companions are lovely enough,

> " With lustie giltin tresses,
> In habit wilde maist like till fostaressis,"

but they are not numerous. The daughter of Jephthah, Polixena, Penthesilea, Iphigenia, and Virginia alone are named, but the poet from his hiding-place saw " vthir flouris of feminitie." They too soon ride past; and apparently with the view of heightening the contrast to the pomp and splendour of the court of Venus, we have a gruesome sketch of the desert to which the poet had been conveyed :—

> " In that desert dispers in sonder skatterit,
> Were bewis bair quhome rane and wind on batterit,
> The water stank, the feild was odious
> Quhair dragouns, lessertis, askis, edders swatterit,
> With mouthis gapand, forkit taillis tatterit,
> With mony a stang and spoutis vennemous,
> Corrupting air be rewme contagious,
> Maist gros and vile, empoysonit cludis clatterit,
> Reikand like hellis smoke sulfurious."

Naturally such a scene makes him melancholy, when suddenly there falls upon his ear the sound of distant music. It rapidly increases in volume and richness, till at last it seems to him as if it were troops of angels

> " With harmonie fordinnand all the skyis."

Then bursts upon his sight a vision of the fairest court ever seen in the world since the creation of Adam :—

> " Quhat sang? Quhat joy? Quhat harmonie? Quhat licht?
> Quhat mirthfull solace plesance all at richt?

> Quhat fresche bewtie ?   Quhat excelland estait ?
> Quhat sweit vocis ?   Quhat wordis suggurait ?
> Quhat fair debaitis ?   Quhat luifsum ladyis bricht ?
> Quhat lustie gallandis did on thair seruice wait ?"

This part of the poem certainly shows the vigour, if not the individuality, of Douglas's genius. His figures have a dazzling beauty, and his verse is full of sweetness, but there is nothing novel in the imagery, or the music. Everything is familiar to us, though the arrangement is new. All poets since Chaucer had spent much of their time in the elaboration of those imaginary courts, and cavalcades, and scenes, in which the middle ages found its ideals; and with the ever increasing influence of the Renaissance, a pseudo-classical air was gradually given to romantic fantasies that really reflected the manners and sentiments of chivalry. Douglas is far above the English allegorists of the fifteenth century, though he is not essentially different from them. It was perhaps impossible for him to reach greater originality in that well-trodden field: but that its resources were not yet exhausted to spirits of the first order, is shown by the *Induction* of Sackville and the *Faery Queene* of Spenser.

We shall not trouble our readers with the long catalogue of lovers who compose the train of the goddess of love. Of course Arcite, Palamon and Æmilia, Dido and Æneas, Troilus and Cressida, Pyramus and Thisbe, Paris and Helen, Cleopatra and Mark Antony, with other celebrities are all there:

> "Ane multitude thay war innumerabill."

Their appearance provokes the poet to sing a ballad about inconstancy in love, for which he is hunted out of his "muskane bowr," struck and buffeted unmercifully, and dragged before the throne of the affronted Queen. His condemnation is pronounced, and he is in momentary expectation of death or of transformation into some beast, when the court of the Muses opportunely arrives. Calliope persuades Venus to pardon the foolish slanderer, on condition that he will recant his calumnies and make a new ballad in her praise and honour, which he hastes to do. Here, as elsewhere throughout the poem, Douglas shows genuine imaginative power, without any peculiar or distinctive imaginative perception. His style is perhaps richer, his eloquence more diffuse, his details more varied and abundant than in most of his predecessors, but he has not yet found out where his strength lies—he has not yet lighted on the theme that will awaken in his spirit an original life and energy. Lines like those which celebrate the "lustie court" of the Muses have indeed a high merit and may favourably compare with other conventional verse of the kind :—

> "Yone is (quod thay) the court rethoricall,
> Of polit termis, sang poeticall,
> And constant ground of famous storeis sweit,
> Yone is the facound well celestiall,
> Yone is the fontane and originall,
> Quhairfra the well of Helicon dois fleit,
> Yone are the folk that confortis euerie spreit,
> Be fine delite and dite angelicall,
> Causand gros leid [1] all of maist gudnes gleit.[2]

> Yone is the court of pleasand steidfastnes,
> Yone is the court of constant merines,
> Yone is the court of joyous discipline,
> Quhilk causis folk thair purpois to expres
> In ornate wise, prouokand with glaidnes

[1] Rude language. [2] Glitter.

> All gentill hartis to thair lair incline,
> Euerie famous poeit men may diuine
> Is in yone rout."

But, after all, the utmost they prove is that Douglas has learned by poetic sympathy and literary culture to do what others did as well as they. Something more is required to make a man one of the ever-shining stars of poesy.

The court of the Muses is of course enriched by the presence of the famous poets. Homer is indeed the only Greek mentioned, but Douglas apologizes for his omissions. The crowd was so great,

> "The hundreth part thair names ar not heir."

He finds room, however, for most of the Latins from Plautus to Claudian; names Petrarch, Boccaccio, Poggio, Laurentius Valla, and other heralds or lights of the Renaissance; nor does he forget that glory of Albion, the "peerless" Chaucer, Gower, Lydgate, and his countrymen Kennedy, Dunbar ("yit vndeid"), and Quintin Shaw. Calliope now hands him over to the care "of ane sweit nimphe maist faithfull and decoir," and along with the rest of her followers he performs one of those miraculous journeys in which the medieval poets delight:—

> "Throw countries seir, holtis and roches hie,
> Ouir vailis, planis, woddis, wallie sey,
> Ouir fludis fair, and mony strait montane,
> We war caryit in twinkling of ane eye."

His geographical nomenclature is superabundant, but it is impossible to trace the course of the visionary riders, who pursue a bewildering flight over all Europe and Western Asia, till at length they alight and repose for a time beside the Castalian fount. Here again we have some fine description of the usual kind, rich but unreal. The meadows yield "all kinde of herbis, flouris, frute, and grane," while ladies go about "playand, singand, dansand ouir the bentis," or crowd the pavilion of the Muses, where they sit on "deissis," are served with "ypocras and meid," and discuss interesting problems of love—

> "Inquyrand quha best in their times had bene,
> Quha traist[1] louers in lustie yeiris grene."

Calliope invites Ovid to discourse on this theme, who repeats the stories of his verse. After he has finished,

> "Vprais the greit Virgilius anone,
> And playit the sportis of Daphnis and Corydone;
> Sine Terence come, and playit the comedy
> Of Parmeno, Thrason, and wise Gnatone;
> Juuenall like ane mowar[2] him allone,
> Stude scornand euerie man as thay yeid by;
> Martiall was cuik till roist, scith, farce[3] and fry,
> And Poggius stude with mony girne and grone,
> On Laurence Valla spittand and cryand fy."

When this extemporized feast has come to an end, the court remount and resume their journey—

> "Ouir mony gudelie plane we raid bedene,
> The vaill of Hebron, the camp Damascene,
> Throw Josaphat, and throw the lustie vaill,
> Ouir waters wan, throw worthie woddis grene."

Suddenly the "Palice of Honour" is seen, crowning a steep marble rock that rises from the midst of a plain, and every one reverently bends his head. Douglas now braces himself up for a supreme effort. The vision far

---

[1] Trusty.   [2] Mocker.   [3] Stuff.

transcends his feeble powers of description. In fact no mortal could imagine the splendour that is disclosed to view. He himself is entranced like St. Paul,

> "For quhidder I this in saull or bodie saw,
> That wait[1] I nocht, bot he that all dois knaw."

Yet the result is not commensurate with the effort. The scenery of the closing part of the allegory is extravagant, confused, and in part even unintelligible. We know that the "Palice of Honour" is only to be reached with extreme difficulty. For the false, the faithless, and the idle there are insuperable obstacles, but these should be set forth in appropriate imagery. The flaming abyss near the top of the hill, full of brimstone and boiling lead, where miserable caitiffs, who loved pleasure more than honour, welter and howl, is a hideous incongruity. Still worse in some respects is the spectacle of the stormy sea of human life which mysteriously presents itself to the poet's view from the summit, and the wreck of a goodly ship, "the Carwell of the State of Grace." Nothing could be more crude or incoherent than this. First of all, the previous tone of the poem is not at all in harmony with this melancholy conception of the world; then, such a ship should not have had a faithless crew and should not have suffered shipwreck; again, a nymph of the Muses' court is not the proper person to give a theological interpretation of the circumstances, though her orthodoxy is unimpeachable; and, lastly, the sudden introduction of the dogmas of the Christian religion in this strange bald fashion seriously disturbs the sympathetic action of the reader's imagination. The

[1] Wot, or know.

"Palice" itself, however, is well described, "that heuinlie Palice all of cristall cleir," but there is really nothing in this part of the work that equals the earlier parts. The nymph guides the poet to a garden where he sees Venus seated on a throne "with stanis riche ouirfret." Before her stands a mirrour—

> "Surmounting far in brichtnes to my dome,[1]
> The coistlie subtell spectakill[2] of Rome,
> Or yit the mirrour sent to Canace,[3]
> Quhairin men micht mony wonders se."

But its brightness is the least of its marvellous properties: everything of moment that has ever happened is visible on its magic surface:—

> "The deidis and fatis of euerie eirdlie wicht,
> All thingis gone like as thay war present,
> All the creatiounis of the angellis bricht."

And so the poet proceeds to catalogue the great events of history from the Fall of Lucifer down to the "nigromansie" of Friar Bacon, with a minuteness of reference that marks at once the fulness and accuracy of his reading. There is little or no poetry in his record. Here and there a stanza rises somewhat above the Dutch level that prevails, for example that which paints the Grecian widows whose husbands lay unburied before Thebes, or that which describes the interview between Æneas and his father in the shades,

> Ouir Stix the flude I saw Eneas fair,
> Quhair Charon was the busteous ferriar,
> The fludes four of hell thair micht I se,

---

[1] Judgment.   [2] Mirror; Lat *speculum*.
[3] See Chaucer's "Squyres Tale." The mirror, however, was for Canace's father.

> The folk in pane, the wayis circulair,
> The welterand stone wirk Sisipho mich cair,
> And all the pleasance of the camp Elise,[1]
> Quhair auld Anchises did commoun with Enee."

But as a rule the historic allusions are not pictorially handled. Most of them do not seem to have any close connection with the rule of Venus, and the explanation given by the attendant nymph is simply unintelligible.

> "Yone mirrour cleir,
> The quhilk thow saw befoir Dame Venus stand,
> Signifyis na thing ellis to vnderstand,
> *Bot the greit bewtie of thir ladyis facis,*
> *Quhairin louers thinks they behald all graces.*"

Venus now reminds the poet of his promise to obey her behests when she spared his life. He acknowledges his obligation, whereupon she places a book in his hand and asks him to turn it into rhyme.

> "Tuitchand this buik perauenture ye sall heir,
> Sum time efter, quhen I have mair lasier."

These are the lines referred to in the passage already quoted from the "Dyrectioun" or "Dedication" of his translation of Virgil to his cousin Lord Sinclair. They reveal that in the very dawn of his poetical career, when he was writing the *Palice of Honour*, he was revolving in his mind the *chef d'œuvre* which was to give him an enduring place in the literature of his country.

When the poet has seen all that was to be seen in the magic mirror, the nymph leads him straight to the

---

[1] The Elysian Field.

palace, where he sees many caitiffs attempting unsuccessfully to force an entrance, among whom he recognizes Simon, Achitophel, Catiline, Jugurtha, and Trypho. The gates are well guarded, and the household of King Honour is a muster-roll of all the virtues. Charity is his major-domo, Conscience his chancellor, Constancy his secretary, Liberality his treasurer, Innocence and Devotion clerks of his closet, Virtue his minion, Discretion his comptroller, Humanity his usher, Peace and Rest his marshals, Temperance his cook, Humility his carver. One looks listlessly at the lifeless figures and passes on with a sense of relief to examine the palace in the company of the poet and his charming guide. Silver pavements, golden doors and windows, roofs of burnished ivory, interspersed with loops of sapphires, diamonds and rubies, stairs of topaz, amethystine floors, tables, trestles, forms and benches of sardius, jasper and emerald, do not dazzle the imagination of modern readers, who may, however, still find a genuine pleasure in contemplating the delight which such fantastic splendours gave to the poets of an earlier world. The sight of the king on his throne, "ane God omnipotent," made the poet swoon with fear. The nymph carries him into the "close" or courtyard, and upbraids him for his timidity. Some curious jangling passes between them. One remark of the lady has a very significant frankness about it when we remember the professed celibacy of the clergy—

"For kirkmen war ay gentill to thair wyifis."

Even the refined and pure-minded Douglas could only find matter for a pleasant jest in the fatal license of his order. When the nymph has explained to him who the folk are that dwell in the palace, she points out the vanity of all earthly glory, and pronounces a fine eulogium on Virtue—the only road to Honour.

> "To papis, bischoppis, prelatis and primaitis,
> Empreouris, kingis, princes, potestatis,
> Deith settis the terme and end of all thair hicht;
> Fra thay be gane, let se quha on thame waitis!
> Nathing remanis bot fame of thair estaitis,
> And nocht ellis bot verteous warkis richt
> Sall with thame wend; nouther thair pompe nor micht.
> Ay vertew ringis[1] in lestand honour cleir,
> Remember than that vertew hes na peir.
>
> For vertew is a thing sa precious,
> Quhairof the end is sa delicious,
> The warld can not considder quhat it is.
> It makis folk perfite and glorious,
> It makis sanctis of pepill vitious,
> It causis folk ay liue in lestand blis,
> It is the way to hie honour I wis,
> It dantis deith, and euerie vice throw micht;
> Without verteu, fy on all eirldlie wicht."[2]

In verses like these we seem to hear the blended tones of the poet and the priest. It would have been well for Douglas if the lesson they teach had been rightly laid to heart by himself, so that he could have triumphantly withstood the temptations of ambition in the evil hour. His personal virtue was indeed never challenged; in the purity of his life and manners he stands far above the Formans and Beatons against whom he struggled or conspired; but still one must regretfully confess that in his later years he sadly forgot the ethics of his youth, and travelled far in directions that never could lead to the Palace of Honour.

[1] Reigns.   [2] Every earthly creature.

The poet is now conducted towards the gardens of the palace. These are encircled by a large foss or ditch, over which a plank is laid. The nymph passes over the perilous bridge with ease, but her companion is less fortunate. Losing his presence of mind, he falls down "into the stank."[1] The fright awoke him from his dream-swoon, and "all the lustie pleasance was away." Nothing could reconcile him to the realities of life—neither song of birds, nor bloom of flowers, nor aught on which the eye could rest. The "fair herbrie" was "maist like to hell"; everything on earth was "barrane and vile."

> "Thus I remanit into the garth twa houris,
> Cursand the feildis with all the fair colouris,
> That I awolk oft wariand[2] the quhile,
> Alwayis my minde was on the lustic ile."

But since it has vanished for ever from his sight, he will at least compose a ballad in "laude of honour" to commemorate the visionary glories of his dream. The stanzas of this ballad bring the poem to an end, and on account of their barbaric plethora of rhymes may perhaps deserve quotation.

> "O hie honour, sueit heuinlie flour degest,
> Gem verteous, maist precious, gudliest,
> For hie renown thow art guerdoun conding,
> Of worschip kend the glorious end and rest,
> But quhome in richt na worthie wicht may lest.
> Thy greit puissance may maist auance all thing,
> And poucrall to mekill auaill sone bring.
> I the require sen thow but peir art best,
> That efter this in thy hie blis we ring.

[1] Pool.   [2] Cursing.

> Of grace thy face in euerie place sa schynis,
> That sweit all spreit baith heid and feit inclynis,
> Thy gloir afoir for till imploir remeid.
> He docht richt nocht, quhilk out of thocht the tynis;
> Thy name but blame, and royal fame diuine is;
> Thow port at schort of our comfort and reid,
> Till bring all thing till glaiding efter deid,
> All wicht but sicht of thy greit micht ay crynis,
> O schene I mene, nane may sustene thy feid.
>
> Haill roiss maist chois till clois thy fois greit micht,
> Haill stone quhilk schone vpon the throne of licht,
> Vertew, quhais trew sweit dew ouirthrew al vice,
> Was ay ilk day gar say the way of licht;
> Amend, offend, and send our end ay richt.
> Thow stant, ordant as sanct, of grant maist wise,
> Till be supplie, and the hie gre of price.
> Delite the tite me quite of site to dicht,
> For I apply schortlie to thy deuise."

As the effort of a youth of twenty-six, *The Palice of Honour* is in some respects a remarkable performance. Its literary execution is of a high order. Douglas already shows himself a master of the art of versification. He has a fine sense of melody and an exhaustless wealth of words. Images rise freely at the summons of his brilliant fancy, but he sees nothing which has not been seen before, or, to put it more exactly, he designs with the same kind of figures and paints with the same kind of colours as his predecessors of the allegorical school. What is chiefly distinctive about the work is not its poetry, but its scholarship. He is the first Scottish poet whose verse breathes the odour of the Renaissance. The ancient world comes to life again, not in its fabulous medieval guise, but in the fairer form of classic legend, and though his imagination is unable to break the fetters which his age imposed, he crowds his poem with incidents of Greek and Roman story, and recites with a scholar's pride the names of the authors in whom he delights. He speaks of Homer like one who knew him at first hand, and it is certain that either then or at a later period he had acquired a knowledge of Greek, for in the prologue to his translation of the first book of the Æneid, he says that he undertook the work at the request of his cousin Lord Sinclair,

> "Quhilk with grete instance diuers tymes seir,[1]
> Prayit me translait Virgill or Omeir."

His familiarity with Ovid is undoubted. It is even probable that his earliest literary effort was a translation of the *Remedia Amoris*; at least we are disposed so to construe the following lines:

> "Lo thus, followand the flowr of poetry,
> The batellis and the man translait haue I:
> Quhilk yoir ago, in myne ondantit yowth,
> Onfructuus idylnes fleand as I couth,
> Of *Lundeis*[2] *Lufe the Remeid* dyd translait;
> And syne of hic Honour the Palice wrait."[3]

But no copy of this work is known to exist, and there must always be some doubt whether "Lundeis Remeid of Lufe" was the classical poem so well known and so suspiciously attractive both to monk and layman in the middle ages. Martial is to Douglas "the mixt and subtell Martiall"; Horace "the morall wise poet." One notices a certain indefinable evidence of direct

[1] Many, several.

[2] Ruddiman changed "Lundeis" into "Ovideis" without any MS. warrant, but his emendation seems a happy one.

[3] Note at end of Book XII. of the Æneid.

knowledge in his language. He speaks of the classic authors with all the reverence of the Renaissance, but with none of the curious hearsay vagueness that older poets often exhibit; and his laudation of the Italian scholars of the fifteenth century, who began the great revolt against the inartistic and graceless literature of the monasteries, strengthens our conviction that Douglas had become imbued at an early date with the new spirit of the time. This seems to us the most interesting feature of the poem now. There is not enough of imaginative vivacity in it to excite a purely poetic enthusiasm, such as stirs us in reading Henryson's *Testament of Cresseid* or Dunbar's *Thrissill and the Rois;* and we follow with a careless indifference the conjectures of critics as to the earlier works from which the Scottish poet may have drawn the design or plan of his own. In truth there is little or nothing to be said for most of these. The *Pinax* of Cebes, the Theban disciple of Socrates, has a similar ethical purpose, and as it was printed at Bologna in a Latin version before the close of the fifteenth century, it might have been known to a scholar like Douglas even in the distant north, but probably no human being except Bishop Sage ever saw any likeness between the two works. The same may be said of the *Trionfi* of Petrarch, a series of poems in terza-rima, on the triumphs of Love, Chastity, Death, Fame, Time, and Deity. From either or both of these, casual suggestions may have been taken, *e.g.*, Petrarch in his *Trionfi d'Amore* passes in review his famous predecessors, the troubadours of Provence and Italy, and this may not have been without its influence on Douglas when he drew his picture of the Court of the Muses. Small thinks that the Scottish poet, when he sketched the outline of the Palace of Honour, had before him Chaucer's *House of Fame*; but there is not the faintest resemblance in style or treatment between the two works, and though Douglas was imbued with the deepest reverence for the great master, he does not seem in this case to have borrowed anything from him. Indeed Douglas is not a plagiarist in any vulgar sense, and he did not need to be one. His fancy, as we have remarked, is wonderfully productive, and he can invent picturesque details with the utmost ease, but he cannot, as yet, transport himself into a world other than the conventional dreamland, though his learning gives him a greater range in his choice of visionary forms than poets of even higher genius. *The Palice of Honour*, for example, is far more densely crowded with historical imagery than *The House of Fame*, but in vividness of representation it is not even distantly to be compared to Chaucer's poem. With quick, subtle strokes, Chaucer brings a scene or a character so distinctly before our imagination that it hardly ever fades from it, while Douglas's personages are almost all shadowy phantasms, *voces et praeterea nihil*. As a landscape painter he has much greater merit, and it was in this department he was destined to reach the height of his excellence as a poet; but it would be an affectation to profess any very genuine interest in scenery which owes nothing to Nature, and such for the most part is the scenery of *The Palice of Honour*.

King Hart, considered as an allegory, is a much more coherent and consistent work than the *The Palice of Honour*. The exact date of its composition is not known, but there is some ground for believing that in

point of time it occupies an intermediate place between
The Palice of Honour and the translation of Virgil.
Its tone is graver than that of the former poem, its
versification is more artistic, and its language more
terse and vigorous, though this may partly be due to
the restrictions imposed by the nature of the narrative,
which does not allow the same license of fanciful
description that is permitted to a dreamer of dreams.
In its essence and purpose *King Hart* is a sermon on
the text, " Remember now thy Creator in the days of
thy youth, while the evil days come not, nor the years
draw nigh, when thou shalt say, I have no pleasure in
them " ; in its outward form it is clothed in the picturesque garb of feudal life, and could not fail to charm
the glittering court of James IV. One cannot say that
Douglas meant to give a lesson to his sovereign in
particular, for there were many men in Scotland who
needed reproof far more than James; but it may be that
the brilliant revels[1] of James's marriage day rose to the
imagination of the poet, when he painted the careless
happiness of Youth and Love, before Old Age had
knocked at the castle gates, and Conscience followed in
his wake.

King Hart has one of the most genuine qualities of
a successful allegory ; the characters and incidents are
depicted with so much vigour and fidelity to nature
that one often forgets the primary purpose of the poem,
and rests content with the graphic imagery of the story.

---

[1] " Successive days of pleasure were diversified with public shows, the feast, the carousal, and the dance. The English added to the entertainments the exhibition of those rude interludes called moralities : nor were the Scottish muses silent, for Dunbar, a poet of deserved reputation, celebrated the nuptials in an allegory of no mean beauty, intituled 'The Thistle and the Rose.' The guests were at length permitted to depart, satiated with pomp and pleasure, with royal generosity, and Scotch hospitality."—Pinkerton, book xi.

The representation of man's body as a castle, in which the heart or soul dwells as a sovereign, and the faculties and passions serve as a royal body-guard and retinue, was not a novelty in the sixteenth century. It had, in fact, long been a familiar mode of symbolizing ethical or religious instruction. Almost every Latin collection of monastic tales has something like it, and examples are not rare in the vernacular poetry of various nations. But no writer has worked out the idea so elaborately or powerfully as Douglas. In him the functions of poet and priest are admirably combined; and the result is one of the most striking and impressive works in early Scottish literature.

"King Hart" sits secure in his "cumlie castell." Nothing mars his happiness. His days are spent in the enjoyment of every pleasure, and he is ignorant of all pain. Yet some of his companions bear names that bode ill for the continuance of his felicity—

> "Want-wyt, Vanegloir, Prodigalitie,
> Vnrest, Nicht-walk, and felon Glutony,
> Vnricht, Dyme Sicht, with Slicht and Subtiltie."

But while "Strenth," "Grein Lust," "Disport," and "Freschness" are at his side no thought of future evil can reach him. Time passes merrily in dance and song and revel,

> "With Bissines all blyth to pleis the lairde."

The "cumlie castell" has a special guard of five servitors, in whom we can recognise, though not quite distinctly, the five Senses. "Sight" and "Hearing" are finely described:

> "Ane for the day, quhilk jugeit certanly,
> With cure to ken the colour of all hew,
> Ane for the nicht, *that harknit bissely*
> *Out of quhat airt that ever the wyndis blew.*"

In the following passage we lose sight of the allegory altogether, and think rather of some border stronghold in which a baron and his train hold a carousal after a successful raid:

> "So strang this king him thocht his castell stude,
> With mony towre and turat crownit hie:
> About the wall thair ran ane water void,
> Blak, stinkand, sowr, and salt as is the sey,
> That on the wallis wiskit,[1] gre by gre,
> Boldning[2] to ryis the castell to confound;
> Bot thai within maid sa grit melody,
> That for thair reird[3] they micht nocht heir the sound.
>
> With feistis fell, and full of jolitee,
> This cumlie court thair king thai kast to keip,
> That noy[4] hes none bot newlie novaltee,
> And are nocht wonnt for wo to woun[5] and weip,
> Full sendill[6] sad, or soundlie set to sleip,
> No wandreth[7] wait,[8] ay wenis[9] welth[10] endure;
> Behaldis nocht, nor luikis nocht, the deip,
> As thaim to keip fra all misaventure.
>
> Richt as the rose vpspringis fro the rute,
> In ruby colour reid most ryck[11] of hew;
> Nor waindis[12] nocht the levis to outschute,
> For schyning of the sone that dois renew
> Thir vther flouris greyne, quhyte, and blew,
> Quhilk hes na craft to knaw the wynter weit,
> Suppois that sommer schane[13] dois thame reskew,
> That dois thame quhile[14] ourhaill with snau and sleit."

Hard by is another castle whose mistress is to become in turn the captor and the captive of "King Hart." It is a structure peerless in beauty and strength, and the

---

[1] Broke with a *whisk* or quick dash.
[2] Swelling—perhaps here "threatening."
[3] A roaring noise. [4] Trouble. [5] Wail. [6] Seldom. [7] Sorrow.
[8] Know (wot). [9] Weens (expects). [10] Prosperity. [11] Rich.
[12] Bears. [13] Sheen. [14] At times.

queen who dwells in it, "Dame Plesance," is supported by a virgin host whose arms are irresistible. One day they ride out for pastime, just as in Douglas's day a gay company might have sallied forth from some well-guarded tower to hunt in greenwood or make merry in the fresh meadows. The picture put before us derives half its charm from its reality and naturalness. The warders of "King Hart's" castle are alarmed at the spectacle, and hasten to inform their master. "Youthheid" and "Delyte" are sent out as scouts to ascertain what is meant by the great array. Almost before they know, "Bewtie" has so dazzled them with her bright beams that they stand speechless in her presence, and are led away unresisting by "Fayr Calling," who

> "Syn to hir castell raid, as scho war woude,[1]
> And festnit vp thir folkis in Venus bandis."

No "bodwarde"[2] coming to "King Hart," he despatches other messengers to bring him news. But "Wantownnes," "Greine Luif," "Disport," "Fule-hardynes" could not be expected to prove very wary spies; and, in fact, they are captured as easily as their predecessors. When the king hears of this fresh discomfiture he is inflamed with anger, and hastily rides out with all his force to chastise the daring Amazons. Their reckless self-confidence is well-portrayed:—

> "Than out thai raid all to a randoun richt,[3]
> This courtlie King, and all his cumlie ost,
> His buirtlie[4] bainer brathit[5] vp on hicht;
> And out thay blew with brag and meckle bost,
> That lady and hir lynnage suld be lost.
> Thai cryit on hicht thair seinze[6] wounder lowde:
> Thus come thai keynlie carpand one the cost,[7]
> Thai preik, thai prance, as princis that war woude."[8]

[1] Mad. [2] Message. [3] At a right swift pace. [4] Large (buirdly).
[5] Flapped noisely. [6] War-cry. [7] Talking of the cost, or damage. [8] Mad.

Of course the king's army is routed. "Beauty" leads the vanguard of his foes, and the bravest succumb to her assaults. The king himself is wounded and taken prisoner. "Dame Plesance" hands him over to the care of the dangerous heroine by whom he has been vanquished; but beauty is not a good leech. She has been ordered

> "His wound to wesche, in sobering of his sair;
> Bot alwayis as scho castis it to clene,
> His malady incressis mair and mair."

Still he is not unhappy, and he submits without murmur to be carried into captivity. The queen and her maidens for a time, however, are content with their victory, and the music of their songs echoes through all the chambers of the palace. The captive monarch is more deeply wounded than ever.

> "King Hart intill ane previe closet crappe,
> Was neir the dungeoun wall, neirby the ground;
> Swas[1] he micht heir and se, sic wes his happe,
> The meikle mirth, the melodie, and sound,
> Quhilk fra the wallis sweitlie can redound
> In at his eir, and sink vnto his hart;
> And thairin wirkis mony previe wound,
> That dois oftsys[2] him stang with stoundis[3] smart."

But deliverance is near at hand. The king and his comrades implore the help of "Dame Pietie";

> "Fair thing! cum doun a quhyle, and with us speik."

"Danger" answers for her

> "That wer grete doute,
> A madin sweit amang sa mony men
> To cum alane, but[4] folk war hir about;
> That is ane craft myself culd never ken."

[1] So as. [2] Ofttimes. [3] Sharp and sudden pains.
[4] Without, unless.

She then hastens to the queen and warns her if she values her own freedom to "keip Pietie fast." That soft-hearted maiden is not to be trusted.

> "May scho wyn out, scho will play yow a cast."

Her fears are well-founded. One night when "Danger" worn out with watching has fallen into a deep slumber, "Pietie" slips from her room—

> "The dure on chare[1] it stude; all wes on sleip;
> And Pietie doun the stair full sone is past.
> This Bissines hes sene, and gave gud keip:
> Dame Pietie hes he hint[2] in armeis fast.
> He callit on Lust, and he come at the last,
> His bandis gart he birst in peces smale:
> Dame Pietie wes gritlie feirit and agast.
> Be that wes Confort croppin[3] in our the wall."

A few minutes serve to effect a revolution in the castle. Douglas has described it with admirable vigour. His abstractions are positively instinct with life, and act with the energy and rapidity of military conspirators.

> "Sone come Delyte, and he begouth to dance;
> Grene Love vpstart, and can his spreitis ta.[4]
> Full weill is me, said Disport, of this chance,
> For now, I traist gret melody to ma.[5]
> *All in ane rout vnto the dure thay ga;*
> And Pietie put thairin first thame befoir.
> Quhat was thair mair, Out! Harro![6] Taik, and slay!
> The hous is wone withoutin brag or schoir.[7]
>
> The courtinis all of gold about the bed
> Weill stentit[8] was quhair fair Dame Plesance lay;
> Than new Desyr, als gredie as ane glede,[9]
> Come rinnand in, and maid ane grit deray.[10]

[1] Ajar; lit. on the turn. [2] Seized. [3] Crept. [4] Take, pick up.
[5] Make. [6] The cries of a surprise party. [7] Threat. [8] Stretched.
[9] Kite. [10] Confused noise.

> The Quene is walknit with ane felloun fray,[1]
> Vp glifnit,[2] and beheld scho wes betraysit;
> Yeild yow, Madame, on hicht can schir Lust say:
> A wourde scho culd nocht speik scho wes so abaisit.[3]
>
> Yeild yow, Madame; grene Lust culd say all sone;
> And fairlie sall we governe you and youris.
> Our lord King Hartis will most now be done,
> That yit is law amang the nether bowris;
> Our lang, Madame, ye keipit thir hie touris;
> Nou thank we none bot Pietie vs suppleit.
> Dame Danger [than] into ane nuk[4] scho kowris;[5]
> And quakand thair the quene scho loy for dreid.
>
> Than Busteousnes[6] come with brag and bost,
> All that ganestude[7] he straik deid in the flure.
> Dame Plesance said, Sall we thus-gate be lost?
> Bring vp the King, lat him in at the dure;
> In his gentrice richt weill I dar assure.
> Thairfor sueit Confort cryit vpone the King:
> Than Bissines, that cunning creature,
> To serve Dame Plesance sone thar can him bring."

Now comes about the result that was foreseen from the beginning. The king and queen were never really at enmity. Ignorance made them rivals; knowledge transforms them into lovers, and the first half of the poem closes with the "roses and raptures" of their bridal feast.

> " So sueit ane swell[8] as straik vnto his hart,
> Quhen that he saw Dame Plesance at his will.
> I yeild me, schir, and do me nocht to smart,
> (The fayr Quene said vpon this wyss[9] him till)
> I sauf[10] youris, suppois it be no skill.

[1] Dreadful fright. [2] Glanced. [3] Abashed. [4] Nook. [5] Cowers.
[6] From busteous, "huge of size." [7] Withstood. [8] Emotion.
[9] Wise, manner. [10] Save.

All that I haue, and all that myne may be,
With all my hairt I offer heir yow till,
And askis nocht bot ye be trew till me.

Till that [quhilk] Love, Desyre, and Lust devysit,
Thus fair Dame Plesance sucitlie can assent.
Than suddandlie Schir Hart him now disgysit,
On gat his amouris clok[1] or euer he stent.[2]
Freschlie to feist thir amouris folk ar went.
Blythnes wes first brocht bodwarde[3] to the hall;
Dame Chastite, that selie innocent,
For wo yeid wode,[4] and flaw out our the wall.

The lustie Quene scho sat in middes the deiss;[5]
Befoir hir stude the nobill wourthy King.
Servit thai war of mony dyuerss meis,[6]
Full sawris[7] sueit and swyth[8] thai culd thame bring.
Thus thai maid ane [richt] mirrie marschalling:
Bewtie and Loue ane hait burde[9] hes begun;
In wirschip of that lustie feist so ding,[10]
Dame Plesance has gart perce Dame Venus tun."

Years pass by unnoticed in this paradise of carnal delight, which the royal lovers think will never be moved. But one morning about sunrise an old man appears at the castle gates and demands admission, at first with courtesy, afterwards, when no heed was paid to his knocking, "he schowted fellonlie." "Wantounnes" looks over the wall and asks his name. He is told that it is "Age." Hurrying to the king with the unwelcome news, the latter sadly recognises his fate.

"He wes to cum. That wist I, be the rude.[11]
It dois me noy,[12] be God, in bane and blude,
That he suld cum sa sone."

[1] Cloak of love. [2] Stepped out. [3] News. [4] Went mad. [5] Dais.
[6] Messes, meats. [7] Savours. [8] Soon. [9] Tussle; Sc. touzle.
[10] Noble; lit. worthy. [11] Cross. [12] Trouble.

"Youthheid" now takes fright, and leaves his master. Even allegory cannot chill the tenderness of the king's farewell.

> "Sen thow man pas, fair Youthheid, wa is me!
> Thou wes my freynd, and maid me gude seruice.
> Fra thow be went never so blyth to be,
> I mak ane vow, [all] thocht that it be nyce,[1]
> Off all blythnes thy bodie beiris the pryce.
> To warisoun[2] I gif the, or thow ga,
> This fresche visar, wes payntit at devyce.[3]
> My lust alway with the se that thow ta.[4]
>
> For saik of the I will no colour reid,
> Nor lusty quhyte, vpone my bodie beir,
> Bot blak and gray; alway quhill[5] I be deid,
> I will none vther wantoun wedis[6] weir.
> Fayr weill my freynd! Thow did me never deir![7]
> Vnwelcum Age, thow come agane my will!
> I lat the wit I micht[8] the weill forbeir.
> Thy warisoun suld be [richt] small, but[9] skill."

"Disport," "Wantounnes," and "Lyflie Delyverance" ride away in the company of "Youthheid." There is something that touches us in the subtle conceit of the poet, when he makes "Fresche Delyte" strive in vain to pass himself off for one who will never return. Through the hollow mask of the allegory we hear distinctly the sound of a human voice, proclaiming the hopelessness of all efforts to perpetuate the lusty vigour of youth.

> "Out at ane previe postrome[10] all thai past;
> And wald nocht byd all-out to tak their leif.
> Than fresche Delyte come rynnand wonder fast,
> And with ane pull gat Youthheid be the sleif:

---

[1] Foolish. [2] For a reward. [3] With great art. [4] Take. [5] Till. [6] Garments.
[7] Hurt. [8] I let thee know that if I could do, etc. [9] Without. [10] Postern.

Abyd! Abyd! Gud fallow, the nocht greif;
Len me thy cloke, to gys[1] me for ane quhyle;
Want I that weid in fayth I will mischeif,[2]
Bot I sall follow the within ane myle.

Delyte come in, and all that saw his bak
They wenit it had bein Youthheid bundin still.
Bot eftirwart, quhen that thai with him spak,
Thay knew it wes ane feinye[3] made thame till.
Sone quhen he had disportit him his fill,
His courtlie cloke begouth to fayd of hew;
Thriftles, threid bair, and reddy for to spill,[4]
Lyk failzeit blak, quhilk wes befoir tyme blew.

Yit wald he nocht away alluterlie,[5]
Bot of retinew feit[6] he him as than;
And, or he wist, he spendit spedellic
The flour of all the substance that he wan:
So wourde[7] he pure and pourit to the pan,[8]
Yit Appetyt, his sone, he bad duell still,
Bot, wit ye weill, he hes ane sory man;
For falt of gude he wantit all his will."

Age now forces his way into the castle at the head of a great crowd of masterful followers. "Queen Plesance" turns from them in mingled rage and grief. Meanwhile a fresh alarm is given. The voice of Conscience is heard sternly threatening vengeance on "the lurdanis"[9] that keep him from the king. When he appears on the scene his first deed is to make a fierce assault on " Syn "—" ane felloun rout[10] he layde on his rig-bone."[11] "Folie" and "Vyce," amazed at his temerity, hide themselves in a corner, while " Falset," " Invy," " Gredie Desyr," " Gamsome Glutony," " Vant," " Vanegloir,"

---

[1] Disguise. [2] Suffer harm. [3] A feint, a deception. [4] Perish. [5] Wholly.
[6] Fed, hired. [7] Became. [8] Impoverished to the very skull. [9] Dolts.
[10] Stroke. [11] Backbone.

"Grene Appetyte" flee in terror from his presence. He now courteously salutes the king, deplores the evils wrought by his wicked counsellors, and upbraids him for following their advice—

> "Thow bird[1] think schame, and of thy riot rew,
> Saw thow thyself into thy colour sad."

While "Conscience" is chiding, "Ressoun" and "Wit" loudly knock at the gates. "Conscience" instantly admits them. The king, however, though sorely abashed has still something to say for himself, and proceeds to vindicate his way of life in a style that reminds us of much later philosophies. He has always tried to do his best. If he has been deceived in his friends, nature is to be blamed for throwing such people in his path—

> "Nature me bred ane beist into my nest,
> And gaif to me Youthheid first seruitour;
> That I no fut micht find, be eist nor west,
> Bot euir in warde, in tutourschip and cure;
> And Wantounness quha wes to me more sure;
> Sic Nature to me brocht, and first devysit
> Me for to keip fra all misaventure.
> Quhat blame serue I, this way to be supprysit?'

He goes even farther in his self-exculpation, and accuses "Conscience" of being slothful in his proper work. If the latter really meant to do him any good he should have come sooner, before "Youth" had fled:

> "The steid is stollin, steik the dure; lat se
> Quhat may avale; God wait![2] the stall is tume."[3]

So that if there is anything amiss in his present state

---

[1] A term of affection common in the ballad literature of Scotland and the English Border. [2] Knows. [3] Empty.

of "drerie indigence," "Conscience" is the cause of the offence, and he boldly invites "Ressoun" to judge between them. "Conscience" defends himself with dignity, declares that he came at the appointed time, and assures the king that he even yet will "blythely reforme" whatever has gone wrong, but that "Ressoun" must first of all "his rollis raithlie to yow reid."[1] These are still worth listening to, and may be quoted :

> "Ressoun rais vp, and in his rollis[2] he brocht.
> Gif I sall say, the sentence sall be plane ;
> Do never the thing that ever may scayth[3] the ocht ;
> Keip mesour and trouth, for thairin lyes na trayne.[4]
> Discretioun suld ay with King Hart remane ;
> Thir vthir young folk-seruandis ar bot fulis.
> Experience mais Knawlege now agane,
> And barnis young suld lerne at auld mennis sculis.
>
> Quha gustis[5] sweit, and feld[6] nevir of the sowre,
> Quhat can [he] say ? How may he seasoun[7] juge ?
> Quha sittis hate, and feld nevir cauld ane hour,
> Quhat wedder is thairout vnder the luge,[8]
> How suld he wit ? That war ane mervale huge !
> To by richt blew, that nevir ane hew had sene !
> Ane servand be, that nevir had seen ane fuge ![9]
> Suppois it ryme it accordis nocht all clene.
>
> To wiss the richt, and to disvse the wrang,
> That is my scule to all that list to leyr.
> Bot Wisdome, gif ye suld duell vs amang,
> Me think ye duell our lang ; put doun your speir ;
> Ye micht weill mak ane end of all this weir,
> Wald ye furth schaw your wourthy document.
> For is thair none that [evir] can forbeyr
> The work of Vice, withoutin your assente."[10]

[1] Quickly read his written laws.
[2] Writings so called because rolled round a wooden or other cyclinder.
[3] Hurt. [4] Snare. [5] Tastes. [6] Felt. [7] Seasoning.
[8] Lodge of leaves. [9] Bundle. [10] Help.

"Wit" also puts in a warning word. "Honour" now rides all round the castle to see if it still harbours anything unworthy. "Dame Plesance" faintly pleads the services of "Eis,"¹ but persuades the king to arrest "Strenth," who is about to depart with his comrade, "Wirschip of Weir." A momentary reaction follows. The king revolts against the authority of "Conscience," and throws himself once more into the arms of the Queen; but his love is no longer sweet:

> "Scho wryit² about, to kyss scho wes full sweir." ³

The more amorous he grows, the more she shrinks from his embraces. No! she must have back the companions of her old felicity if he is to regain her heart.

> "Dame Plesance [said], My freyndis now ar flede;
> The lusty folk that ye furth with yow brocht.
> Methink thir carlis ar nocht courtlie clede!
> Quhat joy haue I of thame? I compt thame nocht.
> Youthheid, and fresche Delyte, micht thai be brocht!
> For with thair seruice I am richt weill kend.
> Fayne wald I that ye send men and thame socht,
> Allthocht it war vnto the warldis end.
>
> The Quene wourde wraythe;⁴ the King wes sore addrede,
> For hir disdane he culd nocht gudlie beir.
> Thai sowpit⁵ sone, and syne thai bownit⁶ to bede;
> Sadnes come in and rounit⁷ in his eir!
> Dame Plesance hes persauit hir new feyr;⁸
> And airlie, affore the sone, scho gan to ryse
> Out of the bed, and turst⁹ vp all hir geir.
> The King wes sound on sleip, and still he lyis."

The flight of the queen soon becomes known. "Ressoun" roughly awakes the forsaken monarch and asks him

¹ Ease.   ² Writhed or twisted.   ³ Reluctant.   ⁴ Became wroth.
⁵ Supped.   ⁶ Went off.   ⁷ Whispered.   ⁸ Companion.   ⁹ Trussed or packed up.

> "Quhair is the thesaure now that ye have woun ?
> This drink wes sweit ye fand in Venus tun ;
> Sone eftir this it sall be staill and soure."

"Wisdom" more gently advises him to seek his old home, and spend his last days in peace and honour. The king consents and orders his men to make ready without delay.

> "Full suddanlie thai can the clarioun blaw ;
> On hors thai lap, and raid then all on raw
> To his awin castell thairin he wes brede."

"Heaviness" bids him welcome, but marvels much at the change in his appearance. "Strength," after lingering for a time, quietly steals away to seek his old "feiris," "Youthheid," and "Delyte." Every day the condition of the king becomes more desolate, feeble, and hopeless. At last a hideous host is seen coming over the moors. The portrait of the leader is boldly drawn :—

> "Decrepitus, his baner schane nocht cleir,
> Was at the hand, with mony chiftanis sture.[1]
> A crudge bak[2] that cairfull cative[3] bure,
> And cruikit[4] war his[5] laythlie lymmis bayth.
> But[6] smirk, or smyle, bot rather for to smvre,
> But scoup, or skift,[7] his craft is all to scayth."

The end is now drawing near. The once "cumlie castell" of "King Hart" is "seigit fast with mony sow and gyne," and after a gallant defence its breastworks are stormed, and its towers topple over. The foe bursts in with "meikle dirdum and deray."

> "Heidwerk,[8] Hoist,[9] and Parlasy,[10] maid grit pay,
> And Murmouris mo with mony speir and targe."

[1] Sturdy.   [2] Humpback.   [3] Wretch.   [4] Crooked.   [5] Loathsome.
[6] Without.   [7] Without purpose or resource.   [8] Headache.
[9] Cough.   [10] Palsy.

"Decrepitus" with his sword inflicts mortal wounds upon "King Hart," whom neither "Ressoun" nor "Wisdom" can any longer help. The poem closes with the dying testament of the hapless monarch. He leaves his proud palfrey, "Vnsteidfastness," to "Dame Plesance"; his servant, "Grein Appetyte," to "Fresch Bewtie"; a cask of "Fantisie" to "Grein Lust"; "Wantounnes" to wait on "Youthheid"; his "meikle wambe" and "rottin levir" to be hung round the neck of "Gluttony"; his "rottin stomak" to "Rere Supper," whom even *in articulo mortis* he praises as "ane fallow fyne," though the reasons he assigns make us doubt it; his broken shins to "Deliuernes"; his conscience to "Chaistite," "that fayr sweit thing, bening in everie bour"; his "threid-bair cloik" to "Fredome"; need to "Waistgude"; a burning fire to "Covatice"; his roomy sleeves to "Vant and Voky"; a stool to "Bissines," "that nevir wes wont to tyre," but whose labours are now at an end; his broken brow to "Fulehardines"; and last of all, he leaves to Dame Danger

"This brokin speir, sumtyme wes stiff and stout."

The outline of the poem now given, together with the quotations, are probably sufficient to exhibit its character and literary merit. No one who compares it with the rest of Douglas's work can fail to be struck by its dramatic vigour. The allegory is full of rapid action, and the *dramatis personæ* play their parts with all the vividness of real life. In this respect *King Hart* is probably unsurpassed by any similar poem in the language, and in our opinion is a much more decisive proof of the author's imaginative power than the *Palice of Honour*. But perhaps the most striking, certainly the most significant feature of the poem is the curious medley of moral feeling that pervades it. It is throughout intensely serious, but the seriousness is that of the Middle Ages—ecclesiastical, almost monkish, not evangelical or humane. To express clearly what one means is difficult, for the Church no longer dominates the ethics of nations as she once did, from chilly heights of austere isolation. For good as well as for evil, the Church and the World have come to live together in friendly intercourse. But in Douglas's time, and for long centuries before it, the Church had a peculiar way of regarding human life outside the sacred precincts as something bright, joyous, delicious, but intrinsically evil, vicious, and doomed to final misery. Happiness was a brief madness from which men were delivered by the dread realities of religion. Out of this came a singular incongruity of sentiment which finds expression in much of the older literature. All that belonged to "the life that now is"—youth, love, beauty, health, strength, pleasure, riches, pomp—was described with an extraordinary zest and relish, as if no language could make it more delightful than it was. There is not a trace of sour severity in the pictures drawn of earthly felicity; only an undertone of regret that such felicity is accursed and cannot endure. When we pass to its counterpart—to scenes where age, sickness, decrepitude, and sadness dwell; where conscience and reason apply their bitter balsams—we seem to hear another voice altogether, one that could never have been lifted up in praise of earthly joys; yet the voice is really the same. The disharmony is not in the individual, but in the prevalent theory of life. The

World and the Church represented antagonistic and irreconcilable ideas, and the age of convenient but pusillanimous compromises had not yet come. Thus it happened that medieval moralists allowed themselves an almost Swinburnian license in their delineations of sensuous delight, which somehow strangely deepened the gloom and dolour of the contrasting pictures.

Nowhere is this contrast more distinctly visible than in *King Hart*. The first canto is a glittering romance of love, the second a ghastly homily on death. No trouveur could be more arch, dainty, and seductive in his turns and suggestions than Douglas in the former part of the poem; no Dominican or Franciscan preacher could set forth the inevitable end of carnal joys in grimmer and more repulsive style than the latter half displays. Yet one sees that the first canto is meant to lead on to the second. The poet is thoroughly in earnest; though he paints the lusty happiness of youth in the brightest colours, and is in fullest sympathy with its passionate emotions, the shadow of the future retribution rests on his soul. "Rejoice, O young man, in thy youth, and let thy heart cheer thee in the days of thy youth, and walk in the ways of thine heart, and in the sight of thine eyes: but know thou that for all these things God will bring thee into judgment."[1] A feeling somewhat akin to this runs through the poem. Of course there are differences. An elaborate and artificial allegory cannot portray an ethical conviction with simplicity and directness of speech, but the differences are only superficial. *King Hart* is essentially a solemn admonition to live "as ever in [the] Great Taskmaster's eye." If the antagon-

---

[1] Ecclesiastes xi. 9.

ism between the flesh and the spirit is too crudely and too severely marked, the work in that respect only more faithfully represents the unnatural asceticism of a Church which misunderstood and perverted the doctrine of St. Paul.

But when everything has been said, we are still unable to resist the conviction that *The Palice of Honour* and *King Hart* possess merely a historical value. Nobody can take very great pleasure in reading them, nor is there much chance that they will ever be read again by any save the most enthusiastic students. We do not mean that they are likely to be forgotten. Their author is too conspicuous and memorable a figure in Scottish history, and they themselves are too important monuments of the national literature, for such a fate to befall them; but the truth is, with all their splendid merits, they lack that personal and human interest that is the only guarantee of immortality. The *Kingis Quhair* is an allegory, but the loves of James and Joanna Beaufort invest it with a perpetual charm. Henryson's *Testament of Cresseid* is a legend of a far-off age, but it is brimful of the same love, sorrow, and despair that still destroy the peace of mortals. Dunbar, in almost every verse he has written, speaks out of the fulness of his heart about what he sees, hears, and suffers in life; but Douglas's allegories have such slight relation to himself, and his capability of expressing natural passion is so small, that it is impossible to feel any permanent interest in the fortunes of his phantoms. The case is different when we pass to his Translation of the Æneid. Apart altogether from the merit of the work as a translation, we are brought into direct and living contact with Douglas himself, in

Prologues and Epilogues, that throw a flood of light upon his literary opinions, sympathies, tastes, pursuits, hopes, and ambitions. The inmost spirit of the scholar and poet is there revealed to us, and for the first time we see and know the man himself. It is hardly an exaggeration to say that the whole nine weary years of his political career after Flodden tell us infinitely less of what he really was than these brilliant additions to his version of Virgil.

His veneration for the great Latin poet was unbounded. Virgil had never ceased to be a magic name from the time of the Roman Empire; even in the darkest days of the Middle Ages, when almost all other classical authors were neglected, he had his readers and admirers. No sooner had the invention of printing come to the help of the Renaissance than his immense popularity was seen. Before the year 1500 his works had passed through ninety editions.

There can be no question that the great literary achievement of Gavin Douglas was his rendering of the "XIII. Bukes of Eneados." It is for this that he is commemorated by Sir Walter Scott—

> "More pleased that, in a barbarous age,
> He gave rude Scotland Virgil's page,
> Than that beneath his rule he held
> The bishopric of fair Dunkeld;"

and though a fuller acquaintance with his life than Scott could possess makes these lines seem ludicrously inappropriate, they no doubt express what ought to have been, if it was not the case.

In two respects this translation marks an era in the history of Scottish culture. From the days of Barbour, that is from its very beginning, the northern literature had been singularly isolated and self-contained. A few southern poets, notably Chaucer, Gower, and Lydgate, had indeed powerfully affected and well nigh founded a Scottish school of poetry. But even their professed followers frequently produced work that was purely native in style and tone; James I., Henryson, Dunbar, are remembered not only for Chaucerian visions, but for homely Scotch ballads and satires. And if the influence of England on Scotland was partial, the influence of Scotland on England was nil. There is no evidence that any Scotch poems of the fifteenth century were so much as known on the other side of the Border; and if they were, they left no trace. But with the publication of Douglas's Æneid this state of things comes to an end. The stream of northern literature begins to find its way into the parent English channel. Douglas may emphasize his patriotism, proclaim on his title page that he has translated into " Scottish Metir," and in his prologue that he is

"Writing in the language of Scottis natioun,"
"Kepand na sudroun bot our awin langage;"

but the fact remains that he is not merely a Scottish poet. He supplies the first link for the chain of English versions of Virgil, the first stone in building up the tradition of what such a translation should be. Surrey's blank verse rendering of the second and fourth books of the Æneid marks a great advance both in theory and execution; but it is easy to show from parallel phrases and passages that Surrey wrote after Douglas and profited by the circumstance.

This of itself is a striking testimony to the success of Douglas's work. Of course his high position served as a good advertisement, and the title page, in this case literally such, takes care to set forth that the author, "the reverend father in God, Mayster Gawin Douglas," is both "Bishop of Dunkel and uncle to the erle of Angus." Of course, too, his residence in the south removed the barrier of distance, and placed him more within the sphere of English readers. Still these circumstances would never have made him an influence in English literature, or conciliated the regard of the fastidious Surrey, had they not been supported by real and conspicuous merits.

Now, of these, the first, and not the least, lay already in the choice of the subject; and this is also Douglas's next great claim to remembrance. It shows how the rising wave of the Renaissance sweeping westward and southward from Italy was at last beginning to beat on the remote shore of Scotland. The opening lines of the introduction run—

> "Laude, honor, prasingis, thankis infynite
> To the and thi dulce ornate fresch endite,
> Mast reuerend Virgill, of Latyne poetis prince."

And in the same tone of exalted admiration he goes on to compare the "Poet Imperial" to a pearl of pearls, a loadstar, a sweet fountain, a palm, a laurel, a cedar. He is never weary of paying these tributes: in prologue after prologue, he breaks out anew in praises of his author.

> "The hie wisdome and maist profound ingyne[1]
> Of myne authar Virgil, poet divyne,
> To comprehend, makis me almaist forvay,[2]
> So crafty wrocht his werk is, lyne be lyne.
> Thairon aucht na man irk, complene, nor quhryne;[3]

[1] Genius. [2] Become bewildered. [3] Murmur.

For quhy ? he alteris his stile sa mony way;
Now dreid, now strif, now luf, now wo, now play,
Langer in murning, now in melody,
To satisfy ilk wichtis fantasy.

Lyke as he had of every thing a feill,[1]
And the willis of every wycht did seill;[2]
And therto eik sa wislie writis he,
Twiching the proffit of the commond weill,
His sawis bene full of sentence every deill,[3]
Of morale doctryne that men suld vicis fle;
Bot gif he be nocht joyous lat us see;
For quha sa list seir[4] glaidsum gemmis[5] leir,[6]
Full mony mery abaittmentis followis heir."

The mere fact that a man felt such an honest enthusiasm about Virgil, and devoted himself to so arduous an undertaking as his interpretation, shows that the middle ages are past. For in them the great classical authors were despised and forgotten. Boethius might be translated as early as the days of Alfred, but then the "last of the Romans" had caught some colours from the Christian faith. Ovid was studied and admired, and even Douglas claims to have rendered his "Remedy of Love," but then Ovid is full of sentimental and almost romantic episodes. Homer was supplanted by Dares and Dictys; and Virgil, if known at all, appeared in far-fetched and corrupted versions which should now be considered artless travesties. One of these, the so-called "Recuyell of the Historyes of Troye" had recently been published by Caxton, and it is interesting to find that Douglas regards this medieval *rechauffée* with feelings of profound and conscious antagonism. With amusing vehemence he attacks and dismembers it, and returns to the charge as

[1] Knowledge. [2] Gladden. [3] Part. [4] Many. [5] Games. [6] Learn.

often as he can find or make an opportunity. Thus in the first prologue he bursts out :—

> "Thocht[1] Williame Caxtoun, of Inglis natioun,
> In pross hes prent ane buik of Inglis gros,
> Clepand it Virgill in Eneados,
> Quhilk that he sais of Frensch he did translait,
> It hes na thing ado therwith, God wait,[2]
> Nor na mair like than the devill and Sanct Austyne."

"In fine," he concludes—

> "Thus schortlie for the nanis,
> A twenty devill mot fall his werk at anis,
> Quhilk is na mair lyke Virgill, dar I lay,
> Na the owle resemblis the papyngay."

Again in the fifth prologue, while celebrating Virgil, he cannot resist a side hit at his perverter.

> "Now harkis[3] sportis, mirthis, and mery playis, . . .
> Endite by Virgile, and heir by me translait,
> Quhilk William Caxtoun knew neuir all his dayis."

Even Chaucer comes in for a share of the translator's wrath for espousing in medieval fashion the cause of Dido against Eneas.

> "He set on Virgile and Eneas this wyte,[4]
> For he was euer, God wait, wemenis frend."

Douglas, therefore, with taste and penetration enough to recognise classical greatness and the greatness of Virgil, has enthusiasm and earnestness enough to make him a missionary of the new faith, and pioneer in the work of classical translation. It was a hard task to undertake, a high movement to inaugurate, and at

---

[1] Though. [2] Wot. [3] Listen to. [4] Blame.

first the translator felt his heart sink. At the outset he exclaims in a kind of despair—

> "Quhy suld I than, with dull forhede and wane,[1]
> With ruide engine and barrand[2] emptive brane,
> With bad harsk speche and leuit[3] barbour tong,
> Presume to write quhar thi sueit bell is rong,
> Or contirfait sa precious wourdis deir?"

As he goes on however he gathers confidence, and at the conclusion is jubilant.

> "Go wlgar Virgill, to euery churlich wycht,
> Say, *I avow thou art translatit rycht;*
> Beseyk all nobillis the corect and amend,
> Beis not afferit to cum in prysaris[4] sycht;
> The nedis nocht to aschame the of the lycht,
> For I have brocht thy purpose to guid end:
> Now salt thou with euery gentill Scot be kend,
> And to onletterit folk be red on hycht,[5]
> That erst was hot with clerkis comprehend."

In another passage he boasts of his extreme accuracy in reproducing Virgil's thoughts.

> "For quha list note my versys, one by one,
> Sall find tharin hys sentens euery deill,[6]
> And almaist word by word, that wait I weill.
> Thank me tharfor, maisteris of grammar sculis,
> Quhar ye syt techand on your benkis and stulis."

Nevertheless he has before told us, and in this case first thoughts were best,—

> "Sum tyme I follow the text als neir I may,
> *Sum tyme I am constrenit ane uther way.*"

The truth is, the Æneid is rather the symptom than the product of that revival which only half a century later, when almost exhausted in the south, was to bring forth

---

[1] Vain. [2] Barren. [3] Ignorant. [4] Critics. [5] Aloud. [6] Part.

its Scottish harvest in the works of George Buchanan. Douglas was no scholar in the sense that Erasmus, a stranger in England at almost the same time with himself, was a scholar. He tries to render his author word for word, or sense for sense, but his literal translations are frequently incorrect, and his paraphrases uncongenial. With all his love for Virgil, he was still an orthodox and "reverend father in God," standing with one foot in the middle ages. He was untouched by that scholarship which was often another name for paganism, and which certainly never minimized the distinction between the antique and the medieval world. He prays,

"Thou virgyne modir and madyne, be my muse;"

and cries to her, after discussing the Cumean Sybil;

"Thou art our sibill, Cristis modir deir."

Strong in the assurance of such Christian celestial help he exclaims—

"From the, bigynning and end bo of my muse,
All other Jove and Phebus I refuse.
Lat Virgyll hald his mawmentis [1] to hymself;
I wirschip noder idoll, stok nor elf,
Thocht furth I wryte so as myne autour dois."

Those who had experienced the real Renaissance fever held different language, and tried to make the Pope himself into a heathen deity. But Douglas, like a true schoolman, sometimes feels, despite all his enthusiasm for Virgil, that really he must apologize for taking such interest in an "unbaptized gentile." At such moments he thinks it necessary to show that his author is

[1] Mahomets, *i.e.*, images.

only in the limbo, not in the lowest hell, and to tell how St. Augustine quoted him in defence of Christianity—

> "Thocht our faith neid nane authorising
> Of gentilis buikis, nor by sic hethin sparkis,
> Zit Virgile writis mony just claus conding,[1]
> Strenthand our belief, to confound payane werkis.
> How oft rehersis Austyne, chief of clerkis,
> In his gret volume of the cetic of God,
> Hundreth versis of Virgile, quhilk he merkis,
> Aganc Romanis, till virtu thaim to brod."[2]

It is another proof that his classical zeal outstripped his classical knowledge, that he has added to the twelve books of Virgil a thirteenth by Mapheus Vegius, an inconsiderable poetaster of the fifteenth century. Douglas indeed makes his excuses for the supplement with a certain amount of sly humour. Mapheus, appearing in a vision, persuades him to the task, partly with a cudgel, partly with the argument—

> "Gyf thou hes afore tyme gayn onrycht
> Followand sa lang Virgill, a gentile clerk,
> Quhy schrynkis thou with my short cristine werk?"

Douglas complies somewhat sarcastically—

> "For, thocht hys style be nocht to Virgill like,
> Full well, I wait, my text sall mony like;
> Quha ever[3] in Latyn has the bruit[4] or glore,
> I speke na wers than I have done before."

Nevertheless, it is easy to see that he does attach some weight to the Christianity of the continuator; and the mere fact that after finishing the Æneid he could take on hand this incongruous appendage, shows that after all he was very much an alien on classic ground.

[1] Condign.   [2] Urge.   [3] Whichever.   [4] Fame.

In the same way some of his renderings of Virgil's text remove us at once from the atmosphere of Virgil. The Sybil is the Holy Nun, and Bacchantes are the nuns of Bacchus—a phrase borrowed and perpetuated by Surrey. Eneas is a "gentle baron," and is on one occasion exhorted to tell his beads with regularity. Every book is divided into chapters, and each chapter is headed with a doggerel couplet, like the following, which are selected quite by chance :—

> " Of Fame that monstre, and Kyng Hyarbas fury,
> And how fra Jove was send the God Mercury."
>
> " Off the scharp wordis queyne Dido did say,
> And how Eneas bownis[1] fast away."
>
> " Our Styx the flud how that Enee did fair,
> And Cerberus in caif hard zell and rair."

Most readers find the opening quatrains of Spenser's cantos a little out of place, but the oddness of such scrappy decorations is much enhanced when they are introduced into the severe structure of a classical epic. Douglas, however, seems to have considered them a success, and coining one for each book strings them together in this most unvirgilian summary of Virgil. " The contentis of every buik following "—

> " The first contenis how the prince Enee
> And Troianis war drive on to Cartage ciete.
> The secund buik schawis the finale ennoy,
> The great mischief, and subversioun of Troye.
> The third tellis how fra Troys ciete
> The Troianis careit war throwout the see.
> The ferd rihersis of fair quene Dido
> The dowble woundis, and the mortall wo.
> The fifth contenis funerale gemmis[2] glaide
> And how the fyir the navy did invaid.

[1] Departs.   [2] Games.

> Into the saxt buik syne doith Virgill tell,
> How that Eneas went and vesyit[1] hell.
> The sevynt Ence bringis to his ground fatall,
> And how Italianis Troianis schupe[2] to assail—
> Vntill Eneas gevis the auchten buke,
> Baith fallowship and armour, quha list luke.
> Dawnus son Turnus in the nynt, tak tent,[3]
> Segeis new Troy, Eneas ther absent.
> The tent declaris, by the coist attanys,
> The battaill betuixt Tuskanis and Rutulianis.
> In the elevynt Rutulianis bene ouersett,
> By the deceiss of Camylla doun bett.
> The twelf makis end of all the were,[4] but dout,
> Throw the slauchter of Turnus, sterne and stout.
> The last, ekit to Virgillis nowmer evyn
> By Mapheus, convoyis Enee to hevyn."

Nevertheless this somewhat barbarous inscription over the portal gives only a partial and unfavourable idea of what is to be found within. Douglas's medievalism may incapacitate him for reproducing some of the characteristic traits of his original; his theology and feudalism may betray him into occasional misconceptions; but for the beauties of very many passages he has the keenest and truest sensibility. He is most delighted with the portraits of men and women, and the descriptions of nature. He is at his best when rendering passages of this kind, and often is so carried away that he cannot help adding touches of his own, most of them truthful and in good taste. Here, for example, is his picture of Camilla, with which the seventh book concludes—

> "Forsuith, ane worthy weriour was she;
> Hir womanly handis nodir[5] rok[6] of tre,
> Na spyndill vsit, nor brochis of Mynerve
> Quhilk in the craft of clayth making dois serve:

[1] Visited. [2] Arranged. [3] Observe. [4] War. [5] Neither. [6] Distaff.

"Bot zit this maid was weill accustumat
To suffyr barganc¹ dourr² and hard debait,
And throu the speid of fut in hir rynning
The swift wyndis prevert and bakwart ding;
Or than also so speidely culd sche fle
Our the cornis, ourtred thair croppis hie,
That wyth hir cours na reid nor tender stra
Was harmit ocht, nor hurt by ony wa;
And, throu the bolnand³ fludis amyd the se
Borne sovyrly,⁴ furth hald hir way mycht she,
The swyft solis of hir tender feyt
Nocht tuicheand anes the watter hir to weyt.
All zoung folkis, on hir for to ferly,⁵
Furth of feildis and houssis flokis in hy.⁶
Litill childring and matronis awundring
On far behaldis hir stout pais in a ling:⁷
So manfully and baldly walkis sche,
With spreit abasit thai gofe⁸ hir for to se,
Quhat wys hir slekit⁹ schulderis war array
Wyth kynglie purpour, honorable and gay;
And how the hair was of this damysell
Knyt wyth a buttoune in a goldin kell;¹⁰
And hou a quavir¹¹ clos scho bair alsua,
Wyth grundin dartis wrocht in Lycia;
And a haill suppline¹² of a gret myrtre,¹³
Quhilk hyrdis mycht ourheild wyth bewis hie,
In maner of a speir in hand scho bayr,
Heidit wyth forgit steill full scharp and squayr."

Again his national love of field sports is excited by the description of the hunt in the fourth book—

"Postquam altos ventum in montes atque invia lustra:
Ecce ferœ saxi dejectœ vertice caprœ
Decurrere jugis; alia de parte patentes

¹ Quarrel.	² Hard.	³ Swelling.	⁴ Surely.	⁵ Wonder.
⁶ Haste.	⁷ Straight line.	⁸ Gape.	⁹ Smooth.	¹⁰ Caul.
¹¹ Quiver.	¹² Sappling.	¹³ Myrtle.		

> Transmittunt cursu campos atque agmina cervi
> Pulverulenta fuga glomerant, montesque relinquunt,
> At puer Ascanius mediis in vallibus acri
> Gaudet equo; jamque hos cursu, jam præterit illos;
> Spumantemque dari pectora inter inertia votis
> Optat aprum, aut fulvum descendere monte leonem."

A few years later, Surrey, profiting by Douglas's experience and recognising better what the duty of a translator should be, could translate more faithfully and therefore more effectively.

> "But to the hills and wild holts when they came;
> From the rock's top the driven savage rose.
> So from the hill above, on th' other side
> Through the wide lawns they gan to take their course,
> The harts likewise in troops taking their flight,
> Raising the dust, the mountain-fast forsake.
> The child Iulus, blithe of his swift steed
> Amid the plain now pricks by them,[1] now these;
> And to encounter wisheth oft in mind,
> The foaming boar, instead of fearful beasts,
> Or lion brown, might from the hill descend."

But who will blame Douglas, that with less knowledge and more unrestrained enthusiasm, he should thus interpolate and expand?

> "And eftir thai ar cumin to the chace,
> Amang the mountains in the wild forrest,
> The ryning hundis of cuplis sone thai kest,
> And our the clewis,[2] and the holtis, belyf,[3]
> The wild bestis down to the daill thai drive.
> Lo! ther the rais, rynning swift as fyre,
> Drevin from the hychtis brekkis out at the swyre;[4]
> Ane vther part, syne yonder mycht thow see
> The hirdies of hartis with there heidis hie,

---

[1] Those.   [2] Rocks.   [3] At once.   [4] Gorge.

> Our spynnerand[1] with swyft cours the plane vaill,
> The hope of dust wpstouring at thair taill,
> Fleand the hundis, leiffand the hie montanis.
> And Ascanyus, the child, amyde the planis,
> Joyus and blyth his stertling steid to assay,
> Now makkis his renk[2] zondir, and now this way,
> Now prekis furth by thir, and now by thaim;
> Langyng, amang faynt frayit beistis vntame,[3]
> The fomy bair doun from the hillis hycht,
> Or the dun lyon discend, recontir he mycht."

Take another similar instance. In the second book, when Pyrrhus and the Greeks break into the palace of Priam, Virgil illustrates their violence by a short simile not four lines long;—

> " Non sic, aggeribus ruptis cum spumeus amnis
> Exiit, oppositosque evicit gurgite moles,
> Fertur in arva furens cumulo, camposque per omnes
> Cum stabulis armenta trahit."

Considering the comparative length of the lines, Surrey rather condenses than amplifies;—

> " Not so fiercely doth overflow the fields,
> The foaming flood, that breaks out of his banks;
> Whose rage of waters bears away what heaps
> Stand in his way, the cotes and eke the herds."

But Douglas was too familiar with a stream in spate not to seize the opportunity of further enlargement and convert the suggestive outline into a finished picture :—

> " Nocht sa fersly the fomy rivair or flude
> Brekkis our the bankis, on spait quhen it is woude,
> And, with his bruscheand faird of watter broun,
> The dikis and the schoiris bettis doun,

---

[1] Running over.   [2] Course.   [3] Wild, shy.

> Oursprcdand croftis and flattis with his spait,
> Our all the feildis that thai may row ane bait,[1]
> Quhill howsis and the flokkis flittis away,
> The corne graingis, and standant stakkis of hay."

But perhaps Douglas excels himself in his description of the storm and its preliminaries in the first book. He finds something congenial in the wildness of Æolus' country :

> "That wyndy regioun,
> Ane brudy[2] land of furious stormy sownn,
> . . . . quhair Eolus the kyng
> In gowstie cavis, the wyndis lowde quhisling,
> And braithlie[3] tempestis by his power refrenis,
> In bandis hard schet in presoun constrenis ;
> And thei, heirat havand full greit disdene,
> Quhill all the hill resoundis, quhryne[4] and plene
> About thar closouris braying with mony rair.
> Kyng Eolus sett hie vpoun his chare,
> Witht septour in hand thair muyd[5] to meis[6] and still,
> Temperis thair ire, les thai suld at thair will
> Beir witht thair byr[7] the skyis, and drive about
> Erd, air, and se, quhenevir thai list blaw out."

Afterwards when Æolus consents to Juno's prayer :

> . . . . "Ane groundin dart lait he glyde,
> And peirsit the bos[8] hill at the braid syde ;
> Furth at the ilk port wyndis braid[9] in a rowt,
> And with ane quhirle blew all the erd abowt,
> Thai vmbesett the seis busteously,
> Quhill fra the deip, till every coist fast by,
> The huge wallis[10] welteris upoun hie,
> Rowit[11] at anis with stormis of wyndis thre,
> Eurus, Nothus, and the wynd Aphricus,
> Quhilkis eist, south, and waist wyndis hait[12] with ws.

[1] Boat. [2] Prolific. [3] Violent. [4] Murmur. [5] Mood. [6] Moderate.
[7] Rush. [8] Hollow. [9] Leap. [10] Waves. [11] Rolled. [12] Are called.

> Sone eftir this, of men the clamour rais,
> The takles graislis,[1] cabillis can freit[2] and frais,[3]
> Switht[4] the cluddis, hevin, sone, and days licht
> Hid,[5] and brest out of the Troianis sicht;
> Dyrknes as nycht besett the seis abowt;
> The firmament gane rummeling rair and rowt,
> The skyis oft lychtnit with fyry lewyne,[6]
> And schortlie baitht air, sea, and hewyne,
> And every thing mannasit[7] the men to de,
> Schawand the deith present tofor thair ee."

The storm strikes the Trojan navy:

> " Ane blusterand bub,[8] out fra the north braying,
> Gane our the foirschip in the bak sail dyng,
> And to the sternys up the fluide can cast,
> The ayris,[9] hachis, and the takillis brast,
> The schippis stewyn[10] frawart hir went[11] can writhe,
> And turnit his braid syide to the wallis swithe,[12]
> Heich as ane hill the jaw of watter brak
> And in ane heip come on thame with ane swak,[13]
> Sum hesit[14] hoverand on the wallis hycht,[15]
> And sum the sownchand[16] see so law gart lycht,
> Thame semit the erd oppinnit amyd the flude;
> The stowr[17] wp bullerit[18] sand as it war wuid."

It is very important to notice the vigour and directness of these passages. The truth is that Douglas by natural genius is a descriptive poet, and is never more at home than when describing a hunt, a storm, a spate, and other natural appearances with which he was familiar in his own northern land. In his earlier works the scenery is the stage scenery of conventional allegory; but tutored perhaps by the classic objectivity of Virgil, he at length discards all this mannerism and comes forward

---

[1] Rattles. [2] Fret. [3] Creak. [4] Soon. [5] Neuter verb. [6] Lightning.
[7] Menaced. [8] Blast. [9] Oars. [10] Stem, prow. [11] Course. [12] Strong waves.
[13] Crash. [14] Were poised. [15] On the top of the waves. [16] Noisy.
[17] Spray. [18] Hurled.

as one of the first and one of the truest of the modern poets of nature.

At the end of his book in very intelligible exultation he exclaims:

> "Throwout the ile yclepit Albioune,
> Red sall I be and sung with mony one.
> Thus up my pen and instrumentis full zoyr [1]
> On Virgillis post I fix for evirmore."

But posterity cannot accept this judgment without modification. In one sense, no doubt, the translation is Douglas's great work, and with it, as we have seen, both by his example in rendering a classic, and by his influence on subsequent Virgilian translators, he has made his deepest mark in literature. Still it is not the work from his pen which is now most read or most worth reading. It is something of an adventure to get through the thirteen books with their quaint language and rugged rhyme, and few there be that achieve it. But Douglas has interspersed his translation with much verse of his own which even now is interesting and fresh to the general reader. In addition to the somewhat unfortunate tags of rhyme already quoted, each book is introduced by an original prologue, and these prologues are of great and increasing excellence. The later ones contain descriptions of some of the chief phases of the year, which, in their feeling and truth, perhaps also in their occasional tendency to cheap classical adornment, might have come direct from the pen of the poet of the *Seasons*. For instance the prologue to the seventh book, following the account in the sixth of the descent to the infernal regions, is intended, as Douglas says, to "smell new come forth of hell," and gives a dreary account of a northern winter.

[1] Ready.

> "The frosty region[1] ringis[2] of the yeir,
> The tyme and sessoune bitter cald and paill,
> Thai schort days that clerkis clepe brumaill;
> Quhen brym[3] blastis of the northyne art
> Ourquhelmit had Neptunus in his cart,
> And all to[4] schaik the levis of the treis,
> The raveand storm ourwalterand wally[5] seis;
> Reveris ran reid on spait with watteir broune,
> And burnis hurlis all thair bankis downe,
> And land brist[6] rumland rudely wyth sic beir,[7]
> So loud ne rummist wyld lioun or beir."

The inhabitant of North Britain can recognise Douglas's realism in his description of

> "The soil ysowpit into wattir wak[8]
> The firmament ourkest with rokis[9] blak,
> The ground fadyt, and fauch[10] wolx all the feildis,
> Montayne toppis sleikit[11] wyth snaw ourheildis,[12]
> On raggit rolkis of hard harsk quhyne stane,
> With frosyne frontis, cauld clynty[13] clewis schane."

He proceeds in his gloomy monotone—

> "Soure bittir bubbis, and the schowris snell,
> Semyt on the sward ane similitude of hell,
> Reducyng to our mynd, in every steid,
> Goustly schaddois of eild and grisly deid,
> Thik drumly scuggis[14] dirknit so the hevyne,
> Dym skyis oft furth warpit feirfull levyne,
> Flaggis of fyir, and mony felloun flawe,[15]
> Scharp soppis of sleit, and of the snypand snawe.
> The dowy dichis war all donk[16] and wait,
> The law vaille flodderit[17] all wyth spait,
> The plane stretis and every hie way
> Full of fluschis,[18] doubbis, myre and clay."

[1] Here referring to the time not to the area of control. [2] Prevails. [3] Fierce. [4] Asunder. [5] Stormy. [6] Surf. [7] Noise. [8] Muddy. [9] Clouds. [10] Brown. [11] Smoothed. [12] Coverings. [13] Stony. [14] Shadows. [15] Blast. [16] Moist. [17] Flooded. [18] Pools.

> Laggerit[1] leys wallowit[2] farnys[3] schewe,
> Browne muris kithit thair wysnit mossy hewe,
> Bank, bra, and boddum blanschit wolx and bair;
> For gurll weddir growyt bestis haire;
> The wynd maid wayfe the reid weyd on the dyk,
> Bedovin[4] in donkis deyp was every syk;[5]
> Our craggis, and the front of rockis seyre,
> Hang gret isch schoklis[6] lang as ony spere."

With the realism of a Netherlands painter, Douglas, high dignitary though he was, ventures to portray objects which were afterwards considered beneath the dignity of poetry.

> " Puire laboraris and byssy husband men
> Went wayt and wery draglyt in the fen;
> The silly scheip and thair lytill hyrd gromis
> Lurkis vnder le of bankis, wodys, and bromys;
> And wthir dantit[7] gretar bestial
> Within thair stabillis sesyt into stall,
> Lic as mulis, horsis, oxin, and ky,
> Fed tuskit baris and fat swyne in sty,
> Sustenit war by mannis gouernance
> On hervist and on symmeris purviance."

His best and most continuous effort in this line is, however, the prologue to the twelfth book, which he himself cannot forbear to commend.

> " The lusty crafty preambill, perll of May,
> I the entitill, crownit quhill[8] domisday;
> And al wyth gold, in syng of state ryall,
> Most beyn illumnit thi letteris capital."

It is the morning of the ninth of May—

> " Furth of hys palyce ryall ischyt Phebus,
> Wyth golden crown and vissage gloryus,
> Crysp haris, brycht as chrysolite or topace,
> For quhais hew mycht nane behald his face,

[1] Bemired. [2] Withered. [3] Ferns. [4] Besmeared. [5] Rill.
[6] Jags, isch schoklis, icicles. [7] Domesticated. [8] Till.

"The fyry sparkis brastyng fra his ene
To purge the ayr, and gylt the tendyr grene,
Defundand from hys sege[1] ethcriall,
Glaid influent aspectis celicall.
Before his regale hie magnificens
Mysty vapour vpspringand sweit as sens,[2]
In smoky soppis of donk dewis wak,[3]
Moich hailsum stovis[4] ourheildand the slak ;[5]
The aureat fanys of hys trone souerane
With glytrand glans ourspred the occiane,
The large fludis lemand all of lycht
Bot with a blenk of his supernale sycht :
Fur to behald it was a gloir to se
The stabillit wyndis and the cawmyt see,
The soft sessoun, the firmament serene,
The lowne[6] illumynat air, and fyrth amene ;
The syluer scalyt fyschis on the greit,[7]
Ourthwort cleir stremis sprynkland[8] for the heyt,
Wyth fynnis schynand brown as synopar[9]
And chyssell talis stowrand heyr and thar."

In the beginning of the quotation the classical imagery is rather offensive to modern taste, but the farther he proceeds the truer and more natural he becomes :—

"Under the bewys[10] beyn[11] in lusty valis,
Within fermans[12] and parkis cloys of palys,
The bustuus[13] bukkis rakis[14] furth on raw;
Heyrdis of hertis throw the thyk wod schaw,[15]
Baith the brokettis, and with brayd burnyst tyndis,[16]
The sprutlyt[17] calvys sowkand the reid hyndis.
The yong fownis followand the dun dayis,
Kyddis skippand throw ronnis eftir rayis.
In lyssouris[18] and on leys litill lammis
Full tait and trig[19] socht bletand to thar dammis.
Tydy[20] ky lowys, veilys by thame rynnis ;
All snog and slekyt worth[21] thir bestis skynnis."

[1] Chair. [2] Incense. [3] Moist. [4] Vapours. [5] Hollow. [6] Still. [7] Gravel. [8] Darting. [9] Cinnabar. [10] Boughs. [11] Pleasant. [12] Enclosures. [13] Boisterous. [14] Run. [15] Shade. [16] Horns. [17] Spotted. [18] Meadows. [19] Tight and trig. [20] Plump. [21] Become.

Sometimes, as in the opening lines of the following extract, the contrast between conventionality and realism gives rise to entertaining explanations; but notice how Douglas's bent to truth makes him quite dramatic towards the close :—

> "On salt stremys wolx Doryda and Thetis,
> By rynnand strandis Nymphis and Nædes,
> *Syk as we clepe wenchis and damysellis,*
> In gresy[1] gravis[2] wandrand by spring wellis,
> Of Blomyt branchis and flowris quhite and rede,
> Plettand thar lusty chaiplettis for thar hede;
> Sum sing sangis, dansis ledys,[3] and roundis,[4]
> With vocis schill,[5] quhill[6] all the daill resovndis;
> Quharso thai walk into thar caraling,
> For amorous lays doith all the rochis rying.
> Ane sang, 'The schip salis our the salt fame,
> Will bring thir merchandis and my lemman[7] hame';
> Sum other singis, 'I will be blyth and lycht,
> Myne hart is lent upon sa gudly wycht.'
> And thochtful luffaris rowmis to and fro,
> To leis[8] thar pane and plene thar joly wo;
> Eftyr thar gys, now syngand, now in sorow,
> With hartis pensyve, the lang symmeris morrow;
> Sum ballettis lyst[9] endyte of his lady,
> Sum levis in hoip, and sum aluterly
> Disparyt is, and sa quyte owt of grace,
> His purgatory he fyndis in euery place.
> To pleis his luife sum thocht to flat[10] and fene,
> Sum to hant[11] bawdry and onlesum[12] mene;
> Sum rownys[13] to hys fallow, thame betwene,
> Hys mery stouth[14] and pastans[15] lait yistrene.
> Smyland sayis ane, 'I cowth in previte
> Schaw the a bowrd,'[16]—'Ha, quhat be that ?' quod he—
> 'Quhat thing ? That moste be secret,' said the tother—
> 'Gude Lord ! mysbeleif ye your verray brother?'—

[1] Grassy. [2] Groves. [3] Lead. [4] Round dances. [5] Shrill. [6] Till. [7] Lover.
[8] Relieve. [9] Pleases to. [10] Flatter. [11] Practise. [12] Unbecoming.
[13] Whispers. [1] Prank. [15] Pastime. [16] Jest.

> 'Na, newyr a deill,[1] bot harkis quhat I wald,
> Thou mon be prevy.'—'Lo, my hand uphald !'—
> 'Than sal thou walk at evin.'—Quod he, 'Quhyddir ?'—
> 'In syk a place heyr west, we bayth togiddyr,
> Quhar scho so freschly sang this hynder [2] nycht;
> Do chois the ane, and I sall quynch the lycht.'—
> 'I sall be thar, I hope,' quod he, and lewch,
> 'Ya now I knaw the mater weill eneuch.'
> Thus oft dywulgat is this schamefull play
> Na thing according to our hailsum May."

Here again from the thirteenth prologue is the description of a June evening drawing on to night:—

> "The lycht begouth to quynkill [3] out and faill,
> The day to dyrkin, decline, and devaill;[4]
> The gummys [5] rysis, doun fallis the donk rym,
> Baith hayr and thar scuggis [6] and schaddows dym.
> Up gois the bak [7] wyth hir pelit ledderyn flycht,
> The lark discendis from the skyis hycht,
> Singand hyr compling sang [8] eftyr hyr gys,
> To tak hyr rest, at matyn hour to rys.
> Owt owr the swyre [9] swymmis the soppis of mist,
> The nycht forthspred hyr cloke with sabill lyst,[10]
> That all the bewtie of the fructuous feyld
> Was wyth the erthis umbrage clein ourheild;
> Baith man and beste, fyrth, flude, and woddis wild,
> Involuit in tha schaddois warrin [11] sild.[12]
> Still war the fowlis fleis in the ayr,
> All stoyr [13] and catall seysit in thar lair,
> And euery thing, quharso thame likis best,
> Bownis to tak the hailsum nychtis rest
> Eftir the dayis labour and the heyt."

These quotations have been given in considerable number, for they show Douglas at his best, and are his most characteristic work. The "Flowers o' the

---

[1] Bit. [2] Yester. [3] Twinkle. [4] Fall. [5] Mists. [6] Shades. [7] Bat.
[8] Song at the last of the canonical hours. [9] Gorge. [10] Border. [11] Were.
[12] Covered. [13] Live-stock.

Forest" has sometimes been ascribed to him, and though this is entirely without justification, we see from these specimens of word-painting that the transformation of the learned bishop to a ballad-monger is not so abrupt as at first sight appears. With all his early taste for allegory, with all his devotion to the great Latin epic, Douglas had yet a popular side to his genius. He writes in Scottish metre for his Scottish countrymen. One of his prologues is in old-fashioned alliterative rhyme; his sympathies are aroused by the rustic sights and sounds of his native land. It is no small praise that the national feeling for external nature first finds expression in him, and that he takes a few steps on the path afterwards to be trodden by so many under the guidance of Thomson and Scott.

CHAPTER VIII.

SIR DAVID LYNDSAY.

His Birthplace.—Position of the Country during his Earlier Years.—He enters St. Salvator's College, St. Andrews.—Passes into the Royal Household.—Flodden.—Lyndsay's Attendance on the Young King, James V.—His Marriage.—James assumes the Government at the Age of Twelve.—Comes under the Power of Angus.—Overthrow of Angus.—Lyndsay begins his Literary Career.—The Dreme.—Analysis and Criticism.—The Complaynt to the Kyng.—Lyndsay appointed Lyon King of Arms.—The Testament and Complaynt of the Kyngis Papyngo.—The Boldness of Lyndsay's Utterance.—His Minor Pieces.—His Masterpiece, Ane Pleasant Satyre of the Thrie Estaitis.—Its Nature.—Outline of the Play.—Critical Estimate.—Lyndsay's Duties as Lyon-Herald.—The King's Marriages.—His Death.—Consequent Changes.—Tragedie of the Cardinall.—Lyndsay's Connection with Knox.—Reasons of his Safety.—Squire Meldrum.—The Monarchie.—The Poet's Death.—Estimate of his Work.

DAVID LYNDSAY was descended from a younger branch of the Lyndsays of the Byers in Haddingtonshire. It is usually assumed that he was born at the Mount, near Cupar-Fife, about the year 1490; but Mr. Laing, his latest and best editor, is of opinion that Garmylton (now called Garleton) in East Lothian, to which the poet succeeded in early life, and which he retained in his own possession, might as likely have had the honour of being the place of his birth. Of his earlier years we know nothing, but the period which they cover is deeply interesting in the history of Western Europe. It was a brief interval of repose and growth after the fiery revolutions of feudal strife had ceased, and before the fiercer struggle of ideas began. In England, the murderous Wars of the Roses were just over, and under the prudent and peaceful rule of Henry VII. the nation was gradually recruiting its shattered strength, and leaving behind it the sentiments and superstitions of the Middle Ages. Hume pronounces this reign to be "the dawn of civility and science" in the island. France, a country in which all the horrors of feudal misrule and perfidy were felt, till Joan of Arc evoked, for the first time in its history, a national spirit, had grown in wealth and power under the astute policy of Louis XI. and his successors, who favoured the burghers at the expense of the barons. The same triumph of monarchy over feudalism was achieved in Spain by Ferdinand and Isabella, but in Scotland the aristocracy was victorious. The monarch who ruled had received his crown at its hands; and when the frightful catastrophe of Flodden took place, the demon of discord was again let loose on the ill-fated land, and the Douglasses, who seemed resolved to ruin the nation of whose liberties they had been the invincible bulwark, added treason to turbulence, and covered with infamy a name that had once been the fairest in Scottish story. So long, however, as James IV. ruled, not only was the evil unfelt, but it could hardly be said to exist. In spite of the rash act, which cost him his crown and his life, and by which he is mainly remembered, he was a thoroughly able and energetic prince. Liberal to the nobility, affable to the commons, and courteous to the clergy, he won golden opinions from all. In his determination to suppress the risings in the Highlands and to weaken the power of the Barons all over the country, especially of the Lord of the Isles, by measures which have already been fully described,[1] we can see that he had the interest of his country at heart. And from this unwonted tranquillity there resulted an unwonted prosperity. At home, agriculture and commerce flourished; abroad, Scotland was made famous by the bold exploits of her seamen. James's treatment of the Lollards of Kyle, to whom reference has already been made,[2] is an evidence that his undoubted sympathy with priests did not greatly mislead him in matters ecclesiastical or deprive him of the sense of justice befitting a king.

Scotland was thus, during Lyndsay's boyhood, under the rule of a gallant and popular monarch, with a friendly neighbour in the English king, who was willing to forget in a matrimonial alliance the angry recollections of the past. In 1505, two years after Margaret Tudor had become James's wife, and the very year in which Knox was born, the poet entered the University of St. Andrews. His name stands in the register of St. Salvator's College next to that of David Beaton, whose tragedy he has exultingly celebrated. It is curious to think that these two may have joyously joined in the customary frolics of student life, without suspicion that a day would come when it would be the pride of the one to defend the murder of the other. Lyndsay seems to have left the University in 1508 or 1509 without taking his degree. Certain writers assert that he thereafter proceeded to the Continent, but there is no evidence to support the assertion. The probability is that he passed from college to the royal household, though the loss of the treasurer's accounts between August, 1508, and September, 1511, prevents us from speaking positively on this point. His name

[1] Page 177.   [2] Page 183.

first occurs in these accounts on the 12th October of the latter year, when the sum of £3 4s. was paid for blue and yellow taffetis, "to be a play coat to David Lyndsay for the play, playit in the king and queen's presence, in the Abbey of Holyrood."

A disastrous change in the foreign policy of Scotland was now impending. James's father-in-law was dead, and Henry VIII. had entered on his passionate and imperious career. It is not necessary here to trace the steps which preceded the rupture between the two proud and sensitive monarchs. It is enough to state that already the war of religious ideas was foreshadowed by the policy of Spain, whose ruler had come forward in the quarrel between Louis of France and the Pope as the champion of the latter. Henry, then a zealous Catholic, was induced to join the emperor in his pious crusade against the head of the Gallican Church; whereupon Louis appealed to the Scottish king to remember the ancient alliance between France and Scotland; and his wife, who knew the romantic gallantry of James, appointed him her knight, and besought him to march for her sake three miles into English ground. So the fatal march to Flodden was undertaken, and England had revenge for Bannockburn. In that same autumn of 1513, in which the French cavaliers made an ignominious display of their horsemanship at the Battle of the Spurs, the Earl of Surrey in one fatal afternoon made havoc for a generation of the prosperity of Scotland. To Lyndsay that "dolent daye" must have been unspeakably distressing. Not only do his works abound with evidences of a stout patriotism, but he knew and loved the fallen king, who, the year before, had made him chief page of honour to the new-born prince. Long afterwards, in his *Complaynt of the Papyngo*, he celebrates the virtues of his ill-fated master, and mourns, in words that are pathetic from their very simplicity, the dismal ruin that had overtaken him :—

> " I never read in tragedie nor storie,
> At one journaye, so mony nobyllis slane,
> For the defence and lufe of thair soverane."

The next eleven years of the poet's life were spent in attendance on the royal youth. He was not exactly his tutor, and yet perhaps James V. derived as much benefit from his familiar intercourse with the keen-witted companion of his leisure hours as from the formal instructions of Dunbar. The employments which fell to Lyndsay are thus described in his *Epistil to the Kingis Grace*, prefixed to his earliest poem, *The Dreme*—

> " Quhen thow wes young, I bure thee in mine arme
> Full tenderlie, tyll thow begouth to gang ;
> And in thy bed oft happit thee full warme,
> With lute in hand, syne, sweitlie to thee sang :
> Sumtyme, in dansing, feiralie I flang ;
> And sumtyme, playand farsis on the flure ;
> And sumtyme, on myne office takkand cure.
>
> And sumtyme, lyke ane feind, transfigurate,
> And sumtyme, lyke the greislie gaist of Gye ;
> In divers formis oft tymes disfigurate,
> And sumtyme, dissagyist full plesandlye.
> So, sen thy birth, I have continewalye
> Bene occupyit, and aye to thy plesoure,
> And sumtyme, Seware,[1] Coppare,[2] and Carvoure.[3]

[1] Steward.   [2] Cup-bearer.   [3] Carver.

> Thy purs maister and secreit Thesaurare,
> Thy yschare,[1] aye sen thy natyvitie,
> And of thy chalmer cheiffe Cubiculare."[2]

Again he says in the *Complaynt to the King*—

> "Quhow, as ane chapman beris his pak,
> I bure thy Grace upon my bak,
> And sumtymes, strydlingis on my nek,
> Dansand with mony bend and bek.
> The first sillabis that thow did mute
> Was 'PA, DA LYN,' upon the lute.
> Than playit I twenty spryngis, perqueir,[3]
> Quhilk wes gret piete fer to heir.
>
> . . . .
>
> And aye, quhen thow come frome the scule,
> Then I behuffit to play the fule."

As his royal charge grew up, and began to display a quick intelligence, and a nature susceptible of imaginative impressions, Lyndsay seems to have taken a more dignified position, and to have led James through the round of classico-romantic legends which fed the wonder of the Middle Ages. In the *Epistil* quoted above he says—

> "Bot now thow arte, be influence naturall,
>   Hie of ingyne, and rycht inquisitive
> Of antique storeis and deidis marciall;
>   More plesandlie the tyme for tyll ouerdryve,
>   I have, at length, the stories done, descryve
> Of Hectour, Arthour, and gentyll Julyus,
> Of Alexander, and worthy Pompeyus;
>
> Of Jasone, and Medea, all at length,
>   Of Hercules, the actis honorabyll,
> And of Sampsone the supernaturall strength,
>   And of leill luffaris stories amiabyll;

[1] Usher. [2] Groom of the bedchamber. [3] Off-hand.

> And oft tymes have I feinyeit mony fabyll,
> Of Troylus, the sorrow and the joye,
> And Seigis all of Tyir, Thebes, and Troye."

It was about the year 1522, and while he was still occupied with the service he has described, that Lyndsay's marriage took place. Chalmers and subsequent writers assign to this event a date ten years later, but Mr. Laing has discovered several items in the treasurer's accounts (1522-24) which leave no doubt on the matter. The name of the lady was Janet Douglas, a name by which she continued to be designated after her marriage. We have no trace of the family to which she belonged, but we know that she did not deem it inconsistent with her dignity as Lyndsay's wife to hold the appointment of seamstress to the king with an annual pension of £10.

Among the other disastrous results of the unhappy marriage of Queen Margaret to the Earl of Angus was the assumption by King James V. of the reins of government at the age of twelve. This of course involved the immediate termination of his studies, and the dismissal of all the learned counsellors of his youth. Lyndsay is vehement in his denunciations—

> " Imprudentlie, lyk wytles fuilis,
> Thay tuke that young Prince frome the scuilis,
> Quhare he, under obedience,
> Was lernand vertew and science,
> And haistelie platt[1] in his hand
> The governance of all Scotland ;
> As quho wald, in ane stormye blast,
> Quhen marinaris bene all agast
> Throw dainger of the seis raige,
> Wad tak ane chylde of tender aige,

[1] Placed.

> Quhilk never had bene on the sey,
> And to his biddying all obey,
> Gevyng hym haill the governall,
> Of schip, marchand, and marinall,
> For dreid of rockis and foreland,
> To put the ruther in his hand :
> Without Goddis grace, is no refuge :
> Geve¹ thare be dainger, ye may juge.
> I gyf thame to the Devyll of hell,
> Quhilk first devysit that counsell,
> I wyll nocht say, that it was treassoun ;
> Bot I dar sweir it was no reassoun.
> I pray God, lat me never se ryng
> In to this realme, so young ane kyng."

Instead of being under the salutary influence of his tutors, the young king soon came into the power of Angus, who, returning from exile and forming an alliance with Lennox and Argyll, took possession of his person and violently established a regency. James was practically a prisoner in his hands for four years. It is frightful to think of the baseness to which this traitor descended in order to maintain his hold upon his ward. Even at this distance of time we cannot read Lyndsay's account of the scandalous artifices employed to corrupt the prince without a sense of burning indignation. For James had a frank and generous soul; he loved his people well, and if his moral sense had not been blunted at this critical period of his life, he might have done as much for the reformation of religion as he did for the suppression of social disorders.

In 1528 the king escaped from the thraldom of the Douglasses. The rough night-gallop from Falkland Palace to Stirling Castle, through the defiles of the Ochils, is the turning-point in his history. Instantly

---
¹ If.

a council was summoned, and Angus was overthrown. When this fortunate event happened Lyndsay had reached the mature age of thirty-eight. In the ordinary sense of the phrase, he had not seen much of the world; he had not been a great traveller: it is even doubtful if he had yet crossed the Border. But he was a good scholar and had read widely; he had a keen eye and a quick ear; and his long residence at court (the hot centre of political and domestic intrigue) had furnished him with an abundance of worldly knowledge. Every poem he has written proves how narrowly he watched the times, and how bitterly he felt the miseries of his country. During the last ascendancy of the Douglasses he probably spent his enforced retirement from court at the family residence in Fife. Wherever he lived he was not idle. It was, perhaps, even fortunate for his fame that he was released from his close attendance on the king, for up to this date he had, so far as we know, written nothing; but now in the safe obscurity of the Mount he sat musing on the things he had seen and heard—the greed and treachery of the courtiers, the vice and simony of prelates, the riot and rapine of nobles, and the general wretchedness of the commonwealth, until the whole took form and shaped itself into the poem called *The Dreme*.

Critics are accustomed to pronounce this first-born of Lyndsay's the most poetical of his productions, and the *Prolog* is in truth not destitute of descriptive beauty, but we look in vain for anything that will bear comparison with the glowing splendours of Dunbar or the diffuse loveliness of Douglas. It is not Lyndsay's imagery or music that rivets us: it is the strength of his moral convictions, the vigour of his political sketches, the audacity of his satire, the broad light that he throws on the age in which he lived, and the assurance we thus derive that, beneath the turbid surface of feudal life, there were still some men in Scotland who loved justice and mercy and peace; whom the outrages of the great fired with indignation, and the miseries of the poor melted with compassion.

There is nothing original in the structure of the poem. The writer follows the fashion of his craft in the Middle Ages when all aspired to imitate Dante. On a bright winter morning, "lansing ouirthorte the landis, toward the see," because the inland scenery was "unblomit," he hears the plaint of the forlorn songstress of the grove and air, and is filled with a spirit of pensiveness—

> "The see was furth, the sand wes smooth and dryc;
> Then up and doun, I musit myne allone,
> Tyll that I spyit ane lyttill cave of stone,
> Heych in ane craig: upwart I did approche,
> But tarying, and clam up in the roche."

While he sat here, looking out upon the deep, the "wolteryng of the wallis"[1] suggested to him the instability of the false world (of which Lyndsay had recently obtained some experience in consequence of the Douglas triumph), and the current of his thoughts began to set in this direction. At last he is lulled asleep "throw the seyis movyng marvellous," and the "bousteous blastis of Eolus," whereupon he has "ane marvellous visioun." A lady of "portratour perfyte" visits him in his dream, and conducts him through Hell, Purgatory, and Heaven. The sting of the poem lies in what he sees in the first of these regions.

[1] Waves.

"Papis," "cairfull Cardinalls," "Achebischopis in thair pontificall," "proude and perverst Prelatis," "Priouris, Abbottis, and fals flatterand Freris," "churle Monkis," swarm in the "painefull poysonit pytt," and although we are also shown a liberal assortment of the laity " rycht furiouslie fryand "—

> "Dukis, Merquessis, Erlis, Barronis, Knychtis,
> . . . .
> Emprices, Quenis, and ladyis of honouris,
> . . . .
> Mansworne merchandis, for their wrangous winning,
> . . . .
> Fals men of law in cautelis rycht cunning
>   Theiffis, revaris, and publict oppressaris;
>   Sum part thare was of unleill lauboraris;
>   Craftismen, thare saw we, out of nummer;"

yet it is with an undisguisedly grim delight that he sees

> "The men of Kirk, lay boundin in to byngis."

Perhaps the martyrdom of Patrick Hamilton, which occurred while Lyndsay was writing his *Dreme*, and which had rekindled after the lapse of a century the flames of persecution in Scotland, intensified that abhorrence of ecclesiastical cruelty, he is never weary of expressing. In the "satiric rage" of our poet, however, we utterly miss the imaginative richness of Dunbar. Throughout the whole piece there is scarcely what may be called a stroke of genius—a *curiosa felicitas*, or memorable phrase. Classes are outlined with a certain broad force, but we lack the vivid incisive individualism of artistic genius. When persons are mentioned they are names and nothing more—

> "Byschope Annas, and the treatour Judas,
> Machomete, that propheit poysonabyll,
> Chore, Dathan, and Abirone thare was."

In this prosaic fashion Lyndsay peoples hell, and if the poem were to be judged only by its literary qualities, we should have little to say in its praise; but when we consider the time and the circumstances in which it was composed, we forget its poetic defects and are struck with admiration at its tone—the earnest, bitter homeliness of accusation against wrong-doers in Church and State, the robust energy of hate, and the intrepidity of speech which Knox himself could not have surpassed. The pictures of the natural capabilities of Scotland, and of the monstrous disorders of the Commonwealth, are the most graphic things in the *Dreme*. But nothing appears to us so characteristic of the courage and sincerity of the author as his "Exhortatioun to the Kyngis Grace" with which he concludes. It is not poetry—but it is something better than poetry. It is the very heroism of patriotic morality. He speaks to his monarch as fearlessly as the old Hebrew prophets spoke to the kings of Judah and Israel; as Knox spoke to Mary, or Melville to her son. The way in which he entreats James to have compassion on the poor is very noble. Nor was his cry uttered in vain. We are fairly entitled to ascribe to Lyndsay, who had much to do with the moulding of his sovereign's character, if not with the direction of his formal studies, the development of those generous and humane instincts which won for him the title of the

"King of the Commons." Lyndsay specially denounces the lawlessness of the Borders—

> "In to the South, allace! I was neir slain;
>   Ouer all the land I culd fynd no releif:
>   Almoist betuix the Mers and Lowmabane
>   I culde nocht knau ane leill man be ane theif.
>   To schaw thair reif, thift, murthour, and mischief,
>   And vicious workis, it wald infect the air;
>   And als langsum to me, for tyll declair."

Now, the very next year James undertook his celebrated expedition to the south, in the course of which Scott of Tushielaw, Cockburn of Henderland, Johnnie Armstrong, and many other "minions of the moon," found to their surprise that Justice had still sufficient rope to hang them.

Quite a different note is struck in Lyndsay's next piece, *The Complaynt to the Kyng*, which was composed in the following year, 1530. It is a rhyming petition in that easy octo-syllabic measure which is so finely adapted to familiar and satirical narrative. It is chiefly interesting as a record of the author's personal fortunes, of the habits and characters of the Scottish courtiers. The *Dreme* is sad and dark with reminiscences of the Douglas tyranny, while the *Complaynt* is bright with auguries of future prosperity which unhappily proved false. The vigour and justice of the king's administration are warmly praised, and contrasted with the corrupt condition of things which preceded, when none could hope for preferment who was not "a Douglas or a Douglas's man." There is no doubt at all that a great change for the better had taken place. James made the moss-troopers feel his power. The burghers were encouraged to throw off their allegiance to the nobles, and transfer it to their monarch; the husbandmen began to pay rent for their farms, and to consider themselves at liberty *not* to "follow to the field some warlike lord"; the impulse which was given to trade and manufactures in the reign of James IV. was broadening and deepening; and an independent middle class was slowly rising on the ruins of that feudalism which Flodden had robbed of its vital force. Only one order in the community was not advancing—the priesthood; and to their still enormous influence must be attributed the disasters which hurried James into a premature grave. Thus glowingly does Lyndsay speak in 1530. James had not forgotten his old friend and gossip. He was always true to Lyndsay and allowed him to say things for which another man would have been burnt. Even to this day we marvel how he escaped when we remember that the king finally threw in his lot with the priests and drifted into a French policy at the very hour when a true insight into the tendencies of the age would have counselled an alliance with England. The only explanation possible is that James, knowing the affectionate loyalty of the poet towards himself, the purity of his motives, and the truth of his satire, had quietly resolved that none of "Baal's shaven sort" (as Knox mockingly terms the monks) should lay a finger on him, come what may! Never was a reformer so fortunate in his relations! And so, perhaps after all, the best thing that could have happened to Lyndsay was that long, irksome, undignified servitude at court, even though it consumed the prime of his early manhood, and withered the freshness of his fancy before he had published a line.

The first result of the *Complaynt* was the appointment of Lyndsay to the office of Lyon King of Arms, and his elevation to the dignity of knighthood. The honour had the effect he predicted. It "rubbed the ruste off his ingyne"; and before the year was out another work was written which must have made the ears of churchmen tingle and the faces of courtiers redden with shame. This was *The Testament and Complaynt of the Kingis Papyngo.*[1] Beginning with a generous panegyric on his great predecessors in poetry, Chaucer and Gower, "quhose sweit sentence throuch Albione bene sung," and his illustrious contemporaries Dunbar and Douglas, the latter of whom he pronounces "the rose of Inglis rethorick," he next modestly laments his own lack of matter and "ingyne," and apologizes for the insignificance of the subject he has chosen.

> "To rurall folke, myne dyting bene directit,
> Far blemit frome the sycht of men of gude ;
> For cunnying men, I knaw, wyll soune conclude,
> It dowe no thyng, but for to be dejectit ;
> And, quhen I heir myne mater bene detractit,
> Than sall I sweir, I maid it bot in mowis,[2]
> To landwart lassis, quhilks kepith kye and yowis."

The argument of the poem is briefly this: The king has a Papyngo "rycht plesand and perfyte," that could

> "Syng lyke the merle,[3] and crawe lyke to the cocke,
> Pew[4] lyke the gled,[5] and chant lyke the laverock,[6]
> Barke lyke ane dog, and kekell[7] like ane ka,[8]
> Blait lyke ane hog,[9] and buller lyke ane bull,
> Gaill[10] lyke ane goik,[11] and greit[12] quhen sho wes wa ;
> Clym on ane corde, syne lauch, and play the fule :
> Scho mycht have bene ane Menstrall agane Yule."

[1] Parrot.   [2] Jest.   [3] The black-bird.   [4] Cry.
[5] The kite.   [6] The lark.   [7] Cackle.   [8] A jack daw.
[9] A year-old sheep.   [10] Chant.   [11] Cuckoo.   [12] Weep.

This wonderfully clever bird is one morning dashed from a tree-top in the royal gardens by a sudden blast of wind and hurt beyond remeid.

> "Upon ane stob scho lychtit on hir breist,
> The blude ruschit out, and scho cryit for a priest."

Her last hours are spent in exhorting the king and courtiers, and in a long sarcastic controversy with her "Holye executouris," the pye, a "channoune regulare," the raven "a blak monk," and the gled "ane holy freir." Sheltering himself under this thin disguise of fable, Lyndsay hurled the javelins of his satire against the clergy with greater force and daring than ever. To the king his language is ever affectionate and free. He counsels him to be honest, diligent, temperate, and virtuous; to gather wise men about him, whether high born or not:

> "Cheis thy Counsale of the most sapient,
> Without regarde to blude, ryches, or rent."

to study the art of government for the sake of the "simple multitude," to treat every "true Barroun" as a brother, and above all to seek for help in his heavy work from "that Roye quhilk rent wes on the Rude." Unfortunately James was in the hands of the prelates, who were on the whole cleverer, better educated, more polished men than his nobles; and, as Knox puts it, "they would rather have gone to hell" than have seen him follow Henry in his anti-papal courses. Many of the nobles, some it may be from honest, others most certainly from dishonest and disloyal motives, were on the English side; and thus, personal intrigue as well as private predilection drove James astray, and left Scotland a generation behind in the march of religious progress. Perhaps, however, the Scottish Reformation was all the more thorough that our ancestors did not imitate the abrupt procedure of England, but waited till the nation was ripe for a change; basing their ecclesiastical action not on the passions of a king, but on the convictions of a people. England in its crisis produced neither a Lyndsay nor a Knox; neither a satirist to expose, nor a preacher to convince; and when the foundations of a new faith are to be raised on the ruins of an old, the services of both are indispensable. Practically Lyndsay helped the English cause, which was the cause of Protestantism; but he was too genuinely patriotic to become a partisan of Angus or Argyll. It was impossible for a Scottish gentleman of honourable spirit, in the reign of James, to countenance the overbearing policy of Henry, or associate himself with the treacherous plots of the exiles. Lyndsay hoped much from the good disposition of his sovereign, and to the moral pressure of his satire, we may trace in some measure that anxiety which James displayed for the reformation of ecclesiastical abuses which had risen in his time to a scandalous height.

The Second "Epystil of the Papyngo," addressed to the courtiers, is a grave and solemn admonition, reminding them by examples, chosen chiefly from the history of Scotland, how precarious is their tenure of prosperity. The arguments have no great originality. That indeed is not a conspicuous quality of our poet. His sincerity makes his thought simple; his earnestness makes his language plain; yet there is at all times in his serious flights a sermonic vigour that must have struck home to the popular heart. The conclusion of this part is one of the few fine pieces of descriptive poetry in Lyndsay.

> "Adew, Edinburgh! thou heych tryumphant toun,
>   Within quhose boundis rycht blythful have I bene,
> Of trew merchandis the rute of this regioun,
>   Moste reddy to resave Court, King, and Quene!
> Thy polecye and justice may be sene:
> War devotioun, wysedome, and honestie,
> And credence, tynt, thay mycht be found in thee.
>
> Adew, fair Snawdoun! with thy touris hie,
>   Thy chapell royall, park, and tabyll rounde!
> May, June, and July, walde I dwell in thee,
>   War I one man, to heir the birdis sounde,
>   Quhilk doith agane thy royall roche redounde.
> Adew, Lythquo! quhose Palyce of plesance
> Mycht be one patrone in Portingall or France!
>
> Fair weill, Falkland! the fortrace of Fyfe,
>   Thy polyte park, under the Lowmound Law!
> Sum tyme in thee I led ane lusty lyfe,
>   The fallow deir, to see them raik on raw.[1]
>   Court men to come to thee, they stand gret awe,
> Sayand, thy burgh bene, of all burrowis, baill,
> Because, in thee, thay nevir gat gude aill."

But it is when he comes to describe the sentiments and conduct of the "Holye Executouris" that Lyndsay's genius begins to scorch. The fearless way in which he mocks the pretensions to sanctity of the religious orders, proves that he did not purchase the favour of the king by the sale of his conscience. Whatever James might do, our poet was staunch to his convictions, and would on no account yield up the right he enjoyed as, an honest man to censure the morals of the Church. In the very dawn of his new prosperity, and thoroughly

---

[1] In a row.

aware of the perils of speech, he burst into a strain of satire, so broad and plain and rasping that he could never hope for absolution at the hands of a priest. His tone is that of a man who has wholly lost faith in the worth of the clergy. He leaves them not a solitary virtue. They are in his eyes conscious hypocrites, who use the privileges of their order to gratify the most earthly cravings. They would fain make the poor Papyngo believe that they are "holye creaturis," and can bring him "quyke to hevin." They are of course distressed to witness his dying agonies—

> "The Ravin come rolpand, quhen he hard the rair;
> So did the gled, with mony pietcous pew."

But the practical conclusion is a greedy advice to the Papyngo to make over to them his "gudis naturall." The rejoinder is a good specimen of Lyndsay's humour—

> "The Papyngo said, 'Father, be the Rude,
>   Howbeit your rayment be religious lyke,
> Your conscience, I suspect, be nocht gude;
>   I did persave, when prevelye ye did pyke
>   Ane chekin from ane hen, under ane dyke.'
> 'I grant,' said he, 'that here was my gude friend,
> And I that chekin tuke, bot for my teind.'"

The unabashed wretches continue their professional babble about the necessity of confession, and promise that—

> "bury we sall your bonis,
> Syne trentalls[1] twenty trattyll[2] all at onis,"

---

[1] Masses for the dead.   [2] Mumble.

besides "cryand for you the cairfull corrynogh,"

> " And we sall sing about your sepulture
> Sanct Mongois matynis, and the meklc creid ;
> And syne devotely saye, I you assure,
> The auld Placebo bakwart, and the beid ;
> And we sall weir for yow the murnying weid ;
> And, thocht your spreit with Pluto war profest,
> Devotelie sall your Diregie be addrest."

The impression left on us by this poem is that the Scottish priesthood as a whole had, in Lyndsay's time, become utterly corrupt; not only dead to the spiritual truth of Christianity, but unconscious that such a thing had ever existed. They had apparently ceased to think and feel about the services of religion, and therefore had lost the very capacity of believing in them; so that the whole affair seemed to them a farce which it was their business to keep going. Lyndsay resolved to stop the success of the farce, which was in his eyes a blasphemous burlesque of a solemn tragedy; and we ought to be grateful to the satirist who caused it to be hissed off the stage of Scottish history, and who prepared the way for the revival of the genuine drama of life under the auspices of John Knox.

Passing over some minor pieces belonging to this period, such as *The Answer to the Kyingis Flyting, The Complaynt of Bagsche, The Justing betuix James Watsoun and Jhone Barbour, Ane Supplicatioun in Contemptioun of Syde Taillis,* and *Kitteis Confessioun,* most of which are mere *jeux d'esprit,* we come upon Lyndsay's master-piece, *Ane Pleasant Satyre of the Thrie Estaitis in Commendatioun of Vertew and Vituperatioun of Vyce.* We do not precisely know when this extraordinary work was composed, nor is it quite certain where it was first performed. Chalmers asserts, without evidence, that the first representation took place at Cupar in 1535. Mr. Laing, on the other hand, with more probability, considering the magnitude of the play and the heavy official duties of the writer, conjectures that the first exhibition was the one at Linlithgow on the feast of Epiphany, 6th January, 1539-40, in presence of the king, queen, the ladies of the court, the bishops, and a great concourse of people of all ranks, "from nine in the morning till six at night." It is not a morality-play, pure and simple; that is to say, the actors are not exclusively personified abstractions. It is rather what is known in the history of our literature as an interlude—something intermediate both in character and time between the morality-play and the regular drama, and representing the transition from the one to the other. It combines in some measure the features of both. Real men and women move about amid allegorical figures. It is at once an echo of the Middle Ages and a prelusion to the "spacious times of great Elizabeth." Lyndsay, however, seems to have properly restricted the term "Interlude" to certain comic and coarse diversions, which were shifted about, altered, multiplied, or diminished, according to the exigencies of time or the inclinations of the audience, and which in no way affected the general movement of the play.

An outline of the play, which is rather a succession of independent scenes than a dramatic evolution of incident, may interest some. The prologue is spoken by "Diligence," who winds up with one of those sly humorous sarcasms for which Lyndsay is notable—

> "Thairfoir till all our rymis be rung,
> And our mistoinit sangis be sung,
> Let everie man keip weill ane toung,
>   And everie woman tway."

"Rex Humanitas" then comes forward, and prays to God for grace to rule himself and his people wisely, but his virtuous desires are rapidly blown to the winds by the allurements of "Wantonness," "Pleasure," and "Solace." These panders introduce the king to "Dame Sensualitie," the star of beauty, and "the fresche fonteine of knichtis amorous"; who describes her own charms with the freedom befitting her character, and assures the monarch that she is nowhere more highly thought of than at the "Court of Rome." When the fatal step is taken and "Rex Humanitas" begins his career of profligacy, "Gude-Counsall" steps on the stage and purposes remonstrance, but he is baffled for the moment by the three villains of the play, "Flatterie," "Falset," and "Dissait," who disguising themselves as "Devotion," "Sapience," and "Discretion," win the ear of the king, and get "Gude-Counsall" expelled from court, and put in prison. While the monarch is in the midst of his wanton revels "Veritie" steps in, and delivers a noble oration on the duties of temporal and spiritual rulers. This excites alarm in the breasts of the three "Vices," who hurry to accuse the new-comer before the spiritualitie of heresy—"in hir hand beirand the New Testament"—and get her put in the stocks. "Chastitie" next makes her appearance, but neither bishop, abbot, prioress, nor parson will acknowledge her, and she is fain to seek refuge among the common people, represented by a "Sowtar" and a "Taylour," whose hospitable intentions, however, are frustrated by the evil passions of their wives, and she finally experiences the same fate as "Veritie." The triumph of wickedness in court and realm now seems secure, when suddenly "Divyne Correction" enters, and a panic seizes the guilty crew, who scurry off in gross disorder, quarrelling as they flee. There is an austere dignity and republican sternness in the speech of " Correction."

> " Be me, traitours and tyrants ar put doun,
>   Quha thinks na schame of thair iniquitie.
>   . . . . . .
>   Quhat is ane king ? nocht but ane officiar
>   To caus his leigis live in equitie;
>   And, under God, to be ane punischer
>   Of tresspassouris against His Majestie."

As he presents anew to the Monarch, "Gude-Counsall," "Veritie," and "Chastitie," he boldly tells him:

> " Now, Schir, tak tent, quhat I will say
>   Observe thir same, baith nicht and day,
>   And let thame never part yow fray,
>   Or else, withoutin dout,
>   Turn ye to Sensualitie,
>   To vicious lyfe and rebaldrie,
>   Out of youre realme richt schamefullie
>   Ye sall be ruttit out."

A proclamation is then issued, summoning a parliament of the Three Estates for the redress of grievances. With this the first part of the satire ends.

The Second Part is more human and is intensely interesting. In it Lyndsay has put forth all his force as a practical reformer. Every mischief, every abuse, every enormity in the national life is pictured, discussed, and condemned. But even this is not enough. He demands reform, and describes the means by which it may be attained. The corruption of the king and the villany of his counsellors form the burden of the first part of the satire; the wrongs, miseries, and wants of the commonwealth, the burden of the second. First enters "Pauper" (The Poor Man), who unfolds to "Diligence" the cause of his wretchedness, and sets forth in touching terms the heartlessness of the clergy in robbing him of his goods in a crisis of domestic agony. Then we have by way of contrast, as if to heighten the pathos of his cry for justice, the brazen-faced proclamation of the "Pardoner" in which Lyndsay's satire of Rome attains its climax of humorous mockery. Take the following as a specimen:—

> "My patent pardouns, ye may se,
> Cum fra the Cane of Tartarie
>   Weill seald with oster-schellis.
> Thocht ye have na contritioun
> Ye sall have full remissioun
>   With help of buiks, and bellis.
> Heir is ane relict, lang and braid,
> Of Fine Macoull, the richt chaft blaid,
>   With teith and al togidder:
> Of Colling's cow, heir is ane horne,
> For eating of Makconnal's corne,
>   Was slane into Balquhidder.
> Here is ane coird, baith great and lang,
> Quhilk hangit Johne the Armistrang:
>   Of gude hemp, saft and sound:
> Gude, halie peopill I stand for'd
> Quha ever beis hangit with this cord,
>   Neidis never to be dround.
> The culum [1] of Sanct Bryd's kow,
> The gruntill [2] of Sanct Antonis sow,
>   Quhilk buir his haly bell;
> Quha ever he be heiris this bell clinck,
> Gif me ane ducat for till drink,
>   He sall never gang to hell,
> Without he be of Balliell borne:
> Maisters, trow ye that this be scorne!
>   Cum win this pardoun, cum.
> Quha luifis thair wyfis nocht with thair hart,

[1] Tail.   [2] Snout.

> I have power thame for till part,
>   Me think you deif and dum.
> Hes naine of yow curst wicked wyfis
> That halds yow intill start and stryfis,
>   Cum, tak my dispensatioun:
> Of that cummer, I sall mak you quhyte,
> Howbeit your selfis be in the wyte,
>   And mak ane fals narratioun.
> Cum, win the pardoun, now let se,
> For meill, for malt, or for monie,
>   For cok, hen, guse, or gryse.
> Of relicts, heir I haif ane hunder;
> Quhy cum ye nocht? This is ane wounder:
>   I trow ye be nocht wyse."

The altercation between the "Pardoner" and "Pauper," in which the former fleeches the latter out of his last "groat," and Pauper in return tumbles the holy relics into the water, is broadly farcical, and was doubtless received with roars of laughter.

By and by, the three Estates, Clergy, Nobles, and Burgesses, come in to assist the king in doing justice; the first of the three, however, urging delay, as if strongly convinced that their interests were most likely to suffer. "Johne, the Commonweill," hereupon shows face, and immediately begins a fierce assault upon the "kirkmen," the "barons," and the "courtiers," whose representatives, the three Vices, are led to the stocks. "Sensualitie" is next banished, to the great sorrow of the "Spiritualitie," who bid her a tender farewell—

> "Adew, my awin sweit hart!
> Now, duill fell me, that wee twa man depart;"

and declare they cannot live without her—for Lyndsay is implacable in his hate, and will not entertain the idea of their reformation. He allows the Temporal

Estates—" to wit, the lordis and merchandis "—to be pricked in their consciences as they listen to the passionate accusations of "Johne, the Commonweill," and to promise that they will—

> " The Commonweill tak he the hand,
> And mak with him perpetuall band."

But the clergy are obstinate to the last. They threaten, swear, foam, and rage; with a truly ecclesiastical obstinacy they will acknowledge no fault, abandon no privilege, promise no reform—

> " Na, na, never till the day of judgement,
> We will want nathing that wee have in use,
> Kirtil nor kow, teind lambe, teind gryse, nor guse."

Then follows an angry and furious discussion on their rights and duties, from which it would appear that in Scotland, as elsewhere, the majority, however worldly-wise or learned in the chicanery of ecclesiastical law, were grossly ignorant of Scripture, and incapable of preaching the Gospel to their flocks—" Dum doggis," as Knox, in imitation of Isaiah, calls them in his wrath.

The flagitious abuses of the consistorial or Church Courts are the subject of endless invective, grave and gay, lively and severe, though these must have been considerably abated by the institution some years before of the Court of Session. Still, the Church had long after this an extensive civil jurisdiction, and it appears to have acted in Lyndsay's time with that singular disregard of justice and humanity which has characterized its judicial procedure in all ages and in all countries of Christendom. There is a merry humour

in this bit of hard hitting, which neither the homely
jingle of the verse nor the rudeness of the dialect can
quite destroy—

> "Marie! I lent my gossop my mear, to fetch hame coills,
> And he hir drounit into the Querrell hollis;
> And I ran to the Consistorie, for to pleinze,
> And thair I happinit amang ane greidie meinze.
> Thay gave me first ane thing, thay call *Citendum;*
> Within aucht dayis, I gat bot *Lybellandum,*
> Within ane moneth, I gat *ad Opponendum,*
> In half ane yeir, I gat *Inter loquendum,*
> And syne I gat, how call ye it? *ad Replicandum:*
> Bot I could never ane word yit understand him.
> And than thay gart me cast out many plackis,
> And gart me pay for four-and-twentie actis:
> Bot or they came half gate to *Concludendum,*
> The feind a placke was left far to defend him:
> Thus, thay postponit me twa yeir with their traine,
> Syne, *Hodie ad octo,* bad me cum againe:
> And than, thir ruiks, thay roupit wonder fast,
> For sentence silver thay cryit at the last.
> Of *Pronunciandum,* they maid me wonder faine;
> But I got nevir my gude gray meir againe."

The complaint of "Chastitie" against the prelates
strikes at one of their vices which had made them
specially odious to the Scottish gentry. Nowhere out
of Italy were the decencies of life so openly outraged, or
the violations of religious vows so gross and shameful
as in Scotland. The traditions of the Borgias, with
whom the century had opened, were there preserved
with shocking fidelity. Not a family was safe—not a
matron or a maid. And so shameless had these transgressors become, that they openly paraded the evidence
of their guilt. Their progeny were so liberally dowered
from the revenues of the Church, that Lyndsay makes

the "Temporalitie" declare it cannot get its own daughters married.

> "For quhy ? the markit raisit bene sa hie,
>   That prelats dochtours of this natioun
> Ar maryit with sic superfluetie :
> Thay will nocht spair to gif twa thowsand pound,
>   With thair dochtours to ane nobill man ;
> In riches sa thay do superabound."

The king next receives "three famous clarks of greit intelligence"—

> "For to the common peopill thay can preich,
> And in the scuilis, in Latine toung, can teich,"

by whose help a further and more searching exposure of the "Spiritualitie" is made. They are forced to describe in detail their manner of life, and thus to pronounce their own condemnation. "Correctioun," who is all through a sort of Master of Ceremony, now asks one of the "famous clarks" to preach a sermon that would really tend to the edification of the laity. The result is a genuine New Testament discourse, "such as Paul, were he on earth, would hear, approve, and own," but the bewilderment and anger of the clergy is something wonderful. They indulge in some captious criticism, but are on the whole stupified and beaten. As a specimen of the picturesque homeliness of Lyndsay's argument, we might quote the clark's reply to the question if the Saviour was really not as rich as a bishop—if he was really a poor man—

> "Yea brother, be Alhallows :
> Christ Jesus had na propertie bot the gallows :
> And left not, quhen he yielded up the spreit,
> To buy himself ane simpill winding scheit."

Finally the "vices" are stripped of their disguise, and the prelates of their dignities; "Johne the Commonweill," who has been long ill-used, is gorgeously apparelled and takes his seat in Parliament; a proclamation of all the new reforms, with a full account of each, is made by sound of trumpet; even " Pauper " is satisfied, and only begs that " Flatterie," " Dissait," " Falset," " Theft," shall be rigorously punished.

It is impossible to form a just idea of the extraordinary merits of the piece from this meagre outline of its contents. Lyndsay's *Satyre* is instinct with life. There is not a dead twig on the whole tree. Under the inspiration of his vital genius, every line quivers like a leaf. His allegorical abstractions are human and speak like men. It is history, not mere poetry, that confronts us in every page. All the phases of Scottish feeling and thought in that perplexed, restless, half-slumbering age which preceded the coming of Knox, are mirrored there with fidelity and homely art. There is not a nation in Christendom which is better off than Scotland in this respect—not one that is in a position to form a clearer notion of the stupidities, superstitions, and impurities from which the Reformation delivered us. Lyndsay's testimony is far above suspicion. If we have set forth his character rightly, he was a man whose opinion was worth more than that of any of his contemporaries—not only because of his moral earnestness, but because of his keen penetration, and deep sagacity. He had nothing to win; he had everything to risk by speaking the truth. He was not a crack-brained enthusiast who courted persecution. On the contrary, he was a careful country squire who wished to add to his estates, and who lost no chance of honestly getting on in the world.

And yet, knowing that some had gone to the stake for a tithe of his plain-speaking—that the clergy, weak in Scripture, but strong in craft, clever, unscrupulous, implacable, would be furious at his conduct, he wrote what he thought, and took his chance of their malice. Nothing is concealed, nothing extenuated: he believes them incorrigible and he paints them so. That his language is occasionally obscene is not to be denied, nor is it always possible to advance the apology that he was filthy in order to be natural. There is a way of caricaturing vice which is as bad as vice itself, and Lyndsay sometimes practises it. Let him bear his measure of blame! It was a coarse age; Scotch humour was peculiarly coarse; and if the ladies of the Court did not blush at what they heard, we can only wonder and be silent.

But coarseness like that at which we have glanced occurs only once or twice in the *Satyre*. A far more essential feature of the work, throwing a strong light on the individual character of the author, is its earnest humanity. Everywhere indeed Lyndsay shows a tender and generous love of poor men, but here he pleads their cause with persistency and warmth. He had witnessed the reckless cruelties of feudal strife, and the bitter wretchedness of down-trodden labour powerless to redress its wrongs: his heart bled at what he saw, and his spirit sprang up to challenge oppression and to champion the weak. He is neither for king, nor baron, nor priest, but for the Commonwealth, and foreshadows in his feelings that genuine Republicanism which Knox and Buchanan were not afraid to advocate, or Cromwell to enact—in spite of "the right divine of kings to govern wrong"! The peasantry

of Scotland long remembered it. It was one of the
causes of Lyndsay's immense popularity in the sixteenth and seventeenth centuries, and it is a reason
why later ages, in which the sentiment of humanity
has acquired greater force, should reverently brush
the dust from his memory.

Meanwhile Lyndsay had not been idle in his official
capacity as Lyon-herald. Twice he visited the Continent; first in 1531, to assist in renewing the treaty
of commerce between Scotland and the Netherlands,
originally concluded by James I. in 1430 for the period
of a century, which had now expired; and again in
1536 to obtain a wife for his sovereign from the prin-
cesses of France. James, who had gone thither himself in the spirit of knightly gallantry, brought home
with him a dying bride. Magdalene of France only
survived her arrival on the chilly shores of Scotland
some forty days, and the poet who would fain have
imitated the joyful strain of Dunbar, on this union of
the *Thistle and the Fleur-de-Lys*, was forced to sing a
funeral dirge. Great preparation had been made to
receive the bride, but, says Pitscottie, "all the great
blytheness was turned into great mourning; and all
the play that should have been, to soul-masses and
dirgies." Lyndsay, however, in his *Deploratioun*, dex-
terously avails himself of the circumstances to describe
what the poor queen-girl would have seen, had death
spared her, and, by the unexpected novelty of the contrast, deepens the shadows of the calamity. The last
two lines are vividly beautiful. Reproaching death
for having slain the "heavenly Flour of France," he
proudly tells the conqueror

" The smell of it sall, in despyte of thee,
    Keip ay twa Realmes in peace and amitie."

Next year the king contracted a second marriage with Mary, daughter of the Duke of Guise, and Lyndsay was officially employed to devise the festive spectacles, the pomps and plays and orations, that welcomed her advent. His personal sympathies could hardly have been in accord with the rejoicings he was called to arrange. She belonged to a house that was intensely Catholic; she was a zealous upholder of the system which Lyndsay so mercilessly satirized. About the time of her marriage Cardinal David Beaton became Archbishop of St. Andrews, and proved a worthy coadjutor of the severely orthodox princess. But Lyndsay was not silenced. The spirit of Knox was in him, and the *Satyre of the Thrie Estaitis* was his answer to the queen's policy. It was before her, as we have seen, that the play was first acted, and she could not possibly affect to misunderstand its meaning; but Lyndsay was safe, for though James had neither the wisdom nor the inclination to ally himself with the Reformers, he was still true to the old memories of his boyhood. Late in the autumn of 1542, when the artifices of the clergy had triumphed, and he had broken with Henry—when he was in the height of his preparations for that priest-begotten war that ended in the shameful disaster of the Solway Moss, he had still leisure to think of his earliest playmate, the companion of his nursery frolics. His gift to Lyndsay: "During all the days of his life, two chalders of oats, for horse corn, out of the King's lands of Dynmure in Fife," is a sort of final bequest or dying legacy. Before the new year came in, the kindly "King of the Commons" had passed away, and Lyndsay, with a grief too deep for verse, directed the ceremonies of his sepulture.

Once more the calamity that had befallen Scotland so frequently since the days of Alexander III., a child-sovereign and a feeble regency, was experienced. Into the troublous politics of the period we need not enter. Lyndsay must have been profoundly chagrined at the course of events, for, owing to the insolent and overbearing policy of Henry, a fatal reaction in public sentiment took place. The old suspicion and hatred of England revived, and to preserve the national independence which seemed to be threatened, Scotland threw herself into the arms of France. The barbarities of Hertford's invasion, when the great abbeys of the Borders were pillaged and burned, deepened the animosity, and crowned with temporary triumph the policy of Beaton and the queen-mother. The Reformation appeared to be thrown back indefinitely, and a golden age of priestly influence to be ushered in. But there was a new life throbbing unseen beneath the surface of society. Although the Scots detested the English alliance, they did not love the clergy a whit the better. Already in various parts of the country there had been popular demonstrations against the monasteries; and in the very noontide of Beaton's success, George Wishart, the gentle, impassioned, mystic enthusiast, began to evangelize the Lothians, John Knox marching before him from place to place bearing, as he tells us himself, a two-handed sword. It is the first historical glimpse we get of the great Reformer. In this heroic attitude he emerges from obscurity—the grand old soldier-priest; fearless, inflexible, scornful of the might that is not based on truth! The man had come, if not yet the hour. Everyone knows the fate of Wishart, and the bloody revenge that was taken for it! Lyndsay did his best to whitewash the assassins, for such justice compels us to designate them, by blackening the memory of the victim, in his *Tragedie of the Cardinall*, in which the ghost of the murdered man appears to the poet in his oratory and recites the story of his life, as a warning to all evil-doers. The author's English sympathies are very marked in the piece—

> "Had we with Ingland keipit our contrackis,
>   Our nobyll men had levit in peace and rest ;
>   Our marchandis had nocht lost so mony packis,
>   Our common peple had nocht bene opprest :
>   On ather syde all wrangis had been redrest ;
>   But Edinburgh sen syne, Leith and Kynghorne,
>   The day and hour may ban, that I was borne."

When the conspirators seized and fortified the Castle of St. Andrews, they were joined by many of the gentlemen of Fife, but Lyndsay was not, as is commonly affirmed, of the number. He was in Parliament at the time, where he sat as commissioner for the burgh of Cupar; but his sympathies were undoubtedly on their side, and we have the testimony of Knox himself that Lyndsay was one of those who, during the siege, were deputed to ask him to preach to the garrison. It was the first interview between the poet who prepared and the preacher who gave birth to the Reformation. The work of the forerunner was almost done, and the founder of the new faith had entered on his career. The time for satire was over ; the time for the Gospel had come. Erasmus may lay aside his pen when Luther has lifted his voice.

Lyndsay was not fated to see the final triumph of his cause, but neither did he suffer the hardships that intervened. There is something miraculous about his good fortune. No doubt he was entirely guiltless of Beaton's blood; but he had done more than any living Scot to make the priests ridiculous and abhorred; and his antipathy to the Franco-Papal policy of the Church was well known. Like Knox, he exulted in the cardinal's destruction, which he compares to the overthrow of Lucifer and Goliath. The king's death had deprived him of his only powerful friend, and yet no one ventured to touch a hair of his head, or even to strip him of the dignity of office. We imagine the true explanation to be that he was a very loyal, if also a very outspoken Scot. He inspired no party with apprehensions of treachery. Even the priests knew that in spite of his avowed predilections he would never sell himself to England, and that his attachment to the new faith was compatible with a generous admiration of France. Whatever the motive, the fact is undoubted, for in 1548, only two years after the assassination of the cardinal, he was sent to Denmark to negotiate a free trade in corn for the Scottish merchants, and to solicit ships for the protection of the Scottish sea-board against English privateers.

Soon after his return home, Lyndsay amused himself by composing a poem on the exploits of Squire Meldrum, a Fifeshire gentleman of his acquaintance, and whose adventures in Ireland, France, and finally at home, both in war and love, were of a very romantic character. It is singularly unlike all his other writings, and is not to be considered a serious performance, but rather as a *jeu d'esprit*, in which Lyndsay seeks relaxation after the grave and earnest labours of his Muse. The ardour of the Reformer and the gravity of the moralist are forgotten for once. No priest is cursed nor vice denounced; we hear nothing of the miseries of the commonwealth, or the errors of kings. The venerable satirist throws aside his scourge and briskly steps forward as a minstrel of chivalry. There is a fine vivacity in the narrative; the pleasant octo-syllabic lines murmur on with easy music. The play of fancy throughout has a mild radiance, as of autumnal afternoons. In all Froissart there is nothing more delightful in picturesque details than the description of the jousts between Meldrum and the English knight, Talbart, on the plains of Picardy.

The last and longest of Lyndsay's works is *The Monarchie: ane Dialog betuix Experience and ane Courteour on the Miserabyll Estait of the World*. It was finished in 1553, but its composition may have extended over many years. It embraces a moral survey of all history, from the creation of Adam to the final Judgment, and closes with a description of the pleasures of glorified saints. As a work of genius or art it is not to be compared with the *Satyre of the Thrie Estaitis*, although particular passages possess great merit; for example, the account "Of Imageis usit amang Christin Men" and the "Exclamatioun aganis Idolatrye." In the pictures of priestly pride and greed, and especially of the Court of Rome, the homely but active fancy of the author arranges and combines with wonderful effect the materials furnished by a wide, keen, and long-continued observation of society, both secular and ecclesiastical. It is a characteristic of Lyndsay, as of Swift, Defoe, and some other writers, that he does not produce a striking result by brilliant flashes of fancy, but by a series of minute, cunning touches. His strength lies for the most part in details; his imagination can work only in prosaic channels; his satiric humour is raciest in petty familiarities. It is only where hatred of priestly hypocrisy impassions his speech that he rises into eloquence; and even then the elevation of his style comes from the Mount of Sinai and not from the heights of Parnassus.

The *Monarchie* is pervaded by a spirit of gloom and sadness, but not of despair. It is the terrible certainty of the Divine Judgments that darkens his vision; not the melancholy conviction that these are the dreams of deluded saints. The clouds that gather on his soul are such as shadowed the imagery of Hebrew bards in evil days. Scotland had been in a miserable state ever since the death of James. A dreary, ruinous, intermittent war of nine years, marked by the desolation of the Borders and the carnage of Pinkie, had been waged, during which Scotland, to secure its political, had seemingly been forced to part with its hopes of spiritual, independence; for the banishment of Knox and the preachers was but an incident of the tangled strife. Though that war was now over, its effects continued to be felt, and Lyndsay saw, in the waning influence of Arran and the increasing power of the Guises, new perils in store for the followers of the Gospel. In the absence of Knox, who dared not return, but who hovered about the Border, preaching zealously to the Northumbrians, probably in the hope that the echoes of his words would be heard across the Tweed, the grey-haired satirist, with failing strength, but not with failing heart, once more set himself to his life-task. It was his last stroke, his final admonition. If there be less sarcasm and more gravity than in his earlier poems, the circumstances of the times, the nature of his subject, and the solemnity of his position at the entrance of the Valley of the Shadow of Death, befit the tone. It is the voice of one who is parting with the world before the struggle is over and the battle won; who cannot see the issues of the future, but who knows that the triumph of the Antichrist will be followed by the terrors of the Lord, and that nations can only hope to flourish by the preaching of the Word. Lyndsay died in 1555,[1] four years before Knox came back to Scotland, and two before the first meeting of the Lords of Congregation. Had he lived to see the triumph of his satire and his scorn, in 1560, when the nation solemnly renounced the idolatries of a thousand years, and the Middle Ages came to an end in Scotland, the undertone of sadness that runs through the *Monarchie* might have been exchanged for the raptures of exultation and the eloquence of devout gratitude. After the completion of the poem he withdrew from public life.

His warfare was over, his work accomplished. Not in vain had he laboured. To him more than to any contemporary we owe that stir of religious thought, that leaven of religious excitement which the eloquence and energy of Knox diffused and impelled to a triumphant issue. He taught his countrymen to regard the Church with courage and honesty and candour, not, as they were wont, with blind servility and ignorant devotion. Institutions and persons were venerable in his eyes only in proportion to their utility and worth. No power on earth could induce this clear-sighted, true-hearted man to worship the false or believe the in-

---

[1] Mr. Laing has the merit of ascertaining the date of Lyndsay's death, ignorance of which led Chalmers into suppositions which are now somewhat ludicrous.

credible. Others might wink at the iniquities of kings and barons and priests, but here was a moralist the strength of whose convictions raised him beyond the vacillations of timidity and doubt: who knew that God took cognizance of all forms of wickedness, who felt that the vials of His wrath were reserved for spiritual wickedness in high places. And as he thought of the vain pretences under which popes veiled their ambition, the insolence with which the clergy maintained their immunity from censure, the prostitution of auricular confession, the drivel of saintly invocations, the rascality of indulgences, the ignorance and debauchery of the strolling friars, a fire of sacred scorn was kindled in his heart. To the solidity of his convictions was added the vehemence of hate, to the vigour of his argument, the blister of sarcasm and the mockeries of ridicule, till men learned to wonder at their folly, and, like Clovis the Frank, were at length prepared to burn what they had reverenced and to reverence what they had burned.

Scotland, it has been said, long remembered him. During the sixteenth, seventeenth, and eighteenth centuries upwards of twenty editions of his works were published. His verses were on almost every tongue. Until Burns appeared he was in fact *the* poet of the Scottish people, and was appealed to as an infallible authority on the Scottish language; "Ye'll no fin' that in Davie Lyndsay" was a fatal objection to any new-coined phrase which a speaker ventured to employ. Nothing can surpass his mastery of the vernacular when the subject is homely and the treatment satiric. Rich in picturesque idioms, happy in colloquial ease, his descriptions remind us in their pith and humour and fancy of the Epistles of the

Ayrshire Bard. If they lack the higher qualities of pathos, imagination, and tenderness, it should not be forgotten that he deliberately circumscribed the sphere of his poetic activity to serve the cause of God. Every Scot who has since lived has derived an unspeakable advantage from Lyndsay's noble sacrifice of literary ambition to religious duty.

INDEX.

Aberbrothock, 113; Douglas, nominated Abbot of, 298.
Acts of the Scottish Parliament, 178.
Adamnan, 18, 103; life of Columba, 26.
Address of the Soul to the Body, 45.
Aelfric's Homilies, 43.
Agriculture in fifteenth century, 100, 121; under James II., 177.
Aidan, coronation of, 30; sent from Iona, 32.
Ailred's life of Ninian, 16.
Alban, vicissitudes of, 4; a kingdom, 24.
Albany, Regent, 99, 110; treachery of, 117; character, 132; death of, 133.
Albany, Murdach, 133; story of, in Boece, 134; execution of, 138.
Albany invited to be regent in minority of James V., 300; accusations against Douglas, 304; makes peace with Angus, 313.
Alcluith, 23.
Alcuin, 103.
Alexander II., his fear of church censures, 233.
Alexander III., Pope, 10.
Alfred's translations from Orosius, Boethius, and Gregory, 43.
Alnwick, capture of William the Lyon at, 38.
Ambrose, 103.
Amiens, Wallace a prisoner at, 66.
Amra, or *Praise of Columcille*, 30.
Anglic, the most important element in Scottish nationality, 2; influence of clergy and nobility on dialects, 11.
Anglo-Saxon Chronicle, 43.
Angus, Archibald, marriage with Queen Margaret, 297, 381; power of, 298; opposition to Albany, 310.
Annales Cambriæ, 18.
Annandale, raid in, 65; Douglas captured by James in, 117.
Architecture unknown before Malcolm, 39.
Ardderyd, battle of, 21.
Arthur the "guledig," 18; his victories over the Angles, 20.
Arundel MS., 69.
Asser's Life of Alfred, 43.
Athole, Earl of, 94, 143.
Auchincruff, 79.

Augustine, 32, 103.
Ayr, 2; Wallace in, 80, 82.
Ayrshire an Anglic possession, 23. 93; abandons the country, 94.
Baliol, Edward, 48; crowned at Scone, Baliol, John, dethroned, 62.
Ballads, mentioned in *Complaynt of Scotland*, 261.
Bannatyne's MS., 129, 158.
Bannockburn, battle of, 12, 49, 53, 107.
Barbour, John, Archdeacon of Aberdeen, 49, 102, 105, 109; *Brus*, 48, 70, 74, 260.
Barton, naval commander, 176.
Beaton, Archbishop, transferred to St. Andrews, 235; seized by Angus, 300; quarrel with Angus, 306; opposition to Douglas, 315; allied with Mary of Guise, 406.
Beaufort, Lady Jane, 136.
Bede, 16, 28, 32; Life of Cuthberht, 33; *Historia Ecclesiastica*, 42; quoted by Fordun, 103.
Bellenden, John, translation of Boece, 224, 240; life, 239; Canon of Ross, 246; translation of Livy, 240; his 'procms,' 246.
Benedict Biscop enriches Northumbrian libraries, 43.
Beowulf, 44.
Bergenroth's *Calendar of Spanish State Papers*, 172.
Berwick, the "Alexandria of the North," 39.
Blackfriars' Church, Edinburgh, 307.
Blair, Wallace's chaplain, 60.
Blind Harry's *Life of Sir William Wallace*, 49, 72, 76, 78, 83, 129, 260; Major's criticism of, 231.
Bludy Serk, The. (See Henryson.)
Boece, Hector, life, 222; friend of Erasmus, 223; pensioned, 226; *Life of Elphinstone*, 124; *Lives of the Bishops of Aberdeen*, 223; *Scotorum Historia*, 224.
Bolingbroke, 99.
Bower (continuator of Fordun), author of *Scotichronicon*, 103, 105, 132; character of James I., 145, 147.
Boyd, Sir Thomas, 112.
Boyd, Robt., Captain of Dumbarton, 113.

Brechin, 113.
Bruce, Robert, 50; denounced by Mr. Freeman, 51, 52; covenant with Comyn, 54; with the English, 62; unsuccessful revolt of, 63.
Bruce, David, 97.
Brude baptised by Columba, 30.
Brus, The. (See Barbour.)
Buchanan, George, pupil of Major, 235.
Buke of the Howlat, by Holland, 126.
Burgess, Scottish, description of, 120.
Burns, Robert, letter to Moore, 76; poems, 89, 159; compared with Dunbar, 212.

Caedmon, reputed author of *Paraphrase*, 44.
Caerlaverock, 67.
Caledonia, Picts of, 1; Celtic, 3.
Calendarium Genealogicum, 69.
Carham, victory of, 6.
Carrick, Earl of, 62.
Carrick's *Life of Wallace*, 77.
Cathedrals founded in all parts of the kingdom, 10.
Cebes compared with Douglas, 333.
Celtic habits of Britons of Cumbria, 2; Celtic ruler of Lothian, 6; Scotland Celtic, 7; Celtic church nearly disappeared, 10; disappearance of Celtic dialect, 13; purely Celtic rule in Scotland ceased, 36.
Chaucer, 123, 260; influence of, 129, 149, 354; Troilus and Creseide, 165; compared with Dunbar, 188, 198, 216; with Douglas, 334,
Christis Kirk of the Greene. (See James I.)
Clement III., Bull in favour of Church of Scotland, 10.
Clifford, Sir Robert, 65.
Cockelbie's Sow, 126.
Colquhouns of Luss, 112.
Columba, contemporary with Kentigern, 18; visits Kentigern, 22; native of Donegal, 24; migrates to Hebrides in 563, 24; reasons why he came, 26; his Life, by Adamnan, 27; his work, 29; death, 32; disappearance of Columban monasteries, 10.
Complaynt of Scotland, authorship of, 247; analysis of, 250.
Complaynt of the Papyngo. (See Lyndsay.)
Comyn, 54, 68.
Confessio Amantis. (See James I.)
Contemporary Account of the Murder of James I., 142.
Cospatrick, 139.
Cottonian MS., 61, 66.
Crawfurd, Sir Ranald, Sheriff of Ayr, 79, 80, 82.
Crawford, Earl of, 111, 113.

Creighton, Castle of, 112.
Cressingham, 63, 90 (note).
Cronykil of Scotland. (See Wyntoun.)
Culbleen, 94.
Culdees, 3, 7, 8, 10, 39, 41.
Culross, Inglis, Abbot of, 246.
Cumberland, invasion of, by Wallace, 64.
Cumbria, Britons of, Teutonized, 2; gifted to Malcolm, by Edward of England, 5.
Cuthberht, prior of Melrose, 33; visits to the poor, 34; his vision, 34.
Cymry of the Clyde, 5, 15, 40.
Cynewulf's *Elene*, 45; *Christ*, 45.

Dacre, Lord, and Queen Margaret, 303, 311, 313, 315, 317.
Dallan Forgaill's *Amra*, 31.
Dalriada, 5, 17, 26, 30, 32.
Damian, John, his attempt at flying, 198.
Dance of the Sevin Deidly Synnis. (See Dunbar.)
Darnley, Earl of, 112.
David I., 7; charter of, 9; his beneficence to Glasgow, 23; at Battle of the Standard, 38; Church of, 102.
David II., 94.
David, St., restores orthodoxy of Wales, 18.
De Brune, 61, 65.
De Cressingham, Hugh, 62.
De Grey, Sir Thomas, 83.
De Haliburton, Ralph, 67.
De la Bastic, slain, 308.
De Muskelburgh, John, 69.
Don Pedro de Ayala on character of James IV., 172; on the state of Scotland, 177.
Dornoch, Abbey of, 10.
Douglas, Gavin, 109, 222; Life, 293; nominated Abbot of Aberbrothock, 298; Bishop of Dunkeld, 302, 305; treachery to the Government, 304; imprisoned, 304; deprived of bishopric, 315; death, 317; *Palice of Honour*, 170, 260, 295, 318; analysis of, 319; translation of Virgil's *Aeneid*, 295, 332, 352; analysis of, 353; influence of the translation on English literature, 354; *King Hart*, 318; analysis of, 334; probably translated Ovid's *Remedia Amoris*, 332; Douglas compared with Dunbar, 295, 318, 352; with Henryson, 333, 352; with Cebes, 333; with Petrarch, 333; with Chaucer, 334; with James I., 352; with Surrey, 354, 364, 365.
Douglas, Sir James, 57.
Douglas, Earls of, with Bruce, 63; power of, 111; intolerance of, 114; banished, 115; invasion of, 117.
Douglas, Sir William, 70, 84, 94.

INDEX. 417

Duan Albanach (chronicle), 42.
Dunbar, William, life, 169; *Lament for the Makaris*, 107, 127, 210; *Freiris of Berwick*, 179; *Twa Maryit Wemen and the Wedo*, 179, 189, 202; *Remonstrance to the King*, 179; minor pieces, 188, 206, 210; *Dance of the Sevin Deidly Synnis*, 189, 200; *The Thrissil and the Rois*, 189; *The Goldyn Targe*, 189, 260; *Fenyeit Freir of Tungland*, 198; *Justis betuix the Tailyeour and the Sowtar*, 199; *The Devil's Inquest*, 204; Pieces on *Discretion*, 207; on *Covetyce*, 208; compared with Henryson, 215; with James I., 215; with Gavin Douglas, 295, 318, 333, 352.
Dunbar, Simon Fraser at, 67; Douglas imprisoned in, 304.
Duncan, fall of, at Lumphanan, 36.
Dundee, Boece native of, 222.
Dunfermline, Henryson at, 160.
Dunkeld, Douglas, Bishop of, 302, 305.
Dunnottar, 94.
Duplin on the Earn, 93.

Eadmer, Bishop of St. Andrews, 9.
Easter and Tonsure Controversies, 32.
Edinburgh, 83; Parliament at, 93, 303; Douglas imprisoned in, 304.
Education, national, 182.
Edward I. acknowledged by barons, 12; his Scottish policy, 46; Claim of Right, 47; account of, by Barbour, 55; invades Scotland, 62; Wyntoun's account of, 105.
Edward III. at York, 92.
Edward IV., 117.
Eglintoun, Schir Hew of, 109.
Ellerslie, Wallace's connection with, 72, 79.
Elphinstone, Bishop of Aberdeen, 123, 299; Life of, by Boece, 124; offered Principalship of Aberdeen, 223; Archbishop of St. Andrews, 302; Death, 302.
Erasmus, contemporary with Dunbar, 171; friend of Boece, 222.
Extracta e Cronicis Scotiae, 137 (note).

Fabyan, 106.
Falkirk, battle of, 65, 69.
Falkland, 94; James' escape from, 382.
Ferdinand and Isabella, 376.
Fergus, fictions of, 230.
Fergus Mor, 26.
Ferrerius, Joannes, editor of Boece, 224.
Feudal institutions modified by "ancient custom," 39.
Finnian of Clonard, founder of greatest monastic school in Ireland, 26.
Flodden, effect of battle on Douglas, 296; on Scotland, 376.

Florence of Worcester, 45, 65.
Flowers o' the Forest, 373.
Fordun's *Chronicle*, 9, 39, 76, 102, 105, 110, 225.
Forman, Archbishop of St. Andrews, 306; death of, 315.
Forrester, Sir John, of Corstorphine, 112.
Freeman on Bruce, quoted, 50, 52.
Fraser, Simon, 67.
French used in time of Alexander III., 40.
Froissart's *Chronicle*, 98, 101.

Gaelic abandoned in Lowlands, 11.
Gaelic language, 40.
Gaels, Picts and Scots become, 1; valour of, 14.
Gareloch, Albany at, 310.
Garmylton, birthplace of Lyndsay, 375.
Gawen and Gologras, 107.
Geoffrey de Vinsauf, 46.
Geoffrey of Monmouth, 46, 103.
Gerald de Barri, 45.
Gesta Romanorum, 162.
Gibson, Murdoch, 112.
Gildas, 103.
Glasgow, 19, 21, 23; Bishop of, 63; Wallace in, 69; University of, 123, 125; Major, Professor of Theology in, 228.
Goloran of Galloway, 107.
Gower, 149; influence of, 354.
Graham, Sir Robert, 142; character of, 143; murder of James I., 144.
Gregory, translation from, 43.

Hailes, Lord, 227.
Halidon Hill, victory of, 93.
Hamilton, Patrick, martyrdom of, 385.
Harlaw, 132.
Hay, Sir Gilbert, 127.
Hebrides subdued by Scandinavia, 5; Columba in, 25; held under the crown, 177.
Hemingford, 61, 63, 65, 68, 77, 90 (note).
Henry IV., 99.
Henry V., 99.
Henry VII., 375.
Henry VIII. supports Queen Margaret, 300.
Henry of Huntingdon, 45, 103.
Henryson, 127, 129; birth, 159; *The Abbay Walk*, 161; *The Praise of Aige*, 161; *The Ressouning betwixt Deth and Man*, 161; *The Bludy Serk*, 162; *The Salutation of the Virgin*, 162; *Robene and Makyne*, 163; *Taill of the Uplandis Mous and the Burges Mous*, 164; *Testament of Cresseid*, 165; compared with Dunbar, 215; with Douglas, 333, 352.
Hesilrig, slaughter of, 63, 69, 83.
Hexham, monks of, 64.
Higden, 103.

2 D

INDEX.

Highlander distinct from Lowlander, 1.
Highlands, condition of, under James I., 138; under James IV., 177, 376.
Highland Host, persecution of the Covenanters, 13.
High Steward of Scotland, 62, 63, 97.
Historia Ecclesiastica of Bede, 42.
Holdelm (Hoddam), 21.
Holland's *Buke of the Howlat*, 126.
Holyrood, 139.
Homildon Hill, battle of, 99, 110, 140.
Huchowne, 107, 126.
Humes of Wedderburn, The, 308.
Huntly, Earls of, 113.

Incheolm, Bower, Abbot of, 103.
Inglis, James, Abbot of Culross, 246.
Inglis, Schir James, reputed author of *The Complaynt of Scotland*, 247.
Innes, Mr. Cosmo, 57, 73, 124, 182.
Inverness, Edward III. at, 94; James I. at, 139.
Iona, 24, 25, 29, 31, 32, 34.
Ireland, Scots of, 1; Kentigern's disciples in, 22; civil strife in, 25; poets of, 30.
Irvine, 63.
Isles, Islesmen of, 112; earldom of Ross wrested from them by James III., 116; Donald, Lord of the Isles, 132; lords of, under James I., 139; lordship of, broken up, 177, 376.

James I., capture of, on voyage to France, 99, 132; released, 134; marriage of, 136; murder of, 144; as a writer, 129; character of, 145, 147; *Kingis Quhair*, 136, 148, 193; analysis of, 150; *Confessio Amantis*, 149; *Christis Kirk of the Grene*, 157; *Peblis to the Play*, 157; compared with Dunbar, 215; with Douglas, 352.
James II., 111, 114.
James III., 111, 115; marriage of, 116; conspiracy of his nobles, 118; murder of, 119; a merchant, 121.
James IV., 171, 297, 335; marriage with Princess Margaret, 177, 377; character of, 181.
James V., king at age of twelve, 381; marriage with Magdalene, 405; with Mary of Guise, 406; his death, 406.
Joan of Arc, 376.
Jocelin, his account of Kentigern, 18.
Joseph of Exeter, 46.
Judith, 45.

Kennedy, Bishop of St. Andrews, 114; death of, 115.
Kentigern, 17; noticed in 'Annales Cambriae,' 18; origin of his name Munghu, 19; settlement in Glasgow, 19; banishment to Wales, 20; recall and meeting with Rhydderch, 21; wider missionary expeditions, 22.
Kinclaven, 94.
King Hart (see Douglas).
Kingis Quhair (see James I.).
Kintyre, 26.
Knox, John, 34; *Reformation in Scotland*, 183; his influence on Scotland, 220; pupil of Major, 229; first sermon of, 237; connection with Wishart, 407.

Laglyne Wood, Ayrshire, 80, 82.
Laing, David, Life of Henryson, 159; Dunbar's poems, 207; Works of Lyndsay, 375.
Lament for the Makaris (see Dunbar).
Lanark, 2; Wallace in, 75, 83.
Lanercost, chronicle of, 54, 55, 61, 63, 69.
Langland's *Vision of Piers the Plowman*, 188, 202.
Langtoft, 61, 65, 69.
Lappenberg, 64.
Lauder Bridge, murders at, 111, 117.
Laurieston, 94.
League between Scotch and French, effects of, 96.
Lennox, Wallace in, 83.
Leo, Pope, Queen Margaret's letters to, 298, 299.
Leuchars, 94.
Leyden, edition of *The Complaynt of Scotland*, 247, 250.
Liber Pluscardensis, 137.
Lindisfarne, see of Aidan, 32.
Lindesay, Robert (see Pitscottie).
Lindores Abbey, 117.
Lindsays, The, 113.
Lionel, Prince, of England, 95.
Lochaber, 139.
Lollards of Kyle, The, 183, 377.
Lothian, peopled by English but ruled by Celts, 6; evangelists in, 39; Malcolm Ceannmor in, 37; wanting in song, 43.
Lundin, Sir Richard, 84.
Lydgate, influence of, 354.
Lyndsay, Sir David, 222; life, 375; marriage of, 381; death, 412; *Complaynt of the Papingo*, 127, 245, 379; analysis of, 389; reputed author of *The Complaynt of Scotland*, 247; *Epistil to the Kingis Grace*, 379; *The Dreme*, 379; analysis of, 383; *Complaynt to the King*, 387; minor pieces, 394; *Satyre of the Thrie Estaitis*, 394; analysis of, 394; *The Declaratioun*, 405; *Tragedie of the Cardinall*, 408; *Squire Meldrum*, 409; *The Monarchie*, 410.

Macalpin, Kenneth, unites Scottish and Pictish crowns, 4.

INDEX.

Macbeth, king of Scotland, 36; his fall marks close of purely Celtic rule in Scotland, 36.
Maclean, Lachlan, 112.
Major (or Mair), Joannes, life, 227; professor in Glasgow, 228; professor in St. Andrews, 235; principal of St. Andrews, 237; treatment of Church question, 232; *De Historia Gentis Scotorum* (or *De Gestis Scotorum*), 59, 77, 157, 229; minor works, 228.
Malcolm Ceanmor, marriage with Margaret, 7; Anglic in sympathy though Celtic king, 7; introduced English tongue to court, 40.
Map, Walter, 46.
March, Earls of, 94, 140.
Margaret, Queen, 170; marriage of, to James IV., 177; in Aberdeen, 179; marries Angus, 297; regent, 297; quarrel with Angus, 308; with Douglas, 312.
Margaret, Queen, wife of Malcolm Ceanmor, influence of, on Scottish history, 37.
Margaret of Denmark, wife of James III., 116.
Matthew of Westminster's *Flores Historiarum*, 61, 66, 70.
Meldrum, Lyndsay's poem on, 409.
Melrose, Abbey of, 10; founded by Aidan, 33.
Menteith, Sir John of, 69.
Mercer, 127, 128.
Merlin, prophecies of, 266.
Mirrour of Magistrates, 166.
Monarchie, The (see Lyndsay).
Monasteries, of Columba, 10; in sixteenth century, 232; unpopularity of, 407.
Moray of Bothwell, 94.
Murray, Dr. J. A. H., 108, 247.

Nennius, 20, 23.
Neville's Cross, battle of, 94.
Ninian, 16.
Norman-French language begins after David I., 40.
Northampton, treaty of, 92.
Northumberland, invasion of, by Wallace, 64.
Northumbria conquered by Scots, 6.
Norway, Kentigern's disciples in, 22.

Ogilvies, The, 113.
Orkney, Kentigern's disciples in, 22; Duncan's aggressions in, 36; acquired by James III., 116.
Ormesby, William, 62, 83, 84.
Ormin, 46.
Orosius, translation from, 43.
Ossian, 44.
Otterburn, battle of, 98.

Oysel, Nicholas, 68.

Palgrave, *Records of Scotland*, 47, 68, 69.
Palice of Honour (see Douglas).
Paraphrase, ascribed to Caedmon, 44.
Paris, Matthew, 45.
Parishes, formation of, 10.
Patrick, St., 20.
Paulinus converts Northern Angles, 23; his influence lost, 32.
Peblis to the Play (see James I.).
Pelham, Sir John, guardian of Prince James, 135.
Pembroke, Earl of, 84.
Penda, victory of, 23.
Percy, Lord, governor of Galloway and Ayr, 78, 79, 82.
Perth, Wallace at, 83; Parliament at, 140; James I. at, 144; Queen Margaret at, 300.
Petrarch compared with Douglas, 333.
Philippe le Bel, 66, 96.
Phoenix, The, 45.
Picts blended with Scots as Gaels, 1; crowns united under Kenneth Macalpin, 4; of Orkney, 4; of Galloway, 9, 16; disappearance of Pictish tongue, 11; conversion of Picts, 24.
Pictish Chronicle, 30, 41.
Pinkerton's *History of Scotland*, 91 (note), 101 (note), 116, 227, 312, 335.
Pitscottie's *History*, 112, 114, 129, 176, 405.
Pius II., Pope, picture of Scotland in 1435, 100.
Pomfret, 134.
Pystyl of Swete Susane, 107.

Quintyne, 127.

Raa, Ralph, 69.
Ragman Roll, 62.
Ramsay of Dalwolsie, 94.
Randolph, Regent, 93.
Ramsay, Sir J. H., note on arrest of the barons at the accession of King James I., 137.
Ramsay's *Gentle Shepherd*, 164.
Red Book of St. Asaph's, 20.
Register of Glasgow, 183.
Rhydderch Hael in Strathclyde, 20.
Riccarton, 72, 81, 82.
Richard II., 98.
Robene and Makyne (see Henryson).
Robene hude and litil Jhone, 260.
Robert II., 97, 101.
Robert III., 98, 101, 110, 133.
Robert of Gloucester, 46.
Roger of Hoveden, 45.
Roger of Wendover, 45.
Roman Church, authority of, 19.
Roslin, 67.

Ross, Earl of, 111.
Rouen, Treaty of, 306.
Roull's Curnying, 128.
Roxburgh, won by James III., 116; siege of, 142.
Rymer's *Foedera*, 135.

Sackville's *Induction*, 321.
Salutation of the Virgin (see Henryson).
Satyre of the Thrie Estaitis (see Lyndsay).
Sauchieburn, battle of, 111, 119, 122.
Scalacronica, 225.
Scone, 83, 84, 93, 95 (note).
Scot, Michael, 42.
Scotichronicon, 60, 72, 75, 95 (note); authorship of, 104; on James I., 137 (note), 145 (note).
Scotland, mythical origin, 225.
Scots blended with Picts as Gaels, 1; crowns united under Kenneth Macalpine, 4.
Scott, Sir Walter, 107, 133; on Dunbar, 216; on Douglas, 296, 353.
Scrymgeour, Sir Alex., 64 (note).
Sennachy, Highland, 39; Celtic of Irish origin, 43.
Ship 'Michael,' largest of James IV.; description of, 176.
Simpson, Andrew, the grammarian of Perth, 183.
Sinclair, Bishop, 93.
Skene, quoted, 8; on *Scotichronicon*, 104.
Slaves in Lothian, 37.
Solway Moss, 406.
Spenser, influence of, 129; *The Faery Queene*, 166, 321.
St. Andrews, 94; University of, 123, 132; Major Professor in, 235; Bellenden in, 239; Douglas at, 294; Douglas imprisoned in, 304; Lyndsay at, 377.
St. Giles, Edinburgh, Douglas, Dean of, 294.
St. Molaisi of Inishmurry, 25.
St. Serf's, Wyntoun, Prior of, 71, 104.
Stewart, Chamberlain of James I., 144.
Stewart, Andrew, installed in palace at Dunkeld, 303; opposition to Douglas, 305.
Steyle, Kirk of, 310.
Stirling, battle of, 63; Queen Margaret at, 300; James' flight to, 382.
Strathclyde gifted to Malcolm, 5; Britons of, abandon Welsh tongue, 11; victories in, by Arthur, 20; becomes a kingdom, 21; church in, 22; comes into hands of Scottish kings, 23; English tongue spoken in, 40; wanting in poetry, 43.
Stuart, James, of Auchmynto, 113.
Surrey compared with Douglas, 354, 364.

Surrey, Earl of, 62.
Taill of Rauf Coilzear, 108, 126, 260.
Tales of the Priests of Peebles, 119 (note).
Testament of Cresseid. (See Henryson.)
Thomas of Ercildoune, 107.
Three Deid Powis, 128.
Trade, did not exist before Malcolm, 39; growth after Alexander III., influences language, 41.
Trivet, Nicholas, 45.
Turgot, quoted by Fordun, 103.
Universities, foundation of, 123; influence of, 125.
Vergil, Polydore, account of, Douglas, 316, 317.
Virgil's *Aeneid*, translation of (see Douglas).

Wales, Kentigern in, 20.
Wallace Papers, 69.
Wallace, William, of Cymric descent, 6; War of Independence, 12, 48, 63; letter to magistrates of Lübeck and Hamburg, 64; in France, 66; feats of, 75, 79, 81; and Marion Braidfute, 130.
Wallace Family: Waleuse, Richard (origin of Riccarton), 72; Henry, 72; traceable in counties of Renfrew and Ayr, 72; Sir Richard Wallace of Riccarton, 79.
Warbeck, Perkin, 176.
Wars of the Roses, 110.
Wedderburn, Robert, reputed author of *The Complaynt of Scotland*, 247.
Welsh, dialect of Britons of Cumbria, 1; of Cymry of Clyde, 5; abandoned in Strathclyde, 11.
Wireker, Nigel, 46.
Wiclif, influence of, 184.
William of Malmesbury, 45, 103.
William of Newbury, 45.
William the Lion, quarrel with the Pope, 10; captured at Alnwick, 38; effect of capture on the unity of the kingdom, 38.
Williamson, Adam, letters to Douglas, 301.
Wishart, George, in the Lothians, 407.
Woden, worship of, 21, 23.
Wolsey, Cardinal, Douglas's letters to, 310, 311, 314.
Wood, Sir Andrew, 176.
Wyntoun, Andrew, prior of St. Serf's, 104, 110; *Cronykil of Scotland*, 71, 73, 83, 95, 98, 104; praises character of Albany, 132.

York, muster at, 65; Parliament at, 92; release of Prince James settled at, 134.